BELIEVING AGAIN

BELIEVING AGAIN

Doubt and Faith in a Secular Age

Roger Lundin

William B. Eerdmans Publishing Company
Grand Rapids, Michigan / Cambridge, U.K.

Published 2009 by
Wm. B. Eerdmans Publishing Co.
2140 Oak Industrial Drive N.E., Grand Rapids, Michigan 49505 /
P.O. Box 163, Cambridge CB3 9PU U.K.
www.eerdmans.com

Printed in the United States of America

15 14 13 12 11 10 09   7 6 5 4 3 2 1

Library of Congress Cataloging-in-Publication Data

Lundin, Roger.
Believing again: doubt and faith in a secular age / Roger Lundin.
p. cm.
Includes bibliographical references.
ISBN 978-0-8028-3077-7 (pbk.: alk. paper)
1. Christianity and culture — History — 19th century.
2. Christianity and literature — History — 19th century.
3. Secularism — History — 19th century. 4. Christianity and culture —
History. 5. Christianity and literature — History.
6. Secularlism — History. I. Title.

BR115.C8L92 2009

270.8 — dc22

2008046503

To

Nathan Hatch

Mark Noll

James Turner

Contents

Acknowledgments

THIS BOOK had its origins in research I undertook during my tenure as a Senior Fellow at the Erasmus Institute at the University of Notre Dame. While I labored away on a different book, which has long since been published, the thought of this one was born during that year at the Institute. I thank Jim Turner, the founder and first director of the Erasmus Institute, and Bob Sullivan, his successor, for their unstinting support of my work in particular and of religiously-situated scholarship in general.

The first drafts of many of these chapters were written as lectures and delivered at the following colleges and universities: Calvin College, Pepperdine University, Regent College, Seattle Pacific University, the University of Tennessee at Chattanooga, the University of British Columbia, the University of Notre Dame, Valparaiso University, and Wheaton College. I benefited from the stimulating exchanges I had at each of these institutions, and for the roles they played in organizing three of these different university events, I would like to give particular thanks to Greg Wolfe, Richard Hughes, and Bill McClay.

Portions of chapters 1, 7, and 8 have appeared in significantly different form in *Image*, the *Sewanee Theological Review*, and *The Cresset*. A much earlier version of chapter 2 was published in *Religion, Education, and the American Experience*, edited by Edith Blumhofer, as was a version of chapter 6 in *The Beauty of God*, edited by Daniel Treier, Mark Husbands, and Roger Lundin. In each of these instances, I am grateful for permission to use this material in its revised and expanded form.

It has proved to be the case with this manuscript, as with others, that my ideas have been strengthened and nuanced in countless ways through my interaction with students and colleagues alike. During the time that I have been at work on these chapters, I have had the privilege of leading seminars for undergraduates, graduate students, and faculty at Calvin College, the University of Notre Dame, and Wheaton College. My debts here are too numerous to be catalogued in full or detailed with precision, but I do wish to give special mention to Hal Bush, Martha Eads, Anthony Wilson, Reggie Young, Kremena Todorova, James Ryan, Linda Mills Woolsey, Dale Brown, David Congdon, Benjamin Ekman, and Joel Sheesley.

In the past year, two student assistants at Wheaton College have done extensive work to check each of the citations in this book. I am grateful that both Mark Nagle and Charlie Zagnoli were willing to spend so much time during their respective senior years chasing down references in the library and tracking down bibliographical data on the web. I also wish to thank Wheaton College for its generous ongoing support of my research and writing. A sabbatical freed up an important block of time at the beginning of the project, and as always my department chair, Sharon Coolidge, has been remarkably flexible and accommodating in working with my scheduling needs. At Eerdmans, David Bratt has been a consistently wise and supportive editor, and I appreciate his patience and good sense.

I am a literary scholar with a strong side interest in contemporary theology, so the reader may wonder why I have chosen to dedicate this book to three historians. I could say that I consider them to be three of the most felicitous prose stylists at work in the contemporary academy and leave it at that. But to do so would be to leave so much unsaid. Each of them has been a trusted friend over the years, and much of what I know about the intellectual, social, and religious history of the nineteenth century I have learned from them.

But the debt runs even deeper for me with Nat Hatch, Mark Noll, and Jim Turner. For the past several decades, they have championed Christian scholarship with a passion that has been consistently inspiring and a generosity that has been downright astonishing. Like many others, I have benefitted intangibly from their example but also tangibly from their success in raising funds and establishing programs to support the life of the mind as well as that of the spirit. This book is a token of my heartfelt thanks for their leadership and for their willingness, at so many different times and in so many varied venues, to invite a literary friend along for the historical ride. I trust they will find *Believing Again* to be a worthy indication of what I have learned on those journeys.

Introduction

"IN EVERY WORK of genius, we recognize our own rejected thoughts: they come back to us with a certain alienated majesty," wrote Ralph Waldo Emerson not quite two centuries ago.[1] I have long been enchanted by this Emersonian insight, for it speaks of art's remarkable power to articulate the meaning of our scattered experiences and to sound the depths of our unfathomable lives. A song or a story, a poem or a play, can weave together the strands of that experience to reveal a pattern that had always been there, even though we may never have spotted it until that moment.

That was how it was for me when as a thirteen-year-old boy I read the first story that ever seized my attention and made me take notice of the power of fiction. It was Jack London's "To Build a Fire," and I read it during a long bus ride in my hometown of Rockford, Illinois. I began reading the story because it had been assigned in a class, but by the time I had finished it, I felt as though my life had been taken away from me for a moment, measured and judged, and then returned in the form of an "alienated majesty." I never would have known, of course, to use such fancy terms at the time, but the experience was real, and from it I date the beginnings of my love of literature.

London's is a straightforward tale of a hapless man's fruitless efforts to build a fire and ward off death. Everything that can go wrong does go wrong for this man without a name, as he struggles to survive in the bru-

1. Ralph Waldo Emerson, *Essays and Lectures,* ed. Joel Porte (New York: Library of America, 1983), p. 259.

tally cold Yukon wilderness. When his final efforts fail, the man submits to his fate and falls into a sweet, dreamless sleep of death. The dog that had accompanied him sniffs his freezing body, catches the scent of death, and heads off in search of other food and fire providers.

When I first read this story, I stood on the brink of adolescence, and to a boy from an unchurched, working-class family, Jack London had gotten things exactly right. On the face of it, life did appear to be ruled as this story imagined it, by an uncanny mix of accident and necessity. Things, sometimes terrible things, simply happened — the neighbor's infant daughter killed by a bucket of scalding bath water, my never-to-be-known older sister strangled in the birth canal by her umbilical cord, and my sweet-spirited aunt struck down in her prime by the ravages of multiple sclerosis. These events seemed either to be random — that is, they didn't fit into any discernible pattern — or to be the workings of a divine power so distant and indifferent that the thought of submitting to its dictates or of enduring what it still had in store for me was unbearable.

The events of the next few years deepened my appreciation of literature as well as my fear of what it was confirming. When I was fifteen, my older brother died suddenly after routine surgery, and his death set grief to work with devastating swiftness upon my mother, my father, and me. But that is a story for another time and telling. For now, the point is that in the years immediately following my brother's death, only high-school English classes offered any sustenance for my famished spirit. As I read certain poets and novelists, I heard voices that spoke into the heart of the void my life had become, and in heeding their call, I took my first steps on a long journey to belief.

History, Culture, Theology

This is a book about that journey, but more important, it is about the larger cultural context of that personal trek. There will be three main elements to the argument that will be developed in the chapters to come. They have to do with the historical setting of this book's concerns, the substance of its cultural analysis, and the subject of its theological response. First, the setting: this is a story about origins and consequences of the emergence of unbelief in the nineteenth century. I do not treat that century in strict chronological terms, as though the dates "1801-1900" could comprehend the whole when it comes to thinking about the era. Instead, the nineteenth century as we will consider it runs from 1789 and the start of the French Revolution — about which William Wordsworth was to exclaim, "Bliss was it in that dawn to be alive, but to be young was very Heaven!" — to 1914 and the outbreak of the First World War — which was greeted by Edward Grey's famous lament, "The lamps are going out all over Europe; we shall not see them lit again in our lifetime."

Spanning 125 years, this period opened in a spirit of boundless hope and closed in a mood of impending doom. Many of the major intellectual and cultural figures who will animate these pages — from Immanuel Kant to Emily Dickinson, from Samuel Taylor Coleridge to Fyodor Dostoevsky — wrote their brilliant works in this period, and while their responses to the press of events varied dramatically, they all sensed themselves to be living at a time of bracing change and challenge. In the first chapter I quote George Steiner, who observes that the French Revolution "literally quickened the pace of felt time" in Western experience. Those who lived through it and followed after it "felt that time itself and the whole enterprise of consciousness had formidably accelerated." Throughout *Believing Again,* that nineteenth-century change in historical consciousness will be close to the heart of my concerns. In our discussions we will range more widely than that, of course, with authors and ideas from antiquity, the Middle Ages, and the early modern period joining the conversation, just as contemporary concerns will have their say in the debate. Yet wherever else we move in the pages of this book, the argument and interests will always come back home to the nineteenth century.

In turn, this historical setting has a special relevance for the cultural analysis that will unfold in the following chapters. Several years after I had made my own initial profession of Christian belief, I read an essay that set my particular religious sojourn in the context of a much longer cultural odyssey. Although it was ostensibly a review of Erik Erikson's *Young Man Luther,* the essay I read by W. H. Auden was more a meditation on modernity and belief than a discussion of that particular book. In his consideration of modern belief, Auden zeroes in on the events of the mid-nineteenth century, which he says mark the end of the "Protestant Era" and the beginning of the "Catholic Era." He hastens to note that by "Protestant Era" he means a period "in which the dominant ideology was protestant (with a small p) and catholic ideology the restraining and critical opposition." The crisis of individual and collective identity, however, "has changed, and [it has] changed precisely because of the success of protestantism in all its forms." The "protestant approach" to these difficulties cannot offer a solution, "because it is protestantism which has caused them."[2]

As Auden defines it, Protestantism emphasizes the unique nature of every human being before God, regardless of class or gender, while Catholicism stresses that "we are all members, one with another, both in the Earthly and the Heavenly City." Since the "principal threat" to our sense of identity today has become "our current lack of belief in and acceptance of the existence of others," we stand in desperate need of the "catholic" corrective, Auden argues, for it affirms "that the individual who will not or cannot join with others in saying *We* does not know the meaning of *I*." Yet in speaking of the return of "catholic ideology," Auden, who remained an Anglican to the end of his life, concludes with a word of clarification:

> By catholic community I do not mean the Christendom of the thirteenth century, nor by lutheran individual, a Lutheran of the sixteenth: there is, as [G. C.] Lichtenburg observed, "a great difference between believing something *still* and believing it *again*."[3]

Auden's understanding of the art of *believing again* seemed remarkably pertinent to my own experience, but more enticingly it offered a fresh perspective on the fate of belief in the modern age. His insights, for example, resonate strongly with the compelling accounts that James Turner, George Marsden, and Charles Taylor, among others, have offered of the emergence of open unbelief as an intellectually viable and socially acceptable option in the nineteenth century.[4] Here in the early twenty-first century we have had 150 years or more to absorb the shock of these changes, to tally the losses and to calculate whatever gains came about

2. W. H. Auden, *Forewords and Afterwords,* ed. Edward Mendelson (1973; repr. New York: Vintage, 1989), pp. 86-87.

3. Auden, *Forewords and Afterwords,* p. 87.

4. See James Turner, *Without God, Without Creed: The Origins of Unbelief in America* (Baltimore: Johns Hopkins University Press, 1985); George M. Marsden, *The Soul of the American University: From Protestant Establishment to Established Nonbelief* (New York: Oxford University Press, 1994); and Charles Taylor, *A Secular Age* (Cambridge, Mass.: Belknap Press of Harvard University Press, 2007).

as a result of open unbelief's sudden appearance. We have learned to live with unbelief in our midst and, in many cases, our hearts. Yet when it first broke upon the scene in the mid-nineteenth century, a sense of disruption and disorientation was palpable, even overwhelming for some, as within a matter of decades unbelief went from being an isolated experience on the cultural margins to becoming a central facet of modern life.

As a consequence of this sea change in religious thought and practice, for many men and women since the mid-nineteenth century the journey to belief has come to include a voyage through the straits of unbelief. In terms of personal experience and cultural life, this passage into unbelief fit as a new variation into what Charles Taylor has called "the Puritan tradition of 'leaving home.'" He describes how in the early colonies of Massachusetts and Connecticut all young persons were expected to undergo a conversion and to establish their own unique relationship to God before they were allowed to join the church. Although Puritan theology lost its hold on the American mind, the tradition of "leaving home" not only endured but strengthened its grip on the culture. To this day, we assume that to grow into maturity a young person must leave the "parental background" to make his or her own way in the world. If children are to take on the values of their parents, we expect them to do so only after they have first held those values at a distance and viewed them with skeptical eyes. For those modern persons who are religiously driven, "leaving home" has often involved a sojourn in the far country of unbelief, and the return has become a matter of "believing again."[5]

In a certain sense, "leaving home" had meant for me departing from the land of unbelief, for when I read that story by Jack London, I did so as a confused teenager already living in the suburbs of serious doubt. To be

5. Charles Taylor, *Sources of the Self: The Making of the Modern Identity* (Cambridge, Mass.: Harvard University Press, 1989), p. 39; Taylor acknowledges his indebtedness to Robert Bellah for this insight about "leaving home."

Timothy Larsen covers similar ground in *Crisis of Doubt: Honest Faith in Nineteenth-Century England* (Oxford: Oxford University Press, 2006). His emphasis, however, is on individuals who "reconverted" to Christianity after a crisis of faith, while my concern, like that of Taylor and Turner, is with the shift in the cultural viability of belief that resulted from the "emergence of unbelief" (Turner) and the development of a distinctive "modern cosmic imaginary" (Taylor). Larsen may have it right about individual cases, but Turner and Taylor are tracking the deeper social, cultural, and intellectual changes.

sure, I assumed that some force governed the course of life, but I had no idea what it was like or whether it even had a name, and I clearly did not consider it to be a loving, forgiving, or personal power. Instead, as an unassuming heir of late-nineteenth century naturalism, I took it for granted that the laws of life took no account of the longings of my heart or the destiny of my soul. Further, I regretted that fact, just as I resented everyone who seemed to testify to its truth. Had I read it at the time, John Updike's description of the main character in his 1960 novel, *Rabbit, Run,* would have made perfect sense to me: "He hates all the people on the street in dirty everyday clothes, advertising their belief that the world arches over a pit, that death is final, that the wandering thread of his feelings leads nowhere."[6]

To reach such a conclusion — that the "wandering thread of our feelings leads nowhere" — is to assume several deeply unsettling things about our individual experiences and collective history. To begin, it is to believe that Christian history has been more or less a saga of endless deception, both of the self and of others. "If what is proclaimed by Christianity is a fiction," observes Czeslaw Milosz, the incomparable Polish poet who will factor significantly in this book,

> And what we are taught in schools,
> In newspapers and TV is true:
> That the evolution of life is an accident,
> As is an accident the existence of man,
> And that his history goes from nowhere to nowhere,
> Our duty is to draw conclusions
> From our thinking about the innumerable generations
> Who lived and died deluding themselves,
> Ready to renounce their natural needs for no reason,
> To wait for a posthumous verdict, every day afraid
> That for licking clean a pot of jam they go to eternal torment.[7]

As Milosz's reference to "the evolution of life" notes, Charles Darwin's theory of natural selection nourished the dawning nineteenth-century sense that all who had trusted in God had merely been "deluding themselves." The Darwinian account had no need of a conscious,

6. John Updike, *Rabbit, Run* (New York: Fawcett, 1960), p. 196.

7. Czeslaw Milosz, *New and Collected Poems, 1931-2001* (New York: Ecco, 2001), p. 540.

divine power to explain the origin, intricacy, or destiny of life, and to some, its alternative narrative — which included a comprehensive material explanation of those origins and that destiny — made the "innumerable generations" of those who had once believed look foolish indeed.[8]

To many in the modern world, the truth of material explanation seems self-evident, whether the one considering that truth is the author of "To Build a Fire" in the early twentieth century, a boy desperate to make sense of life in the senseless 1960s, or the Nobel Prize–winning poet grappling with God to the end of his days. "Once the Bible shaped all conversation, then Marx, then Freud, but today Darwin is everywhere," David Brooks ruefully observed in a 2007 *New York Times* opinion column. "We have a grand narrative that explains behavior and gives shape to history. We have a central cosmology to embrace, argue with or unconsciously submit to."[9]

For the past century, with relentless force, the materialist narrative has swept over the landscape of modern culture and into every corner of human life, including religious experience. One of its most important consequences has been to establish and secure a comprehensive alternative to all providential accounts of life's meaning, so that even when we stand in the heart of belief, we sense that there is nearby another vantage-point from which nature and our experience would look entirely different. Consider, for instance, the implications that the narrative of material explanation might have for a person who has shifted from unbelief to belief. Whether he has become an evangelical Protestant or she has converted to Eastern Orthodoxy, even the most fervent convert knows he or she could *choose* to return to the land of unbelief and find within its borders a sweeping account of the origin, grown, decline, and destiny of human life. To be a modern believer is to recognize that in the deepest personal sense, belief is optional; whatever a person is able to accept and affirm he or she is also free to reject and deny. In one form or another, all of us today are what Robert Langbaum calls "romanticists": "It is not this or that political, philosophical, religious or even aesthetic commitment that marks the romanticist. It is the subjective ground of

8. "To the strongest ties that bound science and belief, Darwin applied an ax." Turner, *Without God, Without Creed,* p. 182.

9. David Brooks, "The Age of Darwin," *New York Times,* April 15, 2007.

his commitment, the fact that he never forgets his commitment has been chosen."[10]

There is no point in bewailing this freedom, for lamentation of this kind too easily leads to nostalgia that offers faint illumination for our moral lives and scant support for our cultural labors. A strong countervailing assumption underlies my approach to modernity in this book. It has to do with the wisdom, perhaps even the necessity, of expressing gratitude rather than regret for the fact that we live in the modern era. My thinking on these matters was first prompted by my reading decades ago of Dietrich Bonhoeffer's meditations, in *Letters and Papers from Prison,* on the fate of religion in a secular age. I have come to agree with Bonhoeffer that "the attack by Christian apologetic on the adulthood of the world" is "in the first place pointless, in the second place ignoble, and in the third place unchristian."[11]

In good measure I have come to share Bonhoeffer's perspective on this matter through reflection on my own experience. Shortly after my conversion to Christianity, I began to dream about how much better my life might have been if I had been born in the Middle Ages. Setting aside how misguided my notions of that period were — I had a sweetly naïve sense of the unity of the culture and the clarity of belief in those days — I was foolish to have wished to have been born at that time. Why? Because my life had been saved twice by modern medicine before I reached the age of ten, first by surgery that staved off dehydration and possible starvation (caused by pyloric stenosis) when I was six weeks old, and a second time when penicillin fought off the pneumonia that had attacked my nine-year-old body. If I had lived in the Middle Ages, I would have had the distinct privilege of having died twice by the age of ten. So much for that dream.

A desire to avoid nostalgia informs the argument throughout *Believing Again,* and that is particularly the case in the opening two chapters. The first deals with the disenchantment of the world, a distinctly modern topic, and it focuses upon the rise of historical consciousness and the growth of the modern sense of the self. These two themes are

10. Robert Langbaum, *The Poetry of Experience: The Dramatic Monologue in Modern Literary Tradition* (1957; repr., Chicago: University of Chicago Press, 1985), p. 21.

11. Dietrich Bonhoeffer, *Letters and Papers from Prison,* enlarged ed., ed. Eberhard Bethge (New York: Collier, 1972), p. 327.

tightly interwoven in the modern experience, and in the opening chapter, I concentrate specifically on the response of romantic artists and their modern Protestant heirs to this consciousness and its attendant spirit of disenchantment.

The second chapter charts a parallel course, as it explores the modern intersection between science, literature, and religion. Here too, the concern is to engage the theological and theoretical implications of scientific discoveries — from early modern cosmology to nineteenth-century biology and twentieth-century astronomy. We may debate the details or argue over the importance of a particular development, but we cannot deny that revolutions in scientific thought have burrowed their way into our poems just as they have shaped our stories and reworked our reading of the Bible.

From these first two chapters, titled simply "History" and "Science," we move onto what we might think of as a more subjective ground, as we consider human actions — believing, interpreting, and reading — rather than historical events or scientific facts. "About two hundred years ago," writes Richard Rorty, "the idea that truth was made rather than found began to take hold of the imagination of Europe."[12] From the early nineteenth century to the present day, a hallmark of our modernity has been the manner in which metaphors of *construction* have gradually overtaken those of *discovery* in our understanding of truth.

There is no point in wishing this were not the case or in pretending that we could possibly transport ourselves back to a time when the truth was simply found and humans had nothing to do with the making or the breaking of it. The alternative to such wishful thinking is to consider both the opportunities offered and the risks taken in employing such metaphors of making and to engage them with wisdom, clarity, and cunning.

Throughout *Believing Again,* several key modern poets and novelists figure prominently in our examination of these challenges. The focus will be on artists who lived somewhere on the margins of belief even though they may have longed to rest at its center. Whether through the poems and stories they wrote or through the lives they lived, such writers — Fyodor Dostoevsky and Emily Dickinson, W. H. Auden and Isak

12. Richard Rorty, *Contingency, Irony, and Solidarity* (Cambridge: Cambridge University Press, 1989), p. 3.

Dinesen, Herman Melville and Czeslaw Milosz — disclose the richly textured, intimate nature of the drama of modern belief and unbelief.

At first blush, this may seem to be at best a loosely connected group of writers, for it includes a flamboyant Russian novelist and a reclusive American poet, a British poet and man of letters and a Danish storyteller who spent her formative years in Africa, a nineteenth-century sailor and novelist, and a Nobel Prize–winning Polish poet from the late twentieth century. But there is a pattern here, and the fact that we can trace it across a period of 150 years tells us something vital about the continuing power of belief in our culture and our lives. The conveners of a highly touted recent conference, "Beyond Belief: Enlightenment 2.0," may be convinced that science will soon "create a new rational narrative" to replace a host of now-discredited Christian and Jewish stories.[13] And for John Updike, that remarkably gifted and extraordinarily diffident Christian novelist, contemporary belief may be powerless to do more than "borrow light and lightness from ancient lamps" and provide a sliver of hope for the few who are still driven to "take comfort in the periodic company of like-minded others, who . . . 'share the pride of this ancient thing that will not quite die.'"[14] But to the brilliant modern writers who appear throughout the following pages, belief in God entailed more than hospice care for a dying faith. They took belief and unbelief to be realities of great heft and power, and like Jacob with the angel, they wrestled with God — and in some cases with the shadow cast by his absence.

For some of these artists, such as Dickinson and Melville, it was as though an uncanny metaphorical sense drove them more than a century ago to discover a degree of promise and peril that the rest of us have only recently begun to fathom. In the instance of Dostoevsky, we find one of the greatest dramatic talents in literary history grappling with an exceptional array of pressing intellectual, political, and personal issues. And with Auden and Milosz, we have two of the most gifted poets of the twentieth century who were also powerful public intellectuals and Christian thinkers.

To call Milosz and Auden "Christian thinkers" is not to claim for them an orthodox thoroughness that they neither professed nor prac-

13. "Beyond Belief: Enlightenment 2.0," http://thesciencenetwork.org/BeyondBelief2/about/

14. John Updike, "Response," *Christianity and Literature* 56 (2007): 485.

ticed; even in the case of these two churchgoing poets, the conflicts and uncertainties surrounding belief remained too great for us to hear in them ringing theological clarity and conviction. This is even more the case with those writers from the nineteenth century — Dickinson, Melville, and Dostoevsky — who factor significantly in this book. As I suggest in the chapter on interpretation, these three knew that the theological ground had shifted dramatically in their own lifetimes. Of the three, Melville found the new dynamics of belief most challenging, and he wearied of the pursuit of God more readily than did Dostoevsky or Dickinson. For the latter two, the affirmations were stronger than for Melville, yet the self-dividing doubts remained as well. "On subjects of which we know nothing, or should I say *Beings* — ," Dickinson wrote near the end of her life, "we both believe, and disbelieve a hundred times an Hour, which keeps Believing nimble."[15]

Doctrine and Drama: The Theological Response

The third portion of my argument throughout this book has to do with the theological response to this new modern drama of "nimble believing." In *Believing Again,* theologians join the conversation at many points. Some of the voices to be heard, including those of St. Paul, St. Augustine, and Martin Luther, appear from the distant past, but those who will speak most often are Catholic, Protestant, and Orthodox thinkers of the past century. After all, they are the ones who have faced the particular modern challenge of unbelief, and they have done so with a creative brilliance that has gone largely unnoticed outside the confessional circles of the faith. As we consider the modern drama of belief and unbelief, the Orthodox theologian Alexander Schmemann reminds us that "secularism . . . is a 'stepchild' of Christianity." It may not be "a legitimate child, but a *heresy*"; yet heresies are distortions and exaggerations of the truth, which nevertheless take the form of "a question addressed to the Church." To be answered, such questions require "an effort of Christian thought and conscience. To condemn a heresy is relatively easy. What is

15. Emily Dickinson, *The Letters of Emily Dickinson,* ed. Thomas H. Johnson and Theodora Ward (Cambridge, Mass.: Belknap Press of Harvard University Press, 1958), 3:728.

much more difficult is to *detect* the question it implies, and to give this question an adequate answer."[16]

In the pages that follow, such theologians as Hans Urs von Balthasar, Karl Barth, and Dietrich Bonhoeffer will be called upon to offer adequate responses to the challenges that Dostoevsky, Dickinson, Melville, and Milosz have set in their art. My goal is to bring such powerful theological figures, along with their contemporary successors such as Kevin Vanhoozer, Colin Gunton, and Edward Oakes, into a conversation with these accomplished poets and novelists.

The theological voices weave their way into the argument throughout the chapters of *Believing Again*, but in the final section, their contributions become especially pertinent. These chapters deal with the themes of beauty, story, and memory, and their subjects point to a tacit consensus shared by both the theologians and the artists. It is that in light of our modernity, Christian art and apologetics would do well to rid themselves of any hankerings for the spatial models of the truth that once dominated Catholic and Protestant thought alike. In terms of Catholicism, this entails coming to terms with the disenchantment of the world and overcoming the longing for the lost medieval synthesis or its equivalent, while for Protestants it involves accepting the consequences of the nineteenth-century demise of the argument from design.[17] "We cannot revive old factions," T. S. Eliot wrote in 1942, "We cannot restore old policies/Or follow an antique drum" — and this comes from the pen of an inveterate Anglo-Catholic who had his own powerful nostalgic yearnings.[18] Or as Milosz described the challenge: "It is simply impossible for me to form a spatial conception of Heaven and Hell. . . . But the imagination can function only spatially; without space the imagination is like a child who wants to build a palace and has no blocks."[19]

16. Alexander Schmemann, *For the Life of the World: Sacraments and Orthodoxy,* 2nd rev. and exp. ed. (Crestwood, N.Y.: St. Vladimir's Seminary Press, 1973), pp. 127-28.

17. "Now this change, which has taken place over the last half millennium in our civilization, has been immense. We move from an enchanted world, inhabited by spirits and forces, to a disenchanted one; but perhaps more important, we have moved from a world which is encompassed within certain bounds and static to one which is vast, feels infinite, and is in the midst of an evolution spread over aeons." Taylor, *A Secular Age,* p. 323.

18. T. S. Eliot, *The Complete Poems and Plays, 1909-1950* (New York: Harcourt, 1971), p. 143.

19. Czeslaw Milosz, *To Begin Where I Am: Selected Essays,* ed. Bogdana Carpenter and Madeline G. Levine (New York: Farrar, 2001), p. 320.

With spatial models having been lost to the modern religious imagination, "what remains is the covenant, the Word, in which man trusts."[20] Indeed, to fill the spatial void, the twentieth century's most astute theologians made extensive use of narrative and drama — the genres most crucial to a covenantal faith — to renew and deepen our understanding of the words and ways of God. Barth and Balthasar in particular have provided exemplary — and exhaustive — theological engagements with the full range of thought and experience in a secular age, including the drama of belief and unbelief. "If they want to be the teachers of our times," Balthasar says of modern Christians, "then they must learn to read the signs of our times. This age cannot be purified by fire if Christians are not ready to allow themselves to be tested in the same fire."[21]

Like Dostoevsky, Dickinson, and Milosz, Balthasar and Barth shift the center of their theological attention from spatial and architectural metaphors to those of the stage and the storied page. Indeed, it is stunning to see how crucial to the enterprise of modern theology images from storytelling and the theater have become. As we will see, Barth and Balthasar in particular have argued that as we search for models of beauty and harmony, we would do well to dwell upon those in which the structural intricacy of God's creative and redeeming love can be told, sung, and heard. "The incarnation is the ground for the possibility not only of creation but is also the basis for all other dramas in world history," Edward Oakes says of Balthasar, and the point seems true of Barth as well. "The reason Balthasar can so freely and sovereignly survey the results and artifacts of world drama . . . and find them of such direct theological use is because he sees them as already grounded in the prior drama of salvation history established by God in his predestining love."[22]

As you read this book, you will notice that the title for each chapter consists of a single word, and not one of them is graced (or burdened) with a subtitle. One reason for this is my sense that the age of the ironic, allusive, sardonic, and elaborated title may be nearing its end. When a best-selling book by a leader in the "emergent church" movement comes

20. Milosz, *To Begin,* p. 320.

21. Hans Urs von Balthasar, *The Glory of the Lord: A Theological Aesthetics,* vol. 5, *The Realm of Metaphysics in the Modern Age,* ed. Brian McNeil C.R.V. and John Riches, trans. Oliver Davies et al. (San Francisco: Ignatius, 1991), pp. 654-55.

22. Edward T. Oakes, *Pattern of Redemption: The Theology of Hans Urs von Balthasar* (New York: Continuum, 1994), p. 220.

with a twenty-nine word subtitle — complete with six slash-marked noun combinations and one multiply-hyphenated modifier — something has to give. My hunch is that these breath-stealing exercises may give way at some point to simpler, less self-conscious formulations, just as the plate-piling titles of the seventeenth and eighteenth centuries eventually yielded to the more minimalist cuisine of the titular menu in the nineteenth century.

Despite the frequency with which it moves into the cultural concerns of the twentieth century (and twenty-first), *Believing Again* remains anchored in the literature, history, and religious thought of the nineteenth century. With the likes of Carlyle, Kierkegaard, and Nietzsche excepted — and those exceptions tell us much about the twentieth century to come — that century was in love with unembellished titles that never even nodded in the direction of the arch, the ironic, or the allusive. Instead, the long poems, novels, and essays of that era were graced with titles consisting of nothing but a short phrase or a single word: *Middlemarch, Great Expectations, The Prelude, Song of Myself, Jane Eyre, The Scarlet Letter, Crime and Punishment,* or "Self-Reliance," "Nature," and "Experience."

In following the lead of the nineteenth century on this matter, I do not mean to be presumptuous, but merely to imitate the example of writers I admire. They felt free to set a subject before their readers and to think along with them about it, and this what I seek to do in the pages that follow. To be sure, there are certain other subjects that I would have liked to cover — particularly "Race" and "Orphans" — if time and space had permitted. But the nineteenth century is a vast terrain, and any one book can only map a portion of it.

I trust that at some point, perhaps even soon, that book about orphans will get written, but in the meantime, there is much for us to explore in the modern drama of *believing again.* As Stanley Hauerwas rightly says in a recent book, "it is hard to make God boring or have little significance for the way we live and think." The challenge is not to convince others that theology somehow matters; "The challenge is whether we are capable of performing the work of theology with the joy and confidence the subject of theology requires."[23] The authors we are about to engage are more than up to the challenge.

23. Stanley Hauerwas, *The State of the University: Academic Knowledges and the Knowledge of God* (Malden, Mass.: Blackwell, 2007), p. 32.

CHAPTER 1

History

WE BEGIN with history, a subject that beguiled the greatest minds of the late eighteenth century and seduced their nineteenth-century heirs. "History is the most popular species of writing," Edward Gibbon claimed in 1789, and in the words of a later practitioner of the craft, "he was right, at least for the second half of the [eighteenth] century. People began to read history avidly as never before, and philosophers no longer thought it beneath their notice." Over half of David Hume's works dealt with history; Immanuel Kant stepped away from the writing of his *Critiques* long enough to "dash off" several essays on the subject; and a passion for matters historical courses through the endless pages of Hegel's ruminations on the workings of Spirit. As a result of the work of these singular figures and others, by the beginning of the nineteenth century, history had achieved a remarkable "new and independent status, and a new dignity and popularity."[1]

What were the roots of this dignity, and what fruits did such popularity eventually bear? To address these questions, in this chapter we will focus on the revolutionary eighteenth-century discovery of historical consciousness and the sobering nineteenth- and twentieth-century consequences of that find. We will listen to the vigorous complaints lodged against the disenchanting power of historical consciousness, and we will see how they became rallying cries for the cultural revolution that was to bring the romantic imagination to power. That romantic impulse ruled

1. Franklin L. Baumer, *Modern European Thought: Continuity and Change in Ideas, 1600-1950* (New York: Macmillan, 1977), p. 238.

briefly over the politics of Europe and for a somewhat longer time over its poetics, until, in the latter instance, Darwin unceremoniously dethroned it. Almost two centuries later, this theory of the imagination stills wields considerable influence in curious places, particularly in the cultural provinces of Anglo-American Protestantism. We will train our sights on the implications of this imagination — both in its original guise and in its contemporary form — for the understanding of history and the modern experience of belief.

Dreams of the Future: Getting Beyond the Past

The nineteenth century opened with dreams of history's perfection and closed with nightmares of its ruin. "I like the dreams of the future better than the history of the past. So good night. I will dream on, . . . marking the progress and the obliquities of ages and countries," Thomas Jefferson wrote to John Adams in 1816, giving expression to the romantic hopes and revolutionary aspirations that had become commonplace in his lifetime.[2] By 1883, however, Jefferson's serenity about history had given way to Friedrich Nietzsche's defiant despair: "To redeem those who lived in the past and to recreate all 'it was' into a 'thus I willed it' — that alone should I call redemption." Because it cannot "will backwards" and break the "covetous" hold of the past, the modern will, according to Nietzsche, has an all-but-irresistible urge to seek revenge against time. "This, indeed this alone, is what *revenge* is: the will's ill will against time and its 'it was.'"[3]

Nietzsche's melancholy bravado, rather than Jefferson's sanguine confidence, was to become the dominant twentieth-century attitude towards history, at least among a majority of artists and intellectuals. Such melancholy courses through the fiction and poetry of high modernism, haunts the memoirs of war veterans and Holocaust survivors alike, and serves as the coin of the realm in popular culture. At a personal level, the pressure of the modern sense of time proved too great for some to bear.

2. Thomas Jefferson to John Adams, August 1, 1816, *The Adams-Jefferson Letters: The Complete Correspondence between Thomas Jefferson and Abigail and John Adams,* ed. Lester J. Cappon (Chapel Hill: University of North Carolina Press, 1959), p. 485.

3. Friedrich Nietzsche, *Thus Spoke Zarathustra,* in *The Portable Nietzsche,* trans. and ed. Walter Kaufmann (1954; repr., New York: Penguin, 1976), pp. 251-52.

This was the case, for example, with Quentin Compson, one of the main characters in William Faulkner's *The Sound and the Fury,* published in 1929. The past weighs so heavily upon Quentin that to elude its grasp, he kills himself. On the final day of his life, he awakens to the ticking of his watch and to the memory of his father's description of time as "the mausoleum of all hope and desire." To Quentin's father, history is nothing but an endless succession of pointless incidents, and in the end, all events, even the crucifixion of Jesus, add up to a sequence of senseless moments in the unendurable course of things. "Christ was not crucified," Quentin recalls his father having told him, "he was worn away by a minute clicking of little wheels."[4]

In one sense, there is little that is novel about Quentin Compson's struggle with time and death. Centuries before Christ was ground down by the "clicking" of those wheels, "the Preacher" had concluded in the book of Ecclesiastes that there was nothing new under the sun. Similarly, from the epics of Homer to the tragedies of Sophocles, the pagan culture of antiquity had its attention fixed upon mortality. And even if we lacked any literary records of such attitudes, common sense would tell us that medieval monks and nuns, along with ancient millers and midwives, felt the passing of time and lamented the brevity of life as keenly as we do.

Nevertheless, no matter how soberly the ancients pondered their own mutability, they unquestionably did not think of themselves as creatures whose essence was historical. That view of things, which has burrowed its way deep into the modern mind, would have been unimaginable to Aquinas or Aristotle, to Paul or Plato, or to any of their contemporaries.[5] A robust understanding of human historicity did not emerge until the nineteenth century, and on this score we in the modern world are the heirs not of Plato but of Hegel, who declared at the

4. William Faulkner, *The Sound and the Fury* (1929; repr., New York: Vintage, 1990), pp. 76-77.

5. Owen Barfield notes the absence of a sense of the historical in the premodern world: "In order to enter sympathetically into the outlook of an educated medieval gentleman, we have to perform the difficult feat of undressing, as it were, our own outlook by divesting it of all those seemingly innate ideas of progress and evolution, of a movement of some sort going on everywhere around us, which make our cosmos what it is. This is more difficult even than it sounds, because so many of these thoughts and feelings have become subconscious." *History in English Words* (1953; repr., Stockbridge, Mass.: Lindisfarne, 1985), p. 167.

dawn of that century, "World history is the presentation of the divine." For him, this meant that the Germans (i.e., Hegel himself) would complete by means of exhaustive thought what the French Revolution had initiated in violent practice.

For a time, events on the world stage played themselves out as though they had been scripted in the philosopher's mind. As Hegel prepared to send his greatest work, the *Phenomenology,* to the printer, Napoleon's army launched a crucial offensive outside Jena, where the philosopher was teaching at the time. He set his manuscript aside long enough to watch the emperor and his entourage troop by in a procession. Calling Napoleon a "world-soul," Hegel described him as a man "who, concentrated here at a single point, astride a horse, reaches out over the world and masters it."[6] To the philosopher, we who play upon history's stage are only the valets of "the Spirit" as he progresses "through stages whereby he attains to his truth and self-consciousness about himself." This "Spirit" is not a personal God who reigns over history but a cosmic force that emerges from within it: it is "the infinite drive [*Trieb*] of the world spirit, his irresistible thrust [*Drang*]" to be realized within the unfolding of that history.[7]

Ironically enough, it was the Christian belief in a personal God that long before had prepared the way for the eventual appearance of Hegel's impersonal Spirit. Over the course of centuries, it had transformed the pagan view of cyclical time into what eventually became the modern concept of historical development. In this process, the doctrine of the incarnation proved central. "The uniqueness of the redemptive event introduces the essence of history into Western thought," Hans-Georg Gadamer explains, and in turn that singular event introduced into human thought a radical conception of the nature of all events.[8] By the logic of the incarnation, the life, death, and resurrection of Jesus Christ

6. G. W. F. Hegel, quoted in Terry Pinkard, *Hegel: A Biography* (Cambridge: Cambridge University Press, 2000), p. 228.

7. G. W. F. Hegel, quoted in Charles Taylor, *Hegel and Modern Society* (Cambridge: Cambridge University Press, 1979), p. 96.

8. Hans-Georg Gadamer, *Truth and Method,* 2nd ed., trans. Joel Weinsheimer and Donald G. Marshall (New York: Crossroad, 1989), p. 419. In the words of Walker Percy, "The intervention of God in history through the Incarnation bestows a weight and value to the individual human narrative which is like money in the bank to the novelist." *Signposts in a Strange Land,* ed. Patrick Samway (New York: Farrar, 1991), p. 178.

comprised a unique occurrence that had accomplished human redemption once and for all. The event of the incarnation could not be repeated, because in its singularity it had secured human salvation and made the restoration of nature possible. In addition, through the "unique and irreversible event" of the incarnation, Christianity brought history into the life of God himself. "This is what the doctrine of the Trinity is," one observer notes, for "it incorporates into the timeless God of the Greeks, the God of project and of suffering; that is, the God of love."[9]

As revolutionary as the doctrine of the incarnation had been in the first century, it would take many centuries for its historical implications to be realized. In theological terms, a crucial development in this long process occurred in the late twelfth century, when the Cistercian monk Joachim of Fiore put forward a vision that effectively subordinated the timelessness of the Trinity to the historical drama of redemption. For Joachim, the era of the ancient pagans and the Old Testament saints had been the Age of the Father. Marked by hierarchy, this phase eventually gave way, with the birth of Jesus Christ, to the Age of the Son, in which the emphasis shifted from the patriarchal family to the monastic orders. In the Age of the Son, sonship replaces slavery and law submits to grace. This age represented to Joachim a clear improvement over the previous one, yet for him, "the best was always still to be." And "the best," he believed, was soon to appear in the Age of the Spirit. In this revolutionary time to come, "a new, superior form of life" would free men and women to live in the fullness of mercy and to leave patriarchy and individualism behind. Joachim did not expect this new "form of life" to burst abruptly into the midst of the present age. Instead, he anticipated a seamless evolution, as the Catholic era gradually gave way to a "dawning new age — the egalitarian, communal life of mutual love."[10]

For centuries, Joachim's dynamic view of history exercised little or no influence on mainstream medieval and early modern culture, yet it coursed with energy in the subterranean channels of Christian thought

9. George Grant, *Philosophy in the Mass Age,* ed. William Christian (1959; repr., Toronto: University of Toronto Press, 1995), p. 42. Karl Barth sums up this point succinctly: "Faith has to do with the God who is in Himself historical and has fashioned a decree whose goal is history, and has set this history going and completed it." *Dogmatics in Outline,* trans. G. T. Thompson (1949; repr., New York: Harper, 1959), p. 28.

10. Steven Ozment, *The Age of Reform (1250-1550): An Intellectual and Religious History of Late Medieval and Reformation Europe* (New Haven: Yale University Press, 1980), p. 107.

and cultural life. Eventually, a revitalized Joachimite theory surfaced to play a role in the political life of seventeenth-century England and eighteenth- and nineteenth-century Europe. With the revolutions in America (1776) and France (1789), and with the visionary schemes of the idealist philosophers and romantic poets alike, it appeared that Joachim's dream of the Spirit's reign might become a reality at last, as the long chain of reflection prompted by the doctrine of an incarnate personal God issued at last in a vision of an impersonal Spirit emerging through history.[11]

Although it had been sown in the ancient consciousness and medieval mind by the first- and second-century theology of the incarnation, the radical understanding of historical consciousness did not break into full bloom until the end of the eighteenth century, when events and theories together nourished its sudden flowering. No single quote or set of statistics, explains George Steiner, "can recapture for us what must have been the inner excitement, the passionate adventure of spirit and emotion unleashed by the events of 1789 and sustained, at a fantastic tempo, until 1815." Over that brief period, the modern consciousness of history changed irreversibly, and our modern sense of time was born. The French Revolution and its aftermath "literally quickened the pace of felt time" in the European experience, and those who lived through that period sensed "that time itself and the whole enterprise of consciousness had formidably accelerated."[12]

The French and American revolutions had laid bare the close ties between private experience and public affairs, as historical events suddenly came to matter to the impoverished multitudes as well as to the

11. To some, such as the German essayist Gotthold Ephraim Lessing, Joachim's "Age of the Spirit" appeared to have been realized in the Enlightenment. By that time, writes M. H. Abrams, it had become possible to assume "that there is in human nature an inherent teleology of educational progression, which will lead inevitably to a 'time of perfection' when man 'will do the good because it is the good' — 'the time of a *new everlasting Gospel*,' or 'third age of the world' which, Lessing says, had been prematurely glimpsed by 'certain visionaries of the thirteenth and fourteenth centuries'; that is, in the theory of an earthly millennium which had been proclaimed by Joachim of Flora and his followers." *Natural Supernaturalism: Tradition and Revolution in Romantic Literature* (New York: Norton, 1971), p. 202. See also Marjorie Reeves and Warwick Gould, *Joachim of Fiore and the Myth of the Eternal Evangel in the Nineteenth Century* (Oxford: Clarendon Press, 1987).

12. George Steiner, *In Bluebeard's Castle: Some Notes Towards the Redefinition of Culture* (New Haven: Yale University Press, 1971), pp. 11-12.

privileged few. Some observers, such as Goethe, sensed the magnitude of these changes as they were unfolding. The great German man of letters was present at Valmy in northern France in 1792, during a pivotal battle in the French Revolutionary Wars. The French emerged victorious at Valmy, and had they lost this particular conflict, the Revolution itself might have been doomed. At the end of the battle, Goethe encouraged a dejected group of Prussian officers to take heart, because "from this place and from this day a new epoch in world history begins and you can say you were there to see it."[13]

To be aware of history in this sense meant to greet each day as the dawning of possibly life-changing events. Steiner explains that beginning in the late eighteenth century, "in Western culture, each day was to bring news — a perpetuity of crisis," as military conflict and political upheaval seized the attention of commoners in unprecedented ways. This change in the pace of things was due in part to improvements in the transportation of people and the transmission of information, but the real impetus lay elsewhere, in the altered dynamics of human expectation. Whatever other consequences it may have had, the French Revolution initiated "a deep, emotionally stressed change in the quality of hope." The expectation of progress, as envisioned by Joachim of Fiore and others, had long possessed "a millenary horizon," but that horizon had always receded into the distance. Now it had "suddenly moved very close" and appeared within reach of the makers of history.[14] In Shakespeare's *Henry V,* only a king could conceive of telling his prospective queen, "We are the makers of manners," but in the age of revolution, the millers and midwives began to feel they might be as well.[15]

13. Goethe, quoted in Nicholas Boyle, *Goethe: The Poet and the Age,* vol. 2, *Revolution and Renunciation, 1790-1803* (Oxford: Clarendon Press, 2000), p. 128. Boyle notes that Goethe recalled this quotation thirty years after the event; it is impossible to determine whether he originally offered the sentiment in this form at the time (1792).

14. Steiner, *In Bluebeard's Castle,* p. 13. In France and America, the stress upon the future went hand in hand with an attack on memory: "For France, the French Revolution signified a destruction of historical memory whose effects on public life went far beyond what had up to that point been known in European history as the 'condemnation of memory' *(damnatio memoriae).* Everything that reminded people of the ancien régime was now taboo, and forgetting was the first duty of the citizen." Harald Weinrich, *Lethe: The Art and Critique of Forgetting,* trans. Steven Rendall (Ithaca, N.Y.: Cornell University Press, 2004), p. 109.

15. In the words of Charles Taylor, with the American Revolution "the idea of founda-

Nineteenth-century fiction provides ample support for Steiner's claims, with the new historical consciousness serving as a central theme in such writers as Nathaniel Hawthorne, Herman Melville, and George Eliot. We come upon an early account of this revolutionary sense of time in Washington Irving's "Rip Van Winkle," which appeared in 1819 and had as its setting the Revolutionary period of the late eighteenth century. The story opens in a drowsy colonial village, where each day Rip genially gathers with other "idle personages" in front of the village inn, which is graced by a portrait of King George III. Rip and his compatriots trade gossip and retell "endless sleepy stories about nothing." If, by chance, "an old newspaper [falls] into their hands," they happily deliberate about public events months after the fact. This is a place without news, a time of myth before the birth of historical consciousness.[16]

When Rip slinks back into the village after his twenty-year slumber, the hotel has become a ramshackle place, and a different George — Washington — stares down from its sign. More important, "the very character of the people seemed changed. There was a busy, bustling disputatious tone about it," and instead of reading "an ancient newspaper," the village residents were listening to a "lean bilious looking fellow" who was "haranguing" them about the *news* of the day, "about rights of citizens — election — members of Congress — liberty — Bunker's hill — heroes of seventy-six — and other words that were a perfect babylonish jargon to the bewildered Van Winkle."[17]

The babbling jargon of Rip's day has become the common parlance of our age. We articulate our lives through the grammar of history and fashion their meaning within the syntax of time. This is true even in theology, a discipline we might not be inclined to think of as being historical in any foundational sense. Yet it too has become saturated with history. Hans Urs von Balthasar, for example, opens his multi-volume *Theo-Drama* with a discussion of "Event" and "History," which he terms the un-

---

tion is taken out of the mythical early time, and seen as something that people can do today." *A Secular Age* (Cambridge, Mass.: Belknap Press of Harvard University Press, 2007), p. 197. See also his discussion of the ideal that emerged in the eighteenth century, of "direct-access" societies in which the "simultaneity" of all events (the "news") becomes the standard (pp. 712-15).

16. Washington Irving, "Rip Van Winkle," in *History, Tales and Sketches*, ed. James W. Tuttleton (New York: Library of America, 1983), p. 772.

17. Irving, "Rip," p. 779.

mistakable "trends of modern theology." We have come to fix upon history in modernity, the Catholic theologian claims, because we are torn between two powerful visions of the truth. One sees truth as a timeless entity veiled by our ignorance and obscured by our embodiment; in this view, truth resides on the peaks that soar above history's valleys, or it is to be encountered at the end of a yet-to-be-discovered path that will lead us out of its labyrinth. The other view accepts the fact that the truth is intertwined with time, and it seeks to trace the pattern of that truth within the tangled web of history, or to discover those points at which the truth from beyond time has revealed itself at the heart of time.

If we view truth as timeless, Balthasar says our goal must be to refine our thought and chasten our perceptions so that truth can emerge in all its self-evident glory. He calls this view the "rationalist-idealist ethics of timelessly valid laws" and contrasts it with the biblical concept of *kairos,* or "fullness of time," which points to God's entry into history in the person of Jesus Christ. In the light of this *kairos,* "destiny comes from a point in history in which 'God appears on the stage of world history'" to redirect the course of that history. If it were to be "cut loose from this dramatic context, the 'historical' character of theology would dissolve . . . into mere philosophy." As a result of Christ's death and resurrection, we "exist at the mysterious intersection of the 'aeons' of which [the Apostle] Paul so often speaks." Deadly conflicts still erupt at that junction, as the forces of the old order meet the power of the Kingdom to come, but the final outcome of the battle between good and evil is not in doubt.[18]

On its own, history can neither supply us with an abiding home nor establish a stable framework for our lives, yet God has nevertheless fashioned from its materials the stage upon which the drama of redemption is being acted out.[19] At the dawn of the Christian era, the Apostle Paul reminded the Athenians that one of their poets had said of God that "in him we live and move and have our being" (Acts 17:28). Over the past two centuries, we have come to see it works the other way as well. If we "have

18. Hans Urs von Balthasar, *Theo-Drama: Theological Dramatic Theory,* vol. 1, *Prolegomena,* trans. Graham Harrison (San Francisco: Ignatius, 1988), pp. 28, 30. See also Oscar Cullmann, *Christ and Time: The Primitive Christian Conception of Time and History,* rev. ed., trans. Floyd V. Filson (Philadelphia: Westminster, 1964).

19. Kevin Vanhoozer: "The theo-drama is nothing less than a covenant-comedy of cosmic significance." *The Drama of Doctrine: A Canonical-Linguistic Approach to Christian Theology* (Louisville: Westminster John Knox, 2005), p. 53.

our being in history," so does God, because in Jesus Christ, he "became flesh and dwelt among us." As Karl Barth told a group of students in the ruins of postwar Europe, "God was not ashamed to exist in this accidental state," and as a result of the incarnation, our history has become God's history, and "we are not left alone in this frightful world. Into this alien land God has come to us."[20] For two thousand years, the Christian church has celebrated this fact in its worship of the incarnate Lord and through its participation in the sacramental life. But can the sacraments endure in the context of modern historical consciousness?

Skipping the History

Five centuries ago, at the dawn of modernity, "sacramental" and "incarnational" would have been fighting words. In the wake of the Lutheran Reformation, it did not take much to prompt an angry exchange in the sanctuaries or the streets over what Jesus had meant when he told his disciples on the last night of his life, "Take, eat; this is my body" (Matt. 26:26). Disputes over the meaning of these words divided families as well as regions, and they split the church into ever more numerous factions — and at times, it seemed, into ever-smaller fractions.

In our current state of theological indifference, it is easy to dismiss the finely honed arguments over the sacraments as a great deal of bloody bickering over minor matters. But that is not how the men and women at the time would have viewed them. When they argued over the degree to which Christ was present in the elements of the communion table, the Christians of the sixteenth century "were not splitting hairs," Brad Gregory explains. Instead, they were disputing the most important of subjects, that being how "humanity's one savior, who took away the world's sins, 'through whom all things were made,' was present to them; who had the authority to make him present in this special manner; and how they knew that this was so."[21]

While controversies over the sacraments quickly became part of the

20. Barth, *Dogmatics in Outline,* p. 109.

21. According to Gregory, what was true of the Eucharist was also the case for other doctrines: "The analogous point can be made for virtually every contested issue. *Doctrines were God's teachings.*" Brad S. Gregory, *Salvation at Stake: Christian Martyrdom in Early Modern Europe* (Cambridge, Mass.: Harvard University Press, 1999), p. 344.

Reformation's legacy, over time the contests grew increasingly subdued and came to resemble sparring matches instead of deadly duels. To be sure, to this day Baptists still debate with Presbyterians over the need to dunk versus the right to sprinkle, and Protestant, Catholic, and Orthodox Christians disagree over whether we are celebrating Communion, the Lord's Supper, the Eucharist, or the Mass. Yet in the main, the bloody conflicts have turned into polite debates and are carried on in the pages of denominational journals or across the table at ecumenical seminars, rather than in prisons or on the way to the stake.

In fact, today sharp disagreements about the incarnation and the sacraments are more likely to be found in Protestant arguments about the arts than in ecumenical debates about the church. In recent decades, for example, as some Christian critics and artists have embraced the language of the sacraments to embellish a romantic aesthetic, Samuel Taylor Coleridge's view of the imagination has often proved more divisive than Luther's theory of consubstantiation. Question the wisdom of calling poetry a sacrament, and you will be accused of denying mystery and disenchanting the world; doubt the existence of a quasi-sacred faculty called the imagination, and you are promoting a view of human beings as soul-starved mechanisms.

If we listen for long to contemporary religious arguments about the arts, we see that everything hinges upon the view of history held by each party to the dispute. Those who speak of sacramental art and incarnational poetry, or who see the imagination as the image of God in the human person, consider such designations to be *atemporal, essential,* and *necessary.* They speak of it being the nature of language to be incarnational, or they take it to be the case that human beings across time have possessed a faculty called the imagination. On the other hand, those who question the contemporary usefulness of such discourse take these terms to be *historical, accidental,* and *contingent.*[22] They recognize

22. This opposition — between the *necessary* and the *contingent* — revisits the conflict between the nominalists and the realists in the late Middle Ages. In the main, the realists were supported by the Catholic Church, while the nominalists were forerunners of the Lutheran Reformation. As Steven Ozment explains, "Ockham's theology transformed the church into a strictly historical reality, a creature in time and an object of faith that could no longer present itself as the passageway through which all life necessarily passed en route to a preordained supernatural end." *Age of Reform,* p. 63. For a thorough examination of the influence of nominalism, see Amos Funkenstein, *Theology and the Scientific*

that the imagination as we know it is in good measure a creation of the eighteenth century, and they trace the roots of contemporary sacramental theories of the arts to romantic efforts to sustain a Christian view of culture without the nourishment of explicit liturgical practices or confessional beliefs.

Still, for many in the past two centuries, the language of sacrament and imagination has proved to be central to their understanding of the arts. They have employed it to counter the corrosive power of modern historical consciousness, for this aesthetic adoption of religious imagery has given them a means of "skipping the history" of modernity. I am referring to an attitude towards history embedded in what M. H. Abrams has called the "high argument" of romanticism. In his words, the romantic poets and critics sought to "sustain the inherited cultural order against . . . the imminence of chaos." According to the romantic argument, that state of chaos had been a cultural byproduct of Newtonian science and philosophical rationalism, both of which had disenchanted the world and transformed it into a soulless mechanism. By having called into question both the miracles of Christ and the authenticity of the scriptures, materialism and rationalism had wreaked havoc upon historic Christianity. Abrams says the romantics assessed the damage and decided they were willing to give up "the dogmatic understructure of Christianity," if by doing so they could "save what one could save of its experiential relevance and values."[23]

The romantic "high argument" portrayed modern history as a saga of disenchantment and turned to the imagination to pass over the history of early modernity and restore the mystery that historical consciousness had dispelled. In the words of a contemporary art historian, from the middle of the eighteenth century to the present, the romantic tradition "has invested art with the power to heal a decadent human condition," and its advocates have sought "in works of art what can best be described as an enchantment."[24] The darker the disenchanted world became, the more brilliantly the imagination shined upon it, and more than one romantic poet coupled his "claims to boundless creativity" with

Imagination: From the Middle Ages to the Seventeenth Century (Princeton: Princeton University Press, 1986), pp. 57-72.

23. Abrams, *Natural Supernaturalism,* p. 68.

24. David Morgan, "The Enchantment of Art: Abstraction and Empathy from German Romanticism to Expressionism," *Journal of the History of Ideas* 57 (1996): 317-18.

"his experience of the world as God-forsaken."[25] In 1810, for example, William Blake wrote, "Let it. here be Noted that the Greek Fables originated in Spiritual Mystery & Real Vision," but they have been clouded over and lost, while "the Hebrew Bible & the Greek Gospel are Genuine Preservd by the Saviours Mercy." To recover what has been lost, and to tap into the power that had given life to ancient mystery, Blake turned to the new theory of the imagination. "The Nature of my Work is Visionary or Imaginative it is an Endeavour to Restore what the Ancients calld the Golden Age," he proclaimed. Indeed, "This world of Imagination is the World of Eternity it is the Divine Bosom into which we shall all go after the death of the Vegetated body."[26] If it can restore the Golden Age and raise the dead, who are we to deny the sacred power of such an imaginative faculty?

Several years ago, the fate of the Blakean imagination was discussed in a session at a conference commemorating the founding of Calvin College.[27] To gauge the contingent nature of the idea of a sacred imagination, we need only consider what the state of things would have been if that conversation had taken place in Geneva in 1564 instead of in Grand Rapids in 2001. The meeting in September 1564 would have come three months after the death of John Calvin at the age of 56. (William Shakespeare was a five-month-old infant at the time.) Europe was in turmoil, as the forces unleashed by the Reformation and the reactions to it swept across the continent.

At our imaginary sixteenth-century gathering, it would have been inconceivable to argue about the sacramental nature of literature or to promote a theory concerning the redemptive power of the imagination. For to speak of the sacraments in the mid-sixteenth century would have been to join a great debate over Christ's power, not poetry's, and over the meaning of divine grace rather than the measure of human creativity. Is the Lord's Supper, those participants would have asked, a matter of transubstantiation, consubstantiation, or remembrance? Is baptism a means of grace, a mark of the covenant, or a sign confirming a conscious faith decision?

25. Charles Taylor, *Hegel* (Cambridge: Cambridge University Press, 1975), p. 47.

26. William Blake, "A Vision of the Last Judgment," in *The Poetry and Prose of William Blake,* ed. David V. Erdman (Garden City, N.Y.: Doubleday, 1970), p. 545.

27. The conference was titled "Christian Scholarship . . . for What?: An International Interdisciplinary Conference." See http://www.calvin.edu/scs/2001/conferences/125conf/

On the question of imagination, there would have been no disagreement in 1564, because no one would have believed such a thing existed. Not until the eighteenth century, in fact, did Scottish and German philosophers fashion the concept, with the help of a gifted group of English poets.[28] We have seen how highly William Blake valued this newfound faculty, and to William Wordsworth its development represented something like the divinely appointed goal of his life. Homer had written of the return of Odysseus, Virgil of the birth of Rome, and Dante of the soul's eternal destiny, but Wordsworth had a different subject for his epic, that being the "growth of a poet's mind":

> This love more intellectual cannot be
> Without Imagination, which, in truth,
> Is but another name for absolute strength
> And clearest insight, amplitude of mind,
> And Reason in her most exalted mood.
> This faculty hath been the moving soul
> Of our long labour.[29]

Wordsworth's collaborator and friend Samuel Taylor Coleridge shared his passion for this newfound faculty: "The primary IMAGINATION I hold to be the living Power and prime Agent of all human Perception, and as a repetition in the finite mind of the eternal act of creation in the infinite I AM."[30]

To anyone living in 1564, Wordsworth and Coleridge's praise of the imagination would have generated a quizzical response at best and a hostile rebuke at worst. A sixteenth-century audience would have identified more readily with the Hampole Psalter's warning against "vain imaginations" and would have resonated with William Langland's conclusion

28. The word "imagination" dates back to the fourteenth century, but the idea of it as a human faculty associated with "poetic genius" did not originate until the eighteenth century. Matthew Maguire provides an insightful account of the corollary development of this concept in French culture from the seventeenth century to the nineteenth. See *The Conversion of Imagination: From Pascal through Rousseau to Tocqueville* (Cambridge, Mass.: Harvard University Press, 2006).

29. William Wordsworth, *The Prelude: A Parallel Text,* ed. J. C. Maxwell (New York: Penguin 1971), p. 520.

30. Samuel Taylor Coleridge, *Biographia Literaria,* ed. James Engell and W. Jackson Bate (Princeton: Princeton University Press, 1983), 1:304.

that "supposing is not wisdom, nor is it wise imagination." If they had read the Coverdale Bible carefully, they would have found the following translation of Lamentations 3:61 — "Thou hast heard their despiteful words, oh Lord, and all their imaginations against me." To the people of the sixteenth century, the imagination was not a godlike power with special access to the truth, but a shadowy human capacity for falsehood and fabrication.

Inwardness and the Way to the Imagination

How was it, then, that the imagination moved so boldly from the shadows to the spotlight in early modernity? What brought about such a sudden transformation of a concept as marginal as the imagination had been? Why, over the short span of several generations, did the impulse to spurn such a thing as the imagination turn into an eagerness to embrace it?

A number of observers believe the answers to such questions are to be found at the crossroads where the modern consciousness of history meets the contemporary sense of the self. In *Sources of the Self,* philosopher Charles Taylor has written of the developments surrounding the growth of that consciousness and the birth of the imagination. In that work, Taylor traces the modern self to three major sources, each of which also played a role in the development of a theory of the imagination. These sources include, first, the unprecedented growth of the sense of inwardness that has become central to our understanding of the self; we in the modern world now believe that each of us has what Taylor calls an "inexhaustible inner domain." A second, vital factor in the development of the modern self proved to be the Reformation's affirmation of ordinary life, which broke down countless hierarchical barriers and leveled many longstanding distinctions between the sacred and the secular. For the third major influence, Taylor cites the late-eighteenth-century turn to nature as a moral and spiritual source.

Taylor begins his exploration of inwardness by noting how we have "naturally come to think that we have selves the way we have heads or arms, and inner depths the way we have hearts or livers." We divvy up our experience of the world by establishing a stark opposition between "inside" and "outside," and we situate our feelings, thoughts, and ideas "within" us. We take this vision of things to be a matter of common sense, when it is in actuality a product of our specific historical situation. Although it has become the dominant mode of thinking about the human person in the industrialized world, such an understanding of human inwardness "had a beginning in time and space and may have an end."[31]

To study that beginning, Taylor returns to antiquity. He cites the particular importance of Plato, whose theory of the "unified self" eventually made possible our modern understanding of interiority. To be sure, the Greek philosopher hardly held to a modern understanding of selfhood, because for him "the moral sources we accede to by reason are not within us." Instead, they dwell in the timeless realm of the Forms, far beyond the whirl of the emotions and the world of the body. But at the same time, there was in Plato at least a hint of the self to come, for his view of "self-collected awareness . . . requires some conception of the mind as a unitary space" in which ideas may eventually be considered to "dwell."[32]

On this point, Taylor appears to be largely in agreement with Eric Havelock, who argues that in the generations leading up to Plato, Greek thought was in the process of discovering "the autonomous psyche." Prior to that discovery, the culture of the Greeks had been dominated by the epic tradition, which transmitted vital information from generation to generation through the memorized language of heroic poetry. "Homeric man," writes Havelock, "was a part of all he had seen and heard and remembered." He did not possess anything close to what we would call a critical intelligence, which involves the capacity to distance oneself from one's circumstances and surroundings and to view them with a degree of detachment. "Homeric man" was not expected to form convic-

31. Charles Taylor, *Sources of the Self: The Making of the Modern Identity* (Cambridge, Mass.: Harvard University Press, 1989), pp. 111-12.

32. Taylor, *Sources of the Self*, pp. 120-26. Jerrold Seigel takes exception to Taylor's account of modern identity, which he says "deserves to be challenged both in its particulars and in its general approach to the subject." Seigel's overarching objection is that "Taylor provides a narrow and distorted image of modern thinking about the self" due to "his nostalgia for the lost Aristotelian cosmos." *The Idea of the Self: Thought and Experience in Western Europe Since the Seventeenth Century* (Cambridge: Cambridge University Press, 2005), pp. 42-43. The disagreement between Taylor and Seigel appears rooted in sharply divergent views of the possibility of recovering certain moral or theological resources suppressed in modernity. Whether one sides with Taylor or Seigel will depend in good measure on what one thinks of the possibility, that is, of *believing again*.

tions of his own, but to imitate the examples handed down to him. In sum, his mental condition was effectively one of a passive "surrender accomplished through the lavish employment of the emotions and of the motor reflexes."[33]

In these circumstances, it proved difficult for "the Greek ego" to resist "splitting itself into an endless series of moods," as it was swept along by the images and narratives of the epic tradition. Not until the time of Plato was that ego able to "rally itself to the point" where it could declare, "I am I, an autonomous little universe of my own, able to speak, think and act in independence of what I happen to remember." In resisting the tyranny of memory, Greek thought began to claim that a human being possesses a consciousness capable of discovering within itself reasons for acting that do not depend upon the prompting of the poetic tradition. This "psyche" is hardly the volatile self of our therapeutic culture but is instead a thoughtful agency that is to be distinguished from the "nexus of motor responses, unconscious reflexes, and passions and emotions which had been mobilised for countless time" in the service of cultural memory. For Plato, the fledgling self had to be reflective as well as critical, and Havelock says its emergence marked the discovery of "the activity of sheer thinking."[34]

The Platonic "discovery of intellection" made it possible to distinguish between "subjects" and "objects." To us this distinction seems self-evident, but in the ancient world, it took nothing less than a philosophic revolution to yield the conclusion that although objects come and go, there is within each of us an "I" that endures. According to Havelock, in Plato we find an unprecedented possibility of conceiving that in every situation there is "a 'subject', a 'me', whose separate identity is the first

33. Eric A. Havelock, *Preface to Plato* (Cambridge, Mass.: Belknap Press of Harvard University Press, 1963), p. 199. Havelock's thesis has had considerable influence in the study of orality and literacy, as the work of Marshall McLuhan and Walter Ong readily attests. Its reception in the field of classical studies has been decidedly more mixed. See John Halverson, "Havelock on Greek Orality and Literacy," *Journal of the History of Ideas* 53 (1992): 148-63.

34. Havelock, *Preface*, p. 200. For an illuminating study of the emergence of the concept of the person in ancient Greece, see Arnaldo Momigliano, "Marcel Mauss and the Quest for the Person in Greek Biography and Autobiography," in *The Category of the Person: Anthropology, Philosophy, History*, ed. Michael Carrithers, Steven Collins, and Steven Lukes (Cambridge: Cambridge University Press, 1985), pp. 83-92.

premise to be accepted before" we can begin to conclude anything about that situation.[35] This may not be the self as we know it, but it is clearly one of its ancestors.

Between Plato and us stands Augustine, whose autobiography, the *Confessions,* reads like a "manifesto of the inner world."[36] For this fifth-century saint, inwardness was centered in memory — the same power, according to Havelock, from which Plato had worked to set the Greek ego free. For Augustine, however, the situation is reversed. The memory he cultivates has nothing to do with transmitting collective cultural identity but focuses instead on ordering and preserving the ceaseless, chaotic flood of personal experience. Through memory, Augustine says, "I can recall at will anything drawn in and hoarded by way of my other senses." He can distinguish the scent of lilies from that of violets and the taste of honey from grape juice, as well as the feel of smooth from rough, "without tasting or feeling anything: I am simply passing them in review before my mind by remembering them."[37] Once planted within the mind, those experiences lie buried beneath the surface of conscious life, like so many seeds waiting to blossom and bask in the warmth of memory's sun.

Deep within our memory, we may even glimpse the God in whose image we have been fashioned. "There I come to meet myself," Augustine says of that memory, and "in that same enormous recess of my mind" I weave plans for the future out of the fabric of my past. "This faculty of memory is a great one, O my God," he cries out. "Who can plumb its depth?" We travel far to "admire lofty mountains" and "crashing waterfalls," but we leave the greatest wonder, ourselves and our memories, "behind out of sight." Why should we gape at "vast stretches of ocean, and the dance of the stars," when we already "harbor" within us the "immense spaces of memory?" For within that harbor, we shelter the very presence of God. "Most certain it is that you do dwell in it, because I have

35. Havelock, *Preface,* p. 201. "Plato seems to have been the first person to argue that the core of each person's existence is an immaterial soul, which by its nature is immortal." Seigel, *Idea of the Self,* p. 46.

36. Peter Brown, *Augustine of Hippo: A Biography* (Berkeley: University of California Press, 1967), p. 168. "Before St. Augustine — or at least before Gregory of Nazianzus, as G. Misch pointed out — it is difficult to find autobiographies with the purpose of describing oneself, one's own character and inner life." Momigliano, "Marcel Mauss," p. 90.

37. St. Augustine, *The Confessions,* trans. Maria Boulding, O.S.B. (1997; repr., New York: Vintage, 1998), pp. 205-6. See Maguire, *Conversion of Imagination,* pp. 36-40.

been remembering you since I first learned to know you, and there I find you when I remember you."[38]

Still, this is not yet the *self* as we know it. Plato discovered the self-reflective ego and Augustine plumbed the depths of memory, yet neither of them believed that each of us harbors an internal entity that is extended in inner space and marked by definable boundaries. In fact, Augustine was hesitant to refer to the "recesses" of memory as being in any way our possession. He knew his own memories were lodged in a "someplace," but wherever *that* was, it was to him a "no place." As he explains, "here too are all those things which I received through a liberal education and have not yet forgotten; they are stored away in some remote inner place, which yet is not really a place at all."[39] So, despite the fact that he used the "language of inwardness," Augustine did not intend by it what we do, when we speak of the self, and he did not see "the moral sources as situated within us any more than Plato did."[40]

It was to be more than a thousand years before those moral sources would take up residence within what we now call the "self," and like many before him, Taylor finds René Descartes in the climactic scene of the story of the discovery of that self. He says the French philosopher decisively abandoned the effort to conceive of the cosmic order as embodying a set of Ideas with which human beings must somehow align themselves. Plato's vision of "the Ideas [had] involved a very close relation between scientific explanation and moral vision," and for all their focus on inwardness and the ego, Plato and Augustine had believed unambiguously in "an order of things in the cosmos which is good." Descartes, how-

38. Augustine, *Confessions,* pp. 206-7, 221. Speaking of Augustine's theory of memory and its relationship to God, Harald Weinrich writes: "Memory is the place where God, mindful of his covenant with men, abides even among sinners in order to await, not entirely within the reach of the sinner's forgetting, the day on which the sinner finally finds his way back to him." *Lethe,* p. 23.

39. Augustine, *Confessions,* p. 207. Krister Stendahl's essay on St. Paul and the "introspective conscience" makes a parallel point about the modern origins of the self. Stendahl highlights the "drastic difference" between Luther's sixteenth-century "struggle with his conscience" and Paul's first-century "awareness of sin." Luther wrestles with self-consciousness in a manner that St. Paul could not have done, and according to Stendahl, Augustine "may well have been one of the first to express the dilemma of the introspective conscience." "The Apostle Paul and the Introspective Conscience of the West," *Harvard Theological Review* 56 (1963): 200, 203.

40. Taylor, *Sources of the Self,* p. 143.

ever, followed the lead of Galileo and no longer took this to be the case. Like the astronomer, he pictured the universe as governed by mechanical laws rather than transcendent ideas, and he took it for granted that the new scientific universe was as soulless in its nature as it was predictable in its workings.[41]

Although Descartes made his peace with the explanatory power of Copernicus and Galileo's materialism, he also understood its harsh implications for the moral and spiritual life. To counter the potential danger on this front, he looked to Augustinian inwardness for assistance. Following Augustine's lead, the philosopher sought to draw "the mind away from the senses, through a special kind of contemplation of itself, to a special kind of contemplation of God." As it contemplated the Deity, the soul was to draw upon the resources it needed to reanimate nature.[42] There was no question as to which was the most important element here, for the soul pours life and purpose into nature, rather than drawing them from it. This contemplation removes the mind from its customary habitat in nature and sets it in "a new intellectual space whence it closely attains to God's view of the world."[43]

This detached observer is an immediate ancestor of the self as we know it, and so it was that with his emphasis upon the *Cogito,* whose self-consciousness proves the existence of God and the ego, Descartes made that self an entity and assigned to it a distinctly modern identity. The Cartesian self has heft and reach, along with a permanent address. "The modern, post-expressivist subject really has, unlike the denizens of any earlier culture, 'inner depths,'" Charles Taylor concludes, and it rules over a vast "inexhaustible inner domain."[44]

41. Taylor, *Sources of the Self,* pp. 143-44.

42. Stephen Menn, *Descartes and Augustine* (Cambridge: Cambridge University Press, 1998), p. x. Menn elaborates upon this point: "Descartes, like Augustine, believes that metaphysical knowledge, being purely intellectual, is independent of the testimony of the senses, and even somehow opposed to what the senses habitually conceive. . . . It will be concerned primarily with God and with the human soul, and not with God and the soul as they may be inferred from sensible objects. The human soul will be known primarily as a thing that thinks: not as an act of an organic body, but as something only extrinsically related to a body" (p. 5).

43. Thomas Pavel, "Literature and the Arts," in René Descartes, *Discourse on Method and Meditations on First Philosophy,* ed. David Weissman (New Haven: Yale University Press, 1996), p. 352.

44. Taylor, *Sources of the Self,* p. 390.

Before long, the opulence of that inner domain began to throw into sharp relief the poverty of the world outside the self. Over the course of the eighteenth century, the imbalance between inward imaginings and outward realities grew steadily greater, and it was this disparity, perhaps more than anything else, that eventually prompted the romantic re-conception and expansion of the imagination. Borrowing a phrase from the German poet and philosopher Friedrich Schiller, Max Weber famously described this historical process of impoverishment as "the disenchantment of the world." He defined disenchantment as the belief that "there are [in nature] no mysterious incalculable forces that come into play, but rather that one can, in principle, master all things by calculation."[45]

In the history of modernity, the rise of disenchantment has coincided with a gradual decline in the belief that "the order of things embodies an ontic logos."[46] With this term, Taylor refers to a central premise of Greek and Christian thought, which is that the created order is worded, that meaning animates it, and that a purposeful will is at work within it. Belief in such an order has waned in modernity, and faith in the human mind has correspondingly waxed, as that mind increasingly has been called upon to impart order and grant meaning to a world that it takes to be "without form, and void."

The Self Under Siege: Romantic Responses

The romantic poets and philosophers broke upon the cultural scene in the late eighteenth century, exactly when the modern sense of historical possibility was meeting up with the historical reality of disenchantment.

45. Max Weber, "Science as a Vocation," in *From Max Weber: Essays in Sociology,* trans. and ed. H. H. Gerth and C. Wright Mills (New York: Oxford University Press, 1946), p. 139. For the connections to romantic theories of the arts, see H. C. Greisman, "'Disenchantment of the World': Romanticism, Aesthetics and Sociological Theory," *British Journal of Sociology* 27 (1976): 495-507.

Of the implications of disenchantment, Charles Taylor writes: "We have constructed an environment in which we live a uniform, univocal secular time, which we try to measure and control in order to get things done. This 'time frame' deserves, perhaps more than any other facet of modernity, Weber's famous description of a 'stahlhartes Gehäuse' (iron cage)." *A Secular Age,* p. 59.

46. Taylor, *Sources of the Self,* p. 186.

Along with a number of others, Samuel Taylor Coleridge responded to the confluence of these forces by promoting the powers of the imagination. He shifted from the empiricist view of the mind as a *tabula rasa* on which experience inscribes the truth to the idealists' faith in the imagination's intuitive power to discern truth. His eventual adoption of idealism, writes biographer Richard Holmes, involved "a philosophic conversion from a materialist to a religious view of the world." Coleridge was driven by a powerful religious desire, as he sought deliverance from the state of "spiritual despair" to which a disenchanted world had driven him. "He *needed* to affirm that the human spirit was not mechanically determined" and simply passive in the face of the natural order. Instead of serving as a catalogue of experiences, the mind as Coleridge came to envision it became a power capable of reviving and transforming nature. He set out to assure himself and persuade others that "the creative powers of the human imagination were active and free." These transcendent powers reach "to infinity" and offer proof of the spirit's liberty. As challenging as the task would prove to be, the poet eagerly set about constructing a "staircase from secular to divine epistemology."[47]

To build that staircase, Coleridge used lumber from nature's storehouse and a hammer forged on the anvil of the imagination. In the *Biographia Literaria,* he offered his famous 199-word description of the imaginative faculty, and in doing so, he "defined for the English-speaking world the Romantic concept of creativity." According to Holmes, the definition Coleridge put forward combines "the quality of an algebraic formula and a witch's spell or incantation," as it weaves together strands of psychological, scientific, and religious argument. In Coleridge's words,

47. Richard Holmes, *Coleridge: Darker Reflections, 1804-1834* (New York: Pantheon, 1999), pp. 393-94. As Terry Pinkard observes, conversions such as Coleridge's came at a cost. In the wake of Kant, we discover a "radically new emphasis on human spontaneity and freedom." We are no longer to view ourselves primarily as agents "fulfilling some metaphysical potentiality for [our] own perfection." Instead, "in even the most ordinary perceptions, we find only the results of human spontaneity, expressed in self-imposed conceptual rules, combining itself with the given elements of sensory and intuitive experience, not the preordained results of a perfect order disclosing itself to us. The old world, so it seemed, had melted away under the heat of Kant's *Critique*." *German Philosophy, 1760-1860: The Legacy of Idealism* (Cambridge: Cambridge University Press, 2002), p. 44.

For Coleridge's brief flirtation with the English Jacobins and their ripe sense of historical possibility, see Richard Holmes, *Coleridge: Early Visions, 1772-1804* (New York: Viking, 1989), pp. 47-49.

"the primary IMAGINATION I hold to be the living Power and prime Agent of all human Perception, and as a representation in the finite mind of the eternal act of creation in the infinite I AM." The secondary imagination, the poet says, is "identical with the primary in the *kind* of its agency, and differing only in *degree*." It works like a chemical agent as it "dissolves, diffuses, dissipates" the elements of the world, but like the Spirit of God, it only dismantles "in order to re-create. It is essentially *vital,* even as all objects (*as* objects) are essentially fixed and dead."[48]

In comparing the imagination to God, Coleridge was effectively committing himself to offer a corollary for Jesus the Son, and the analogy appeared to be obvious: just as the Father reveals himself through the incarnate Son, so does the Imagination embody itself in language. For Coleridge, the symbol was the word made flesh; it was to be "characterized by a translucence of the special in the individual, or of the general in the special, or of the universal in the general." In the symbol, the mysterious shines through the mundane, and there is a "translucence of the eternal through and in the temporal."[49] The symbol was to Coleridge an "objective conception transmitted into terms of feeling — the 'union and reconciliation of that which is nature with that which is exclusively human.'"[50] As such, it reconciles the mind to the world beyond itself, because just as time and eternity meet in Jesus Christ, so do they fuse in the symbol.

The Coleridgian legacy inspired countless writers in the nineteenth century before its influence declined markedly in many quarters in the wake of Darwin and Marx. But that story has been told often and well elsewhere. The one we will pursue at this point has to do with the intriguing manner in which Coleridge's categories have lived on in, among other places, Christian poetics, as critics and artists alike have made use of his insights in an effort to reinvigorate the arts and give them a sacred cast.[51] The ties between Protestant spirituality and romantic aesthetics

48. Holmes, *Darker Reflections,* p. 410; Coleridge, in *Biographia,* 1:304.

49. Samuel Taylor Coleridge, quoted in W. Jackson Bate, *Coleridge* (1968; repr., Cambridge, Mass.: Harvard University Press, 1987), p. 164.

50. Bate, *Coleridge,* pp. 164-65.

51. Matthew Maguire speaks of "imagination's remarkable status in modern Western culture — indeed, a status inconceivable in the history that precedes modernity." *Conversion of Imagination,* p. 3. He notes that the concept of the imagination remains a particularly potent force in French poststructuralism.

reach back two hundred years, but in the past half-century, many from the evangelical Protestant tradition in North America have pressed hard to strengthen those connections. They have done so for many of the same reasons that had initially prompted nineteenth-century religious thinkers to embrace romantic premises. That is, these contemporary Christians see the imagination, working in tandem with nature, as providing spiritual resources that are not to be found elsewhere; further, they envision that imagination validating the Christian faith and protecting its spiritual substance from the corrosive effects of rationalism, skepticism, and empiricism.[52]

For an eloquent, forceful example of this appropriation, we might consider the recent efforts of a distinguished Christian poet, Scott Cairns, to elaborate the concept of a "sacramental poetics." In an essay first delivered at that conference at Calvin College in 2001, Cairns seeks to explain the "perceived absence" he encounters in most poems and to point to the "real presence" that genuine poetry should, like the Eucharist, embody. He tells of having grown up in a Baptist church, in which the sacrament was a mere act of commemoration known as "the Lord's Supper." As they consumed crackers and grape juice, he and his fellow Baptists merely expected to be "reminded" of Christ's sacrifice. "Neither the juice nor the cracker were, in themselves, *mysterious*." They pointed back to a first-century meal and ahead to a heavenly banquet but offered scant sustenance in the interim.

To Cairns, most contemporary poems are like so many crackers meant "to be ingested in order that the mind might be thereby directed to another, more real event, an event whose agency is always — by the way — necessarily fixed in the past." Such poems have traded a profound

52. For an account of the union of evangelical Protestant aesthetics and the romantic tradition, see Roger Lundin, "Offspring of an Odd Union: Evangelical Attitudes toward the Arts," in *Evangelicalism and Modern America,* ed. George Marsden (Grand Rapids: Eerdmans, 1984), pp. 135-49.

My focus in this chapter is on Protestant criticism. Although Roman Catholic scholars frequently use the term "literary imagination," they mean by it something different from the idea of imitating God's creative powers. In *Christ and Apollo,* for example, William F. Lynch differentiates his work from those forms of theory that "give literature a basically strange character." The first of these "strange" forms he mentions is "the theory that the literary imagination is absolutely 'creative' and productive of altogether new and self-contained realities." *Christ and Apollo: The Dimensions of the Literary Imagination* (1960; repr., New York: New American Library, 1963), p. xi.

suggestive power for a paltry right to communicate facts and commemorate events. The genuinely *poetic,* on the other hand, is an occasion of "ongoing, *generative* agency" that is *"present-presence,"* and it takes its cues from those Christian traditions that "embrace a sacramental theology." When we consume the elements in an authentic sacramental observance of the Eucharist, we partake in God's "Entire and Indivisible Being," and we bear "his creative and re-creative energy in our sanctified persons." Our poems, in turn, have the power to bear this energy and to embody this Being as well. To Cairns, this "appalling" presence of *Very God of Very God* serves "to exemplify what I would call *the poetic: the presence and activity of inexhaustible, indeterminate enormity apprehended in a discreet space.*"[53]

To be sure, Cairns's Orthodox view of the sacrament represents a substantial tradition within Christian history, and that sacramental theory is not at issue here. What might be questioned, however, is whether an Orthodox understanding of the Eucharist necessarily entails a sacramental understanding of poetry. One can participate in this sacrament without having to believe it illustrates a sacred poetic phenomenon or accept the power of the Eucharist without having to take poetry to be "that unique genre that performs the mystery of word made flesh."[54]

At the same time, it would be as foolish to question Coleridge's theoretical brilliance as it would be churlish to mock the sorrow that drove his search for a spiritual poetics. He and his fellow romantic poets experienced a genuine crisis of spiritual confidence, and for understandable reasons they lamented the loss of spiritual ardor in a world that had been disenchanted by mechanistic science and afflicted by a new historical consciousness. Still, as the history of sacramental poetics has shown, Coleridge's solution had consequences he may never have imagined and created difficulties we cannot avoid. The romantic promotion of the

53. Scott Cairns, "Elemental Metonymy: Poems, Icons, Holy Mysteries." Christian Scholarship . . . for What?: An International, Interdisciplinary Conference, 27-29 September 2001. Calvin College. See http://www.calvin.edu/scs/2001/conferences/125conf/papers/cairnss.htm.

54. See, for example, Alexander Schmemann, *For the Life of the World: Sacraments and Orthodoxy,* 2nd ed., rev. and exp. (Crestwood, N.Y.: St. Vladimir's Seminary Press, 1973). "The time of the world has become the time of the Church, the time of salvation and redemption. And God has made us *competent* . . . to be His witnesses, to fulfill what He has done and is ever doing. This is the meaning of the Eucharist" (p. 46).

quickening spirit fed the growth of the inexhaustible inner domain, and the Coleridgian theory of the imagination fueled the expansion of an imperial aesthetic order in which the imagination often seemed to rival God rather than to serve him. Indeed, many of Coleridge's heirs have learned to train their sights so intently on the inner domain that they blind themselves to the glories of the world beyond the mind.

The Affirmation of Ordinary Life

Even as the burgeoning power of inwardness was radically recasting the conception of the self in the eighteenth and nineteenth centuries, another force was at work, shifting the balance between the world within and the one without. This was the "affirmation of ordinary life," which is Charles Taylor's name for a complex set of beliefs and practices that flowed from the Reformation's understanding of sacred offices and secular callings.

By "ordinary life," Taylor means the facets of our experience that are centered on production and reproduction, "the things needed for life, and our life as sexual beings, including marriage and the family." Throughout most of history, these aspects of human experience had been considered necessary but insufficient for the pursuit of the good. Aristotle, for instance, believed that labor and procreation were essential for providing the "infrastructure" of "the good life," but he was also convinced that in themselves they could not be considered elements of that ideal.[55] Jürgen Habermas notes that in ancient Greece, "the reproduction of life, the labor of the slaves, and the service of the women went on under the aegis of the master's domination." Even birth and death unfolded in the murky "realm of necessity and transitoriness" that comprised the "private sphere." Only in the public sphere, which few were privileged to enter, could one discover freedom and a sense of permanence.[56]

The medieval church adapted these pagan distinctions between spiritual virtues and prosaic necessities. With its monastic orders, its re-

55. Taylor, *Sources of the Self,* p. 211.

56. Jürgen Habermas, *The Structural Transformation of the Public Sphere: An Inquiry into a Category of Bourgeois Society,* trans. Thomas Burger with the assistance of Frederick Lawrence (Cambridge, Mass.: MIT Press, 1989), pp. 3-4.

quirement of priestly celibacy, and its emphasis upon religious vocations, Catholicism gave its special blessing to the idea of selected higher callings. It acknowledged the importance of "the life that the vast majority cannot help leading, the life of production and the family, work and sex," but in the hierarchy of spiritual values, it ranked a life of that kind far below one of contemplative devotion.[57]

Together, the Reformation and the Copernican Revolution served to level this hierarchical order and set ordinary life on an equal footing with the religious callings. From the scientific side, this came through the promotion of a cosmological model that called into question both the contemplative ideal and the social order that supported it. Copernicus dislodged the earth from the center of the universe, and then Newton turned the heavenly mysteries into the laws of motion. In the shadows cast by this new mechanistic order, the cosmos lost its luster and was changed from a subject of spiritual contemplation into an object of mechanical study. The harmonious music of the spheres gave way to the flow of matter in motion, and the ancient ideal of contemplating the beautiful order of the cosmos now appeared "vain and misguided." We should forsake the fruitless search for a spiritual order hidden within reality, Francis Bacon concluded in the early seventeenth century, and turn our attention exclusively to the study of "how things function." The point of scientific learning is to make things better, not *there* but *here,* not *then* but *now:* "To relieve the condition of man: this is the goal."[58]

This scientific attack on the contemplative ideal dovetailed with the Reformers' questioning of the mediating role of the church. If every believer was a priest, as Luther had argued, then Catholic sacerdotalism and sacramentalism had to be rethought entirely. The Reformers rose to the challenge and mounted a brisk assault on the Catholic claim that the sacraments possessed an efficacy that was independent of the faith of the priest who administered them or of the parishioner who received them. In Catholicism, the sacraments had been considered effective *ex opere operato* ("from the work already done"), which meant that Christ's

57. Charles Taylor, *Modern Social Imaginaries* (Durham: Duke University Press, 2004), p. 73. Taylor sees the Protestant "affirmation of ordinary life" as having been particularly "formative in the development of modern civilization." It led to the "central place given to the economic in our lives," and its "anti-elitist" component "underlies the fundamental importance of equality in our social and political lives" (p. 74).

58. Taylor, *Sources of the Self,* p. 213.

sacrifice had established their power once and for all. According to Protestantism, in contrast, that power depended in part upon the spiritual state of the participants, because the sacraments have their force *ex opere operantis* ("from the work being done").

Having concluded that neither the priest nor the host fully conveyed the grace of God, the Reformers saw personal commitment and inner sincerity as the main bridges running from the human to the divine and back again. To be certain, the shift to human inwardness took place gradually, and Luther for one was quick to resist the radical rethinking of communion that some Reformers were already putting forward in his lifetime. "There are two things that should be known and proclaimed" about this sacrament, he wrote in 1526. The first is "what one should believe," or the *"objectum fidei"* (object of faith), which is "the work or thing in which one believes." The other is "the faith itself, or the use which one should properly make of that in which he believes." This is "the attitude which the heart should have toward" the sacrament, and Luther admits it is "the best part" of the sacramental equation. But that does not mean that the "first part" — the objective presence of Christ in the sacraments — is not also important, and Luther regrets that it is "being assailed by many."[59]

Nevertheless, despite Luther's efforts to balance the claims of the *object of faith* against those of the *believing subject,* the scales began to tip in that subject's direction, as the transfer of authority from sacrament to spirit proceeded apace in early modernity. For judging religious experience, motives gradually came to be considered more important than actions or consequences, and the locus of divine activity shifted from the offices of the church to the spirit of the believer. Charles Taylor quotes Joseph Hall's early seventeenth-century admonition that "the homeliest service that we doe in an honest calling, though it be but to plow, or digge, if done in obedience . . . is crowned with an ample reward; whereas

59. Martin Luther, "The Sacrament of the Body and Blood of Christ — Against the Fanatics," in *Martin Luther's Basic Theological Writings,* ed. Timothy F. Lull (Minneapolis: Fortress, 1989), p. 314. Steven Ozment describes the tension between object and subject: "The options in late medieval religion were not, however, 'subjective' religious emotion and 'objective' church ritual and authority," for Protestantism had its own "irrational, magical, and purely ritualistic side. What Protestants set out to overcome was perceived oppressive superstition — teachings and practices that burdened the consciences and pocketbooks of the faithful." *Age of Reform,* p. 210.

the best workes for their kinde (preaching, praying, offering Evangelicall sacrifices) if without respect of God's injunction and glory, are loaded with curses. God loveth adverbs; and cares not how good, but how well."[60]

In ways the Reformers never fully anticipated, the adverbial culture of Protestantism hastened the displacement of the center of spiritual activity from the cosmos arrayed outside the self to the labyrinthine world enfolded within it. The further we travel into the Protestant era, the less likely we are to find God turning the heavenly wheel, and the more likely we are to encounter him plumbing the depths of our souls. We move from Dante's fourteenth-century praise of that "Love that moves the sun and the other stars" to William Blake's nineteenth-century glorification of the imagination in "The Vision of the Last Judgment": "What it will be Questiond When the Sun rises do you not see a round Disk of fire somewhat like a Guinea O no no I see an Innumerable company of the Heavenly host crying Holy Holy Holy is the Lord God Almighty."[61]

As the nineteenth century unfolded, the imaginative powers Blake had celebrated drew ever greater praise and had ever more lofty expectations placed upon them. With trenchant brilliance, Ralph Waldo Emerson summarized in 1837 the revolutionary steps that had led from Martin Luther's sixteenth-century discovery of faith to the late-eighteenth-century invention of the imagination. He did so by means of his "theory of books," which was grounded in the only "thing in the world, of value, . . . the active soul." Where Luther and Calvin had viewed the Bible as the Word of God meant to be read and obeyed, Emerson saw it as one of many once-inspired works that must now be supplanted. In itself, a book possesses no power, because it is nothing but an inert record of a once-vital activity. "The scholar of the first age" received the world into himself and gave it "the new arrangement of his own mind." Throughout history, Emerson says, the pattern has repeated itself:

> It came into him, life; it went out from him, truth. It came to him, short-lived actions; it went out from him, immortal thought. It came to him, business; it went from him, poetry. It was dead fact; now it is

60. Joseph Hall, quoted in Taylor, *Sources of the Self,* p. 224.

61. Dante, *Paradiso,* XXXIII: 145, in *The Portable Dante,* trans. and ed. Mark Musa (New York: Penguin, 1995), p. 585; Blake, *Poetry and Prose,* p. 555.

quick thought. . . . Precisely in proportion to the depth of mind from which it issued, so high does it soar, so long does it sing.[62]

Nature and the Imagination of Wonder

From the beginning, the Reformation's dual emphasis upon the vitality of inner faith and the affirmation of ordinary life often appeared in key respects to work at cross-purposes. For Luther, both nature and the human will had miraculous significance. His vow to become a monk, for example, was offered at the age of twenty-one and came in response to a thunderstorm that struck while he was returning to the university after a visit with his parents. He pleaded to be spared and cried out to St. Anne, the patron saint of travelers in distress. Because she protected him, he fulfilled his vow, forsook the study of law, and entered the Augustinian monastery immediately upon the completion of his journey.[63] To Luther there was little difference between the inner promptings of the spirit and the outward workings of ordinary experience. Both were charged like "shook foil" (Hopkins) with the awful grandeur of God.

Little more than a century after Luther's death, travelers had come to be equipped with more pedestrian explanations for the storms that rained down upon them. Taking these things to be natural phenomena in a physical order ruled by fixed laws, the people of the eighteenth century were considerably less inclined to read them as messages from a meddling God. By the time of the Enlightenment, deists across Europe were denying the reality of miracles and claiming that the God who had constructed the mechanism of the universe would never break its laws simply to impress a wayward soul or two. The God of the deists was too committed to the independence of ordinary experience to make an extraordinary intervention in it, and as a result, "miracles and prophecy, and all particular religious rites and beliefs, [appeared to be] mere superstition."[64]

Yet as we have seen, not everyone was content with a world that had been disenchanted by the discoveries of physics and the powers of his-

62. Ralph Waldo Emerson, *Essays and Lectures,* ed. Joel Porte (New York: Library of America, 1983), pp. 57, 56.

63. Ozment, *Age of Reform,* pp. 225-26.

64. John Herman Randall Jr., *The Making of the Modern Mind: A Survey of the Intellectual Background of the Present Age* (Boston: Houghton, 1926), p. 291.

torical consciousness. "The sculptors and poets were half-sad," W. H. Auden wryly observed in a poetic meditation on these developments, "And the pert retinue from the magician's house/Grumbled and went elsewhere."[65] Indeed, by the end of the eighteenth century, that "retinue" had become part of a cadre of artists and intellectuals who were crying out for a world that could match in its external splendor the marvels created by the imagination in its internal wonder.

As the nineteenth century unfolded, these disenchanted artists were discovering, to their regret, what Jay Gatsby was to learn a century later. In F. Scott Fitzgerald's classic study of the disparity between the visionary imagination and everyday reality, Gatsby is constantly confronting, but never understanding, the poverty of ordinary experience in contrast to the opulence of personal desire. His idealized lover, Daisy Fay Buchanan, ultimately "tumbled short of [Gatsby's] dreams — not through her own fault but because of the colossal vitality of his illusion." Of those illusions Fitzgerald could only conclude, "no amount of fire or freshness can challenge what a man will store up in his ghostly heart."[66]

Jay Gatsby was a late romantic, and the contrast that vexed him — between the fathomless depths of the human spirit and the shallow surfaces of ordinary life — had already troubled the first generation of romantic poets and philosophers. They proposed to solve the problem of disenchantment by listening to "the voice of nature," which Charles Taylor identifies as the third main source of the modern self's identity. They turned to nature to replenish the spiritual stores that science and history had depleted, and they supplemented their faith in it with an emphasis upon the mind's dynamic role in its interplay with the creation. In the words of Abrams, the romantics exercised "a revolutionary mode of imaginative perception" and sought to bring about "nothing less than the 'creation' of a new world." They expected the imagination to heal the wounds of individuals, but their ultimate hope was that this "re-creative way of seeing [would] in the course of time become available to 'the progressive power . . . of the whole species.'"[67]

The breathtaking sweep of the romantic vision is on full display in a

65. W. H. Auden, *Collected Poems,* ed. Edward Mendelson (New York: Modern Library, 2007), p. 188.

66. F. Scott Fitzgerald, *The Great Gatsby* (1925; repr., New York: Scribner, 1995), p. 101.

67. Abrams, *Natural Supernaturalism,* p. 338.

poem Wordsworth published in 1814 as a "Prospectus" to a longer work in which he planned to develop his "high argument" concerning the union of spirit and nature. Writing in Miltonic blank verse, the poet claims that nothing in the world or beyond it — not "Jehovah with his thunder," not the "choir of shouting Angels," nor even "Chaos" or the pits of Hell — "can breed such fear and awe/As fall upon us often when we look/Into our Minds, into the Mind of Man." History has clouded the memory of Eden and blighted our hopes of ever returning to it, but even with the loss of "Paradise, and groves/Elysian, Fortunate Fields," the question remains,

> why should they be
> A history only of departed things,
> Or a mere fiction of what never was?
> For the discerning intellect of Man,
> When wedded to this goodly universe
> In love and holy passion, shall find these
> A simple produce of the common day.[68]

In Judaism and Christianity, marriage has long symbolized God's faithful love for a faithless human race and has served as a promise of his coming kingdom. In using the marriage analogy to describe the relationship of the mind to nature, poets such as Wordsworth were declaring that imaginative artists might at last achieve what God had failed to accomplish. The romantics sought "to save traditional concepts, schemes, and values which had been based on the relation of the Creator to his creature and creation" by recasting them within a "two-term system of subject and object, ego and non-ego, the human mind or consciousness and its transactions with nature."[69] In this marriage, nature would spur the passions of the spirit and provide fertile ground for its operations. But at the same time, it will no longer be seen "as the order which defines our rationality. Rather we are defined by purposes and capacities which we discover within ourselves. What nature can now do is awaken these."[70]

As nature awakened such capacities within the self, the romantic poets and philosophers took it to be participating in a drama of redemp-

68. William Wordsworth, quoted in Abrams, *Natural Supernaturalism,* p. 467.

69. Abrams, *Natural Supernaturalism,* p. 13.

70. Taylor, *Sources of the Self,* p. 301.

tion patterned after the Christian theme of the *fortunate fall (felix culpa).* By means of this theory, the church had sought to explain how Christ's sacrifice could turn Adam's fall from a woeful fact into a fortunate occurrence.[71] If we had not lost Eden, we would never have gained the New Jerusalem, the argument went, and in romanticism, the fortunate fall was used to render the torments of consciousness as blessings in disguise. The loss of unselfconscious innocence may have led to the conflicts and divisions of self-consciousness, but those proved in turn to be the necessary precursors of a higher consciousness. According to this line of reasoning, if our modern historical consciousness had not disenchanted us, we would never have discovered the expansive, liberating powers of the imagination.

Yet how little gratitude those powers were to show towards nature, once she had awakened them from their slumbers! As the nineteenth century opened, the imagination spoke in gentle tones to nature, but by the end of century, spirit's language had grown menacing and its tone violent.[72] Wordsworth had promoted the marriage of spirit and nature, but Nietzsche now talked of rape. "Nature, artistically considered, is no model. It exaggerates, it distorts, it leaves gaps. Nature is *chance*," according to him. "To study 'from nature' seems to me a bad sign: it betrays subjection, weakness, fatalism — this lying in the dust before *petty facts* is unworthy of a *complete* artist." The "essence of intoxication," he claimed, "is the feeling of plenitude and increased energy. From out of this feeling one gives to things, one *compels* them to take, one rapes them — one calls this procedure *idealizing*."[73]

71. For a clear expression of this theological insight, see Colin Gunton's brief summary of Irenaeus in *The Christian Faith: An Introduction to Christian Doctrine* (Malden, Mass.: Blackwell, 2002), pp. 24-25.

72. The classic treatment of romantic marriage imagery remains Abrams's *Natural Supernaturalism:* "It begins to be apparent, that Wordsworth's holy marriage, far from being unique, was a prominent period-metaphor which served a number of major writers, English and German, as the central figure in a similar complex of ideas concerning the history and destiny of man and the role of the visionary poet as both herald and inaugurator of a new and supremely better world" (p. 31).

73. Friedrich Nietzsche, *Twilight of the Idols/The Anti-Christ,* trans. R. J. Hollingdale (New York: Penguin, 1990), pp. 82, 83. Kai Hammermeister outlines Nietzsche's "aestheticization of philosophy": "Much like the good, the beautiful for Nietzsche consists of an increase of power; ugliness is what brings man down, depresses him, depletes his energies, in short, everything that Nietzsche considers decadent and unhealthy. Nietzsche

Nietzsche's late-nineteenth-century rapaciousness shows us how quickly the "purposes and capacities" aroused in romanticism began to overtake nature. Indeed, the past two centuries have witnessed a relentless growth of inner capacities and a continuing impoverishment of the outside world. To be sure, this process has also been hastened along by scientific and technological developments, particularly the Darwinian revolution. Yet at the heart of the shift from cosmos to self has been the prolific growth of the "inexhaustible inner domain."

History, Christianity, and the Arts

As we have already seen in the case of sacramental poetics, contemporary Christian artists and critics have continued to tap into the power of the self (and its language) through a romantic view of the imagination as a quasi-redemptive force. This theory wields considerable force, and numerous examples of such appropriation abound in Christian poetry, fiction, and criticism from recent decades. Some of the most illuminating cases, however, are to be found in popular culture and the activities of the mass market.

Consider, for instance, the opening page of notes to the remarkably popular *Student Bible*. "The Bible begins with words that have become famous," explain editors Tim Stafford and Philip Yancey: "In the beginning God created." That is to say, "God, like an artist, fashioned a universe. How can we grasp the grandeur of this?" How can we comprehend the power God exercised when he made the universe from scratch, out of nothing? Stafford and Yancey suggest that we turn to the artist we know to understand the God we can hardly fathom. To comprehend the miracle of God's creation, we need only ponder the mystery of the artist's acts. They implore us to consider "Michelangelo, perhaps the greatest artist in history. . . . He painted Rome's famous Sistine Chapel to retell Genesis' story of creation. His experience proves one thing: Creativity is work."[74] That Stafford and Yancey felt compelled to use the artist to explain God's

---

does not shy away from regarding artistic production as a spin-off of sexual creation: 'To make music is also a way to make children.'" *The German Aesthetic Tradition* (Cambridge: Cambridge University Press, 2002), p. 146.

74. *The NIV Student Bible, Revised* (Grand Rapids: Zondervan, 2002), p. 1.

creativity tells us something revealing about the continuing vitality of romantic metaphors in Christian thought.

Several decades ago, M. H. Abrams explored the ironies entailed in such efforts to press the romantic language of imagination and creativity into the service of Christian belief. In all learning, he explained, the process of association is at work, as "the mind moves from the better known to the less known, assimilating new materials through metaphor and analogy." As we employ these analogies, we reveal what it is that we take to be self-evident, and we hint at what has become opaque to our understanding. To illustrate this point, Abrams cites a passage from *God and the Astronomers,* by William Ralph Inge, the Dean of St. Paul's Cathedral in the early twentieth century. "The analogy of a poet and his work — say Shakespeare and his plays — is the most helpful in forming an idea of the relation of God to the world," Inge wrote. The universe "is the expression of His mind," and whatever we can manage to learn about nature will teach us "something about God."[75]

Abrams says Inge's use of creativity points to a most intriguing irony of modern intellectual history. It is that when it comes to the idea of the imagination, it is God's relation to creation, rather than the artist's relation to his or her work, that requires explanation. In the sixteenth century, a few daring souls had tentatively put forward a case for thinking of human creative ability as an analogue of the far more readily understood concept of God's power to create *ex nihilo.* Yet now, Dean Inge must appeal "to the concept of the creative poet in order to illuminate the very analogue from which it had once been engendered."[76] To Stafford and Yancey, the concept of God's power was clear, but to explain this to young people, they felt God needed Michelangelo's assistance to make sense of the labor of creation.

Dean Inge and the *Student Bible* appear at the end of a long historical road down which we in the modern world have been traveling for centuries. At the start, in the fifteenth and sixteenth centuries, belief in the creative power and covenantal faithfulness of God set the coordinates to keep the journey on track towards its ultimate destination. But as the travelers moved ever deeper into modern territory, signs that had once

75. M. H. Abrams, *The Mirror and the Lamp: Romantic Theory and the Critical Tradition* (London: Oxford University Press, 1953), p. 262.

76. Abrams, *Mirror and Lamp,* p. 262.

pointed clearly to the divine gradually became opaque, and a once-enchanting landscape turned desolate and forbidding. Over the past century, many who have approached the trail's end have questioned the wisdom of the trip and have longed to return to a time before such a weary wandering began. They have felt as Ralph Waldo Emerson did in 1844, when he ruefully compared "our party promises to western roads, which opened stately enough, with planted trees on either side, to tempt the traveller, but soon became narrow and narrower, and ended in a squirrel-track, and ran up a tree." So does "culture" run a similar course in modernity, according to Emerson, for "it ends in head-ache. Unspeakably sad and barren does life look to those, who a few months ago were dazzled with the splendor of the promise of the times."[77]

So it has been that when faced with an "unspeakably sad and barren" modern landscape, many in the past two centuries have set out to retrace our collective steps in search of a lost past. Since the mid-nineteenth century, a number of Protestants have sought to recover that past by turning to the Roman Catholic Church or Eastern Orthodoxy. For others, including nineteenth-century poets and contemporary Christian theorists alike, a nostalgic return to an enchanted past has involved soaring on the wings of the imagination in search of a land hidden from the view of our disenchanted modernity.

Bearing Witness

However useful the romantic conceptions of the imagination may have been in the nineteenth century, they remain contingent responses to a particular situation and are not necessary categories for a Christian view of the arts. As any number of writers in the twentieth century brilliantly demonstrated, one can mount a vigorous theological defense of the arts without having to depend on a romantic poetics of sacrament and imagination. The poets and storytellers I am about to discuss do not make up anything as elaborate as a school of criticism or theory, and they certainly would not have seen eye-to-eye on many theological issues. Yet taken together, their works provide rich metaphors for fresh approaches to Christian aesthetics.

77. Emerson, *Essays,* p. 478.

For decades the poetry of Richard Wilbur has sharply questioned the idea of the romantic imagination, even as it has clearly demonstrated Wilbur's own impressive inventive powers. In place of a sacramental poetics, he has promoted what we might call a modest *poetics of testimony.* When an interviewer once asked Wilbur about William Meredith's judgment that he, Wilbur, "obviously believe[s] that the universe is decent, in the lovely, derivative sense of that word," the poet replied, "Well, yes. To put it simply, I feel that the universe is full of glorious energy, that the energy tends to take pattern and shape, and that the ultimate character of things is comely and good." As Wilbur sees things, a poet who searches for the good, the true, and the beautiful will be more concerned with *discovery* than *invention,* and more passionate about the marvels that swim before our eyes than those that lie buried within our selves. Simply put, beauty does not need to be conjured *out of nothing.* "My feeling," he said, "is that when you discover order and goodness in the world, it is not something you [as a poet] are imposing — it is something which is likely really to be there, whatever crumminess and evil and disorder there may also be." However disenchanted the world may appear to be, Wilbur refuses to "take disorder or meaninglessness to be the basic character of things."[78]

He particularly has resisted using the work of the poet to explain the power of God. In one poem he does so brilliantly by heightening the disparity between invention and discovery. The poem is called "Lying," and it opens with a simple falsehood. If, at a "dēad party," Wilbur writes, you try to spice things up by saying that you have "spotted a grackle" when in fact you haven't, there is little chance you will do any harm with your fabrication. Nor in doing so are you likely to damage "your reputation for saying things of interest" or rupture "the delicate web of human trust."[79] The grackle is a common bird, and there is nothing special about the claim to have seen one.

Yet if a claim like this is so trivial as to be insignificant, why would anyone bother to make it? Wilbur answered that question in an essay written years after the publication of "Lying." He explained that the poem had had its origin in his Harvard friendship with André de Bouchet, a fel-

78. Richard Wilbur, *Conversations with Richard Wilbur,* ed. William Butts (Jackson: University Press of Mississippi, 1990), pp. 190-91.

79. Richard Wilbur, *New and Collected Poems* (New York: Harcourt, 1988), p. 9.

low graduate student who went on to become one of France's leading poets. Wilbur says he and his friend were "quite besotted with poetry, writing it constantly, continually theorizing about it, and translating each other's work," and they longed to write a "poetry which should be pure, disrelated, autotelic." This poetry was to have no end beyond its own existence, and to describe its purpose, Wilbur relates a conversation he once had with Bouchet. The latter had observed that it would be "a pure creative act" to announce that one had seen a squirrel in front of Harvard's Fogg Museum, precisely when "one had *not* seen a squirrel there; one would thus harmlessly and disinterestedly introduce into the minds of one's friends a squirrel which had never existed."[80]

This was the source of "Lying's" grackle, because it occurred to Wilbur that a poem about "truth and poetry" could begin with a "piddling and ludicrous instance of fraudulent 'creation,' and then proceed to take its implications seriously." The point was not to offer "an indictment of [his friend] Bouchet," but to see where such a view of the imagination might lead. Poetic "lying" intrigued Wilbur, because of the power of poetry to "charge and heighten the world in language." The incantatory powers of language leave the poet "prone to the illusion that he can make or unmake the world, or create an alternative reality." But in reality poets do not possess such power, and when a poet ends up being beguiled by the dream that he does, he becomes "timid about doing what he *can* do," which is to "interact with the given world, see and feel and order it newly."[81]

Hans Urs von Balthasar once wrote that Christianity was for Karl Barth "the immense revelation of the eternal light that radiates over all of nature and fulfills every promise; it is God's Yes and Amen to himself and his creation."[82] So, too, for Wilbur are creation, light, and witness intertwined. To Wilbur, the artist, like John the Baptist, is not the "Light, but [the one who] was sent to bear witness of that Light" (John 1:8):

In the strict sense, of course,
We invent nothing, merely bearing witness

80. Richard Wilbur, *The Catbird's Song: Prose Pieces, 1963-1995* (New York: Harcourt, 1997), p. 138.

81. Wilbur, *Catbird's Song,* pp. 138-39.

82. Hans Urs von Balthasar, *The Theology of Karl Barth: Exposition and Interpretation,* trans. Edward T. Oakes (San Francisco: Ignatius, 1992), p. 26.

To what each morning brings again to light:
Gold crosses, cornices, astonishment
Of panes, the turbine-vent which natural law
Spins on the grill-end of the diner's roof,
Then grass and grackles or, at the end of town
In sheen-swept pastureland, the horse's neck
Clothed with its usual thunder, and the stones
Beginning now to tug their shadows in
And track the air with glitter. All these things
Are there before us; there before we look
Or fail to look.[83]

Where Wilbur takes issue with the nineteenth-century's doctrine of the godlike imagination, the Danish fiction writer Isak Dinesen (Karen Blixen) interrogates the isolating aestheticism that century had embraced. She is skeptical of the romantic use of the language of symbol and sacrament, because it privileges the lyric mode and diminishes the value of temporal experience. We cannot expect to discover the truth, Dinesen suggests, if we take our experience to consist of a unique series of discrete events separated from any larger context. To counter the isolating powers of aestheticism, she offered in her stories an alternative vision involving what she called the "play of the Lord."

As one of Dinesen's characters muses — he has the stately name of Count Augustus von Schimmelmann — "truth, like time, is an idea arising from, and dependent upon, human intercourse.... What is the truth about a man on a desert island? And I, I am like a man on a desert island." For Dinesen, the truth about that man is to be found in the innumerable stories spun about him in the mysterious web of telling, both human and divine. "The truth about this road is that it leads to Pisa, and the truth about Pisa can be found within books written and read by human beings."[84]

Although he will claim to have learned the lessons of spiritual dependence and reciprocity that are taught by narrative, Schimmelmann never takes these lessons to heart. He sits through a puppet show one evening and is attracted to the moral a character draws near the story's close. "The truth," she explains, "is that we are, all of us, acting in a mario-

83. Wilbur, *New and Collected Poems,* p. 9.

84. Isak Dinesen, *Seven Gothic Tales* (1934; repr., New York: Vintage, 1991), p. 165.

nette comedy. What is important more than anything else in a marionette comedy, is keeping the ideas of the author clear." Schimmelmann appears to agree: "Yes, he thought, if my life were only a marionette comedy in which I had my part and knew it well, then it might be very easy and sweet."[85] Nevertheless, in the concluding scene of the story, the count stubbornly refuses to play his part when the chance comes to do so. An elderly woman named Carlotta has shown him a small smelling-bottle she received in her youth from a friend. He holds in his pocket a matching bottle, which that same Carlotta gave his aunt, who is the friend in question. Schimmelmann knows he should show this bottle to Carlotta, because "he felt that this would have made a tale which she would forever have cherished and repeated." Yet he refuses to share his storied treasure, believing instead "that there was, in this decision of fate, something which was meant for him only — . . . which belonged to him alone, and which he could not share with anybody else any more than he would be able to share his dreams."[86] According to Robert Langbaum, Schimmelmann failed to learn "that you do not find out who you are by introspection, by looking into a mirror, but by putting on a mask and engaging in an action with such intensity that you step from a human story into God's story, from your own relative to God's absolute purpose."[87]

"Nothing sanctifies," claims a character in another Dinesen story, "nothing, indeed, is sanctified, except by the play of the Lord, which is alone divine." The players and pieces in a chess game are not sacred in themselves, "but the game of chess is a noble game, and therein the knight is sanctified by the bishop, as the bishop by the queen." The character who says this also informs his conversational partner that she is like a person who would declare only half of the musical scale — "say, *do,*

85. Dinesen, *Seven Gothic,* p. 199.

86. Dinesen, *Seven Gothic,* p. 216.

87. Robert Langbaum, *The Gayety of Vision: A Study of Isak Dinesen's Art* (London: Chatto, 1964), p. 19. Dinesen questioned nineteenth-century aestheticism, but to do so she also drew on resources from that tradition. Langbaum describes how art is for Dinesen "the back door to Eden — art that delivers us from self-consciousness through ritual or, in Yeats's phrase, dying into a dance." She uses the marionette image and the romantic theory of the fortunate fall to show how "art recaptures for consciousness the data of unconscious knowledge and thus regains for us our lost unity of perception through an expansion of consciousness" (pp. 51, 52).

re and *mi* — to be sacred, but *fa, sol, la,* and *si* to be only profane." Yet it is not the separate notes that are sacred, for "it is the music, which can be made out of them, which is alone divine." Sanctification is not an internally generated process of virtue but a gratuitous — that is, free and unmerited — product of the "play of the Lord." "The lion lies in wait for the antelope at the ford," and that "antelope is sanctified by the lion, as is the lion by the antelope, for the play of the Lord is divine."[88]

In her understanding of history and the mysteries of identity, Dinesen was articulating an understanding of narrative strikingly similar to the views later suggested by the Catholic moral philosopher Alasdair MacIntyre and the Lutheran philosopher Hans-Georg Gadamer. "Man is in his actions and practice, as well as in his fictions, essentially a story-telling animal," argues MacIntyre in *After Virtue.* "He is not essentially, but becomes through his history, a teller of stories that aspire to truth. . . . I can only answer the question 'What am I to do?' if I can answer the prior question 'Of what story or stories do I find myself a part?'" We enter into social life playing the various roles "into which we have been drafted," and only through the telling and retelling of stories can we learn how to respond to the world that beckons and surrounds us. Because this is the case, there is no way for us to understand "any society, including our own, except through the stock of stories which constitute its initial dramatic resources."[89]

In a similar manner, Gadamer has questioned "the aesthetic myth of freely creative imagination" and "the cult of genius," and he has ar-

88. Dinesen, *Seven Gothic,* pp. 14-15. In a later chapter (on beauty), we will explore in depth the theological importance of play and drama as two of the greatest theologians of the twentieth century, Hans Urs von Balthasar and Karl Barth, understood them.

89. Alasdair MacIntyre, *After Virtue: A Study in Moral Theory,* 2nd ed. (Notre Dame: University of Notre Dame Press, 1984), p. 216. According to François Furet, a distinctive of the nineteenth century was its disdain of the "stock of stories" that made up the "initial dramatic resources" of the West: "Another element of the revolutionary idea, the illusion of the tabula rasa, also helped universalize it. The tabula rasa was an expression of the spontaneous 'constructivism' of public opinion in the democratic era, and of the tendency to envision social issues merely as products of volition; it represented a rejection of tradition, an obsession with the present, and a passion for the future." The myth of the "tabula rasa" grew out of the "history of a great beginning, that of the French [Revolution], which had sparked the imaginations of all nineteenth-century Europeans." *The Passing of an Illusion: The Idea of Communism in the Twentieth Century,* trans. Deborah Furet (Chicago: University of Chicago Press, 1999), p. 69.

gued that "for the writer, free invention is always only one side of a mediation conditioned by values already given." Human beings possess no such thing as a creative imagination, if by that is meant a faculty that creates new worlds *ex nihilo.* Gadamer says the invention of the imagination two hundred years ago shows simply "that in the nineteenth century mythical and historical tradition was no longer a self-evident heritage." As a result, the imagination was called upon to revitalize a world disenchanted by historical consciousness, "but even so the aesthetic myth of the imagination . . . does not stand up to reality. Now as before, the choice of material and the forming of it still do not proceed from the free discretion of the artist" and are not the expression of the artist's inner life. Instead, it remains the case that the artist "addresses people whose minds are prepared and chooses what promises to have an effect on them."[90]

Gadamer proposes that we forsake the romantic "cult of genius" and turn instead to what he calls "play as the clue to ontological explanation." He employs the concept of play as a powerful counterweight to the romantic preoccupation with consciousness and its creative powers. In play, the primary concern is not the subjectivity of the player but the play itself. Seen from its vantage point, a work of art is "not an object that stands over against a subject for itself," but it finds its true identity instead in the fact that the work "becomes an experience that changes the person who experiences it." The subject remains "the work itself" and not the "subjectivity of the person who experiences it," for the experience of a work of art includes the play of appropriation and interpretation that follows upon its productions, and "play has its own essence, independent of the consciousness of those who play."[91]

The mysteries Gadamer explores here have some remarkable analogues in the trinitarian debates of the past two centuries, because the self assumed in the romantic theory of the imagination is like the ghostly God envisioned in the modalist understanding of the Trinity. Modalism was an early Christian heresy that denied that God was "three persons, separate and distinct." The modalist deity is a singular entity that manifests itself in the three *modes* of Father, Son, and Spirit. According to the modalists, God is never fully present in any of those forms, but remains in

90. Gadamer, *Truth,* p. 133.
91. Gadamer, *Truth,* p. 102.

the background, safe and secure above the fray. This view differs rather dramatically from the historic understanding of the incarnation, which holds that Christ is not one of God's *modes,* but his *Son;* when Christ suffers, so does God, and when Christ dies, God, in some mysterious sense, also dies. "It is by the incarnation that God has revealed His truly immutable being," Barth writes in the second volume of his *Church Dogmatics.* "God is 'immutably' the One whose reality is seen in His condescension in Jesus Christ, in His self-offering and self-concealment, in His self-emptying and self-humiliation." There is no hidden God shrouded in "a majesty behind this condescension, behind the cross on Golgotha," Barth argues. Instead, that cross is the very sign of "the divine majesty," and this sacrificial "free love is the one true God himself."[92]

When we enter fully into the play of human experience, we resemble, however faintly, Jesus Christ, who cast himself into the drama of the world, enjoying its mysteries, enduring its uncertainties, and suffering its cruelties. According to both Barth and Gadamer, the image of play enables us to understand the incarnation better than the model of the sacramental imagination does. In the to-and-fro of play, we temporarily set aside our self-conscious identity, only to have it returned to us, deepened and renewed by the play in which we have taken part. The work of art is a form of play, Gadamer says, and in play "the player, sculptor, or viewer is never simply swept away into a strange world of magic, of intoxication, and of dream; rather, it is always his own world, and he comes to belong to it more fully by recognizing himself more profoundly in it."[93]

To supplement the vision of art as witness to the story that is the play of the Lord, we might add a final image, that of the poet as the loving secretary of the invisible. This homely metaphor is a conflation of images from poems by W. H. Auden and Czeslaw Milosz, arguably two of the greatest Christian poets of the past century. Auden's image comes from "The More Loving One," a poem whose speaker faces the silent heavens with resolve rather than regret. Aware of the fact that he lives in a disenchanted world, the speaker in this poem gazes at the stars and knows that "for all they care, I can go to hell." Yet, as dispiriting as this situation may be, the speaker of the poem concludes that "on earth indifference is

92. Karl Barth, *Church Dogmatics,* ed. G. W. Bromiley and T. F. Torrance (Edinburgh: T. & T. Clark, 1956-62), II.1.517.

93. Gadamer, *Truth,* pp. 133-34.

the least/We have to dread from man or beast." What would we do, he asks, "were stars to burn/With a passion for us we could not return?" In the end, perhaps their silence is not so unbearable, so the poet concludes, "If equal affection cannot be,/Let the more loving one be me."[94]

In this poem, Auden recasts the debate about poetry in a disenchanted world by treating it as an ethical challenge instead of an aesthetic dilemma. So, he in effect says, let us assume that everything Charles Taylor says about modern identity is true. That is, we can grant that philosophy since Descartes and science since Newton have left us living in a barren world where disembodied minds wrestle with a soulless nature. Further, we will accept that in the late eighteenth century, men and women began to detect a growing imbalance between the complex richness of their inner lives and the uniform poverty of the world outside their selves. Still, according to Auden, even if this is true, when I face a hostile or indifferent natural order, the only real question is whether I will respond in anger or with love. Do I cry out against the heavens, or do I vow to make "the more loving one be me"?

Auden believed romanticism had distorted our view of poetry with its images of the poet as the vital resuscitator of a lifeless world. Throughout his career he remained wary of the romantic impulse, according to Edward Mendelson, because it "glorified the lyric as the highest mode of poetry, and made it the vessel for philosophical and historical subjects few earlier ages would have tried to force into it." In the face of a disenchanted world and under the pressures of historical consciousness, poetry abandoned its public role at the start of the nineteenth century. Like its sister arts, it shifted its attention from speaking to specific audiences on particular occasions and became instead its "own sufficient reason for being." Having freed itself from its local contexts and commitments, art "established itself instead in the neutral international context of the museums and concert halls that sprang up as its temples, bastions of its newly won autonomy."[95] From within those bastions, for two centuries, many in the arts have been seeking to re-enchant the world.

94. Auden, *Collected Poems,* p. 582. Edward Mendelson notes that when Auden wrote this poem in 1957, he was referring, among other things, to his difficult affair with Chester Kallman: "Auden lived with the adult knowledge that his own love would not be satisfied, and . . . he preferred it that way: 'If equal affection cannot be,/Let the more loving one be me.'" *Later Auden* (New York: Farrar, 1999), p. 200.

95. Edward Mendelson, *Early Auden* (New York: Viking, 1981), pp. xvi-xvii.

Yet poetry paid a price for its freedom. Stripped of its civic dimensions, "the quest [of poetry] now became the allegory of inner discontent," and as a result, "the price art paid for its autonomy was its desperate isolation." Mendelson says Auden was the "first English writer" to have absorbed fully the lessons of modernism, even as he set out to move beyond those limits. He successfully challenged "the vatic dynasty after more than a century of uncontested rule," and promoted instead a vision of "civic poetry." In civic poetry, poets write not as "geniuses in exile" but "as citizens, whose purpose is to entertain and instruct, and who choose subjects that would interest an audience even if a poet were not there to transform them into art."[96]

Like Auden, Czeslaw Milosz sought to move beyond the vatic tradition and its praise of the poet as prophet. The Nobel Prize–winning poet chose to present himself as "a secretary of the invisible thing/That is dictated to me and a few others." Such "secretaries" walk the earth "Without much comprehension," with their task being the simple one of taking dictation, "Beginning a phrase in the middle/Or ending it with a comma." They do not know the full meaning of the snippets they record, nor can they comprehend the greater story in which their lives play such a small part. "And how it all looks when completed/Is not up to us to inquire, we won't read it anyway."[97]

But humility for Milosz did not mean passivity. To the end, he remained an active seeker after truth and an aggressive questioner of God. Not long before he died, he offered a brief reflection on his spiritual persistence: "Instead of leaving to theologians their worries, I have constantly meditated on religion. Why? Simply because *someone* had to do this." In his own lifetime, which spanned virtually the entire twentieth century, "Heaven and Hell disappeared," and belief in life after death weakened considerably. The distinction between humans and the animal kingdom became blurred, the notion of absolute truth was undermined, and "history directed by Providence started to look like a field of battle between blind forces."[98]

96. Mendelson, *Early Auden,* pp. xvii, xx, xv.

97. Czeslaw Milosz, *New and Collected Poems, 1931-2001* (New York: Ecco, 2001), p. 343.

98. Czeslaw Milosz, *To Begin Where I Am: Selected Essays,* ed. Bogdana Carpenter and Madeline G. Levine (New York: Farrar, 2001), p. 329. In his Norton lectures at Harvard in 1981-82, Milosz placed the modern transformation of poetry's relationship to religion in the second half of the nineteenth century, and he named Darwin as a key player in the

As a result of these wrenching changes, Milosz says, the "huge edifice of creeds and dogmas" that had been erected over a period of two thousand years abruptly collapsed. That system painstakingly constructed by great intellects "from Origen and Saint Augustine to Thomas Aquinas and Cardinal Newman" disappeared, seemingly overnight, and "the age of homelessness has dawned." To Milosz, it is not remarkable that he, like a secretary of the vanishing invisible thing, charted the course of this loss: "How could I not think of this? And is it not surprising that my preoccupation was a rare case?"[99]

In his struggle with God and with historical consciousness, Milosz was hardly isolated among the artists of his day. Along with Wilbur, Dinesen, Auden, and others, he sought to tap into the religious power of literature without relying upon romantic theories of the imagination and the self. At this point in our history, Christian thought has much to gain from images of the kind these writers provide; it has much to learn from a poetics that is modest in its assumptions, communal in its concerns, and creative in its understanding of the role of the arts. Whether by portraying poetry as an art of witness or fiction as a celebration of the play of the Lord, or by offering a vision of the poet as the secretary of the invisible, these writers encourage us to engage the history in which we find ourselves and to forsake all attempts to skip over that history, as though we could soar above time, weightless on the wings of the sacramental imagination, endlessly searching for an enchanted, irrecoverable past.

---

change. See *The Witness of Poetry* (Cambridge, Mass.: Harvard University Press, 1983), pp. 41-57.

99. Milosz, *To Begin,* pp. 329-30.

CHAPTER 2

Science

YOUNG Ralph Waldo Emerson had no interest in a modest poetics of any kind as he raced to complete his first major work, *Nature*, in the summer of 1836, and his ambitions were far too great for him ever to be satisfied as a mere "secretary of the invisible thing." In fact, in *Nature*, Emerson was proposing to account for nothing less than the "relation between the mind and matter," which he called the "standing problem which has exercised the wonder and the study of every fine genius since the world began." Pythagoras, Plato, and Leibniz, to name a few, had tried their hand at solving the riddle and failed. Now it was time for a new generation of nineteenth-century aspirants — including Emerson, the pastor turned poet, prophet, and essayist — to take a crack at it. "There sits the Sphinx at the road-side, and from age to age, as each prophet comes by, he tries his fortune at reading her riddle."[1]

From the beginning, some questioned whether Emerson was anything but a purveyor of platitudes who possessed at best a muddled understanding of science. Yet his great essays, beginning with *Nature*, repeatedly give lie to that claim; in fact, he had an extensive knowledge of scientific history and was keenly aware of the revolutionary potential of

1. Ralph Waldo Emerson, *Essays and Lectures*, ed. Joel Porte (New York: Library of America, 1983), pp. 24-25. Emerson's brother Charles, who died shortly before *Nature* was published, gave him the image of the Sphinx, as Waldo reported in a journal entry from August 1, 1835: "There sits the Sphinx from age to age, in the road Charles says[,] & every wise man (in turn) that comes by has a crack with her." *The Journals and Miscellaneous Notebooks of Ralph Waldo Emerson*, ed. Merton M. Sealts Jr. (Cambridge, Mass.: Belknap Press of Harvard University Press, 1965), V:76.

the scientific changes underway. Only months after he had quit the pastorate along with the active practice of the Christian faith, Emerson stood ecstatically before the exhibits in the Paris "Cabinet of Natural History."

> The Universe is a more amazing puzzle than ever as you glance along this bewildering series of animated forms, — the hazy butterflies, the carved shells, the birds, beasts, fishes, insects, snakes, — & the upheaving principle of life everywhere incipient in the very rock aping organized forms. Not a form so grotesque, so savage, nor so beautiful but is an expression of some property inherent in man the observer, — an occult relation between the very scorpions and man. I feel the centipede in me — cayman, carp, eagle, & fox. I am moved by strange sympathies, I say continually "I will be a naturalist."[2]

In seeking to counter the "stereotypes that have dogged critical and popular opinion [about Emerson] for 150 years," Laura Dassow Walls asks us to view him as a truly dynamic scientific thinker who discovered in "the creative method of science" nothing less than "the key to the universe." To most modern people, religion, literature, and science appear to be cut from different cloths entirely, but to the nineteenth-century Emerson, they were all threads woven into a seamless tapestry of spirit and nature. He "was perfectly at ease folding scientific truth into moral truth," and he was always eager to announce the spiritual insights he had garnered from scientific facts.[3]

Nevertheless, Walls says there was a problem with Emerson's method: he assumed others possessed a knowledge of science equal to his own. But most did not, and as a result of his having taken scientific literacy for granted, Emerson's scientific metaphors were destined to "sink out of sight," and even "worse, from his time to ours, the divorce between 'the two cultures' of literature and science has made his deep debt to science virtually invisible." As a result of this "divorce," the goals that "once yoked poetry and science as allies in a common cultural enterprise" have become obscured, Emerson's achievement "has been swept

2. Emerson, *Journals and Miscellaneous Notebooks,* IV:199-200.

3. Linda Dassow Walls, *Emerson's Life in Science: The Culture of Truth* (Ithaca, N.Y.: Cornell University Press, 2003), pp. 2-3.

into 'literature,'" and the "common roots of literary and scientific thought in America" have been forgotten.[4]

With this complaint, Walls joins a chorus of critics who have long bemoaned the modern world's drive to separate science, religion, and the arts. As we will see, the barriers between these fields rose ever higher in Emerson's own lifetime and appeared to have become insurmountable by century's end. "Nineteenth-century science was unremittingly hostile to any notion of religion," Czeslaw Milosz notes. "And we are, to a large extent, children of the nineteenth century."[5] As the twentieth century opened, the reigning assumption was that science and religion had become irreconcilable antagonists, and the arts were left to make a lonely choice between hard facts and sweet fancies. Only in the final decades of the twentieth century did gaps begin to appear in the walls, making limited commerce and hesitant communication a viable option once again.

Beyond the Boundaries: Literature and the Disciplines

"Something there is that doesn't love a wall," intones the speaker in Robert Frost's "Mending Wall," a poem that reads like a charter for a program in interdisciplinary studies:

> Something there is that doesn't love a wall,
> That sends the frozen-ground-swell under it,
> And spills the upper boulders in the sun;
> And makes gaps even two can pass abreast.

4. Walls, *Emerson's Life,* p. 3. For an insightful discussion of the Emersonian tradition and science, see Robert Faggen, *Robert Frost and the Challenge of Darwin* (Ann Arbor: University of Michigan Press, 1997), pp. 13-51. The separation between literature and science is a subset of the larger divorce of science and religion. A curious recent trend has involved the mass marketing of materialist accounts of reality that try to reconcile religion and science by suggesting, or demanding, that the former capitulate to the latter. For representative titles, see Steven Weinberg, *The First Three Minutes: A Modern View of the Origin of the Universe,* updated ed. (New York: Basic, 1993); Richard Dawkins, *Unweaving the Rainbow: Science, Delusion and the Appetite for Wonder* (Boston: Houghton, 1998); and Daniel C. Dennett, *Breaking the Spell: Religion as a Natural Phenomenon* (New York: Viking, 2006).

5. *Czeslaw Milosz: Conversations,* ed. Cynthia L. Haven (Jackson: University Press of Mississippi, 2006), p. 176.

> The work of hunters is another thing:
> I have come after them and made repair
> Where they have left not one stone on a stone,
> But they would have the rabbit out of hiding,
> To please the yelping dogs. The gaps I mean,
> No one has seen them made or heard them made,
> But at spring mending-time we find them there.
> I let my neighbor know beyond the hill;
> And on a day we meet to walk the line
> And set the wall between us once again.[6]

"Mending-Wall" is about the impulse to build barriers as well as the need to break through them, and what it says is as true of the divisions between academic disciplines as it is of the old stone walls that to this day dot the landscapes of rural New England. For more than a century, American colleges and universities have parceled out the domains of knowledge into distinct fields of study. They have marked the boundaries between the fields with care, and they have trained generations of specialists to tend ever-narrower patches of ground.

This has been as true for literature as for any other field. From the romantic poets and philosophical idealists, argues Terry Eagleton, modern poets and critics alike inherited the "assumption that there [is] an unchanging object known as 'art'" and "an isolatable experience called 'beauty' or the 'aesthetic.'" In the centuries prior to the romantic age, men and women had "written poems, staged plays or painted pictures" for countless different reasons, while others had read and watched their productions for any number of purposes. Yet only in the eighteenth century did critics begin to distinguish certain productions from others, labeling one group as the *fine* arts and the other as the *useful* ones.[7]

As we will see in a later chapter, this distinction took hold in the late eighteenth century and soon became a powerful organizing principle for

6. Robert Frost, *Collected Poems, Prose, and Plays,* ed. Richard Poirier and Mark Richardson (New York: Library of America, 1995), p. 39.

7. Terry Eagleton, *Literary Theory: An Introduction* (Minneapolis: University of Minnesota Press, 1983), p. 21. For a lively discussion of the concept of "disciplines as distinct 'fields' of study," see Anthony T. Kronman, *Education's End: Why Our Colleges and Universities Have Given Up on the Meaning of Life* (New Haven: Yale University Press, 2007), pp. 91-136.

literature and criticism. In this paradigm, the useful arts fashion tools for our daily lives, while the fine arts give us objects that we are free to contemplate but not to use. The *useful* products include everything from the bowls in which we serve our food to the blades with which we mow our fields, while the *fine* arts produce the paintings that adorn our walls and the poems that delight our hearts.[8]

In separating the fine from the useful arts, the romantic poets and philosophers were trading on a distinction set down 1400 years earlier in St. Augustine's *On Christian Doctrine.* In that work, Augustine defined the difference between things that are meant to be *used* and those that are intended to be *enjoyed:* the latter "make us blessed," while the former "sustain us as we move toward blessedness." We are wanderers who have strayed from home, and if we are to return to the land God intended us to enjoy, we need to use "vehicles for land and sea." If, however, we turn these items of use into objects of enjoyment, we become "entangled in a perverse sweetness" and lose sight of our true blessedness and real home. Countless things are there before us to be used as means, but only God should be enjoyed as an end in himself. "The things which are to be enjoyed," Augustine says, "are the Father, the Son, and the Holy Spirit, a single Trinity, a certain supreme thing common to all who enjoy it."[9]

As happened to a number of other facets of Christian thought, the Augustinian distinction between use and enjoyment underwent a transformation in the eighteenth century. In this instance, the category of enjoyment was shifted from God to the fine arts, with all other crafts being consigned to the category of the useful. Powerful social and economic forces hastened this transformation.[10] With the advent of the printing press and the growth of the capitalist economy, literature in early moder-

8. While many recent theorists have questioned Kant's classic view of the "fine arts," Paul Guyer argues that "the non-reductionist but hardly uninformative theory of Kant continues to offer greater enlightenment than any of its more single-minded successors." *Kant and the Claims of Taste,* 2nd ed. (Cambridge: Cambridge University Press, 1997), p. 366.

9. St. Augustine, *On Christian Doctrine,* trans. D. W. Robertson Jr. (New York: Bobbs-Merrill, 1958), pp. 9-10. For understanding this Augustinian distinction's importance for the modern arts, I am indebted to Tzvetan Todorov, *Theories of the Symbol,* trans. Catherine Porter (Ithaca, N.Y.: Cornell University Press, 1982), pp. 36-44.

10. For an illuminating discussion of the issues at stake, see Walter Benjamin's acclaimed essay, "The Work of Art in the Age of Mechanical Reproduction," in his *Illuminations: Essays and Reflections,* ed. Hannah Arendt, trans. Harry Zohn (New York: Schocken, 1969), pp. 217-51.

nity no longer found itself bound to the church or indebted to the patron. With its rhetorical purposes discounted and its didactic potential dismissed, literature's essential uselessness was now sometimes considered its greatest asset. An art that had no worldly purpose might nevertheless serve otherworldly ends, and by offering itself as a haven, literature could rationalize its loss of a public role as a private boon. "Having lost his patron, the writer discovered a substitute in the poetic," Eagleton observes. Literature was "extricated from the material practices, social relations and ideological meanings in which it is always caught up, and raised to the status of a solitary fetish."[11]

As we saw in our opening chapter, a number of nineteenth-century apologists were to claim that in becoming isolated, literature had mysteriously acquired saving powers. "Life is such a hideous business that the only method of bearing it is to avoid it," wrote the French novelist Gustave Flaubert in an 1857 letter. "And one does avoid it by living in Art, in the ceaseless quest for Truth presented by Beauty." If "you read the great masters" with an eye towards the beautiful alternative they provide to ordinary life, "you will be like Moses descending Sinai, with the light shining from his face because he had seen God."[12]

But mountaintop experiences do not last for long in the valleys below, and as lustrous as Flaubert's aesthetic ideal may have seemed in the nineteenth century, the events of the twentieth tarnished it almost beyond recognition. In particular, two world wars — marked by carnage and genocide on an unimaginable scale — did a great deal to dull any romantic claims made on behalf of literature. In *The Great War and Modern Memory,* Paul Fussell documents the devastating impact of the First World War in particular. Nineteenth-century optimism could not ac-

11. Eagleton, *Literary Theory,* p. 21. Modernist views of literature gravitated to spatial rather than temporal models for their understanding of literary purpose and form. T. S. Eliot, for example, described literary tradition as a timeless body rather than a developing form: "The historical sense involves a perception, not only of the pastness of the past, but of its presence; the historical sense compels a man to write . . . with a feeling that the whole of the literature of Europe from Homer and within it the whole of the literature of his own country has a simultaneous existence and composes a simultaneous order." *The Sacred Wood: Essays on Poetry and Criticism* (London: Methuen, 1920), p. 49.

12. Gustave Flaubert, "Letter to Mlle. Leroyer de Chantepie," in *The Modern Tradition: Backgrounds of Modern Literature,* ed. Richard Ellmann and Charles Feidelson Jr. (New York: Oxford University Press, 1965), p. 72.

count for twentieth-century terror, Fussell writes, and that terror transformed the English language and its literature. To find a vocabulary adequate to describe the realities of the twentieth century, "it would take still another war, and an even worse one, before such language would force itself up from below and propose itself for use."[13]

Fussell's image recalls the "frozen-ground-swell" that Frost says "spills" the boulders to make the gaps in the wall. And so it has been that over the past century, no matter how vigilantly literature's defenders have patrolled its boundaries, historical events and scientific discoveries have continued to break holes in the walls between the disciplinary fields. Something there is, after all, that doesn't love a wall. As one who treasures the field of English and the crops it yields, I understand the urge to wall it off from outside dangers and influences. Indeed, to a degree, I honor these boundaries, and I have no desire to treat literature as a subset of history or philosophy. Yet I also believe it makes little sense any longer to think of literature as "a set of ciphers, an agenda of mysteries, a collection of secular scriptures" that can remain somehow untouched by scientific and historical change.[14]

If openings have indeed appeared in the walls dividing literature, science, and religion one from another, then religiously inclined critics would do well to move through the openings and welcome the renewal of commerce between the fields. For do not those who believe that "in Christ everything in heaven and on earth was created" have a responsibility to care about the yield of other fields and what they may reveal about the one who "holds all things together" (Col 1:16-17)? And when the occasion arises, would it not be wise to accept the gifts that may come our way through the gaps in the wall?

A "Ground-Swell of Knowledge": History in the Heavens

In the mid-1990s, there was a particular "frozen-ground-swell" that spilled over and broke through disciplinary boundaries. I am referring to

13. Paul Fussell, *The Great War and Modern Memory* (New York: Oxford University Press, 1975), p. 174.

14. David Hollinger, *In the American Province: Studies in the History and Historiography of Ideas* (1985; repr., Baltimore: Johns Hopkins University Press, 1989), p. 81.

the remarkable case of the Hubble telescope, which in 1996 began beaming back to earth photos that were as stunning in their beauty as they were staggering in their implications. We awoke one morning to learn that the universe as we knew it had grown five times larger overnight. In the Hubble images, astronomers discovered forty billion new galaxies, and further studies more than doubled that figure. At the beginning of the twentieth century, scientists were not sure that more than one galaxy existed. Now, at the century's end, we found ourselves with more than a hundred billion of them on our hands.

In ways we can barely imagine, the knowledge acquired through the Hubble will influence cultural life for decades to come. It will change our readings of certain poems, shape the history of our ideas, and deepen our understanding of the human psyche. Such claims may seem extravagant, but I make them confidently, because of what we know about the history of modern cosmology. From the sixteenth century to the present, changes in the scientific picture of the universe have coincided with dramatic shifts in the ideas and images that drive the life of the culture. Thomas Kuhn was right to argue that metaphors shape the way we picture the universe, but it is just as true that our knowledge of the heavens colors the metaphors in our poems and the narratives of our lives. As Charles Taylor points out, the history of the past 500 years is the story of an intimate, reciprocal relationship between "scientific discovery and profound cultural change."[15]

As a case in point, the intricate relationship between metaphor and cosmology is on full display in the recently renovated Hayden Planetarium in New York City. As Edward Rothstein explained shortly after the reopening of the planetarium in 2000, in the previous exhibit at the Hayden, the earth had been at the center of things. "There was no question about where one was or who one was in that artificial cosmos. One was a child of Earth," and the exhibit had been built with the intention of making its visitors feel at home. At its center, a large projector had cast on the planetarium ceiling "images in which humanity could see a reflection of itself." To Rothstein, this earlier display had been driven too much

15. Charles Taylor, *A Secular Age* (Cambridge, Mass.: Belknap Press of Harvard University Press, 2007), p. 349; for an extended treatment of the role of "cosmic imaginaries," see pp. 322-51. For Kuhn, see *The Structure of Scientific Revolutions* (Chicago: University of Chicago Press, 1962).

by metaphor and guided too little by science. It permitted the mind to humanize the alien universe but did not allow the universe in turn to make a truthful imprint upon that mind.[16]

But according to Rothstein, with the recent renovation at the Hayden, everything has changed. Copernicus and Galileo had dislodged humans from the center of the universe, and "here humanity is not even at the center of the planetarium." The designers have done nothing to encourage the viewer's imagination to project itself upon the heavens but have sought instead "to project that cosmos inward, imprinting it on the human imagination, stupefying it." They have used various methods of "de-centering," including the creation of a walkway in which each inch represents the passage of 3.6 million years. After traveling the length of a football field — a journey of thirteen billion years — the visitor arrives at the point where human history begins, and the span of that history is the width of a single human hair. "Instead of bringing the cosmos home, the home has been thrust, untethered, into the cosmos," Rothstein explains.

One innovation at the Hayden involves using data from the Hubble for computer simulations that reveal behind the torn scrim of the planetarium's sky "a stunning three-dimensional cosmos" in which the earth is nothing but a mite of stardust. "The overall effect is humbling," Rothstein says, as he compares the ambitions of the planetarium with those of "the great cathedrals: all resources are devoted to inspiring humility before greater forces." Yet in the world of modern cosmology those forces are wholly impersonal, and in the renovated Hayden, the heart can only bow in awe and terror before a regally silent universe. Like the cathedral, the new Hayden Planetarium is "also meant to inspire a kind of faith," but not one centered in a personal God. "The faith is in the human capacity to make sense of it all, to give order to the overwhelming."

The early responses to the Hubble's discoveries often highlighted the power of technology to exalt the mind rather than humble it. By revealing that the universe is even more staggeringly vast than we had imagined, the Hubble images "show that we are even less significant than we ever thought," writes journalist Peter Kendall. In describing their exhilarating effect, he used images similar to those Edward Rothstein was to employ in his story on the Hayden Planetarium. But instead of driving

16. Edward Rothstein, "Cut Loose in the Cosmos, Mites of Dust Without a Home," *New York Times,* February 19, 2000.

home the point about human insignificance, those photos "somehow have exactly the opposite effect," Kendall says. "They show just how clever we are, that if we noodle away at a problem long enough we can pry the lid off secrets we have no earthly right to know."[17]

These accounts of the Hubble's significance caught my eye because they seemed to echo a passage I had read years earlier in a book by Karl Barth. In it, Barth observes that modern science simultaneously exalts and diminishes the human subject. To understand this paradox, he goes back to the eighteenth century, whose inhabitants were the first to realize "that Copernicus and Galileo were right." The earth, the "theater" of human action, was no longer the "centre of the universe" but only "a grain of dust amid countless others in this universe." The eighteenth-century thinkers "clearly saw the consequences" of this dramatic transformation of their view of the universe. Yet did this shift lead to "an unprecedented and boundless humiliation of man?" No. Instead, it put human beings more securely than ever in the center of things, because it had been human instruments that had made the discoveries and human theories that had provided the frameworks to make sense of them. The world "expanded overnight into infinity — and without anything else having changed, without his [eighteenth-century man's] having to pay for it in any way." So it was that in the eighteenth and early nineteenth centuries, "the geocentric picture of the universe was replaced as a matter of course by the anthropocentric."[18]

17. Peter Kendall, "Discoveries in Deep Space: Infinity," *Chicago Tribune,* January 21, 1996. In one of his final essays, Walter Ong wrote of the spiritual significance of modern cosmology: "We know that the universe we live in is now more or less 12 to 14 billion years old. Over the past several decades this has been news to all human beings, including scientists, nonbelieving or believing, Christian or other believers. . . . But despite the massive study and research that has brought humankind this relatively new knowledge . . . , [that] knowledge has hardly been assimilated theologically or otherwise by many human beings inside or outside communities of Christian believers." "Where Are We Now? Some Elemental Cosmological Considerations," *Christianity and Literature* 50 (2000): 7.

18. Karl Barth, *Protestant Theology in the Nineteenth Century,* new ed., trans. Brian Cozens and John Bowden (Grand Rapids: Eerdmans, 2002), pp. 23-24. Barth argues that the Christian faith cannot claim any particular cosmology as its own. "In so far as faith itself is true to itself, . . . its association with this or that worldview will always bear the marks of the contradiction between the underlying confession and the principles of the system with which it is conjoined." Cosmology "can arise only in the sterile corner where the Word of God with its special revelation has not yet found, or has lost again, hearing

According to Barth, the "anthropocentric" vision triumphed because men and women had become aware at last of their "capacity for thinking which was responsible to no other authority" than themselves. Buoyed by their understanding of abstract thought, many eighteenth-century thinkers embraced "the ideal of a science of history and of natural science, without presuppositions and possessing supreme intellectual dignity in virtue of this very absence of presuppositions."[19] They envisioned a self as unencumbered by obligations as it was uninformed by presuppositions. Secure in its autonomy, that self would be free to manage the complex affairs of its inner domain and to catalogue the vast, silent reaches of the universe arrayed beyond its bodily boundaries.

Literature, Science, and the Retreat from the Word

Still, there was a price to be paid for the freedom of living under the hushed Copernican heavens, and that cost came for some in the form of a spiritual and emotional bankruptcy. "The eternal silence of these infinite spaces fills me with dread," Blaise Pascal confessed in the mid-seventeenth century.[20] In expressing that anxiety, he was intuiting the consequences of what George Steiner would much later describe as a "si-

---

and obedience on the part of man." *Church Dogmatics,* ed. G. W. Bromiley and T. F. Torrance (Edinburgh: T. & T. Clark, 1956-62), III.2.10-11.

In Barth's understanding, the anthropocentric vision granted anthropology the right to determine theological truth. In the nineteenth century, Ludwig Feuerbach argued that all statements about God had to be considered as "nothing but statements about human nature. . . . Feuerbach, Barth believed, had accurately diagnosed the logical dilemma of modern liberal theology. . . . No theological method (such as that of liberalism) which wanted to maintain the existence of God strictly on the basis of certain anthropological phenomena would, logically speaking, ever get beyond mere assertions about anthropological phenomena — regardless of their theological form." George Hunsinger, *How to Read Karl Barth: The Shape of His Theology* (New York: Oxford, 1991), p. 35.

19. Barth, *Protestant Theology,* pp. 25-26. Hans-Georg Gadamer has offered a trenchant critique of the Enlightenment prejudice against prejudice. "The overcoming of all prejudices" is what he calls "the global demand of the Enlightenment." According to Gadamer, this goal "will itself prove to be a prejudice," because it is impossible for finite human beings to set aside all their prior judgments in the quest for understanding. *Truth and Method,* 2nd ed., trans. Joel Weinsheimer and Donald G. Marshall (New York: Crossroad, 1989), p. 276.

20. Blaise Pascal, *Pensées,* trans. A. J. Krailsheimer (New York: Penguin, 1995), p. 66.

lencing" of the cosmos brought on by a general "retreat from the word" in the thought and experience of the West. Until the seventeenth century, mathematics had remained tethered to human experience and ordinary language, so there was no substantial rift between the mathematical and the moral sciences. Both described the same world, although in different ways, and both were part of a sustained cultural and theological effort to contain that world within the boundaries of ordinary language. This ideal of a comprehensive *verbal universe* was embodied in the concept of the *Logos.*[21]

For both classical thought and the Christian faith, "all truth and realness — with the exception of a small, queer margin at the very top" — were considered "housed inside the walls of language." Yet everything changed with the invention of calculus in the seventeenth century and the elaboration of Newton's mechanistic understanding of the universe. From that point on, mathematics ceased being dependent upon nature and human experience, and once it had been cut off from these sources, it became a rich and dynamic language that was a world unto itself. *"And the history of that language is one of progressive untranslatability,"* Steiner writes. In the century after Newton, mathematics continued to extend its dominion over an ever wider expanse of human thought, and its imperial ambitions eventually "broke Western consciousness into what C. P. Snow calls 'the two cultures,'" one anchored in the humanities, the other in the sciences.

The heirs of that cultural division occupy the contemporary academy, and to a significant extent the disciplines as we know them are the product of the early modern divorce of which Snow and Steiner have written. The divide between ordinary language and mathematical language grows ever wider, and the people on each side have become, "in respect of each other, . . . illiterate."[22] On one side of the gap huddle the hu-

21. George Steiner, *Language and Silence: Essays on Language, Literature and the Inhuman* (New York: Atheneum, 1970), p. 14.

22. Steiner, *Language and Silence,* pp. 14, 16-17. Hans Jonas has pointed to this chasm with his comparison of modern naturalism and ancient Gnosticism. The modern isolation of the human presence within nature "constitutes the utter loneliness of man in the sum of things." As embodied creatures, we share in the "mechanical determination" of nature, and we view spiritual aspirations and intellectual capacities as accidents in the impersonal scheme of things. As a consequence, "that by which man is superior to all nature, his unique distinction, mind, no longer results in a higher integration of his being into the

manities; across the way are the hard sciences; and on the bridge that sways precariously between them shuttle the social sciences, not certain where they belong.

Since the eighteenth century, advocates of the arts have tirelessly defined them in opposition to the proponents of science who stand on the other side of the gap. For a considerable period, at least until the end of the nineteenth century, the artists appeared to many to have the upper hand in this argument, as they promoted the spiritual virtues of their domain. While science starved the spirit, they said, music fed it; where mathematics undermined ethical ideals, literature sustained them; and even as hard facts stifled the emotions, poetry gave free rein to human feelings.[23]

In opposing literature to science, the romantic poets and philosophers were effectively dismantling a consensus that had held together Western thinking about the arts for more than two thousand years. From Aristotle to the eighteenth century, most critics and artists alike had defined literature as a mimetic activity whose goal was to *re-present* reality. The meaning of mimesis varied over time, as art's proponents debated whether it should represent objects or embody ideals. Yet in the main, theorists from ancient Greece to early modern England believed art was meant, as Hamlet says, "to hold the mirror up to nature."[24]

In *The Republic,* Plato had argued the mimetic point in classic fashion by claiming that those who make objects ought to fashion them according to the Ideal plan of the One who has made "the earth and heaven, and the things which are in heaven or under the earth." According to Socrates, the artist has a unique way of imitating the divine maker:

---

totality of being, but on the contrary marks the unbridgeable gulf between himself and the rest of existence." *The Gnostic Religion: The Message of the Alien God and the Beginnings of Christianity,* 2nd ed. (Boston: Beacon, 1963), pp. 322-23.

23. What I describe as "interdisciplinary" exchange, however, differs considerably from the "postdisciplinarity" discussed (and criticized) in an essay by historian Thomas Haskell. The essay is one of several included in a "roundtable" discussion of Louis Menand's *The Metaphysical Club.* See Bruce Kuklick et al., "Roundtable: Louis Menand's *The Metaphysical Club* and the Problem of Pragmatism." *Intellectual History Newsletter* 24 (2002): 84-125.

24. "'Imitation' continued to be a prominent item in the critical vocabulary for a long time after Aristotle. . . . Through most of the eighteenth century, the tenet that art is an imitation seemed almost too obvious to need iteration or proof." M. H. Abrams, *The Mirror and the Lamp: Romantic Theory and the Critical Tradition* (London: Oxford University Press, 1953), p. 11.

And there is another artist, — I should like to know what you would say of him.

Who is he?

One who is the maker of all the works of all other workmen.

What an extraordinary man!

. . . Do you see that there is a way in which you could make them all yourself?

What way?

An easy way enough; or rather, there are many ways in which the feat might be quickly and easily accomplished, none quicker than that of turning a mirror round and round — you would soon enough make the sun and the heavens, and the earth and yourself, and other animals and plants, and all other things of which we were just now speaking, in the mirror.[25]

After it had been in use for so many centuries, what happened to this mirror? Isaiah Berlin says it was shattered by early modern science. From Homer to Hume, the doctrine of mimesis had presupposed the existence of timeless principles and patterns that it was the duty of poetry and the other arts to "imitate." In the seventeenth and eighteenth centuries, this mimetic ideal was at last overthrown by "what Whitehead once called 'the revolt of matter,'" as the scientific method substituted material laws for Platonic forms, and there was nothing left for art to mirror but matter in motion. In the early modern period, the method of studying the physical sciences particularly undermined "faith in the *a priori* axioms and laws provided by theology [and] Aristotelian metaphysics." It replaced theological assertions with scientific laws "validated by empirical evidence," and in doing so, it fueled the growth of "a spectacularly increased capacity . . . to predict and control nature, and men as natural beings."[26]

According to Berlin, concerns about this power of manipulation, coupled with a fear that "men as natural beings" might become cogs in a machine, eventually led to the romantic revolution at the dawn of the nineteenth century. The earlier "revolt of matter" had been anything but

25. *The Dialogues of Plato,* trans. Benjamin Jowett (1892; repr., New York: Random House, 1937), 1:853.

26. Isaiah Berlin, *The Crooked Timber of Humanity: Chapters in the History of Ideas,* ed. Henry Hardy (1990; repr., Princeton: Princeton University Press, 1997), p. 214.

an outright rebellion against the concept of law, for "the domination of mathematics" had been stronger than ever in the eighteenth century. In response to this newfound power of mathematical and physical laws, romanticism developed a "violent scorn for rules and forms as such" and pressed passionately for the free "self-expression of groups, movements, individuals, whithersoever this [freedom] might carry them." Romanticism swept aside established patterns and rushed to embrace the "source of all life and action, of heroism and sacrifice, nobility and idealism both individual and collective — the proud, indomitable, untrammeled human will."[27]

Fashioned by Immanuel Kant and others in the late eighteenth century, this romantic will was put to use in the nineteenth by Friedrich Schiller and Johann Gottlieb Fichte to pry the human spirit free from the grip of natural necessity. For these idealists, nature was not to be imitated but transcended. "Spirit leaves the bounds of reality behind it," wrote Fichte, "and in its own special sphere there are no bounds. . . . In the pure, clear aether of the land of its birth there are no vibrations other than those it creates with its own wings."[28] In Fichte's work, the theory of the will reached the "novel and audacious" conclusion that "ends are not, as had been thought for more than two millennia, objective values, discoverable within man or in a transcendent realm by some special faculty." Instead, for the romantic idealists, our deepest values and ultimate destinies are not discovered but made, "not found but created."[29]

This revolutionary view moved at gale force through nineteenth-century thought and culture. It swept aside all theories that had assigned the poet the primary task of tracing preexisting patterns, because the romantic imagination does not copy old forms but generates new worlds. "Art is not a mirror held up to nature," Berlin says of the romantic view, nor does it involve creating pleasing and harmonious objects governed by the standards of taste. Instead, art has become a means of "self-expression for the individual spirit." Whether a work of art accurately represents nature is immaterial, for only the authenticity of its inten-

27. Berlin, *Crooked Timber,* pp. 214-15.

28. J. G. Fichte, "On the Spirit and the Letter in Philosophy," in *German Idealist Philosophy,* ed. Rüdiger Bubner (London: Penguin, 1997), pp. 119-20.

29. Berlin, *Crooked Timber,* p. 227. For the relationship of Fichte's idealism to modern science, see Robert J. Richards, *The Romantic Conception of Life: Science and Philosophy in the Age of Goethe* (Chicago: University of Chicago Press, 2002), pp. 72-84.

tions matters. In the romantic view of the creative will, the consequences of my actions may be beyond my control, but "my own motives, my goals, my attitude to men and things" still belong to me. As a mixture of flesh and spirit, I live in two worlds. One, which I do not control but cannot ignore, is physical; the other is spiritual and "is in my power," and it is this world that I can bring under the sway of my will and within the scope of my imagining.[30]

If nature is a scene of bondage and a system of necessity, why should I trouble myself with trying to mirror its reality? If values do not somehow inhere in objects but only emanate from subjects, should not poetry express the needs of those subjects rather than represent the limitations of those objects? M. H. Abrams says the eighteenth-century rejection of mimesis led to the replacement of the image of the poem as mirror with "that of the poem as heterocosm, 'a second nature,' created by the poet in an act analogous to God's creation of the world."

Throughout the nineteenth century, this new view became a part of most Anglo-American aesthetic theories. For a time, it remained loosely tethered to a waning belief in the correspondence of the order created in art and the order to be found in God's creation. But belief in such a correspondence declined rapidly in the nineteenth century and had all but disappeared by its end. As a consequence, by the middle of the twentieth century, the "poem as heterocosm" had come to mean simply that the world of poetry is absolutely distinct from that of science, for poetry belongs to a "self-contained universe of discourse, of which we cannot demand that it be true to nature, but only, that it be true to itself."[31]

In the early nineteenth century, Samuel Taylor Coleridge had given the romantic doctrine of poetry its best-known formulation in his *Biographia Literaria.*[32] In the fourteenth chapter of that work, he argued

30. Berlin, *Crooked Timber,* p. 228.

31. M. H. Abrams, *Mirror and Lamp,* p. 272. Many Catholic and Protestant critics embraced the idea of the poem as "heterocosm," despite the fact that it has a profound tension between theological judgment and formal standards built into it. Henry James offered a famous expression of this tension: "Questions of art are questions (in the widest sense) of execution; questions of morality are quite another affair, and will you not let us see how it is that you find it so easy to mix them up?" *Literary Criticism: Essays on Literature, American Writers, English Writers,* ed. Leon Edel (New York: Library of America, 1984), pp. 62-63.

32. Walter Jackson Bate cautions against reading Coleridge's arguments as though

that science and history share with poetry an ultimate concern for truth but differ as to their immediate goals. For science, the aim is to discover "truth absolute and demonstrable," and for history, it is to narrate the truth by means of "facts experienced and recorded." As we search for scientific and historical truths, we may experience pleasures along the way, but our enjoyment of them can never be the purpose of the journey. Because truth is not the immediate goal of poetry, however, poetry is free to pursue pleasure with a passion — even with a method. Poetry is allowed to operate in this manner, because it is that species of composition "which is opposed to works of science, by proposing for its *immediate* object pleasure, not truth; and from all other species . . . it is discriminated by proposing to itself such delight from the *whole,* as is compatible with a distinct gratification from each component *part.*"[33]

In the history of Christian thought, the relationship of part to whole had customarily encompassed the whole of reality, as each object in nature and each event in history became part of a larger story of creation and redemption. The whole consisted of the triune God and all that he had freely created. Everything in heaven and on earth was assumed to play a role in the drama of creation and redemption.

Coleridge thought the pleasures of poetry might revive the disenchanted spirit, but his promotion of its powers stopped far short of the extravagant claims many of his intellectual descendants would later make. Some of them were to argue that poetry could supplant historic Christianity as a source of truth and as an agent of redemption, because it could uniquely discern both the spirit that courses through nature and the moral structure that undergirds it. Ralph Waldo Emerson made this case early in his career:

---

they were more consistent than they are. Because his critical remarks "are so fragmentary, they have the attraction of allowing us to turn them into anything we want, if we take them up in isolation. That is a legitimate use of his insights. Where we err is in trying to construct from them a general theory that we then attribute to Coleridge." *Coleridge* (1968; repr., Cambridge, Mass.: Harvard University Press, 1987), pp. 157-58.

33. Samuel Taylor Coleridge, *Biographia Literaria,* ed. James Engell and W. Jackson Bate (Princeton: Princeton University Press, 1983), 2:12-13. Engell and Bate explain Coleridge's distinction between poetry and science: "'Truth', broadly conceived, may very well be the *ultimate* object of poetry. . . . When we say that pleasure is the immediate object, we mean that each 'part' (each phrase, cadence, image, metaphor, episode) is, ideally speaking, providing a pleasure in and through itself as well as contributing a further pleasure as it adds architectonically to the 'whole'" (p. cviii).

> For, as it is dislocation and detachment from the life of God, that makes things ugly, the poet, who re-attaches things to nature and the Whole, — re-attaching even artificial things, and violations of nature, to nature, by a deeper insight, — disposes very easily of the most disagreeable facts.[34]

For Emerson, poetry comforted the modern soul without requiring it to subscribe to discredited doctrines or maintain antiquated practices. The time had arrived, he announced in 1836, for nature and the human spirit to complete what the Christian God had failed to accomplish, and everything required for the task lay within reach. According to Emerson, "it is not words only that are emblematic; it is things which are emblematic. Every natural fact is a symbol of some spiritual fact. Every appearance in nature corresponds to some state of the mind."[35] And the poet was able to detect those correspondences better than anyone else could.

This breathtaking vision of a spiritualized nature — Thomas Carlyle called it "natural supernaturalism" — flourished at the start of the nineteenth century but faded quickly at its close. It could not survive the trauma of the Civil War or the shock of the Darwinian revolution. Alfred Kazin notes that up until the war, the Bible had remained an essential personal resource for most Americans, but after the war, few felt confident any longer invoking God's purpose to support a particular political course. "Everything so long festering in the American heart" over the aching desire to believe that God rules over history — "everything that was to be threatened after the war by the idea of nature as a self-operating mechanism — now flamed out with all the passion of war itself."[36] The Civil War, in short, brought on a "hermeneutical crisis" that called into question "the adequacy of the Bible itself."[37] And in the wake of this crisis, both romantic idealism and sentimental Christianity were

34. Emerson, *Essays*, p. 455.

35. Emerson, *Essays*, p. 20.

36. Alfred Kazin, *God and the American Writer* (New York: Knopf, 1997), p. 132.

37. Mark A. Noll, *America's God: From Jonathan Edwards to Abraham Lincoln* (Oxford: Oxford University Press, 2002), pp. 396-400. Noll explains how "the Civil War's division of the country's ardent Bible believers called into question the reputation of the Bible as an omnicompetent, infallible authority for life now and forever, at least as that adequacy had been formulated by Protestants since the Reformation" (pp. 397-98).

soon to be swamped by the surge of scientific naturalism that still flows into our cultural and spiritual lives.

As curious as it might at first seem, one consequence of this surge proved to be the advent of the academic study of literature as we know it in American colleges and universities. The discipline of "English" did not exist in America or anywhere else until the late nineteenth century. The teaching of literature in the vernacular had taken place sporadically on campuses in the years before the Civil War, but the practice did not spread widely until the years immediately after the war. The impulse that prompted this growth had something in common with Coleridge's earlier ideal of a "clerisy," a distinct class of learned and literary people who were to provide spiritual leadership to a culture that had lost its traditional spiritual guides.[38] By teaching literature in the vernacular, the fledgling English departments sought to minister to the human spirit through a rigorous study of that spirit's literary productions. Under the considerable influence of the philological tradition, scholars of literature saw themselves as providing a viable alternative to the now discredited religious framework of knowledge. The aim of humanistic study, wrote a leading classicist in 1911, "is to enrich the heart and mind of the student by leading him to live over in thought and feeling the complete spiritual unfolding of a great people by repeating in imagination the experience of their sensuous environment, of their religious sanctions, their social and political life, their poetry and formative art, their philosophy and science."[39]

As firmly as they resisted naturalism's spiritual and cultural implications, these humanistic scholars largely accepted its methodological presuppositions, which had been put forth in Darwin's *On the Origin of Species* in 1859. Half a century after that work first appeared, John Dewey said it "marked an epoch in the development of the natural sciences." With the theory of natural selection, Darwin overturned "conceptions that had reigned in the philosophy of nature and knowledge for two thousand years." Those ideas had "rested on the assumption of the supe-

38. For the "clerisy" analogy, I am indebted to James Turner, *The Liberal Education of Charles Eliot Norton* (Baltimore: Johns Hopkins University Press, 1999), p. 12.

39. Paul Shorey, quoted in Jon H. Roberts and James Turner, *The Sacred and the Secular University* (Princeton: Princeton University Press, 2000), p. 105; for a fuller discussion of these issues, see pp. 95-106. See also James Turner, *Language, Religion, Knowledge: Past and Present* (Notre Dame: University of Notre Dame Press, 2003), pp. 100-106.

riority of the fixed and final" and had treated "change and origin as signs of defect and unreality."[40] As Dewey saw it, Darwin freed nature from the shackles of superstition by making development the standard for spiritual experience as well as for biological life.

In effecting this revolutionary change, Darwin undermined the argument from design and decimated natural theology as a force in Protestant thought. Following the lead of Greek philosophy, Christian thought had for many centuries emphasized its belief in the *teleological* nature of human life; there is, the faith held, a divinely appointed *telos,* a given purpose and goal to human life and the natural order. Darwin dramatically turned our sights from providential ends to impersonal origins; he was interested in the *arche,* that point of origin from which life and order emerged in the ceaseless struggle for survival. The survival of the species, as brutal as the process might be, was the only *telos* nature had in mind for life, human or otherwise. After Darwin, to understand the meaning of a life one did not attempt to trace the arc of its journey forward to a destined ethical or spiritual end. Instead, one followed the trail back to its biological origins. Darwin made it obvious that modern science had "to narrow its focus to physical reality alone."[41]

That left the world of the spirit — intangible as it was — to the poets and artists. If, to paraphrase Dylan Thomas, reality was to hold them green and dying, then they might as well sing in their chains like the sea. Or to return to our metaphor from Robert Frost, if a great wall now separated the domain of matter from the kingdom of the spirit, then so be it. The artists could tend to their own gardens in splendid isolation and try their best not to worry about what — or who — was being planned, invented, or executed on the other side of the wall.

That many of these artists were content to till the literary soil with quasi-scientific implements may seem odd, but it does make sense in its own way. By the beginning of the twentieth century, the authority of science had become so great that many writers and critics alike were eager to appropriate its methods and trade upon its authority, even as they spun aesthetic alternatives to the web of material explanation. For ex-

40. John Dewey, *The Influence of Darwin on Philosophy and Other Essays* (1910; repr., Amherst, N.Y.: Prometheus, 1997), p. 1.

41. James Turner, *Without God, Without Creed: The Origins of Unbelief in America* (Baltimore: Johns Hopkins University Press, 1985), p. 186.

ample, both T. S. Eliot and Ezra Pound sought the sanction of science even as they promoted poetry as the antidote to the poisonous effects of scientific materialism. They claimed that the writing of poetry and criticism resembled scientific inquiry in that both activities "required long study and preparation" and made discoveries that had significance beyond the realm of the merely local or personal.[42] "Consider the way of the scientists rather than the way of an advertising agent for a new soap," Pound advised aspiring poets in 1913. "The scientist does not expect to be acclaimed as a great scientist until he has *discovered* something."[43]

In literary criticism, Cleanth Brooks followed the lead of Pound and Eliot in calling for poetry and criticism to be as rigorous as science in their methods yet as comforting as religion in their message. In a classic text of the New Criticism, *Modern Poetry and the Tradition,* Brooks describes science as an "abstract" but undeniably "powerful" form of knowledge that does its work efficiently and tells its story convincingly. But the knowledge it yields is partial and speaks only to one part of human experience, while poetry addresses the whole person. Poetry moves beyond "those elements which make the knowledge 'useful,'" and adds "other 'useless' elements as well." In Brooks's words, "science is power-knowledge" that enables us to heat our homes and print our books, but it may also "contribute to *hubris;* whereas poetry (as an element of religion or merely as poetry), . . . constantly reminds man that the thing described lies outside man's control, and thus rebukes *hubris.*"[44] In keeping human pride in check, literature stands in for the now-departed gods of Greek tragedy.

In identifying the "useless" as the definitive "extra" that belongs to poetry, Brooks looks back to Kant and Coleridge and forward to the dominant mid-twentieth-century defense of poetry. Modernism promoted literature as a heated cry of the heart against the wintry indifference of a disenchanted world. So defined, poetry had little to say to a culture in crisis and could do nothing for one beyond repair.[45] Instead, it

42. Gail McDonald, *Learning to Be Modern: Pound, Eliot, and the American University* (New York: Oxford, 1993), p. 76.

43. Ezra Pound, "Imagism," in *Modern Tradition,* ed. Ellmann and Feidelson, p. 144.

44. Cleanth Brooks, *Modern Poetry and the Tradition* (Chapel Hill: University of North Carolina Press, 1939), pp. 91-92.

45. David Hollinger sets modernism's pursuit of pleasure, and its rejection of the didactic and rhetorical, in context: "If 'modernism' was not a 'world-view' for the critics of

offered irony and aesthetic distance as art's saving graces. John Keats had given this ironic stance a telling name when he wrote in an 1817 letter that he was trying to identify the quality that "a Man of Achievement especially in Literature" possessed: "I mean *Negative Capability,* that is when man is capable of being in uncertainties, Mysteries, doubts, without any irritable reaching after fact & reason." Or as Oscar Wilde put the matter at the end of the nineteenth century:

> We can forgive a man for making a useful thing as long as he does not admire it. The only excuse for making a useless thing is that one admires it intensely.
>
> All art is quite useless.[46]

In this scheme of things, to be saved is to hover in a state of suspended judgment, holding every ultimate question in abeyance, deciding nothing and consigning all to the power of irony and the liberty of uncertainty. In turn, this veneration of irony made it possible for a number who held no discernible religious beliefs to treat literature with a feeling akin to awe. Modern literature may offer no theological system, and it may not subscribe to any creed, but Lionel Trilling says "its ethic is by no means obscure." Diffident as it may be about staking a claim to any specific set of beliefs, literature nonetheless "asks us if we are content with ourselves, if we are saved or damned — more than with anything else, our literature is concerned with salvation. No literature has ever been so intensely spiritual as ours," writes Trilling, who taught for decades at Columbia University. He might not call it "religious, but certainly it has the special intensity of concern with the spiritual life which Hegel noted when he spoke of the great modern phenomenon of the sec-

---

the mid-century decades, it was certainly a *set of suspicions* about human beings and their world, a collection of senses *that could be explored the most safely if kept out of propositional form,* and outside the realm of prosaic argument. It was a function of the scripture of modernism to create and maintain for the exploration of these suspicions *a privileged foundation:* a base free from the obligation to specify and to take a stand upon the political, moral, and metaphysical implications of those suspicions. . . . Now, literature was to be about society but not subject to it: *of* the world, but not *in* it." *In the American Province,* p. 85.

46. John Keats, *Selected Poems and Letters,* ed. Douglas Bush (Boston: Houghton, 1959), 261; Oscar Wilde, "The Improvidence of Art," in *Modern Tradition,* ed. Ellmann and Feidelson, p. 103.

ularization of spirituality." There is an "extravagant personal force" in modern literature, and Trilling confesses, "for me it makes difficulty." Trilling's particular difficulty is that of confronting "the necessity of bearing personal testimony." Talking about "formal matters" alone — about such things as "verse-patterns, metrics, prose conventions, irony, tension, etc." — will no longer suffice. The teaching of literature demands commitment from its readers as well as commentary upon the turbulent world that seethes outside its walls.[47]

Literature, Science, and the Pyrrhic Victory of Theory

Trilling wrote his celebrated essay in 1961, and in less than a decade, American literary studies were to be altered radically, as political forces and social upheavals blew gaping holes in the walls between the academic disciplines. Literary theorist Tzvetan Todorov, for example, identifies the transformation as having taken place in that most volatile of years, 1968. "Until roughly 1968," he claims, "most American critics seemed preoccupied by one key question: 'What does the text mean?'" When confronted with a difficult work, he says, they believed "their most important task was to discover as exactly as possible what the text meant." Yet according to Todorov, after 1968, the question "What does the text mean?" was rendered moot in American criticism by deconstruction's response — "Nothing at all" — and pragmatism's answer — "Anything whatsoever."[48]

Todorov's account may oversimplify a complex history, but it does point to a genuine change in theorizing about literature in the final decades of the twentieth century. This involved an abrupt abandonment of literature's defensive stance vis-à-vis science and the adoption of a markedly more aggressive posture. Nietzsche had prepared the ground for this approach a century earlier, with his animated admonitions against "lying in the dust before [the] *petty facts*" of nature. Still, it is not clear that his depiction of science as a fictive discourse would have resonated

47. Lionel Trilling, *Beyond Culture: Essays on Literature and Learning* (1965; repr., Oxford: Oxford University Press, 1980), pp. 190, 8.

48. Tzvetan Todorov, *Literature and Its Theorists: A Personal View of Twentieth-Century Criticism,* trans. Catherine Porter (Ithaca, N.Y.: Cornell University Press, 1987), pp. 182-83.

as it did without the political and cultural upheavals of the 1960s. The social revolution of that decade reinforced the epistemological skepticism that had begun at last to undercut the authority of science.

For many writers and critics who had been long inured to a twilight struggle with science, this newfound skepticism proved liberating. It meant that literature no longer needed to take shelter behind disciplinary walls but could break through them and move on to seize the ground held by its scientific adversaries. As the epistemological equal of science and its moral superior, literature could now claim for itself the power to alter our perceptions — and even to transform our world.

In recent decades, Richard Rorty has served as an avid champion of the "linguistic turn" that led to the putative triumph of the poetic impulse. As the twentieth century drew to a close, he argued that literature had replaced philosophy as the central intellectual discipline just as philosophy had supplanted science a century earlier. In their nineteenth-century battle with science, the philosophical idealists had argued that "nothing exists but ideas," and now "there are people who write as if there were nothing but texts." Both nineteenth-century idealism and contemporary textualism "adopt an antagonistic position to natural science" and insist that we cannot compare human thought with an unmediated reality. Science offers no privileged view of that reality but is only a tool for predicting natural processes. In Rorty's words, the idealists and textualists agree that scientific knowledge no longer has pride of place in the intellectual scheme of things. They insist instead that "there is a point of view other than, and somehow higher than, that of science."[49]

As we have seen in the case of Coleridge and Emerson, the idealists had argued that poetry trumped science by providing access to the hidden reaches of spirit. But contemporary textualists claim it is irony that makes poetry supreme, for "the ironic modernist's awareness that he is responding to texts rather than to things, puts him one up on the scientist." The naïve scientist searches for truths hidden in nature, but the savvy poet realizes there are none to find. Twentieth-century textualism built upon the romantic revolution and sought to make literature the central discipline, and to think of "both science and philosophy as, at best, literary genres." For Rorty, genres are flexible and can be changed

49. Richard Rorty, *Consequences of Pragmatism: Essays, 1972-1980* (Minneapolis: University of Minnesota Press, 1980), p. 139.

through force or by an act of genius. In his words, "it is a feature of what I shall call 'literature' that one can achieve success by introducing a quite new genre of poem or novel or critical essay *without* argument." Literature is not disputatious but irenic, and it colonizes not through the rigorous force of argument but through the seductive appeal of metaphor.[50]

The romantics, according to Rorty, were the first to posit that what matters is not the "propositions we believe but what vocabulary we use." Although metaphysical idealism did not survive the challenges of the nineteenth century, it did make it possible in the following century for "the literary culture . . . to assert its spiritual superiority to science." Specifically, Kant had paved the way by relativizing the vocabulary of science. In his wake, Hegel consciously nurtured the fledgling literary culture by showing "that everything can be changed by talking in new terms." But in the end, it was William James and Friedrich Nietzsche who "gave up the notion of truth as a correspondence to reality" and made the eventual triumph of literary culture inevitable. Rather than arguing "that the discovery of vocabularies could bring hidden secrets to light, they said that new ways of speaking could help get us what we want." James, Nietzsche, and the others became "pragmatists" who stripped romanticism of its epistemological anxieties and metaphysical pretensions. They abandoned the "notion of *discovering the truth*," which is the foundation of theology and science, and embraced the imaginative power to create the truth, which is the cornerstone of poetry and the arts.[51]

These post-romantic figures spurned the fixity of truth and embraced the flexibility of texts. In Rorty's terms, there are "weak" textualists and "strong" ones. Among the weak textualists would be the modernist poets and critics who dominated literature from the First World War through the 1960s; they respected the intellectual seriousness of science and did their best to "imitate science" by searching for a "*method* of criticism." They believed that each great work of literature is governed by a secret code, unique to it alone. The weak textualists were eager to hunker down within the compound of poetry and stay "within the boundaries of a text." They did break "with the myth of language as mirror of re-

50. Rorty, *Consequences of Pragmatism*, pp. 140-42.

51. Rorty, *Consequences of Pragmatism*, pp. 142, 149-51. For William James on truth, see Robert D. Richardson's superb *William James: In the Maelstrom of American Modernism* (Boston: Houghton, 2006), pp. 484-88.

ality," but they also longed "to imitate science" through the methodical analysis of poetry and fiction. Weak textualists long for the "comforts of consensus, even if only the consensus of readers of literary quarterlies," and they find in irony a god worthy of their devotion.[52]

The strong textualists, on the other hand, seek not to worship the word but to use it. About texts, they ask themselves the same questions that the engineer asks about physical reality: "how shall I describe this in order to get it to do what I want?" The strong textualists believe we need a vision for transforming reality rather than a means of adjusting to it. "Occasionally a great physicist or a great critic comes along and gives us a new vocabulary which enables us to do a lot of new and marvelous things," Rorty notes. Only when we have forsaken the search for a *"privileged vocabulary,"* can we create a new one to extend our verbal dominion over the wilderness that is our world.[53]

The linguistic turn represents a triumph of "the literary culture" so complete that Wordsworth and Coleridge would blush at its audacity. They had resisted science not because they sought to silence the story it told but because they believed it to be possible, and necessary, to supplement that story. Their struggle against science was an agonistic contest in which each party was defined in good measure by its adversary. To them, the truth of science was one thing, that of poetry and religion another, but neither truth in itself could comprehend the whole. The romantic poets would have cast a cold eye on a definition of literature as the art of constructing selves and fabricating truths, and they would have spurned any attempt to reduce religious experience to a therapeutic regimen. To those poets, the triumph of literature over science would have seemed to be a Pyrrhic victory indeed.

The Poets' Response

In recent decades, literary theorists have often behaved like courtiers as they have curried the favor of the poets and have sought to sidle up to the literary throne. Yet perhaps surprisingly, many poets have been hesitant

52. Rorty, *Consequences of Pragmatism,* p. 152. See also Frank Lentricchia, *After the New Criticism* (Chicago: University of Chicago Press, 1980), pp. 29-60.

53. Rorty, *Consequences of Pragmatism,* pp. 152-53.

to return the favor or to appreciate the fawning. In good measure, they have spurned such theoretical flattery out of a sense of modesty about their craft, as we saw with Czeslaw Milosz and Richard Wilbur's refusal to regard poetry as a sacrament or the imagination as an incarnational power.

Hesitant to make bold religious claims on behalf of poetry, the likes of Wilbur and Milosz would be equally reluctant to celebrate any putative triumph of literature over science. They and others may question the imperial presumption of science, but at the same time, they seem to have little desire to make it a servant in the court of the poetic. Instead of pitting religion, poetry, and science against each other in a pitched cultural battle, poets such as Milosz, Emily Dickinson, and W. H. Auden took a different tack. Each had a passion for science that rivaled his or her passion for belief, and each in turn has offered a rich poetic response to the vexing questions modern science has often put to that belief.

Consider the case of Dickinson, the only one of these poets to have been active at the height of the nineteenth-century revolutions in biology and geology. Because she grew up before *On the Origin of Species* was published, her early, formative judgments were shaped by the eighteenth-century argument from design rather than by the naturalism of the late nineteenth century. To a significant extent, that fact accounts for the sense of shocked immediacy one feels in her poems and letters, as they register how things felt on the ground, when the Darwinian quake rocked the religious foundations of the culture at mid-century.

In Dickinson's childhood, many scientists and Christian apologists alike had still taken the "Book of Nature" and the "Book of Scripture" to speak with one voice. At the Amherst Academy, Emily was taught by Edward Hitchcock, a renowned Christian geologist who drew extensive analogies between biblical passages and natural processes. For example, in a popular book, Hitchcock drew an extensive comparison between the resurrection of Christ and the renewal of life in spring. "Spring presents us with numerous examples of life emerging from apparent death," he wrote, for it "opens upon us brighter displays of Divine Power, Wisdom and Goodness."[54] To the young Emily Dickinson, such messages were reassuring, as she told a friend years later: "When Flowers annually died and I

54. Edward Hitchcock, *Religious Lectures on Peculiar Phenomena in the Four Seasons* (Amherst, 1851), pp. 33, 42.

was a child, I used to read Dr Hitchcock's Book on the Flowers of North America. This comforted their Absence — assuring me they lived."[55]

The wellsprings of that comfort dried up in Dickinson's lifetime. When she was born in 1830, the argument from design ruled over a six-thousand-year-old earth; by the time she began writing poetry in the late 1850s, that earth had grown much, much older. Copernicus and Galileo had expanded the universe spatially in the sixteenth and seventeenth centuries; now Darwin and his contemporaries were stretching its temporal limits beyond imagining. In one of her most perfect poems, Dickinson sets the brevity of human life within the new understanding of the vast expanse of geological and biological time. She does so by considering the status of the dead who are "Safe in their Alabaster Chambers" while they await the promised resurrection of the body. As they sleep beneath their "Rafter of Satin and Roof of Stone,"

Grand go the Years,
In the Crescent above them —
Worlds scoop their Arcs —
And Firmaments — row —
Diadems — drop —
And Doges — surrender —
Soundless as Dots,
On a Disc of Snow.[56]

Here the heavens move with dreadful slowness, while death claims its victims relentlessly, and the entire drama unfolds before a silent audience. Although this poem does not so much deny the resurrection as announce its indefinite postponement, there are in it more than a few hints of that "boundless humiliation" Karl Barth described in his reflections on modern cosmology.

As she responded to scientific developments in her day, and particularly to Darwin, Dickinson questioned sharply the intellectual substance

55. Emily Dickinson, *The Letters of Emily Dickinson,* ed. Thomas H. Johnson and Theodora Ward (Cambridge, Mass.: Belknap Press of Harvard University Press, 1958), 2:573.

56. *The Poems of Emily Dickinson,* reading ed., ed. R. W. Franklin (Cambridge, Mass.: Belknap Press of Harvard University Press, 1999), #124; all further references to Dickinson's poems will be cited in the text with the number assigned to them in the Franklin edition.

of Christian belief even as she prized the emotional resources it offered for her spirit. In an age of sentimentalized eschatology, she put forward a stark vision of human vulnerability that had much in common with the wisdom literature of the Hebrew Bible, *The Confessions* of St. Augustine, and Jonathan Edwards's sobering reflections on the freedom of the will. Lutheran theologian Helmut Thielicke refers to this broad Augustinian tradition when he describes human life as being situated "at the place where [two geometrical lines] intersect." One line represents the intelligible world of human relationships, the other the timetable of the universe, in which the human person appears as "an infinitely insignificant quantity." When cast against a backdrop of innumerable galaxies or inserted onto a timeline stretching out billions of years, an individual life seems like "an almost unimaginable trifle."[57] To be human is to live in the space between heaven and earth. From this vantage point we may be able to imagine eternity, but we cannot escape mortality.

As Thielicke understood, the problem with such a bracing view of human nature was that, in and of itself, it could not imagine anything more than a stiff and distant God to rule over this world. Dickinson describes this God in a late poem as one who looks on as the frost "beheads" a "happy Flower" one morning. The cold, "blonde Assassin" passes on to other flowers, while "The sun proceeds unmoved/To measure off another Day/For an Approving God-" (#1668). At best, Dickinson was able to manage a strained relationship with the "Eclipse" that her sister and parents called "their 'Father.'" Whatever meaning he had for her family, her neighbors, or her contemporaries, God remained for her an "Adamant, " a "God of Flint" who seemed to "refuse" to give her even the smallest signs of "Grace" (#478).

In search of the comfort she craved, Dickinson turned her back on God the Father and her face towards Jesus the Son, and in making this Christological turn she was a harbinger of the theological future. Half a century after Dickinson, Karl Barth would also come to see nineteenth-century liberal theology as sterile and bankrupt. Like her, he found little to warm to in the thought of a mechanistic deity. It was the heartlessness of natural theology that drove him to develop a richly textured doctrine of Jesus Christ.

57. Helmut Thielicke, *Nihilism, Its Origin and Nature — with a Christian Answer,* trans. John W. Doberstein (New York: Harper, 1961), pp. 106-7.

Dickinson, for her part, had scant knowledge of the history of Christian doctrine, but she knew her Bible well, and sensed that she could somehow turn to Christ for care. Her affection for Jesus often proved to be as palpable as her fear of God was strong, and for her, Christ was the "Largest Lover," the "Tender Pioneer," and the "Man that knew the News." Vexed by the callous indifference of nature, she nevertheless could take heart in the fact that

The Savior must have been
A docile Gentleman —
To come so far so cold a Day
For little Fellow men — (#1538)

Jesus can give us comfort because he suffered as we do and underwent the death that each of us must endure. "When Jesus tells us about his Father, we distrust him," Dickinson wrote to a neighbor late in life. "When he shows us his Home, we turn away, but when he confides to us that he is 'acquainted with Grief,' we listen, for that also is an Acquaintance of our own." Or as she explained to a friend, when they were grieving the death of a mutual acquaintance, "the crucifix requires no glove." We can grasp the cross of Jesus because suffering is familiar to our touch, and our hands have a hold on a grief of which they will not let go.[58]

Where Dickinson focused largely on the personal, emotional implications of modern science, Auden and Milosz divided their attention between the public questions science raised and the private dilemmas it prompted. In their twentieth-century engagement with a disenchanted world, these two poets focused more on what I termed earlier the ethical question — "How am I to respond to a disenchanted world?" — than on the aesthetic one — "How might I bring into being the more beautiful world that I have imagined?"[59] They had no hankering for a "literary cul-

58. Dickinson, *Letters,* 3:837, 2:603. For my understanding of Dickinson's response to the life, and death, of Jesus Christ, I am indebted to Dorothy Huff Oberhaus, "'Tender Pioneer': Emily Dickinson's Poems on the Life of Christ," *American Literature* 59 (1987): 341-58. "When read together as a group allowing each to illuminate the others, these meditations on Jesus' birth, life, Crucifixion, and Resurrection form something like a nineteenth-century American Gospel" (p. 341).

59. That is not to say that Auden and Milosz disparaged imaginative longing, for both of them wrote of the heart's desire to find an enduring realm. Aleksander Fiut writes of Milosz's attempt to interpret the "book of the world": "The Book that the poet tirelessly at-

ture" of the kind that Rorty and others have envisioned, and both resisted any efforts to pattern our social life after a poetic model. Indeed, according to Auden, a society that resembled a good poem in that it embodied "the aesthetic virtues of beauty, order, economy and subordination of detail to the whole, would be, a nightmare of horror." Given human nature, such a society could only come into being "through selective breeding, extermination of the physically and mentally unfit," absolute obedience to its rulers, and "a large slave class kept out of sight in cellars." But the opposite holds true as well. "Vice versa, a poem which was really like a political democracy — examples, unfortunately, exist — would be formless, windy, banal and utterly boring."[60]

To avoid a forced choice between brutality or banality, Auden suggests an alternate view of art as a gratuitous activity that has an aura of the sacred about it. He notes that most premodern cultures considered the gratuitous to be sacred, while the contemporary world is governed by "the values appropriate to Labor" and sees leisure not as a sacred thing but as "a respite from laboring, a time for relaxation and the pleasures of consumption." In modern culture, the making of art can have a political as well as a religious potential, insofar as it affirms "that *Homo Laborans* is also *Homo Ludens*." For Auden, both the poet who writes verses and the plebeian who plays cards should be able to subscribe to the belief "that among the half dozen or so things for which a man of honor should be prepared, if necessary, to die, the right to play, the right to frivolity, is not the least."[61]

---

tempts to decipher is a representation, a repetition in words of the entire universe. It is a text that discloses the method for its own reading only to the initiated. It is a prefiguration of the world that like a parchment scroll God will roll up at the end of human history. Only then will the chasm between the subjective and the objective, the sign and the signified, be bridged." *The Eternal Moment: The Poetry of Czeslaw Milosz,* trans. Theodosia S. Robertson (Berkeley: University of California Press, 1990), p. 195.

60. W. H. Auden, *The Dyer's Hand, and Other Essays* (1962; repr., New York: Vintage, 1989), p. 85.

61. Auden, *Dyer's Hand,* pp. 74, 88, 89. Auden's thoughts on gratuity and the sacred are echoed in a speech Robert Frost delivered shortly before his death. Frost drew poetry, religion, and science together to praise the "extravagance" of creation, divine and otherwise. "I was thinking of the extravagance of the universe, you know, what an *extravagant* universe it is," he explained. "And the most extravagant thing in it, as far as we know, is man." Take out a telescope and scan the heavens, Frost says, and you will see "how much of a universe was wasted to produce puny us." Poetry itself, like the countless galaxies swim-

As to the specific relationship between poetry, science, and the Christian faith, Arthur Kirsch explains that Auden took the effects of modern science to "have been both admirable and pernicious." Science, Auden said, "has liberated men from a misplaced humility before a false god." The god whose death Nietzsche announced in the late nineteenth century was not the Christian God but a cultural deity, "a Zeus without Zeus's vices." To Auden, the singular achievement of science in the modern world "has been to demythologise the Universe. Precisely because He created it, God cannot be encountered in the Universe," so the disenchantment of the world may be seen as a gift from a gracious God. "A storm" is just "a natural phenomenon, not as in polytheism, the wrath of Zeus — just as when I read a poem, I do not encounter the author himself, only the words he has written which it is my job to understand."[62]

Like Dickinson, Auden on occasion turned to Christ in hopes of resolving the spiritual difficulties science had raised. Initially, this took for the poet the form of trust in the moral authority of Jesus. Over time, however, admiration for the ethical Jesus gave way in Auden's poetry to affection for the suffering Christ. "Faith for Christianity means the power to endure the paradox that Jesus, the individual historical man, was and is, as He claimed, Christ, the only begotten Son of the Father," he wrote in 1942.[63]

One of his ambitious poems along these lines, "Friday's Child," focuses upon the relationship of Jesus Christ to the radical freedom God has granted to men and women in the modern age. The poem, which is dedicated to Dietrich Bonhoeffer, deals with the paradox of human power and divine powerlessness, or at least divine permissiveness. Perhaps God "frowns" at our sins, Auden muses; perhaps he "grieves" over

ming through the silent heavens, "is a sort of extravagance, in many ways. It's something that people wonder about. What's the need of it? — you know. And the answer is, no need — not particularly." "On Extravagance," in *Collected Poems,* p. 902.

62. Arthur Kirsch, *Auden and Christianity* (New Haven: Yale University Press, 2005), p. 162. The Auden citations are from an unpublished manuscript and are quoted from the transcription given on pp. 162-63 of *Auden and Christianity.* As for the pernicious effects of modern science, Auden observes: "We are finding out to our cost that we cannot enslave nature without enslaving ourselves. If nobody in the universe is responsible for man, then we must conclude that man is responsible, under and to God, for the Universe. . . . This means re-introducing into the sciences a new notion of teleology, long a dirty word."

63. W. H. Auden, quoted in Edward Mendelson, *Later Auden* (New York: Farrar, 1999), p. 255.

the fact that we have harnessed the atom and acquired the power to destroy the world. But in the end, we simply do not know whether it is God's "anger" or his "compassion" that "leaves/The bigger bangs to us." Whichever it is, how are we to pay reverence to a "Divinity so odd/He lets the Adam whom He made/Perform the Acts of God"?

"Friday's Child" shows that Auden, like Dickinson, found the argument from design wanting. "The analogies are rot/Our senses based belief upon," and since that is the case, "We have no means of learning what/Is really going on." Auden was unable to affirm unambiguously the central doctrine that is the source of Christian hope: "Now, did He really break the seal/And rise again? We dare not say," but even "unbelievers feel/Quite sure of Judgment Day." When we look at the suffering Christ, we meet "a silence on the cross" that "speaks of some total gain or loss." But which one it is — gain or loss — that silence does not say, and we can only try

> To guess from the insulted face
> Just what Appearances He saves
> By suffering in a public place
> A death reserved for slaves.[64]

This is a minimalist Christology. Faith may point the way, but like science, it cannot deliver us to any sound assurance beyond this guess or any definite place beyond this face.[65]

64. W. H. Auden, *Collected Poems,* ed. Edward Mendelson (New York: Modern Library, 2007), pp. 673-75. Auden wrote "Friday's Child" under the considerable influence of Owen Barfield's *Saving the Appearances:* "Barfield proposed instead a new (yet also ancient) understanding based on imaginative 'participation' between observer and observed, a participation culminating in the 'final participation' of full religious faith, when all the idols of detached observation are swept away." Mendelson, *Later Auden,* p. 428.

Auden questioned the wisdom of modernist efforts to make religion and poetry as methodically rigorous as the sciences: "Any defense of the poetic and personal realms must fail, Auden believed, if it adopts the methods of its adversaries. Most modern literature and thought had done precisely that: had insisted on plainspoken realism in art and on scientific detachment in ethics, or had withdrawn into opiate symbolism in art and existential drama in ethics." Mendelson, *Later Auden,* p. 429.

65. For a helpful discussion of the religious background to "Friday's Child," see Alan Jacobs, *What Became of Wystan: Change and Continuity in Auden's Poetry* (Fayetteville: University of Arkansas Press, 1998), pp. 94-95. Jacobs quotes Auden's remark to Ursula Niebuhr concerning the resurrection: "It does make a difference if it really happened,

As they wrestled with the idea of an isolated self housed within an indifferent universe, Dickinson and Auden revealed the limits of an exclusive concentration on the sufferings of Christ. Indeed, their poetry gives evidence in places of a tendency towards "anthropological overcompensation" that has become a dominant motif of modern theology. The term is Helmut Thielicke's, and with it he describes an effort, originating in the nineteenth century, to counter the "cold and uninvolved" dogmatism of orthodox Christology with an emphasis upon the passion of Christ. The intention, Thielicke holds, was lofty, perhaps even noble: "Our own suffering is softened by seeing the similar suffering of others," particularly that of Christ. ("The crucifix requires no glove.") Yet the unintended consequences proved to be troubling, for in time the stress on a weak and suffering Christ led to an "increasing transformation of theology into anthropology."[66] The anthropological Christ may have good intentions, but he is an ineffectual savior, for no matter how deeply he suffers, he cannot do so on our behalf, and he remains trapped with us within finitude and powerless alongside us in the face of death.

In his poetic portrayals of Christ, Milosz also wavered between affirmation and doubt, as he grappled with the idea of an "anthropological" savior. "Christ has risen," a late poem begins, only to have this assertion qualified at every turn through the remainder of the poem. If we believe "Christ has risen," we ought not to "behave as we do," muddling on "in cars, in beds,/Men clutching at women, women clutching at men," even as they (and we) "plod on with hope." Our actions reveal both our cosmic disorientation and our moral confusion, for we "have lost the up, the down, the right, the left, heavens, abysses." It is as though we live in a cave and are warmed by fires, "while outside the golden rain of stars is

---

doesn't it" (p. 148 n. 17). But on this score, Auden was never confident. Late in life, in a set of unpublished notes on religion and theology, he bluntly concluded: "To-day, we find Good Friday easy to accept: what scandalises us is Easter: Modern man finds a happy ending, a final victory of Love over the Prince of this World, very hard to swallow." Quoted in Kirsch, *Auden and Christianity,* p. 21.

Auden's ambivalence about the resurrection is consistent with a tendency in the Western church to stress the *theologia crucis* (theology of the cross) at the expense of the *theologia gloriae* (theology of glory). For a concise examination of this question, see Karl Barth, *Dogmatics in Outline,* trans. G. T. Thompson (1949; repr., New York: Harper, 1959), pp. 114-20.

66. Helmut Thielicke, *The Evangelical Faith,* vol. 2, *The Doctrine of God and of Christ,* trans. and ed. Geoffrey W. Bromiley (Grand Rapids: Eerdmans, 1977), pp. 385-86.

motionless." Our "theologians are silent," and our philosophers "don't even dare ask: 'What is truth?'" The speaker of the poem will not deny the resurrection, but he also cannot affirm it in the poem's closing lines: "And now let everyone/Confess to himself. 'Has he risen?' 'I don't know.'"[67]

In interviews and essays alike, Milosz often traced his theological uncertainties to their roots in his scientific anxieties. Increasingly, he reported late in life, "I am more concerned with the erosion of the religious imagination because of the impact of science."[68] In his reading of the modern condition, it was Copernicus who first unhoused the human race by evicting it from its secure "central place in the universe." Several centuries later, Darwin stripped the homeless self of its dignity by calling into question "the very singularity of being human" and by undermining the "meaning of human death." In documenting nature's "incredible prodigality," Darwin had convincingly demonstrated that nature spawns individuals solely to sustain the species. For him, nature remains "absolutely indifferent to the fate of the individual"; to nature, an isolated man or woman is not a sinner for whom Christ died but a simple and expendable "statistical cipher."[69]

As a result of Darwin, Milosz says, the "imagination . . . [became] lost to certain varieties of religious belief," as the framework that had supported Christian art for centuries collapsed under the weight of naturalism. Over the course of the nineteenth century, the three-tiered universe of Dante's *Divine Comedy* disappeared, and the rapid "erosion" of the concepts of heaven and hell touched "every human being's perception of life in terms of salvation and damnation." As the century came to a close, "strange things happen[ed]" to poetry as a result of these losses. Several "solitary rebels" sought to elevate the art form "so high as to remove from it any goals whatsoever and began to glorify it as a thing unto itself, *l'art pour l'art*." And so it is that "in the very midst of a universal weakening of values deprived of their metaphysical foundations, there arises the idea of a poem outside that crisis." Thus envisioned, the poem becomes a self-sufficient entity governed by its own laws and set apart as "a peculiar

67. Czeslaw Milosz, *New and Collected Poems, 1931-2001* (New York: Ecco, 2001), p. 498.

68. *Czeslaw Milosz: Conversations,* p. 153.

69. Czeslaw Milosz, *The Witness of Poetry* (Cambridge, Mass.: Harvard University Press, 1983), p. 43.

anti-world." For this "cult of sovereign, haughty poetry," the only goal is "the fulfillment of the poet's personality, as if he were leaving forever a cast of his own face."[70]

Milosz had too high a regard of science to endorse the idea of a "sovereign poetry," but he also banked too heavily on religious belief to accept a scientific view of reality unquestioningly. Hence his ambivalence. On the one hand, he welcomed the humbling of poetry by science, for in certain moods, he considered a poem to be "no more than a broken whisper, quickly dying laughter."[71] Our poems are but "abundantly draped silks/To brighten the dance of skeletons," and when a poet dies, his poetry is left to wander "through the world,/Forever, clear." While others have been called to suffering or sainthood in the twentieth century, Milosz has faced a different destiny: "I empty glasses, throw myself on food,/And glance greedily at the waitress's neck." He desires greatness but experiences instead "what was left for smaller men like me:/A feast of brief hopes, a rally of the proud,/A tournament of hunchbacks, literature."[72]

Yet at the same time, the heart needs more than "a feast of brief hopes" to sustain it, and as he searched for spiritual sustenance, Milosz kept returning to the Emersonian riddle of the mind's relationship to nature. What he found there made him highly suspicious of nature and her consort, science. "I am with all those people who have proclaimed their distrust of Nature (it's contaminated) and relied solely on the boundless freedom of the divine act, or Grace," he explained. We live at a time when the sacred is accessible to us "only through negation and repudiation of what is anti-sacral."[73]

In his poetry, Milosz never really gave up his flirtation with Gnosticism, the ancient heresy that claims that the world was created by a secondary power, a lesser God. As a case in point, in the last decade of his life, he wrote a witty poetic rejoinder to an unnamed "Mrs. Professor," who had apparently mounted a verbal or written attack upon cats. In his response, Milosz declared his cat — like all of nature — innocent of the guilt that only humans can bear for their cruelty. His meditation then moves from the specific case to a general view:

70. Milosz, *Witness of Poetry,* pp. 43, 46.

71. Milosz, *Witness of Poetry,* p. 46.

72. Milosz, *New and Collected Poems,* pp. 462, 725, 461.

73. Czeslaw Milosz, *To Begin Where I Am: Selected Essays,* ed. Bogdana Carpenter and Madeline G. Levine (New York: Farrar, 2001), pp. 321-22.

Nature devouring, nature devoured,
Butchery day and night smoking with blood.
And who created it? Was it the good Lord?

We humans, "alone in the pale anthill of galaxies," trouble ourselves to put our "hope in a humane God" who is like us, in that he thinks and feels as we do:

Yet if it is so, then He takes pity
On every mauled mouse, every wounded bird.
Then the universe for him is like a Crucifixion.[74]

In the end, Milosz's view of science was so acute that to survive spiritually he was forced to deny what he sensed empirically. This denial enabled him to answer the question — "How to resist nothingness?" — with a confidence fueled by a spirit of resistance and the persistence of desire. In a poem that pays tribute to his deceased wife, Janina, he calls upon "Fire" as an agent of "liberation from gravity." Yet, "Do I believe in the Resurrection of the Flesh? Not of this ash," he concludes. Instead, he "beseech[es]" the "elements, dissolve yourselves!/Rise into the other, let it come, kingdom!/Beyond the earthly fire compose yourselves anew." Or as another poem notes, we cannot *know* the truth about Christ's life and death, but must simply be about the business of "Trying to do good within our limits,/Forgiving the mortals their imperfection. Amen."[75]

At the Theological Limits

As decisive as they were in their judgments about science, Dickinson, Auden, and Milosz remained tentative in their treatment of religious belief. They found it easier to chart the loss of God than to clear a path for

74. Milosz, *New and Collected Poems,* pp. 631-32.

75. Milosz, *New and Collected Poems,* pp. 469-70, 541. Some take Milosz's modest uncertainty to be evidence of his denial of Christian hope, but I think of it in terms similar to those used by Ludwig Wittgenstein in a related context: "Within Christianity it's as though God says to men: Don't act a tragedy, that's to say, don't enact heaven and hell on earth. Heaven and hell are *my* affair." *Culture and Value,* ed. G. H. von Wright, in collaboration with Heikki Nyman, trans. Peter Winch (Chicago: University of Chicago Press, 1980), p. 14e.

belief. "It is true that the unknown is the largest need of the intellect," Emily Dickinson wrote to her cousins, "though for it, no one thinks to thank God," and she remained uncertain as to whether this need could ever be met.[76] In like manner, when W. H. Auden embraced the Christian faith, he did so as a Kierkegaardian ever alert to the "infinite qualitative difference" between God and humanity. We know Christ was a suffering servant, but we "dare not say" whether he was raised from the dead.[77] And although Czeslaw Milosz remained a practicing Catholic to the end of his life, he also never stopped wondering whether "one should constantly meditate on who Jesus was./ What can we, ordinary people, know of the Mystery?"[78]

In response to such questions, the New Testament asserts that we are able to know everything we need to know of that mystery, for in sharp contrast to Gnosticism, orthodox Christianity has never thought of the gospel as a secret to be kept, but rather a gift to be shared. At the core of the New Testament, there is a ringing confidence in the reconciling love of God as it has been embodied and revealed in Jesus Christ. "In the New Testament a mystery is a secret which has been, or is being, disclosed," and it is mysterious "not because it offers so little to our understanding, but because its superabundant wealth overwhelms our understanding (Col. 2.2; cf. Phil. 3.8)."[79] The Apostles preached about Jesus Christ openly in the Book of Acts, as they proclaimed the good news of a God who doesn't love the wall of sin and death but "wants it down." In speaking of Jesus, St. Paul and others tell of that "Docile Gentleman" who, "though he was in the form of God, did not regard equality with God as something to be exploited, but emptied himself, taking the form of a slave, being born in human likeness." He "humbled himself" and accepted "even death on a cross" (Phil. 2:6-8).

Yet suffering and death are but part of the gospel story. If we limit ourselves to those elements of the divine drama, we end up agreeing with Auden

> that the Bard
> Was sober when he wrote

76. Dickinson, *Letters,* 2:559.

77. Auden, *Collected Poems,* p. 674.

78. Milosz, *New and Collected Poems,* p. 541.

79. G. S. Hendry, "Mystery," in *A Theological Word Book of the Bible,* ed. Alan Richardson (New York: Macmillan, 1950), p. 156.

That this world of fact we love
Is unsubstantial stuff:
All the rest is silence
On the other side of the wall;
And the silence ripeness,
And the ripeness all.[80]

There is more to the story than this, however, for a comforting word has filled the silence and a disruptive love has broken through the wall. In first-century Athens, the Apostle Paul told the Stoics and Epicureans he understood "how extremely religious you are in every way" (Acts 17:22). He had come across an altar with the inscription "To an unknown god" who dwelt in security on the other side of the wall. Paul told those Athenians of a God who would "have that wall down": "What therefore you worship as unknown, this I proclaim to you" (Acts 17:23). He spoke of Jesus Christ, the "man whom [God] has appointed" to judge the world and the one of whom "he has given assurance to all by raising him from the dead." When the hardened determinists of first-century Athens "heard of the resurrection of the dead, some scoffed; but others said, 'We will hear you again about this'" (Acts 17:31-32).

It is easy to understand why the flinty materialists of late antiquity took exception to the claim that a personal God ruled the universe and did his saving work not in the guise of "an extra metaphysical entity" but as "Mary's child, the hanged man of Golgotha."[81] The scriptures report that when the Epicureans and Stoics scoffed at him, "at that point Paul left them. But some of them joined him and became believers" (Acts 17:33-34a). So it was that the first Christians began to follow that hanged man through the breach in the wall between darkness and light, between death and eternal life. So it is that countless others, from all nations and lands, continue to do so to this day.

80. Auden, *Collected Poems,* p. 404.

81. Robert W. Jenson, *Systematic Theology,* vol. 1, *The Triune God* (New York: Oxford University Press, 1997), p. 145.

CHAPTER 3

Belief

FOR GOOD REASON, we think of history and science as realities that are, in Richard Wilbur's felicitous phrase, *there before us* in time and space. We may dispute certain historical facts or argue about their meaning, but whatever our views may be, we consider history to be comprised of events that have unfolded over time. In like manner, although we may puzzle over the movement of galaxies or debate the moral significance of the genetic code, we agree that stars and microbes, like elephants and asteroids, live and move and have their being in a world starkly independent of our inner needs and longings.

By the end of the nineteenth century, we were to learn just how independent of those needs and longings the world of nature could be. In the fiction of Thomas Hardy and Kate Chopin, as in the poetry of Stephen Crane and Robert Frost, nature and the self never meet or mingle, but stand apart, separate and silent. But that had not been the case, of course, when that century began. At that point, every facet of culture and experience appeared to remain, however tenuously, under the jointly held rule of nature, scripture, and sacrament, with a delicate balance holding between the power of creation and the wonder of discovery.

Written in 1798, William Wordsworth's "Tintern Abbey" shows just how delicate this equilibrium was. The poem tells of Wordsworth's return to a place he had visited five years earlier. The beauty of the surroundings is beyond dispute, yet the poet is surprised by how little his moral imagination depends upon the actual presence of the scene. "These forms of beauty have not been to me,/As is a landscape to a blind man's eye," he writes, for

oft, in lonely rooms, and mid the din
Of towns and cities, I have owed to them,
In hours of weariness, sensations sweet,
Felt in the blood, and felt along the heart,
And passing even into my purer mind
With tranquil restoration.[1]

When he first roamed the hills above Tintern Abbey, nature had been to Wordsworth "all in all." It had "had no need of a remoter charm,/ By thought supplied, or any interest/Unborrowed from the eye." But now, a new, curious force has risen up within the poet to challenge the sufficiency and supremacy of the landscape: "I have felt/A presence that disturbs me with the joy/Of elevated thoughts." Under the sway of this power, the poet no longer merely receives what nature gives; he also creates blessings she cannot offer. At the outset of his adulthood and the end of a century, Wordsworth seeks to infuse nature with something of his own spiritual vitality:

Therefore am I still
A lover of the meadows and the woods,
And mountains; and of all that we behold
From this green earth; of all the mighty world
Of eye and ear, both what they half-create,
And what perceive.[2]

Are our most intimate thoughts, values, and beliefs things that we "perceive," or do we "half-create" them? Or even fully create them? Is knowledge a gift to be received or a task to be accomplished? Each of the three following chapters will explore a different facet of this singular modern struggle between the mind's power to *create* the truth and the heart's longing to *discover* it. And *belief* stands at the heart of any effort to balance the labor of the subject with the gift of the object.

1. William Wordsworth, *William Wordsworth*, ed. Stephen Gill (Oxford: Oxford University Press, 1984), p. 132.

2. *William Wordsworth*, pp. 133-34.

Back to Belief

Belief is back. After several decades of self-imposed exile during the reign of suspicion, it has returned from the far country to reclaim a place in modern cultural studies. In recent years, it has made its presence known in many different forms in criticism and theory alike, ranging from the soberly provocative final works of that *enfant grise,* Jacques Derrida, to the probing, occasionally anguished meditations of Andrew Delbanco, to Alfred Kazin's *God and the American Writer,* the capstone *cri de coeur* of an extraordinary six-decade career. Although Stanley Fish is not usually thought of as a religious stalwart, he recently reported that "when Jacques Derrida died I was called by a reporter who wanted [to] know what would succeed high theory and the triumvirate of race, gender, and class as the center of intellectual energy in the academy. I answered like a shot: religion."[3]

There are complex reasons behind the renewal of theoretical interest in religious belief, but the most important factor involves a truth our theorists may have forgotten, even though our poets and novelists never did: it has always been "there before us."[4] When we discuss the important role played by religious belief in the literature of America, we are "merely bearing witness/To what each morning brings again to light."[5] Richard Wilbur is referring here, of course, to the act of testifying to the sheen-swept world that comes to light each day and goes its vital way, whether or not we notice or acknowledge it. Yet as a poet, Wilbur is a maker of artifacts, as he is a student of culture, and he takes seriously the role the human mind plays in the greater play of things. In the history of American culture, what is "there before us" and to which we "bear witness" includes a vast record of spiritual experience and discovery. Many of the culture's most accomplished artists — from Dickinson to Frost to Milosz, from Melville to Baldwin to O'Connor — have wrestled with belief and unbelief

3. Stanley Fish, "One University Under God?" *Chronicle of Higher Education,* January 7, 2005, http://chronicle.com/jobs/2005/01/2005010701c.htm.

4. For a brilliant examination of how it was that "religion" became an "invisible domain" within the late-twentieth-century academic study of American literature, see Jenny Franchot, "Invisible Domain: Religion and American Literary Studies," *American Literature* 67 (1995): 833-42.

5. Richard Wilbur, *Collected Poems, 1943-2004* (Orlando, Fla.: Harcourt, 2004), p. 83.

for the past two centuries, and they will no doubt continue to do so in the decades to come.[6]

Such a passion for belief and its conflicts, however, appears odd, even uncouth, to many who live outside the borders of the United States or beyond the pale of religion within it. Novelist Robert Stone found this out when he heard Alfred Kazin give a lecture on *God and the American Writer* shortly after its publication in 1997. The setting was the Harbourfront literary festival in Toronto, and the subject of the talk was "American writers and their uneasy relations with the numinous." According to Stone, Kazin's performance that day was animated by his longstanding passion for "the God-infused, post-Calvinist literature of America."[7] Yet not everyone in his Toronto audience shared Kazin's fervor. As the critic concluded his talk, a listener seated behind Stone "remarked with bitter humor to his companion, 'Why do they have this thing about themselves and God?'" The novelist reports that "at that point the Holy Spirit descended upon me and I was moved to reply," but he hesitated, thought twice about where he was, and kept his polite silence. This was, after all, Toronto, a city in which everything is "clean," "everything works," "crime is discouraged," and "the subway routes are comprehensible." In such a place, how could he, Robert Stone, an American, begin to explain his nation's obsession with "the power of Almighty God" or its terrifying sense of its own failure? Take a look at the United States from a Canadian vantage point, Stone says, and "it's impossible not to wonder: Where did we go wrong?"

Yet at the same time, the novelist mused, was it possible that this Canadian man somehow did "not know, after all, that the Lord had led Americans, alone among all peoples, out of bondage" for the purpose of redeeming the whole world? Did this man not realize that to humble "these fawners, parading with baubles, heathen honors, and jeweled

6. In recent decades, historians of American religion have played a vital role in renewing interest in the influence of religious belief upon the national culture. The examples are legion, but three of the most important works of recent decades are: Nathan O. Hatch, *The Democratization of American Christianity* (New Haven: Yale University Press, 1989); George M. Marsden, *The Soul of the American University: From Protestant Establishment to Established Nonbelief* (New York: Oxford University Press, 1994); and Mark A. Noll, *America's God: From Jonathan Edwards to Abraham Lincoln* (New York: Oxford University Press, 2002).

7. Robert Stone, "American Apostle," *New York Review of Books,* March 26, 1998.

crosses" in Toronto and elsewhere, "we [the people of America] had been raised up, appointed a City on a Hill, a light unto the nations?" "Probably not," Stone surmises. No doubt this man from the North "had come of age during the Vietnam War. All the rest" — all that stuff about God, human destiny, and the City upon a Hill — "would probably have been news to him. He might even, in invincible ignorance of the Word, have rejected it."

"Why do they have this thing about themselves and God?" The answer to this question can better be discovered by tracking the course of specific historical realities than by finding abstract reasons. We can pick up one of the important trails in the mid-nineteenth century, when open unbelief became for the first time an intellectually viable and socially acceptable option in the countries of the North Atlantic. It was not until 1869, for example, that Thomas Huxley coined the term *agnosticism* to describe what was at that point a strange phenomenon having to do with the sudden, widespread loss of belief. Whatever this new reality was, Huxley recognized its emergence as a turning point in cultural history. To some, the appearance of open unbelief represented a hard-fought victory. It stood as the culmination of "two centuries of struggle between those who sought to secure belief by fixing it in comprehensible reality and those who denied that God fit those familiar terms."[8]

Agnosticism entailed both a "permanent suspension of belief in God" and a stubborn inability to rest in the reality of God. It quickly "became the distinctively modern unbelief" and established itself as a "self-sustaining phenomenon" in the decades after the American Civil War, explains historian James Turner. Unbelief had become at last "plausible enough to grow beyond a rare eccentricity and to stake out a sizable permanent niche in American culture" and the British Isles.[9]

8. James Turner, *Without God, Without Creed: The Origins of Unbelief in America* (Baltimore: Johns Hopkins University Press, 1985), p. 171.

9. Turner, *Without God,* p. 171. Walter Houghton connects agnosticism to the "rise of the critical spirit," which he defines as a drive to subject "all authority to the judgment of reason." In the mid-nineteenth century "age of transition," a "breakdown of traditional beliefs and the declining prestige of both the clergy and the aristocracy tended to throw the individual back upon himself, whether he would or no. 'As the old doctrines have gone out, and the new ones have not yet come in, every one must judge for himself as he best may' [Mill]." *The Victorian Frame of Mind, 1830-1870* (New Haven: Yale University Press, 1957), pp. 94, 96.

Turner's use of the word "niche" is instructive. Agnosticism did indeed set up its stall to claim a corner in the marketplace of ideas, but if it harbored monopolistic aspirations, it lacked monopolistic powers. It was more like Apple to theism's Microsoft. The "thriving agnostic subculture" of the late 1800s served as a "community of ideas, assumptions, and values," and it gave its adherents a coherent view of reality without the benefit, or burden, of God.[10] The agnostic product was undeniably stylish and sleek, but like the computer technology produced in Cupertino, it was only the preference of a small but passionate coterie of advocates.

Yet as Turner, Jon Roberts, and George Marsden have argued in recent studies, the "permanent suspension of belief" would prove to have an influence far greater than its numbers appeared to have warranted, because, again like the Macintosh, it made its greatest inroads among Anglo-American cultural elites.[11] In the colleges and universities of the North Atlantic region, emerging unbelief was quickly assigned a role in the dominant narrative of secular liberation, which took the form of what Charles Taylor calls a "subtraction story."[12] This involved a narrative of progress in which the shackles of religious belief and practice had finally been loosed in the nineteenth century. In this story, religion played the role of a once-powerful character now down on his luck, and to some agnostics, it was only a matter of time before religion would be written out of the script entirely. "The first doubt," wrote the firebrand Robert G. Ingersoll in 1872, "was the womb and cradle of progress, and from the first doubt, man has continued to advance." As each religious idea has "been placed in the crucible of science, . . . nothing but dross has been found." In a spirit of triumphalism, Ingersoll announced that although the supernatural was rapidly disappearing, "the natural remains. The gods have fled, but man is here."[13]

10. Turner, *Without God,* p. 171.

11. George Marsden, *Soul of the American University;* Jon H. Roberts and James Turner, *The Sacred and the Secular University* (Princeton: Princeton University Press, 2000).

12. "I mean by this stories of modernity in general, and secularity in particular, which explain them by human beings having lost, or sloughed off, or liberated themselves from certain earlier, confining horizons, or illusions, or limitations of knowledge." Charles Taylor, *A Secular Age* (Cambridge, Mass.: Belknap Press of Harvard University Press, 2007), p. 22.

13. Robert G. Ingersoll, *The Gods and Other Lectures* (Washington, D.C., 1900), pp. 81, 84.

The accounts offered by Marsden, Turner, and Roberts show a gap opening in the nineteenth century between an educated loss of belief and an artistic passion for it, and that gap has widened ever since.[14] Contemporary theorists based in the university may have rejected the nineteenth-century narratives of progress, but they continue to embrace the tacit dismissal of belief embedded in those narratives. A central assumption of both modernist and postmodernist accounts of culture is that in the nineteenth century we entered a new phase of history, one that is *beyond* belief.[15] Whether we are poststructuralists, postcolonialists, post-industrial Marxists, posthumanists, or just plain postmodernists, we may not be certain of what we believe or what the future holds, but we know what we have moved beyond and left behind.

Many novelists and poets, however, neither embraced the glossy narrative of progress nor accepted the curt dismissal of belief. As they witnessed the emergence of unbelief in the nineteenth century and tracked its progress through the next century, these writers saw it as something more than a decisive turning point in the history of personal and cultural liberation. In their creative works and personal lives, unbelief often emerged as a facet of belief itself rather than a replacement for it. When viewed in this manner, unbelief took the form of a new variation upon the longstanding modern theme of inwardness, liberty, and choice. That is why, more often than not in the literature of the past 150 years, the conflict between belief and unbelief has played itself out more readily within the private struggles of individuals than in public battles between the forces of progress and those of reaction.

14. As the study of philosophy became specialized in the nineteenth-century universities, the discipline effectively ceded to poetry and fiction much of its interest in metaphysical questions. Bruce Kuklick notes that "as philosophy became a profession, its nature and the character of the men it attracted changed." In the decades after the Civil War, the generalists with broad metaphysical, ethical, and political concerns were all but banished from the profession. The professionals who replaced them abandoned "concerns outside the discipline," and their attention was "narrowed to a domain of more arcane interests" than those pursued by the amateur metaphysicians of the past. *The Rise of American Philosophy: Cambridge, Massachusetts, 1860-1930* (New Haven: Yale University Press, 1977), p. xxii.

15. Robert Bellah, *Beyond Belief: Essays on Religion in a Post-traditional World* (New York: Harper, 1970).

The Rise of Indifference and the Roots of Unbelief

The flowering of unbelief in the last decades of the nineteenth century was in many respects a natural outgrowth of a spirit of religious indifference that had been sown on the cultural winds several decades earlier. This indifference appeared specifically within the history of American Protestantism, and when we track its origins, we find that many of the most heavily traveled paths lead to and from the early career of Ralph Waldo Emerson. Dating from his 1832 resignation from the Christian ministry to the 1838 delivery of "The Divinity School Address," that portion of Emerson's career has become the part that stands for the whole when we speak of the rise of religious indifference in American culture.[16]

Emerson broached the topic of indifference when he resigned from the pastorate of Boston's Second Church in 1832 at the end of a struggle over the sacrament of communion. He had taken issue with the particularity of the sacrament, because he found it offensive to think that any ritual could possess an intrinsic power or play a mediating role in a person's relationship to God. Emerson wished to be done with the sacraments, and when his church board refused to let him abstain from administering them, he decided to resign from the ministry and leave the Christian church forever.

On his final day in the pulpit, Emerson preached on the Lord's Supper. In this sermon, he marshals extensive historical and theological evidence to refute the very idea of a sacrament. Yet in the end, he chooses to clinch his argument not with a fact from history or a point of logic but with the unassailable claim of indifference: "I have no hostility to this institution." Others may happily administer it, but he refuses to be required to do so. "That is the end of my opposition, that I am not interested in it."[17] Without apology, Emerson made boredom his main reason for dispensing with the sacrament and with the historic faith it is meant to encapsulate, and in doing so, he elevated "distaste into a principle of criticism."[18]

16. For a survey of Emerson's place in American religious history, see E. Brooks Holifield, *Theology in America: Christian Thought from the Age of the Puritans to the Civil War* (New Haven: Yale University Press, 2003), pp. 439-47.

17. Ralph Waldo Emerson, *Essays and Lectures,* ed. Joel Porte (New York: Library of America, 1983), p. 1140.

18. Barbara Packer, "Signing Off: Religious Indifference in America," in *There Before Us: Religion, Literature, and Culture from Emerson to Wendell Berry,* ed. Roger Lundin

Although he claimed to have no abiding interest in the sacrament or in the theological reasoning behind it, long after he left the ministry, Emerson remained decidedly interested in indifference. Perhaps surprisingly for a man who had resigned from the church, he was especially agitated about the decline of worship in his own day. No one, he told the group of Harvard divinity students in 1838, can go intelligently "into one of our churches, without feeling, that what hold the public worship had on men is gone, or going." The good have no affection for the church, the bad no fear of it. "In the country," Emerson reported, "neighborhoods, half parishes are *signing off,* — to use the local term. It is already beginning to indicate character and religion to withdraw from the religious meetings." A "devout person" who once "prized the Sabbath" now tells Emerson bitterly, "On Sundays, it seems wicked to go to church."[19]

This is a mild form of the ironic, oppositional thinking that was to become a central feature of self-articulation in the Transcendentalist line. The stance that Emerson struck in a series of pithy and barbed sentences, Henry David Thoreau was to master in a narrative voice that expressed sustained, sardonic contrariety:

> The greater part of what my neighbors call good I believe in my soul to be bad, and if I repent of any thing, it is very likely to be my good behavior. What demon possessed me that I behaved so well? You may say the wisest thing you can old man, . . . — I hear an irresistible voice which invites me away from all that. One generation abandons the enterprises of another like stranded vessels.[20]

(Grand Rapids: Eerdmans, 2007), p. 9. See the entirety of Packer's essay (pp. 1-22) for a superb analysis of the rise of religious indifference in nineteenth-century America.

19. Emerson, *Essays,* p. 87. Although the irony of Emerson and Henry David Thoreau was meant to expose abuse and prompt reform, it also hinted at the sense of *cosmic* irony that the nineteenth-century eclipse of belief was nourishing. Ernst Behler describes a "notion of 'God's irony' and 'irony of the world'" which "results from the disappearance of the conviction of reasonable order in this world and derives from that 'great rupture through the world' which has 'torn asunder the world, right through the middle,' but also goes right through the center of the heart of the poet, which, like the 'center of the world,' has been 'badly torn asunder.'" *Irony and the Discourse of Modernity* (Seattle: University of Washington Press, 1990), p. 92.

20. Henry David Thoreau, *Walden,* in *A Week, Walden, The Maine Woods, Cape Cod,* ed. Robert F. Sayre (New York: Library of America, 1985), p. 331.

Thoreau's most famous expression of this contrariety comes in the account he gives, in "Resistance to Civil Government," of his refusal to pay a fee for the support of the Congregational church. Although a Massachusetts constitutional amendment had disestablished the church in 1833, individual parishioners still had to "sign off" from the church rolls to avoid paying a levy to support it. Thoreau did just that in his declaration: "Know all men by these presents, that I, Henry Thoreau, do not wish to be regarded as a member of any incorporated society which I have not joined." Had he known how to name them all, Thoreau explained, "I should then have signed off in detail from all the societies which I never signed on to; but I did not know where to find a complete list."[21]

In lauding the act of signing off, Thoreau and Emerson evidenced their debt to Protestant patterns of self-development, even as they declared their freedom from specifically Christian beliefs and practices. That is, they followed in the footsteps of their Puritan ancestors but eventually went down paths those early New Englanders could never have imagined exploring. As Edmund Morgan explains, the seventeenth-century Puritans had pressed to the limit the Reformation's "powerful impulse toward free consent as the basis of both state and church."[22] The Puritans viewed the church as a covenantal and contractual community that a person had to "sign on" to through a rigorous process of conversion and from which, at least in theory, one could "sign off" as well.

With its distinct view of conversion, New England Puritanism coupled an emphasis on rupture with a stress on assent. Before they could assume their parents' faith, Puritan children first had to resist or reject it. Only then could they appropriate that faith and turn it into a product of their own choosing. Both Robert Bellah and Charles Taylor have observed that later American culture borrowed liberally from the Puritan tradition of "leaving home," and through the pervasive influence of

21. Henry David Thoreau, "Resistance to Civil Government," in *Transcendentalism: A Reader*, ed. Joel Myerson (New York: Oxford University Press, 2000), pp. 557-58. Although Thoreau's irony hints at "cosmic irony," Robert D. Richardson correctly reminds us, "'Resistance to Civil Government' is . . . both abolitionist and pacifist at the same time. The essay is essentially an antiwar, antislavery piece, not a theoretical defense of individual rights and not primarily an autobiographical document." *Henry Thoreau: A Life of the Mind* (Berkeley: University of California Press, 1986), p. 177.

22. Edmund S. Morgan, *Visible Saints: The History of a Puritan Idea* (1963; repr., Ithaca, N.Y.: Cornell University Press, 1965), p. 29.

American models of self-development, modern culture remains deeply indebted to those Puritans.[23]

For the seventeenth-century Calvinists, the brief departure involved in "leaving home" was meant to serve as a prelude to a grand return. The child might have to journey into the far country, but he or she was always expected to come home in the end. In signing off, however, Emerson, Thoreau, and their compatriots were announcing that they planned never to return to a home that no longer interested them. In his "Divinity School" address, Emerson lamented the New England church's failure to explore the "Moral Nature" whose "revelations introduce greatness" and "God himself, into the open soul." A passion for this moral nature requires indifference towards those "traditionary" sources of belief, which have brought men and women "to speak of the revelation as somewhat long ago given and done, as if God were dead."[24] Only the lifeless traces of a once-vital God, Emerson had concluded, could be found in the pages of the scriptures or the practice of the sacraments.

For several decades — say, between 1835 and 1860 — this passion for indifference served well the needs of a small band of Anglo-American men and women struggling to find a way out of the confines of belief. First-generation indifferentists that they were, Emerson and Thoreau were able to salvage countless tropes from the ruins of the Christian scriptures, beliefs, and practices. Theirs was a mission of both rescue and discovery, and in their works a fruitful, disruptive energy is palpable. But in the refined prose and aestheticized tastes of a second-generation Emersonian such as Charles Eliot Norton, or in the work of a late Victorian such as Walter Pater, one senses what modern literature might have become if religious indifference had been successful in spreading its benign influence and tightening its lifeless grip on the minds and pens of American artists.[25]

23. On the subject of "leaving home," see Robert Bellah et al., *Habits of the Heart: Individualism and Commitment in American Life* (Berkeley: University of California Press, 1985), pp. 56-62, and Charles Taylor, *Sources of the Self: The Making of the Modern Identity* (Cambridge, Mass.: Harvard University Press, 1989), pp. 38-40.

24. Emerson, *Essays,* pp. 82-83.

25. Pater coupled indifference towards Christianity with a passion for aesthetic experience: "To burn always with this hard, gemlike flame, to maintain this ecstasy, is success in life. . . . While all melts under our feet, we may well grasp at any exquisite passion, or any contribution to knowledge that seems by a lifted horizon to set the spirit free for a mo-

"The Secret of Our Paternity": Orphaned Souls in an Indifferent World

But such was not to be the case. Too many powerful forces — slavery and Civil War in the United States, unprecedented industrialization and urbanization on both sides of the Atlantic, as well as disruptive developments in the scientific, philosophical, and theological thought of the era — were roiling the sea of faith, and mere indifference stood little chance of calming the troubled waters of the American mind.

In fact, for a number of authors, including Herman Melville and Emily Dickinson, the melancholy roar of that sea proved all but deafening. These writers knew the same cultural narratives and read the same books as Emerson and Thoreau but drew a different lesson from them. Where the Transcendentalists believed they had established an equilibrium of indifference, Melville and Dickinson found themselves restlessly driven by the instabilities of indecision. While Emerson and Thoreau were content to "sign off" from the creedal history of the church, Dickinson and Melville could not stop looking for a belief to "latch on to." In their refusal to accept religious indifference as the goal of cultural activity and religious experience, Melville and Dickinson proved to be forerunners of some of the twentieth century's greatest writers.

Because he himself was unsettled about the question of belief, Nathaniel Hawthorne seemed especially alert to the spiritual volatility of the younger Melville. These two met for their last extended conversation in November 1856, when Melville visited his friend near Liverpool, England, where Hawthorne was serving at the American consulate. They walked the beaches overlooking the Irish Sea before retreating to a hollow among the sand hills, where they "smoked a cigar" while talking of "Providence and futurity, and of everything that lies beyond human ken." Melville said "he had 'pretty much made up his mind to be annihilated,'" yet Hawthorne noted:

> But still he does not seem to rest in that anticipation; and, I think, will never rest until he gets hold of a definite belief. It is strange how he

---

ment, or any stirring of the senses, strange dyes, strange colours, and curious odours, or work of the artist's hands, or the face of one's friend." "The Intensity of the Moment," in *The Modern Tradition: Backgrounds of Modern Literature,* ed. Richard Ellmann and Charles Feidelson Jr. (New York: Oxford University Press, 1965), p. 183.

> persists — and has persisted ever since I knew him, and probably long before — in wandering to-and-fro over these deserts, as dismal and monotonous as the sand hills amid which we were sitting. He can neither believe, nor be comfortable in his unbelief; and he is too honest and courageous not to try to do one or the other.[26]

Hilton Obenzinger observes that this "restlessness for definite belief" shapes the "dialogic qualities" of Melville's fiction; it leads to the frequent juxtaposition of deadly serious assertions and comically absurd asides. This pattern produces the exquisitely balanced tensions of Ishmael's and Ahab's separate universes in *Moby Dick,* along with the frenzied shuffling between reality and illusion in *Pierre.* It also provides the structural framework for *Clarel,* a long poem whose characters engage in "an *agon* of questions, a dialog of oppositions, a deliberate intellectual and theological test of our ability to hold contesting ideas in the mind at once." Melville struggled to develop new poetic and fictional forms that could incorporate the deep religious uncertainties that had settled upon him and the age in which he lived. In the words of James Wood, on the question of belief, Melville "was like the last guest who cannot leave the party; he was always returning to see if he had left his hat and gloves." And yet he did not really want to be at the party, for he had no desire to submit to the hard dignities and sobering demands of belief. "It is just that he had nowhere else to be, and would rather be with people than be alone."[27]

In a meditation demonstrating the impossibility of spiritual indifference, Melville has Captain Ahab muse in *Moby Dick* on those "grassy glades" and "ever vernal endless landscapes in the soul" in which "men yet may roll, like young horses in new morning clover; and for some few fleeting moments, feel the cool dew of the life immortal on them." Yet these moments cannot last, for "the mingled, mingling threads of life are woven by warp and woof: calms crossed by storms, a storm for every

26. Nathaniel Hawthorne, quoted in Hershel Parker, *Herman Melville: A Biography,* vol. 2, *1851-1891* (Baltimore: Johns Hopkins University Press, 2002), p. 300.

27. Hilton Obenzinger, *American Palestine: Melville, Twain, and the Holy Land Mania* (Princeton: Princeton University Press, 1999), p. 71; Stan Goldman, *Melville's Protest Theism: The Hidden and Silent God in "Clarel"* (DeKalb: Northern Illinois University Press, 1993), p. 15; James Wood, *The Broken Estate: Essays on Literature and Belief* (New York: Random, 1999), p. 29.

calm." Ahab concludes by summarizing life not as the stately progression of a secular Bildungsroman but as a dynamic cycle endlessly retracing the unresolved struggle between belief and unbelief:

> There is no steady unretracing progress in this life; we do not advance through fixed gradations, and at the last one pause: — through infancy's unconscious spell, boyhood's thoughtless faith, adolescence' doubt (the common doom), then skepticism, then disbelief, resting at last in manhood's pondering repose of If. But once gone through, we trace the round again; and are infants, boys, and men, and Ifs eternally.

The meditation closes with an image that turns the serenity of indifference into the fear of abandonment: "Where is the foundling's father hidden? Our souls are like those orphans whose unwedded mothers die in bearing them: the secret of our paternity lies in their grave, and we must there to learn it."[28]

The poetry and letters of Emily Dickinson offer abundant evidence of a similar struggle between the desire to be free of God's judgment and the fear of being orphaned by his death. Like Melville, Dickinson found the idea of "signing off" appealing, but also like him, she dreaded the thought of being forsaken by God and robbed of divine promises. An agonizing ambivalence is on display throughout her poetry, and her individual works constantly pit conflicting views of belief one against the other.

For example, any number of Dickinson poems chart the course of a confident romantic narrative of self-development. She writes of having finished with the use of "The name They dropped opon my face/With water, in the country church" and of having chosen "consciously" her new identity (#353). In a poem from 1863, she sounds positively Thoreauvian, as she depicts a self that achieves perfection, after it "signs off" from creedal belief. "The Props assist the House/Until the House is built," the poem begins. Eventually those props drop away, leaving behind a House, which being "adequate" can "support itself." Yet that house also ceases to "recollect/The Augur and the Carpenter." Such is the "retrospect" of a "perfected Life": "A Past of Plank and Nail/And slowness — then the scaffolds drop/Affirming it a Soul — " (#729). When Dickinson's

28. Herman Melville, *Moby Dick*, 2nd ed., ed. Hershel Parker and Harrison Hayford (New York: Norton, 2002), p. 373.

poetic voice sounds this particular note, she seems to dispense with belief readily, because a self in which the principles of growth are already embedded has no need of a divine power to plant them within it.[29]

Such heroic secularity, however, is only part of the story of unbelief for Dickinson. While the subject of "The Props assist the House" does not care to recollect the past, the speakers in other poems cannot forget it. In a famous poem written late in her life, for example, the loss of belief involves a gruesome maiming and leads to a general diminishment and a violent disenchantment of the world. Through the use of a bloody image like the one employed by Nietzsche in his depiction of the "death of God," Dickinson presents a mangled deity whose absence haunts a lonely humanity. "Those — dying then,/Knew where they went — ," begins this poem:

> They went to God's Right Hand —
> That Hand is amputated now
> And God cannot be found — (#1581)

Dickinson refuses here to place the blame for the loss of belief. She renders the amputation of God's hand in the passive voice, and with the word "abdication" she leaves it unclear whether God's disappearance is a result of a divine self-mutilation or a parricidal act of human aggression. What is clear is that belief's abdication has created a void in the lives of many who had once rested in its assurances.

In a letter written in the same year as this poem (1882), Dickinson spoke of the passionate questioning that continued to weary and inspire

29. Robert J. Richards sees spiritual continuity between the romantic poets and Darwin: "When Darwin abandoned the Creator God, he did not, as I will argue, eviscerate living nature of teleological structure; rather his nature had exactly the same Romantic look as that depicted by thinkers like Alexander von Humboldt. And creative power would be transferred to nature in the gradual, evolutionary unfolding of telic purpose." *The Romantic Conception of Life: Science and Philosophy in the Age of Goethe* (Chicago: University of Chicago Press, 2002), p. 518.

Whether or not Darwin believed in a spiritualized nature, many who read him took a different message away from his work. Dickinson, for example, took him to be preaching something other than the "gradual unfolding of telic purpose." She wrote to a friend in 1882, "Mrs Dr Stearns called to know if we didn't think it very shocking for [Benjamin F.] Butler to 'liken himself to his Redeemer,' but we thought Darwin had thrown 'the Redeemer' away." *The Letters of Emily Dickinson*, ed. Thomas H. Johnson and Theodora Ward (Cambridge, Mass.: Belknap Press of Harvard University Press, 1958), 3:728.

her at the same time. Like Melville, she viewed the struggle between belief and unbelief as an internal drama of the self more than as a saga of historical development. "On subjects of which we know nothing, or should I say *Beings* — ," she explained, "we both believe, and disbelieve a hundred times an Hour, which keeps Believing nimble."[30]

Dickinson's shuttling uncertainty on this point is a sign of a particularly modern dilemma that Hans Urs von Balthasar has called the inability of "even great, normative individuality [to] escape the contradiction at the heart of the phenomenon of life." For those who waver between belief and unbelief, "life's contradiction, with 'its ubiquitous constant rhythm, its simplest symbol being that of our breathing in and out,' pulsates in every living being." In an age of nimble believing, it is the essence of life, Balthasar says, quoting Georg Simmel, "to produce that which contradicts the content of every moment; the opposite produces what it posits and is complemented by it."[31]

As Dickinson grappled with these internal contradictions, like Melville, she intuitively understood the indifference of those who had "signed off" from Christian belief in her lifetime. She felt the emotional appeal of this position, with its promise of deliverance from the misguided strife of Christian history. But at the same time, she was chastened and frightened by a lesson she seemed to learn again and again, which was that if "a person goes out into a world that is not only ungodly but hostile to God, he will be led to the experience of Godforsakenness."[32] That was an experience she knew in certain moods, but hardly one that she welcomed.

Art in the Age of Unbelief

Emily Dickinson died in 1886, Herman Melville in 1891. Their deaths came at the precise historical point at which philosophical naturalism took hold of the literary imagination of the cultures of the North Atlantic. This mixture of scientific and social theory was presented to the late

30. Dickinson, *Letters,* 3:728.

31. Hans Urs von Balthasar, *Theo-Drama: Theological Dramatic Theory,* vol. 1, *Prolegomena,* trans. Graham Harrison (San Francisco: Ignatius, 1988), p. 617.

32. Balthasar, *Theo-Drama,* 1:647.

nineteenth-century mind as a "complex social philosophy, deterministic, Darwinistic, and fatalistic," and it quickly filled the void that had been created among the cultured elites by the rise of unbelief.[33] As a system of thought, naturalism traced the origins of religious belief to the shadowy regions of human need, and it dismissed out of hand the possibility that religious claims might actually be true.

Thus, after having made an initial blushing appearance at the middle of the nineteenth century, by the century's close unbelief had become brazen about its doubts and its spirit of denial. With naturalism in the ascendancy, artists and intellectuals no longer felt the pressure to reconcile new insights with established beliefs, but instead considered themselves free to move ahead boldly without concern for a discredited creed. In a study of the American reception of Darwin, Jon Roberts locates "a host of factors in the cultural milieu of the United States" that led in the last decade of the nineteenth century to a "growing tendency among literate Americans to ignore the categories of Christian theology in interpreting their experience." Having conceded so much ground to scientific determinism over the course of the nineteenth century, many Protestants "found themselves defending a very attenuated view of God's role in the universe," and the thinned-out forces backing the God of liberalism could muster no more than a flimsy defense against the assault of naturalism.[34]

In this intellectual climate, on matters of religious belief literature often seemed to assume a valedictory air. Poets, novelists, and essayists found themselves bidding adieu to a no-longer forbidding deity. Some writers of this period, such as Edith Wharton and Stephen Crane, took the loss in stride; throughout most of her adulthood, Wharton took the "late nineteenth-century scientific rationalism" of her youth to be her guide, while Crane found what shelter he could under the cover of cosmic irony.[35] Others, such as Theodore Dreiser and Jack London, readily

33. Martin Travers, *An Introduction to Modern European Literature: From Romanticism to Postmodernism* (New York: St. Martin's, 1998), p. 62.

34. Jon H. Roberts, *Darwinism and the Divine in America: Protestant Intellectuals and Organic Evolution, 1859-1900* (1988; repr., Notre Dame: University of Notre Dame Press, 2001), p. 238. Colin Gunton wrote extensively about the need for a theological response to what he termed "the pathos of modernity." See *The One, The Three, and the Many: God, Creation and the Culture of Modernity* (Cambridge: Cambridge University Press, 1993), pp. 11-40.

35. R. W. B. Lewis, *Edith Wharton: A Biography* (New York: Harper, 1975), p. 510.

embraced the liberating power of materialism; in a deterministic world, sin became a vacuous concept and guilt a largely useless cipher.

At the same time, other writers at the end of the nineteenth century, Henry Adams and Mark Twain among them, found themselves torn between their disdain for traditional Christianity and their dismay over the heartlessness of a God-less world. While Adams wrote in sorrow, Twain masked his pain with sarcasm. "*Nothing* exists; all is a dream. God — man — the world — the sun, the moon, the wilderness of stars: a dream, all a dream — they have no existence," he wrote in *The Mysterious Stranger*. "*Nothing exists save empty space and you!*"[36] Consciousness and the empty void made for a lonely, mismatched pair, and Twain eventually came to believe life would be unendurable without the gift of death: "Whoever has lived long enough to find out what life is, knows how deep a debt of gratitude we owe to Adam, the first great benefactor of our race. He brought death into the world."[37]

Twain's plaintive desperation proved to be the exception rather than the rule for many authors in the early twentieth century. Following the lead of Flaubert and Baudelaire, a number of English and Irish writers turned instead to the ideal of a self-contained aesthetic world cut off from the turmoil of ordinary life. To be certain, for most authors in that period, the passion for aesthetic development and cultural criticism proved too all consuming to allow for more than a fleeting concern for the passing of belief. In England, in Ireland, and in exile, William Butler Yeats, Ezra Pound, and James Joyce were busy breaking new literary ground and forsaking the cultivation of overtly Christian concerns. Denis Donoghue sums up this state of affairs with his description of Yeats as a "residual Christian" and a "Protestant of an unexacting theological persuasion" who propounded ideas that were "heterodox indeed but not entirely a scandal to Christians."[38] With certain exceptions, the

36. Mark Twain, quoted in Alfred Kazin, *God and the American Writer* (New York: Knopf, 1997), p. 192.

37. Mark Twain, *Pudd'nhead Wilson*, in *Mississippi Writings*, ed. Guy Cardwell (New York: Library of America, 1982), p. 929. For Mark Twain's late despondency, see Justin Kaplan, *Mr. Clemens and Mark Twain: A Biography* (1966; repr., New York: Simon and Schuster, 1983), pp. 341-48; for a balanced treatment of Twain's complex religious views, see Harold K. Bush Jr., *Mark Twain and the Spiritual Crisis of His Age* (Tuscaloosa: University of Alabama Press, 2007).

38. Denis Donoghue, *Adam's Curse: Reflections on Religion and Literature* (Notre Dame: University of Notre Dame Press, 2001), p. 119. Of the writers discussed in this para-

modernist poets and novelists had little sympathy for religious orthodoxy, and they took the legacy of Christian belief to be a curious residue coating the ruins of the Western tradition. The central events and symbols of that tradition had become the fragments that the speaker of T. S. Eliot's *The Wasteland* says he has "shored against my ruins."

Across the Atlantic, American culture appeared too preoccupied with the acquisition of wealth and the pursuit of pleasure to be concerned about rummaging in the ruins of the European and Christian past. In the words of F. Scott Fitzgerald, "America was going on the greatest, gaudiest spree in history and there was going to be plenty to tell about it."[39] Malcolm Cowley, who was both a keen participant in this gaudy spree and a noted chronicler of it, described the turmoil of the post–World War I generation as "a moral revolt," and he was convinced that "beneath the revolt were social transformations." Young people of that era "had a sense of reckless confidence not only about money but about life in general." They were determined to break with the beliefs and values of their parents' generation, and in this time of rapid change, "puritanism was under attack, with the Protestant churches losing their dominant position" in the culture at large.[40]

The period that stretched from the death of Dickinson to that of Fitzgerald — from 1886 to 1940 — is the era that Alfred Kazin covers in *On Native Grounds,* the 1942 book that launched his distinguished career. In it Kazin rarely mentions historical developments in American Christianity,

---

graph, Eliot alone remained committed to historic Christianity. In 1929, Yeats wrote in his journal: "I agree with Ezra [Pound] in his dislike of the word belief. Belief implies an unknown object, a covenant attested with a name or signed with blood, and being more emotional than intellectual may pride itself on lack of proof." Something other than belief was needed, he concluded: "We, even more than [T. S.] Eliot, require tradition and though it may include much that is his, it is not a belief or submission, but exposition of intellectual needs." *Modern Tradition,* ed. Ellmann and Feidelson, pp. 99, 100.

39. F. Scott Fitzgerald, quoted in Malcolm Cowley, *A Second Flowering: Works and Days of the Lost Generation* (1973; repr., New York: Penguin, 1980), p. 25.

40. Cowley, *Second Flowering,* pp. 26, 25. By "Protestant churches" Cowley meant mainline churches, not the fundamentalist ones supplanting them. Of the modernist impulse, Kazin wrote: "Modernism would become its own tradition after the 1920s, the only chic tradition left in the academy. But modernism as the expression of an elite that believed in nothing so much as freedom and venerated nothing but the individual personality would soon dissipate into the modern American passion for equality." *An American Procession* (New York: Knopf, 1984), p. 395.

nor does he discuss the theological significance of the myriad literary movements and arguments he examines along the way. He dates the manuscript "1937-1942," and the book reads as though the press of economic, political, and military history in those terrible years crowded out any other possible concerns. "Yes, the pressure of the times is too great; it beats upon all of us," the book's remarkable final paragraph begins. "Literature today lives on the narrow margin of security that the democratic West, fighting for its life, can afford; and that margin may grow more narrow every day." The challenges of a world at war made it "imperative . . . not to sacrifice any of the values that give our life meaning; never was it so imperative for men to be equal to the evil that faces them and not submissive to its terror." A world at war waits for a "new order" and a "new truth," and "we have not even begun to see it all — and what it may become."[41]

Conditions had changed markedly by the time Kazin came to write what proved to be his final book, *God and the American Writer,* near the end of the twentieth century. That work deals with major American writers and their ceaseless struggles with God and the question of belief. One does not feel the weight of contemporary history in its pages, and in the America it describes an imperiled populace no longer clings to a "narrow margin of security." When *God and the American Writer* appeared, it had been more than fifty years since the defeat of the Nazis and almost a decade since the fall of the Berlin Wall. With politics having receded into the background, Kazin trains his attention instead on those writers whom he calls, borrowing a phrase from Emily Dickinson, the "strange minds" behind America's greatest literature. And despite his background as an agnostic Jew, he keeps his focus in this book almost exclusively upon authors caught in the throes of Protestant decline.

As he moves from Emerson and Dickinson to Frost and Faulkner, Kazin uncovers a preoccupation with religion in general and Christianity in particular among the writers of his nation. (He finds this passion in the writers of every period of American history, including that of the half-century from 1890 to 1940 covered in *On Native Grounds.*) But Kazin believes the Christianity he finds in the culture's major writers is markedly different from the faith professed by most Americans. According to him, the writers of the United States have always been at odds with the

41. Alfred Kazin, *On Native Grounds: An Interpretation of Modern American Prose Literature,* abridged ed. (1942; repr., Garden City, N.Y.: Doubleday, 1956), pp. 405-6.

culture, and he is convinced those writers would view contemporary popular religion as he does — that is, as "publicly vehement, politicized, and censorious." What does it mean, he asks, to "love and praise God" in a country in which "the great majority go to church, synagogue and mosque, where many confess to believe in the Devil," and "where fundamentalists have captured the Republican party South and West" even as they have been tearing down the wall between church and state?[42]

Kazin has a simple answer. He cites Emerson, who is quoting Plotinus, and he then applies the insight to Emily Dickinson: the "love and praise of God" in authentic American religion is always the story of "the flight of the alone to the Alone."[43] It is an exploration of the soul by the self, conducted in private and intended for personal ends alone. This authentic religion has no bearing upon our life in history, and it dares not make any claims upon our social practices or public values. For Kazin, the ideal literary representation of belief involves tracing the fading contours of covenantal faith and listening for the faint echoes of a retreating God. Although he has regrets about the absence of any full-throated profession of faith among contemporary American writers, Kazin is on balance content with the prospects of divine silence in a post-Christian world. "Genuine belief is lacking" in the modern United States, and the nation's greatest writers are "apostle[s]" who are required to believe in nothing "except the unlimited freedom that is the usual American faith."[44]

42. Kazin, *God and the American Writer,* pp. 257, 21-22. Kazin's own religious beliefs seem to place him closest to Herman Melville, out of all the major writers treated in this book. In his journals, Kazin describes himself waking in "the terrible middle of the night": "I pray to a God who cannot be very real, since he seems to be only a word, a name, a hope, a reach. Yet I pray." Quoted in Richard M. Cook, *Alfred Kazin: A Biography* (New Haven: Yale University Press, 2007), p. 404.

43. For Kazin on Dickinson, see "Emily Dickinson: The Alone to the Alone," in *God and the American Writer,* pp. 142-60. When he traveled to Europe at thirty, Emerson spoke disparagingly of the weight of the past in the Old World and praised the lonely American resistance to it: "Here's for the plain old Adam, the simple genuine Self against the whole world. Need is, that you assert yourself or you will find yourself overborne by the most paltry things." *Emerson in His Journals,* ed. Joel Porte (Cambridge, Mass.: Belknap Press of Harvard University Press, 1982), p. 99.

44. Kazin, *God and the American Writer,* pp. 258-59.

Believing Again

Although he never rid himself either of his hankering for a monotheistic God or his regrets about the "psychologizing" of American culture, Kazin remained an Emersonian to the last in his interpretation of the literature of the United States. "There was nothing strange or unexpected in 1938," he explained near the end of his life, "about my being both critical of 'the system' and crazy about the country."[45] He did not warm to the narrative of religious indifference, but he accepted its account of the fate of religion in his native land. To Kazin it was self-evident that American artists had indeed "signed off" from the doctrines of Christianity and the demand structures of Judaism. For him, there was no turning back from the secular course of history, however hard the losses had proved to be along the way.

To clinch his argument at the close of *God and the American Writer,* Kazin introduces Czeslaw Milosz, whom he calls "the wonderfully harmonious Polish poet." He views Milosz as a representative of a cultural order in which "genuine belief is lacking, [but] 'religion' as a social experience fills the bill." Here "religion is heritage, is institution, is teaching, company, and safety," and Kazin takes Milosz to be a great muse of this formal faith. He quotes the poet — "Nothing could stifle my inner certainty that a shining point exists where all lines intersect" — and reads this "inner certainty" as a clear sign of Milosz's "European heritage [stemming] from centuries of common worship in relatively homogeneous societies." To Kazin, the rooted quality of Milosz's life contrasts sharply with the cultural homelessness of the typical American writer.[46]

Kazin seriously misreads Milosz at this point, because as we have seen, the poet's faith in the "shining point" had more to do with his gnostic inclinations than his European heritage, and his passion for belief yoked him with Dickinson and Melville more than with the "common worshippers" of a lost "homogeneous" past. Like those two descendants of New England Calvinism, the Polish Catholic poet took the struggle with unbelief to be an inescapable element of the modern experience of belief. When Pope John Paul II once questioned him about his religious uncertainty, Milosz offered a Dickinsonian response. "You always take

45. Alfred Kazin, quoted in Andrew Delbanco, "On Alfred Kazin (1915-1998)," *New York Review of Books,* July 16, 1998.

46. Kazin, *God and the American Writer,* p. 258.

one step forward and one step back," the pope told him. "To which I replied, 'Can one write religious poetry in any other way *today?*'"[47]

In responding to the pope, Milosz was echoing G. C. Lichtenburg's point about the great difference between believing something *still* and believing it *again.* As a poet and public intellectual living in the late twentieth century, Milosz was well aware that most of his peers no longer struggled to believe *again* but had resigned themselves to believing *no longer.* "If only this could be said," began an essay he wrote in 1991: "I am a Christian, and my Christianity is such and such." Many people can make such a statement, but Milosz says he lacks "that gift. The power of dispossession, of disinheritance, is so great that language itself draws a boundary line" between him and the confident confession of belief. Quoting the poet Theodore Roethke on the absence of God — "In that dark world, where gods have lost their way" — Milosz suggests that if we are to speak about God today, only the *via negativa,* the way of negation, can provide a path to him.[48]

Milosz reports that for him the greatest obstacles to belief "derive from shame." Since shame is an emotion we experience in relation to others, in describing its effects he says he feels compelled to "picture the faces of people before whom I am ashamed." These faces belong to his "contemporaries," the educated and cultured members of his "milieu" who are scattered in cities and centers of learning around the world. In general, they are people who treat religious faith with a modicum of respect, but to them it always remains "something held by others that they have rejected for themselves." Milosz says such contemporaries of his are at peace with the "radical changes" that turned ancient customs and beliefs into antiquated curiosities in a matter of decades. They simply "experience these changes both as progress and as a loss about which nothing can be done."[49]

Like Dickinson and Melville before him, Milosz found it harder to sense the progress on this front than to detect the loss. "Once upon a time," he writes, the most intimate realities of human existence were "consecrated by rituals marking a person's entrance into life, fertility, and death."

47. Czeslaw Milosz, *A Year of the Hunter,* trans. Madeline G. Levine (New York: Farrar, 1994), p. 21.

48. Czeslaw Milosz, *To Begin Where I Am: Selected Essays,* ed. Bogdana Carpenter and Madeline G. Levine (New York: Farrar, 2001), 314.

49. Milosz, *To Begin,* pp. 314-15.

A child was born into the Mother Church, received the sacrament of baptism, and matured through the rites of initiation (confirmation, communion) on the way to adulthood. Yet in only a matter of years over the course of the twentieth century, such milestones were no longer "perceived as self-evident," and became optional activities that "require a decision." And even when the rituals continued to be observed, their specifically Christian significance was undermined "by the impression the surrounding scientific-technological civilization makes upon the imagination."[50]

Many other artists of Milosz's generation noted a similarly abrupt transformation of belief, practices, and mores. John Updike's *In the Beauty of the Lilies* documents the sudden loss of belief that Reverend Clarence Arthur Wilmot undergoes one afternoon in 1910, as he explicitly feels "the last particles of his faith leave him." We learn that for him it had been the reading of the nineteenth-century biblical scholars that finally "undermined Christianity's ancient supporting walls and beams." Similarly, Ingmar Bergman's 1962 film, *Winter Light,* examines the sudden loss of faith that a Swedish Lutheran pastor — and, by extension, the larger culture — experienced in a matter of years in the 1950s. In a delicate, understated scene, the pastor has a brief exchange with a young boy whose older brother is about to be confirmed. "Will you go to class too?" he asks the boy, who says "No." When the pastor questions, "Why not?" the child replies with an eyes-averted, Emersonian insouciance: "I don't know." And in a poem titled "Annus Mirabilis," Philip Larkin wittily pegs a profound change in values and practices to a very specific point in time:

> Sexual intercourse began
> In nineteen sixty-three
> (Which was rather late for me) —
> Between the end of the *Chatterley* ban
> And the Beatles' first LP.[51]

Milosz sees the decline in faith and ritual as having proceeded in tandem with sweeping changes in sexual values and practices. In his words, "the sundering of the link between sex and fertility" has not only

50. Milosz, *To Begin,* pp. 315-16.

51. John Updike, *In the Beauty of the Lilies* (New York: Knopf, 1996), pp. 5, 15; *Winter Light,* directed by Ingmar Bergman (1962; Criterion Collection, 2003); Philip Larkin, *Collected Poems,* ed. Anthony Thwaite (New York: Farrar, 1989), p. 167.

undermined marriage but has reached "much deeper, into the very definition of man." If the sexual drive conflicts with an emerging definition of "a human way of life" and if the urge must be "cheated" by technological means, then a host of longstanding convictions about "what is natural behavior and what is unnatural fall by the wayside." In turn, the "distinction between the natural and unnatural was based on the harmony of Nature, which enfolded and supported man. Now we are forced to recognize that anti-naturalness defines man's very nature." Shakespeare anticipated this shift centuries ago, with his play upon the words "nature" and "natural" in *King Lear,* and Milosz says the transformation of our understanding of what is "natural" became complete in his own twentieth-century lifetime. If human nature is "unnatural" in some fundamental sense, what will be the fate of ritual and liturgy? For "isn't a belief in salutary cyclicity inherent in every ritual? . . . And isn't every kind of ritual dealt a blow when a species has to oppose the cycles of nature?"[52]

Shame also comes into play for Milosz when he describes how he shares the embarrassed confusion of his contemporaries over matters of belief and practice. "How can I make a profession of faith in the presence of my fellow human beings?" he asks. "I am just as confused. I have no idea at all how to relate to the rituals of initiation." How should children be catechized? When should young people prepare to take the Eucharist? What should a Catholic make of the modern confusion about marriage and sexual morality? Milosz says he has "no opinion" on these matters, not because he is indifferent to them, but because he has been a party to these and other changes and cannot imagine how they might be undone.[53]

52. Milosz, *To Begin,* p. 316. In *King Lear,* Shakespeare's characters shuttle between two vastly different conceptions of "nature." To the illegitimate Edmund, nature is his "goddess," for he thinks of it as an amoral arena in which he can fight to satisfy his voracious appetite for power. For other characters, "natural" carries the opposite connotation of that which it is fitting and appropriate for human beings to do, in light of their natures, their destinies, and their obligations.

53. Milosz, *To Begin,* pp. 317-19. In the same year that he wrote "If Only This Could Be Said," Milosz gave an interview in which he offered a considerably more appreciative appraisal of the Catholic Church: "The Church is, above all, the sacrament. In other words, the Church is based on the mystery of the Eucharist, the mystery of transubstantiation and the Eucharist. . . . I have no time for any philosophy that has no sense of respect. For me, the Church embodies respect for — we can call it by its general name — God." *Czeslaw Milosz: Conversations,* ed. Cynthia L. Haven (Jackson: University Press of Mississippi, 2006), p. 126.

Only on the question of death does Milosz "part ways with many people with whom I would like to be in solidarity but cannot be. To put it very simply and bluntly," when he is asked whether he believes the "four Gospels tell the truth," Milosz answers, "Yes." So too with the greatest "absurdity, that Jesus rose from the dead." Here again, the answer is "Yes," and "by that response," he says, "I nullify death's omnipotence." This assurance comes at a price, however, because it depends for its validity on the power of the will. A desire for immortality, more than anything else, provides the foundation for whatever confidence Milosz can muster on this front, as he mounts his quixotic "challenge to the Spirit of the Earth."[54]

In the end, like Dickinson and Melville, Milosz found it difficult, if not impossible, to see the force that rules nature and the power that raised Jesus from the dead as one. In the face of nature and death, he lamented "how weak an act of faith in the incarnate God seems to be."[55] And as critical as he was of the romantic tradition, Milosz frequently followed its lead in opposing the realm of freedom (spirit) to the rule of necessity (nature). In this vision of reality, spirit and nature are not lovers on their way to marriage but a husband and wife who live apart and are no longer on speaking terms.

Milosz blames "the methodology of science," which "carries atheism with it," for having broken up that marriage. Modern science has explained reality with such breathtaking comprehensiveness that he wonders whether literature, in contrast, can be anything but "a frivolous, godless occupation." It is frivolous because even though it claims to transform reality into language, very little in the way of reality penetrates it, and it is godless, because "what else could it be" at a time "when litera-

54. Milosz, *To Begin,* p. 320. Milosz was attracted to the gnostic promise of deliverance from bondage to the created order. In describing the present age, he explains, our descendants "will probably make use of the term 'neo-Manichaeanism' to describe our characteristic resentment of evil Matter to which we desperately oppose value, but value no longer flowing from a divine source and now exclusively human." Ewa Czarnecka and Aleksander Fiut, *Conversations with Czeslaw Milosz,* trans. Richard Lourie (San Diego: Harcourt, 1987), p. 123.

55. Milosz, *To Begin,* p. 320. I have examined elsewhere the roots of this split between the God of nature and the Lord of spirit, as it appears in the nineteenth-century fascination with the theme of orphaned humanity. See Roger Lundin, Anthony C. Thiselton, and Clarence Walhout, *The Promise of Hermeneutics* (Grand Rapids: Eerdmans, 1999), pp. 25-41.

ture and art have separated from religion" in an unsuccessful effort to "worm their way into the embrace of science"? This situation has left literature stranded "somewhere between religion and science, primarily exploring various forms of atheism." In this position, literature can only give "expression to the agitated struggling of men trapped by the power of science but for whom science is insufficient."[56]

Such struggles animated, and agitated, Milosz's religious life and poetic work. "No matter how hard I try," he told an interviewer in the 1980s, "I cannot get my hands on the world, which keeps eluding my grasp."[57] At funeral services, he finds that his imagination has been "rendered powerless" to imagine the resurrection, because "it comes up against a blank wall." He longs for eternity but finds it "impossible" to form a convincing picture of heaven and hell, and "the images suggested by the world of art or the poetry of Dante and Milton" prove to be of little help to his efforts to imagine the afterlife. Still, the needs of the spirit remain, and poets continue their search for the forms that might give suitable shape to their religious imaginings. "The imagination can function only spatially," and "without space the imagination is like a child who wants to build a palace and has no blocks."[58]

In *The Discarded Image,* C. S. Lewis illumines the spiritual and artistic difficulties faced by modern poets such as Milosz when they set out to represent religious experience and belief in their work. Lewis does so by asking us to try to imagine the vastly different universe that confronted the medieval viewer and the way it "affected those who believed in it." To understand the medieval cosmos, he says, "you must go out on a starry night and walk about for half an hour trying to see the sky in terms of the old cosmology." When you do so, you find yourself faced with an "absolute Up and Down." As you stand on earth, you are in the very center of all created reality. To understand the size of the medieval universe, Lewis says, you must substitute for the category of distance a quite different concept, that of *height,* "which speaks immediately to our muscles and nerves. The Medieval Model is vertiginous." It is immaterial that the height of the medieval universe seems so slight and insignificant when compared to the distances of the modern cosmos. "For thought and

56. Milosz, *A Year of the Hunter,* pp. 73-74.

57. Czarnecka and Fiut, *Conversations,* p. 303.

58. Milosz, *To Begin,* p. 320.

imagination, ten million miles and a thousand million are much the same," he writes. "Both can be conceived (that is, we can do sums with both) and neither can be imagined; and the more imagination we have the better we shall know this."[59]

When we set the medieval and modern models side by side, Lewis explains, we are struck by how orderly the one appears and how disorienting the other proves to be. The medieval universe may have been "unimaginably large," but it was also "unambiguously finite." It possessed a "perfect spherical shape" and held within itself "an ordered variety":

> Hence to look out on the night sky with modern eyes is like looking out over a sea that fades away into mist, or looking about one in a trackless forest — trees forever and no horizon. To look up at the towering medieval universe is much more like looking at a great building.

The "space" of modern astronomy may arouse feelings of terror or reverie, but it provides no form within which the modern mind may rest or the spirit dwell. The "spheres" of the medieval universe, on the other hand, offer just such a place, for they "present us with an object in which the mind can rest, overwhelming in its greatness but satisfying in its harmony."[60]

The differences between these models explains "why all sense of the pathless, the baffling, and the utterly alien — all agoraphobia — is so markedly absent from medieval poetry when it leads us" into the heavens.[61] Such imagery, of course, is decidedly present in the work of such modern writers as Melville, Dickinson, and Milosz. With their images of the alien, the homeless, and the orphaned, the poets and novelists of the past 150 years have registered that shock of spiritual displacement which Karl Barth says their Enlightenment predecessors utterly failed to sense or anticipate. The shift from medieval to modern involves a move "from living in a cosmos to being included in a universe," in the words of Charles Taylor. Like the medieval cosmos, the modern universe has an order of its own, but it does not involve "a hierarchy of being," nor does it require eternity as the source of its cohesion. Instead, the universe as we now understand it and live in it simply "flows on in

59. C. S. Lewis, *The Discarded Image: An Introduction to Medieval and Renaissance Literature* (Cambridge: Cambridge University Press, 1964), p. 98.

60. Lewis, *Discarded Image,* pp. 98-99.

61. Lewis, *Discarded Image,* p. 99.

secular time," and its principles of order have little or nothing to do with human meaning.[62]

In contemporary theology, the pressure of "the pathless and the baffling" has led to a pronounced shift in Christian imagery away from spatial models towards temporal schemes.[63] Over the past two centuries, this change in imagery has prompted intense interest in the theology of history and has led to much stronger emphases upon eschatology and the incarnation. To believe in the forgiveness of sins, the resurrection of the body, and the life everlasting, one does not need to assume that hell dwells at the center of the earth or that heaven lies just beyond the stars. In fact, Colin Gunton argues that the loss of the spatial model has enabled the modern church to overcome the "false eternity" that has dogged Christianity for centuries. Throughout much of Christian history, theology has remained "ambivalent about the reality and value of time," he explains. Only with the collapse of medieval cosmology did we see in Christian thought a concerted reaffirmation of the goodness of creation and its temporal dimensions. What modernity has made possible — or necessary — is a recovery of the theme of "recapitulation," which expresses "the narrative structure of the Christ-history . . . [as] that history . . . takes up into itself the whole of created reality."[64]

So it has been that time has replaced space as the central dimension of theological aesthetics. Or as Milosz writes, with the disappearance of viable spatial imagery, "what remains" for the Christian artist and thinker "is the covenant, the Word, in which man trusts."[65] This "Word" has a decidedly temporal dimension, and it frames human life within a narrative of God's creative and redemptive love. Over the past century, the covenantal theology of the Word has provided a firm foundation for Christian thought and artistic activity at a time when Catholicism's hier-

62. Taylor, *A Secular Age,* pp. 59-60.

63. This shift from the spatial to the temporal will be a significant theme in chapter six. For an excellent introduction to this subject, see Edward T. Oakes, *Pattern of Redemption: The Theology of Hans Urs von Balthasar* (New York: Continuum, 1994), pp. 211-28.

64. Gunton, *The One, the Three, and the Many,* p. 80. See also the superb discussion of Irenaeus in David Bentley Hart, *The Beauty of the Infinite: The Aesthetics of Christian Truth* (Grand Rapids: Eerdmans, 2003), pp. 325-27, and for an insightful philosophical exploration of the modern dimensions of this question, see Taylor, *Sources of the Self,* pp. 296-302.

65. Milosz, *To Begin,* p. 320.

archies have been eroded and the Protestant argument from design has been swept away.

As a case in point, Hans Urs von Balthasar concludes his seven-volume *Theological Aesthetics* with a meditation that portrays transcendence temporally rather than spatially; "no innerworldly hope," he says, "has a power for transcendence like that of the Christian hope, which has the 'down-payment' of the new aeon in the midst of the old aeon, to which it gives an orientation that carries it up beyond itself in all its dimensions." All the "futility and decay of earthly existence" can become fruitful, if they are understood to be "the 'pangs' of the new aeon and as a sharing in Christ's sufferings."[66] In like manner, Karl Barth begins his massive treatment of the "doctrine of creation" by setting the theme of "creation" specifically within that of "covenant." "As God's first work," he argues, "creation stands in a series, in an indissolubly real connexion, with God's further works," and these works have at their center "the institution, preservation and execution of the covenant of grace." As important as it is in its own right, creation simply "sets the stage" for the drama of grace, which "requires a stage corresponding to it; the existence of man and his whole world."[67]

Covenantal Promise in a Homeless Age

The covenant, the Word, trust, the stage and drama of grace — these terms bring us back to the categories and commitments from which Emerson and Thoreau had sought to "sign off" in the middle of the nineteenth century. Nevertheless, more than a century later, we find Czeslaw

66. Hans Urs von Balthasar, *The Glory of the Lord: A Theological Aesthetics,* vol. 7, *Theology: The New Covenant,* ed. John Riches, trans. Brian McNeil, C.R.V. (San Francisco: Ignatius, 1989), p. 519.

67. Karl Barth, *Church Dogmatics,* ed. G. W. Bromiley and T. F. Torrance (Edinburgh: T. & T. Clark, 1956-62), III.1.43-44. Another representative work on this topic is Oscar Cullmann's influential *Christ and Time:* "The Christian absolute norm *is itself also history* and is not, as is the philosophical norm, a transcendent datum that lies beyond all history." *Christ and Time: The Primitive Christian Conception of Time and History,* rev. ed., trans. Floyd V. Filson (Philadelphia: Westminster, 1964), p. 21. For a creative, thorough exploration of the doctrinal implications of Balthasar's and Barth's imagery of drama and the stage, see Kevin J. Vanhoozer, *The Drama of Doctrine: A Canonical-Linguistic Approach to Christian Theology* (Louisville: Westminster John Knox, 2005), esp. pp. 363-97.

Milosz yearning to "sign on," that is, to *believe again* in a Source of life secure beyond all human imagining. "*Someone* had to do this," he wrote of his lifelong struggle with belief; *someone* had to consider what it meant for Heaven and Hell to disappear all but overnight at the end of the nineteenth century, just as *someone* had to make sense of the fact that the intellectual structure that had housed Christian thought for more than 1500 years — from Augustine to Cardinal Newman — had collapsed suddenly in the twentieth century. "The age of homelessness has dawned," Milosz concluded, and the Christian artist must report what he sees, or cannot see, in the dim light of that dawn.

In the mid-nineteenth century, Thoreau and Emerson had seen the departure from home as a gesture of release and experience of liberation. "The nonchalance of boys who are sure of a dinner, and would disdain as much as a lord to do or say aught to conciliate one, is the healthy attitude of human nature," a casually confident Emerson declared, while Thoreau told his fictional "old man" that *"one generation abandons the enterprises of another like stranded vessels."*[68] For the "boys and girls" who came after them, however — for Melville and Dickinson, Kazin and Milosz — the joy of liberation had turned into the terror of abandonment. Orphans rarely throw a party to celebrate their discovery of post-parental freedom.

For a century or more, some of the Christian church's most astute theologians have wrestled with this sense of forsakenness and have puzzled over the silence of God. Helmut Thielicke, for one, wrote with passion and insight on this theme during the Second World War and in the decades after it. In a series of books, many of them based upon his sermons, Thielicke carried the fear of abandonment into the heart of God. "In the suffering, crucified Jesus Christ, God himself steps up beside us," and on the cross, God takes "everything human upon himself," including "suffering and anxiety, loneliness and the fear of death." He does so by taking the weight of history upon himself through the incarnation, which involves God's entering fully into our finite, forsaken condition. "Golgotha hurts God," Thielicke writes, and "God himself suffers there where the Crucified hangs. . . . When he cries, 'My God, my God, why hast thou forsaken me?' the eternal Heart abandons itself to all the forsakenness and despair that a man suffers in his separation from

68. Emerson, *Essays*, p. 261; Thoreau, *Walden*, p. 331.

God."[69] Thielicke was drawing on an ancient tradition. The logic of this suffering, wrote Irenaeus of Lyons in the late second century, is that without it, Christ's exhortation to his disciples that they take up their cross and follow him (Matt. 16:24) would have been meaningless. "In fact," Irenaeus explained, "we should be 'above the Master', were we to suffer and sustain what the Master Himself had not suffered and sustained beforehand."[70]

Thielicke's explorations of divine suffering anticipate the fuller development of this theme in the work of Eberhard Jüngel and Hans Urs von Balthasar among others. Collectively, these thinkers offer a theological parallel to the anthropological approach Dickinson and Milosz took to belief. That is, they situate suffering within the redemptive work of the triune God, just as the poets sought to include the apprehension of unbelief within a deepened understanding of belief. Suffering is no more foreign to divine knowledge than unbelief is to the human experience of belief. Balthasar addressed this matter by focusing in particular upon the theme of the descent into hell, which is mentioned directly in the Apostles' Creed and alluded to in a number of places in the New Testament (see especially Acts 2:17-36; 1 Pet. 3:18-22, 4:5-6; and Rom. 10:6-8). In his solidarity with the dead, Jesus Christ carries the supreme human experience of rupture, loss, and abandonment into the life of the trinitarian God:

69. Helmut Thielicke, *I Believe: The Christian's Creed,* trans. John W. Doberstein and H. George Anderson (Philadelphia: Fortress, 1968), pp. 116-17. See also Helmut Thielicke, *The Silence of God,* trans. Geoffrey W. Bromiley (Grand Rapids: Eerdmans, 1962), and Eberhard Jüngel, *God as the Mystery of the World: On the Foundation of the Theology of the Crucified One in the Dispute between Theism and Atheism,* trans. Darrell L. Guder (Grand Rapids: Eerdmans, 1983).

Milosz wrote an extraordinary poem on the silence of God. It construes that silence to be God's speech and takes his refusal to punish to be his judgment. God has "humble[d] people to the quick,/allowing them to act whatever way they wished,/leaving to them conclusions, saying nothing." As a consequence of the divine silence, the very materiality of the world itself seems to dissolve into nothingness, and "People, afflicted with an incomprehensible distress,/were throwing off their clothes on the piazzas so that nakedness might call for judgment./But in vain they were longing after horror, pity, and anger." *New and Collected Poems, 1931-2001* (New York: Ecco, 2001), p. 263.

70. Irenaeus of Lyons, *The Scandal of the Incarnation: Irenaeus Against the Heresies,* ed. Hans Urs von Balthasar (San Francisco: Ignatius, 1990), p. 16.

> In Sheol, in the Pit, all that reigns is the darkness of perfect loneliness. But to be without contact with God *means* to be without the inner light of faith, hope and love. . . . If Jesus has suffered through on the Cross the sin of the world to the very last truth of this sin (to be forsaken by God), then he must experience, in the solidarity with the sinners who have gone to the underworld, their (ultimately hopeless) separation from God, otherwise he would not have known all the phases and conditions of what it means for man to be unredeemed yet awaiting redemption.[71]

"Every Christian," writes W. H. Auden, "has to make the transition from the child's 'We believe still' to the adult's 'I believe again.' This cannot have been easy to make at any time, and in our age it is rarely made, it would seem, without a hiatus of unbelief."[72] As we have seen, Auden and others have dealt with this "hiatus of unbelief" by recasting it, by changing it from a story of secular liberation into one of dynamic spiritual struggle. For these modern writers in the Christian tradition, the question was not a matter of *either-or* — either believing in the Christian faith or unbelievingly dismissing it. Instead, to them it is a story of belief *and* unbelief, an art of "nimble believing."

For those who have a deep spiritual hunger, "nimble believing" may taste like meager fare, and the concept of a suffering God may offer little lasting nourishment. David Bentley Hart, for instance, has taken much of modern theology to task for its fascination with "tragic" motifs. He writes of the "current theological fashion," in which Christian thinkers of all kinds have acquired a "taste for tragedy," singling out for criticism Balthasar and his "Christ of the cadavers" as well as Jüngel and the "ghastly Wagnerian opulence" of his "cult of *Verwesung*" (putrefaction). In the words of Hart, the tragic impulse cannot "inspire any ethos but one that hovers disquietingly between resignation and masochism." In its fascination with the idea of "a miserable, imperfect, shadowy god," modern uncertainty misses what "the ancient and medieval church had the wisdom and strength" to long for, which was "a God of superabounding and eternal might, life, joy without any trace of pain, the inexhaustible

71. Hans Urs von Balthasar, "Abstieg zur Hölle," quoted in Oakes, *Pattern of Redemption,* p. 245.

72. W. H. Auden, *Forewords and Afterwords,* ed. Edward Mendelson (1973; repr., New York: Vintage, 1989), p. 518.

fountainhead of life and light and beauty, a God of infinite ontological health."[73]

Hart has legitimate theological concerns on this point, but the critique is best reserved for the theologians who expound upon the faith from within the church and perhaps ought not to be leveled at the poets who hesitate on its threshold. In our opening chapter, we encountered Milosz's image of the poet as a "secretary of the invisible thing." He transcribes the "dictation" of the gods and concludes, "how it all looks when completed/Is not up to us to inquire, we won't read it anyway."[74] Might we not see this as an admission of humility, instead of as a sign of hopelessness? (We recall what Wittgenstein said: "God says to men: . . . Heaven and hell are *my* affair.") Poetry can do many things, but it cannot forgive sins and raise the dead. Only God has the responsibility, and power, to do that.

No less passionate a Christian than T. S. Eliot made this point repeatedly in his *Four Quartets.* "For us," he wrote at the close of "East Coker," "there is only the trying. The rest is not our business." The "rest" is both the *everything else* that is not our business and the *Sabbath rest* that awaits the Church in God's Kingdom. At the end of "Dry Salvages," Eliot explains that the effort to "apprehend/The point of intersection of the timeless/With time, is an occupation for the saint." For most of us, there

> are only hints and guesses,
> Hints followed by guesses; and the rest
> Is prayer, observance, discipline, thought and action.
> The hint half guessed, the gift half understood, is Incarnation.[75]

In the aftermath of the nineteenth-century emergence of open unbelief, Emily Dickinson, Herman Melville, and Czeslaw Milosz may have only "half guessed" the meaning of the divine "hints" hidden within nature and human experience. For a robust understanding of the meaning of those "hints," the Christian student of nature and culture must look to the scriptures and to those — from Irenaeus to Karl Barth and beyond — who are part of the great "communion of the saints." The "strange minds"

73. Hart, *Beauty of the Infinite,* pp. 373-75.

74. Milosz, *New and Collected Poems,* p. 343.

75. T. S. Eliot, *The Complete Poems and Plays, 1909-1950* (New York: Harcourt, 1971), pp. 128, 136.

who have written brilliantly about belief in modern literature may not proclaim Christian truth as vigorously as the theologians might wish, but that should not obscure — for us as well as for them — the importance of their restless, ceaseless, and nimble efforts to "believe again."

CHAPTER 4

Interpretation

SHORTLY AFTER Christmas in 1882, Emily Dickinson wrote to one of her closest friends, Elizabeth Holland, to thank her for the words of comfort she had offered in the wake of Emily's mother's death a few weeks before. As was often the case with Dickinson, this letter's concrete references to friends and family abruptly gave way to a set of broader, cryptic reflections on life's larger mysteries and meaning. "The Fiction of 'Santa Claus,'" Dickinson wrote, "always reminds me of the reply to my early question of 'Who made the Bible' — 'Holy Men moved by the Holy Ghost,' and though I have now ceased my investigations, the Solution is insufficient —."[1] Shaken by the biblical criticism of the nineteenth century, Dickinson could only conclude, as a poem written in the same year puts it, "The Bible is an antique Volume —/Written by faded Men/At the suggestion of Holy Spectres —" (#1577).

Herman Melville fared no better than Dickinson in his efforts to chart a course through the turbulent seas of the higher criticism. His case, like hers, shows how intricately intertwined were the rise of unbelief and the crisis of interpretive authority in the late nineteenth century. As Andrew Delbanco describes the situation, in mid-life, Melville arrived reluctantly at the conclusion "that the Bible was a collection of improbable fictions, and he cursed the secular scholars who had lately exposed it as an unreliable book compiled over time by fallible men rather than written by God."

1. Emily Dickinson, *The Letters of Emily Dickinson,* ed. Thomas H. Johnson and Theodora Ward (Cambridge, Mass.: Belknap Press of Harvard University Press, 1958), 3:756.

The novelist "heartily wish[ed]" biblical critics "to the dogs," and he complained bitterly that "they have robbed us of the bloom."[2]

In this chapter, we will focus first on nineteenth-century writers whose lives and works were thrown into interpretive confusion by the rise of unbelief. Here Herman Melville and Fyodor Dostoevsky will be at the center of our attention, and we will see their spiritual struggles as acts in a larger drama being played out on the cultural stage of late modernity. We will then move from their fiction to the work of two of the twentieth-century's most influential theorists of interpretation, Paul Ricoeur and Mikhail Bakhtin. It was Ricoeur who gave the name "the conflict of interpretations" to the consequences of the struggle between belief and unbelief, and along with Bakhtin he recaptured that "bloom" of Christian understanding whose loss Melville had lamented so bitterly. Bakhtin went about his work as one attracted to Christian belief even if he did not embrace it fully, while Ricoeur was open about his commitment to the faith. In their work and that of the imaginative writers who inspired them, we find compelling examples of how to engage the conflict of interpretations with charity and to imagine its resolution with hope.

The Narrative of Heroic Secularity

Brokenhearted and bereft of the buoyant energy that had sustained him through a decade of frantic yet brilliant novel writing, Herman Melville sailed out of New York Harbor on October 11, 1856. With a number of intermediate stops before him, the thirty-seven-year-old writer had as his final destination the eastern Mediterranean and the Holy Land. Exhausted by the never-ending clash of ideas within himself, Melville sought rest and something more, perhaps a sign of the divine presence or an assurance of the divine favor to be discovered somewhere in the desolate landscape that had served as the cradle for Judaism and Christianity. As sorely disappointed as he was in the course of his career and the turmoil of his domestic life, the novelist continued to be driven by "a relentless desire to fathom the ineffable essence of creation, to possess secrets that could only be unveiled in the East or at the edge of madness."[3]

2. Andrew Delbanco, *Melville: His World and Work* (New York: Knopf, 2005), p. 257.

3. Hilton Obenzinger, *American Palestine: Melville, Twain, and the Holy Land Mania* (Princeton: Princeton University Press, 1999), p. 64.

To fund his trip, Melville had to turn to his father-in-law, Judge Lemuel Shaw of the Massachusetts Supreme Court, for support. Shaw was willing to cover his son-in-law's expenses because he recognized the precarious state of Herman's emotional health. "I suppose you have been informed," he wrote to his own son, "how very ill, Herman has been." In a series of letters, Shaw's daughter had told him of her "great anxiety about" her husband's health. "When [Herman] is deeply engaged in one of his literary works, he confines him to hard study many hours in the day, — with little or no exercise," Shaw reported. This overwork "brings on severe nervous affections," and the proposed trip "would be highly beneficial to him & probably restore him."[4]

Lemuel Shaw was in fact as oblivious to his son-in-law's actual spiritual state as he was generous in his efforts to meet Herman's financial needs. He was no more able to understand his son-in-law's malaise than the loyal Starbuck had proved capable of comprehending the agony of Ahab in *Moby Dick.* Where Melville's father-in-law thought exercise and a change of scenery might cure his ills, Starbuck believes Ahab needs to concentrate on practical matters and set reachable goals, and everything else will fall into place. He pleads with his Captain to abandon the fruitless pursuit of Moby Dick: "Why should any one give chase to that hated fish! Away with me! let us fly these deadly waters! let us home! . . . How cheerily, how hilariously, O my Captain, would we bowl on our way to see old Nantucket again!" Yet the maimed spirit of Ahab needs more than a change in location or disposition to be healed, for he has "piled upon the whale's white hump the sum of all the general rage and hate felt by his whole race from Adam down; and then, as if his chest had been a mortar, he burst his hot heart's shell upon it." Ahab tells Starbuck, "I feel deadly faint, bowed, and humped, as though I were Adam, staggering beneath the piled centuries since Paradise," and he begs him to "stand close to me" and "let me look into a human eye; it is better than to gaze into sea or sky; better than to gaze upon God."[5]

4. Lemuel Shaw, quoted in Hershel Parker, *Herman Melville: A Biography,* vol. 2, *1851-1891* (Baltimore: Johns Hopkins University Press, 2002), p. 289.

5. Herman Melville, *Moby Dick,* 2nd ed., ed. Hershel Parker and Harrison Hayford (New York: Norton, 2002), pp. 156, 406. With his mixture of rage and tenderness, bravado and terror, Ahab is a clear descendent of Satan in Milton's *Paradise Lost.* For example, when he first spies Adam and Eve in the Garden of Eden, at the start of Book IV, Satan's bit-

Ahab's agony cut deep; so did Melville's own anxiety as he sailed to Europe in 1856. On his way to the Mediterranean, the novelist stopped in the British Isles to do casual research into his ancestral roots and to visit Nathaniel Hawthorne. It was at this time that the two friends had their conversation about "Providence and futurity, and of everything that lies beyond human ken." In every respect, Hawthorne saw his friend's life as a ceaseless round of pointless motion and his mind as a kind of mental handcar hurtling back and forth on the rails of doubt without a destination in sight. "He [Melville] can neither believe, nor be comfortable in his unbelief; and he is too honest and courageous not to try to do one or the other," Hawthorne concluded.[6] This description, says Andrew Delbanco, "captures perfectly Melville's uneasy suspension between faith and skepticism, a yearning that gave him the air of distractedness that some found trying."[7]

Melville found little to satisfy his yearnings when he reached the Middle East. The hardscrabble landscape provoked in him one bleak response after another, and he was repulsed by the mixture of crassness and vulgarity he discovered at the holy sites. "*Talk of the guides* 'Here is the stone Christ leaned against, & here is the English Hotel.' Yonder is the arch where Christ was shown to the people, & just by that open window is sold the best coffee in Jerusalem. &c&c&c." When he visited the Pyra-

---

terness is tempered by his pity, and his jealousy is muted by his admiration of the beauty of these two:

> "O Hell! what do mine eyes with grief behold,
> Into our room of bliss thus high advanc't
> Creatures of other mould, earth-born perhaps,
> Not Spirits, yet to heav'nly Spirits bright
> Little inferior; whom my thoughts pursue
> With wonder, and could love, so lively shines
> In them Divine resemblance, and such grace
> The hand that form'd them on their shape hath pour'd."

Paradise Lost and Paradise Regained, ed. Christopher Ricks (New York: New American Library, 1968), pp. 130-31.

6. Nathaniel Hawthorne, quoted in Parker, *Herman Melville,* p. 300. Brenda Wineapple reports that by the time of this meeting, which proved to be their last, "the flowers of friendship had faded" between the two men. "I do not know a more independent personage," remarked Hawthorne, who was himself not given to light-hearted sociability. *Hawthorne: A Life* (New York: Knopf, 2003), p. 293.

7. Delbanco, *Melville,* p. 253.

mids, Melville found himself not inspired but dispirited, even terrified. "A feeling of awe & terror came over me," he reported. "I shudder at the idea of ancient Egyptians. It was in these pyramids that was conceived the idea of Jehovah. Terrible mixture of the cunning and awful. . . . The idea of Jehovah born here." Long given to bold, even bizarre metaphorical flights, Melville seemed by the end of his trip to be bent under the weight of a leaden despair, and his prose labored to put one word down after another. "This day saw nothing, learned nothing, enjoyed nothing, but suffered something," he wrote in Rome in March 1857.[8] Within weeks he sailed to the United States in a state of "spiritual exhaustion" and uncertain as to whether he would ever write again.[9]

Despite his disappointment, for the rest of his life — he died in 1891 — there remained in Melville an odd mixture of longing and patience as far as belief was concerned. In the words of Michael Colacurcio, this was "not quite Job's 'I will love him though he slay me.'" Instead, it was something more like, "I trust he will not destroy me for pursuing without cynicism" the moral evidence that calls our metaphysical proofs into question. This was not the "definite belief" that Hawthorne had prescribed for his friend, yet it was "a position that left ample room for faith, should it ever be given."[10] Perhaps this was Melville's way of meeting the nineteenth-century challenge of unbelief, his own version of "nimble believing," hammered out, in this case, on the anvil of a broken heart.

Unlike Melville, a considerable number of writers in the late nineteenth century greeted unbelief with relief instead of regret. They considered it a product of an irreversible process and took it to be a sign of an unmistakable gain. To them, the appearance of unbelief represented a turning point in the long struggle on behalf of "a human being's privilege to fashion his inner life for himself."[11] This latter phrase is found in the final sentence of Edmund Gosse's *Father and Son,* an autobiographical account of a Victorian son's bitter struggle to free himself from religious

8. Herman Melville, *Journals,* ed. Howard C. Horsford with Lynn Horth (Evanston and Chicago: Northwestern University Press and The Newberry Library, 1989), pp. 89, 75, 112.

9. Delbanco, *Melville,* p. 257.

10. Michael Colacurcio, "Charity and Its Discontents: Pity and Politics in Melville's Fiction," in *There Before Us: Religion, Literature, and Culture from Emerson to Wendell Berry,* ed. Roger Lundin (Grand Rapids: Eerdmans, 2007), p. 79.

11. Edmund Gosse, *Father and Son: A Story of Two Temperaments,* ed. Peter Abbs (London: Penguin, 1983), p. 251.

oppression and parental control. Gosse pitched his story as a battle between the progressive power of art and the reactionary force of religion:

> This book is the record of a struggle between two temperaments, two consciences and almost two epochs. It ended, as was inevitable, in disruption. Of the two human beings here described, one was born to fly backward, the other could not help being carried forward.[12]

Faced with a religiously intransigent parent, a modern child has only two choices, according to Gosse: "Either he must cease to think for himself; or his individualism must be instantly confirmed, and the necessity of religious independence must be emphasized." Philip Gosse had offered "no compromise" to his son and "no proposal of a truce," so "it was a case of 'Everything or Nothing.'" And "Nothing" it was to be for Edmund Gosse. "Thus desperately challenged, the young man's conscience threw off once for all the yoke of his 'dedication', and, as respectfully as he could, without parade or remonstrance," he set about fashioning his inner life.[13]

In its loftiest version, the narrative of secularization often struck a note of chastened wisdom like the one sounded at the conclusion of George Eliot's *Middlemarch,* as the narrator sums up the life of Dorothea Brooke:

> But the effect of her being on those around her was incalculably diffusive: for the growing good of the world is partly dependent on unhistoric acts; and that things are not so ill with you and me as they might have been, is half owing to the number who lived faithfully a hidden life, and rest in unvisited tombs.[14]

Everything in this judgment is carefully modulated. Dorothea's influence is undeniable yet *incalculable* and *diffuse;* progress is dependent upon *unhistoric* acts, things are *not so ill* as they *might* have been, and *the good of the world* is *half* attributable to the *hidden* lives of those who now rest in *unvisited* tombs. This is a modest triumphalism, to be sure, and it serves

12. Gosse, *Father and Son,* p. 35.

13. Gosse, *Father and Son,* p. 251.

14. George Eliot, *Middlemarch,* ed. Rosemary Ashton (New York: Penguin, 1994), p. 838.

as a high water mark of sorts for the subtraction story and secularization narrative. Having entered adulthood as an ardent evangelical Christian, Dorothea Brooke will die as an admirable agnostic. This is the inevitable course of the world, and for George Eliot and many others in her day, there was but one grand story to be told, a single all-encompassing interpretation to be offered for the myriad facets of human experience.[15]

The assumptions informing the narrative of heroic secularity have largely governed the writing of modern literary history. The appeal of such a cultural story is evident, for example, in the writings of M. H. Abrams, whose *The Mirror and the Lamp* and *Natural Supernaturalism* stand as two of the most important works of literary criticism from the second half of the twentieth century. In the preface to the latter work, Abrams sets the framework for this narrative. "It is a historical commonplace," he writes, "that the course of Western thought since the Renaissance has been one of progressive secularization." That is not to say that secular thinkers had somehow worked "free of the centuries-old Judeo-Christian culture." Instead of dismissing or replacing religious concepts, modern poets and novelists have assimilated and reinterpreted those "religious ideas, as constitutive elements in a world view founded on secular premises."[16] Taking the decline of theistic belief as a given, writers in the romantic tradition set out to secure ethical and spiritual values upon the bedrock of mind and nature rather than in the debris scattered on the modern shore by a retreating sea of faith.

15. Gillian Beer makes what may seem at first to be the opposite point in her summation of *Middlemarch:* "Most important of all, she [George Eliot] uses these immanent worlds to indicate that any single interpretation of experience will mislead. The self, to be valid, must stand as pars pro toto. The single focus contains; the one candle makes for introspective vision." *Darwin's Plots: Evolutionary Narrative in Darwin, George Eliot and Nineteenth-Century Fiction,* 2nd ed. (Cambridge: Cambridge University Press, 2000), p. 167. Yet the longer one considers it, the more this account of difference sounds like a narrative having to do with the principle of an expansive, universal principle of secular singularity. The *one story* to be told about human life is that no single story can encompass it.

16. M. H. Abrams, *Natural Supernaturalism: Tradition and Revolution in Romantic Literature* (New York: Norton, 1971), p. 13. It is easy to overlook the debt that the novel owes to "the Christian ethos," writes Walker Percy. "It underwrites those very properties of the novel without which there is no novel: I am speaking of the mystery of human life, its sense of predicament, of something having gone wrong, of life as a wayfaring and a pilgrimage, of the density and linearity of time and the sacramental reality of things." *Signposts in a Strange Land,* ed. Patrick Samway (New York: Farrar, 1991), p. 178.

The Conflict of Interpretations

The rule of the secularization narrative proved to be short-lived, for it depended upon the union of mind and nature, and as we have seen, those two had filed for a divorce by the end of the nineteenth century. At the same time that mind and nature were falling asunder, the human mind itself was being divided from itself by fresh challenges that undermined our confidence in consciousness and discredited the narratives of progress that relied upon that confidence. It was these challenges that Ricoeur gathered under the rubric of "the hermeneutics of suspicion," his name for the method of reading texts and human actions that flowered in the nineteenth century and bore sometimes-bitter fruit as "the conflict of interpretations" in the twentieth.

With this term, Ricoeur was labeling the work performed by the masters of a very particular craft. Each of the great "masters of suspicion" — Karl Marx, Friedrich Nietzsche, and Sigmund Freud — put forward a comprehensive account of history, human nature, and culture in the final decades of the nineteenth century. As different as they proved to be in many respects, each of the narratives of suspicion situated *desire*, as anarchic and unselfconscious as it may be, at the center of human action and cultural activity. In doing so, they called into question both the narrative of secular progress and its great antagonist, the biblical account of God's providential care.[17] Yet even as they cast a skeptical eye on the theistic accounts that had set the cultural boundaries for almost two millennia, these accounts of suspicion were at the same time calling each other into question, as each vied for a position of supreme explanatory power.[18]

17. "If we go back to the intention they had in common," writes Ricoeur of the masters of suspicion, "we find in it the decision to look upon the whole of consciousness primarily as 'false' consciousness." These newfound doubts about consciousness subverted the narrative of progress that had dominated Western thought from Descartes to the Victorian age. *Freud and Philosophy: An Essay on Interpretation,* trans. Denis Savage (New Haven: Yale University Press, 1970), p. 33. See also Hans Frei, *The Eclipse of Biblical Narrative: A Study in Eighteenth and Nineteenth Century Hermeneutics* (New Haven: Yale University Press, 1974).

18. Gillian Beer writes of Darwinism's effect on nineteenth-century fiction: "It is its ability to propose a total system for understanding the organisation of the natural world which has been its most powerful influence. The all-inclusiveness of its explanation, stretching through the differing orders of the natural world, seemed to offer a means of understanding without recourse to godhead. It created a system in which there was no

According to Ricoeur, the hermeneutics of suspicion sought to overcome the pretensions of the Cartesian *cogito,* which in the early seventeenth century had set the standards for modern thought. Descartes had held that it was possible to prove God's existence through the certainty of self-consciousness; hence his *Cogito, ergo sum* ("I think, therefore I am"). The Cartesian proof held sway for almost three centuries, until Freud and others began to question whether consciousness itself was indeed a clear, self-constituting power. To the contrary, they argued that self-awareness is too dependent upon desire to be free and transparent. "Existence, we can now say, is desire and effort," Ricoeur explains. We use *effort* to designate the "positive energy" and "dynamism" of existence, while we refer to *desire* to acknowledge the sense of "lack" and "poverty" that we also find at the heart of that existence. Once its dependence upon desire has been exposed, the self can no longer indulge "its pretension of positing itself," for "it appears as *already* posited in being."[19] For the hermeneutics of suspicion, such "being" is not the personal God of Judaism and Christianity, but a primordial power of necessity and unconscious desire.

If such a definition of suspicion sounds too abstract, it might help us to think of it differently, with the aid of Melville's meditation on the pyramids. When the novelist said he "shuddered" at the "idea of ancient Egyptians," what upset him was the realization that the "idea of Jehovah" came not as a revelation from beyond delivered on Mount Sinai, but it had been "conceived" instead in the miasmal experience of the slaves who built the pyramids. This judgment was standard mid-nineteenth-century fare, in that it considered God to be a concept that had been *made* rather than a personal power who had been *found.* The hermeneutics of suspicion merely carried the categories of conception and construction into the very citadel of self-consciousness. If bondage and brutality produced the idea of a redemptive Jehovah, suspicion would say, then so too do the murky forces of will and desire lurk just below the surface of our seemingly lucid self-reflection. There, in silence and secrecy,

---

need to invoke a source of authority outside the natural order: in which instead of foreknown design, there was inherent purposiveness." Darwinian theory has proven to have "an extraordinary hermeneutic potential — the power to yield a great number of significant and various meanings." *Darwin's Plots,* pp. 12, 8.

19. Paul Ricoeur, *The Conflict of Interpretations,* ed. Don Ihde (Evanston: Northwestern University Press, 1974), p. 21.

they shape the values, judgments, and beliefs that we in our naïveté take to be clear, secure, and self-evident.

Since self-consciousness is not capable of understanding itself immediately or fully, it requires the mediating work of interpretation to make sense of what it cannot understand. The task of interpretation is to demonstrate "that existence arrives at expression, at meaning, and at reflection only through the continual exegesis of all the significations that come to light in the world of culture." To become a "self" requires deciphering and appropriating the meaning "which first resides 'outside'" ourselves in the history of culture and in its works. When they are taken together, Ricoeur argues, even "the most opposite hermeneutics point, each in its own way, to the ontological roots of comprehension," and each "affirms the dependence of the self upon existence." That dependence manifests itself in different guises — with "its dependence on desire glimpsed in an archaeology of the subject, its dependence on the spirit glimpsed in its teleology, its dependence on the sacred glimpsed in its eschatology." Ricoeur acknowledges that "rival hermeneutics" may become "mere 'language games,'" but he also holds that this need not be the case, as long as those who hold "equally valid interpretations" remain capable of recognizing "that each interpretation is grounded in a particular existential function."[20]

In a broader sense, the conflict of interpretations has come to stand for the pervasive phenomenon of interpretive competition in modernity. From the fifteenth century to the present, Western societies have witnessed an ever-accelerating movement of persons and information across political borders and cultural boundaries. This free flow of individuals and ideas has pressed longstanding beliefs and practices into constant contact and frequent conflict with one another. In many cases, from the late seventeenth to the late nineteenth century, such conflicts were resolved through assimilation into an established narrative of secular development, because as Ricoeur notes, modernity had been marked from the start by a "forgetfulness of the signs of the sacred." Forgetfulness of this kind "is the counterpart of the great task of nourishing men, of satisfying their needs by mastering nature through a planetary technique."[21]

20. Ricoeur, *Conflict,* pp. 22-24.

21. Paul Ricoeur, *The Symbolism of Evil,* trans. Emerson Buchanan (1967; repr., Boston: Beacon, 1969), p. 349.

In the unfolding story of the "forgetfulness of the sacred," ancient beliefs repeatedly clashed with modern discoveries, with reason and the scientific method most often cast as the heroes of the story, and religious rituals and beliefs as its villains.

The hermeneutics of suspicion was to usher in a new type of intellectual conflict at the close of the nineteenth century. In these battles, the distinctions between allies and enemies became confused, and the virtues of friends appeared to be as ambiguous as the vices of foes had once seemed unmistakable. And as we have seen in the story of the rise of unbelief, for the most part, these new dramas were played out not on the fields of Gettysburg or in the labs of Louis Pasteur but within the confines of the human heart. "Ourself behind ourself, concealed —/Should startle most — ," Emily Dickinson wrote in 1862. "Assassin hid in our Apartment/Be Horror's least —" (#407). With the modern self divided against itself, the conflict of interpretations has increasingly taken the form of a struggle between plausible visions of reality, each of which claims validity for its reading of human nature, social reality, and the inner life.

From the vantage point of contemporary history, the advent of suspicion in the late nineteenth century may be seen as a new phase of a longstanding conflict that Jeffrey Stout has called "the problem of many authorities." In the early modern period, new claims to religious authority had proliferated, as a teeming brood of Protestant children took leave of the mother church. These theological siblings in turn quickly established their own scriptural and sacramental rivalries. So it was that as new churches and interpretive schemes continued to spring up at an astounding rate, Stout writes, any "conventional means for resolving disputes arising from such competition became less and less effective," and the "'problem of many authorities' [became] the central social and intellectual difficulty of the Reformation."[22]

Originally intended to provide Protestantism with a regulative ideal for the faith, the doctrine of *sola scriptura* proved incapable on its own of calming the interpretive storms sweeping across the modern ecclesiastical landscape. In the wake of the Reformation, explains Jaroslav Pelikan, the actual interpretation of Scripture turned out to be a more difficult ex-

22. Jeffrey Stout, *The Flight from Authority: Religion, Morality, and the Quest for Autonomy* (Notre Dame: University of Notre Dame Press, 1981), p. 41.

ercise than the formulation of an abstract doctrine of inspiration had been. It soon became apparent that a proliferating series of biblical interpretations were proving too difficult to reconcile one with another, while fixed rules or interpretive ideals, such as the recovery of the author's intentions or the bracketing of presuppositions, appeared to provide few real checks on interpretive liberty. With considerable difficulty, the children of the Reformation learned there was no such thing as a "'nonpartisan' exegesis but the 'systems and formularies of their several communions' determined how confessional exegetes interpreted Scripture."[23]

For the first several centuries of the Protestant era, pastors and philosophers alike labored to channel the flood of new interpretive practices safely within the banks of specific intellectual streams. From the seventeenth to the nineteenth centuries, they turned first to Cartesian reason, then to Kantian intuition, and, finally, to the romantic understanding of nature. Yet each scheme in its turn failed to establish its authority over interpretive practice, while the culture as a whole continued to live "on the capital of absolutist belief amassed by Christian tradition without ever feeling the need to replenish it." By the time the writers of the nineteenth century "came to take their share" of that capital, "there was practically nothing left."[24]

At mid-century Herman Melville and others were left to choose between the ruins of the ancient beliefs and the possibilities of present discoveries. Melville, for one, both looked back with regret and forward with hope. Delbanco credits him with being "the first to understand that if a literary work is to register the improvisational nature of experience, it must be as spontaneous and self-surprising as the human mind itself."[25] Caught between his intellectual exhilaration and his spiritual exhaustion,

23. Jaroslav Pelikan, *The Christian Tradition: A History of the Development of Doctrine,* vol. 5, *Christian Doctrine and Modern Culture (since 1700)* (Chicago: University of Chicago Press, 1989), p. 73. Employing a metaphor from drama, Kevin Vanhoozer offers a concise description of the primacy of Scripture and the importance of tradition: "*Sola scriptura* does not preempt the need for church tradition but merely asserts the primacy and finality of the script as a norm for evaluating subsequent performances." *The Drama of Doctrine: A Canonical-Linguistic Approach to Christian Theology* (Louisville: Westminster John Knox, 2005), p. 235.

24. William C. Spengemann, *The Adventurous Muse: The Poetics of American Fiction, 1789-1900* (New Haven: Yale University Press, 1977), p. 200.

25. Delbanco, *Melville,* p. 146.

Melville set the conflict of interpretations at the heart of his fiction. In the opening sections of *Moby Dick,* for example, he explored that conflict by dividing his attention between the amiable openness of the narrator, Ishmael, and the monomaniacal fervor of Captain Ahab. These two men split the world between them, and their differences seem irreconcilable, as do those between the captain and the crew of which Ishmael is a member. At its center, the conflict involves a struggle between Ahab's determination to hunt only Moby Dick and the crew's eagerness to kill whales of any kind to make a living. Ahab has nothing but contempt for their mercantile interests, for all that matters to him is getting "vengeance on a dumb brute" and finding relief for the torments of his God-riddled mind.

The conflict of interpretations becomes particularly pointed in *Moby Dick* in an incident involving a gold doubloon. Ahab has the coin nailed to the masthead, and it is to go to the first sailor to spot the white whale. One day he pauses before the doubloon, "as though now for the first time beginning to interpret for himself in some monomaniac way whatever significance might lurk" in its symbols:

> And some certain significance lurks in all things, else all things are little worth, and the round world itself but an empty cipher, except to sell by the cartload, as they do hills about Boston, to fill up some morass in the Milky Way.

The coin depicts "the likeness of three Andes' summits; from one a flame; a tower on another; on the third a crowing cock." As he ponders these peaks, Ahab names each as his own, as though he himself were each person of the Trinity, the Godhead all rolled into one, for "all are Ahab; and this round gold is but the image of the rounder globe, which, like a magician's glass, to each and every man in turn but mirrors back his own mysterious self."[26]

At this point, each of the ship's three mates pauses before the doubloon and reads its meaning through the prism of his own idiosyncratic imagination. When they have finished with their interpretive tasks, it falls to Pip, the crazed cabin boy who serves as court jester to the overbearingly regal Captain Ahab, to make sense of this flurry of hermeneutical activity. Having heard the disparate readings, Pip simply conjugates

26. Melville, *Moby Dick,* pp. 331-32.

the verb "to look" three times: "I look, you look, he looks; we look, ye look, they look." His intention in doing so is clear; he wishes to show that as each man reads the world, it "but mirrors back his own mysterious self." Or as the ship's mate Flask explains, "There's another rendering now; but still one text. All sorts of men in one kind of world."[27]

Although the interpretive divisions among the crew interested him, Melville's deepest concern was for the unique case of Captain Ahab, a living embodiment of "the conflict of interpretations." In an early chapter of the novel, the novelist grants us first-person insight into the agonies of this self-divided man. As he gazes at the sunset on a beautiful evening, Ahab explains, "time was, when as the sunrise nobly spurred me, so the sunset soothed." Yet that is the case no more. He laments that everything lovely has become a source of anguish to him. "Gifted with the high perception, I lack the low, enjoying power; damned, most subtly and most malignantly! damned in the midst of Paradise!" It is Ahab's burden to recognize the validity of every interpretation and the authority of none save his own monomaniacal vision.[28]

Like Dickinson, Melville had a heightened sensitivity to the new dynamics of belief and unbelief, and like her, he also viewed the conflict of

27. Melville, *Moby Dick,* p. 335. In the lifetime of Dickinson and Melville, one of the Christian tradition's most powerful tropes all but completely lost its force. The figure of the "Book of Nature," which dates back to the early medieval period, wielded particular influence in Protestant apologetics in the eighteenth and early nineteenth centuries. Under pressure on many fronts, that trope lost its justifying context in the decades after 1850, and nature changed from a loquacious book to an inscrutable text. As Emily Dickinson wrote of nature in 1864:

> We pass, and she abides.
> We conjugate Her Skill
> While She creates and federates
> Without a syllable — (#798)

28. Melville, *Moby Dick,* p. 143. Richard Brodhead explains the to-and-fro quality of Melville's handling of belief and its interpretive consequences: "Like the Puritans of *The Scarlet Letter,*" Ahab "takes the meanings he perceives to be sanctioned by a cosmological order. Melville's contrast of fixity and flexibility of selfhood and interpretation" is, in the end, "a conflict between a force that assigns determinate meanings to experience felt as derived from a higher order and a force that generates meaning from within the processes of its actual experience, entertaining these not as final truth but for the sense they make of that experience, and recognizing them as the products of its own angle of perception." *Hawthorne, Melville, and the Novel* (Chicago: University of Chicago Press, 1976), p. 156.

interpretations as a matter of internal struggle rather than one of public dispute. As they zeroed in on this inward conflict, these two became intrepid explorers of that "inexhaustible inner domain" that Charles Taylor has located in the modern self. Over the past several centuries, he argues, we "modern, post-expressivist subject[s]" have come to see ourselves as possessing "inner depths" that we can study but never plumb completely. Our sense of those depths goes hand in hand with our feeling that we contain within us resources we can never deplete, for we are convinced that however much we draw up from our fathomless selves, "there is always more down there."

Possessing such "inner depths," we also think of ourselves as having significant "expressive powers." Under the inspiration of romanticism, a sense of self-articulation grew expansively in the nineteenth century, and it came to compete with the power of "disengaged rational control," which represents for Taylor the other dramatic innovation of modern selfhood. Through the exercise of rational control, we seek to hold our selves and our world in abeyance, as we turn everything, including our own experience, into an *object* to be scrutinized by the *subject* that is human consciousness. Such a detached standpoint informs Cartesian epistemology and Newtonian science and is at the center of those techniques that are meant to establish "a stance of disengagement from [our] own nature and feelings." Yet disengagement of this kind alienates us from ourselves even as it enhances our sense of power. Were we to disengage completely — from our world as well as from ourselves — Taylor says we would be too weak to tap into the sources of the inner domain. As a result, we are torn between two options, and in our relationship to ourselves and the world, we alternate between a hunger for detachment and a longing for immersion.[29]

Or to put this another way, since the nineteenth century, we have come to think of our *selves* as both the vast wonders that are waiting to be explored and the intrepid adventurers who are about to embark upon a voyage through those inner domains. "Volcanoes" may be found in "Sicily/And South America," Dickinson wryly noted, but she had learned from her personal "Geography" of a "Volcano nearer here." And this was "A Crater I may contemplate/Vesuvius at Home" (#1691). There was little

29. Charles Taylor, *Sources of the Self: The Making of the Modern Identity* (Cambridge, Mass.: Harvard University Press, 1989), p. 390.

need for Dickinson to sally forth from Amherst, for whenever she wished to do so, she could climb any "Lava step" she liked or peer into the "Crater" of any inner "Vesuvius" she wished to examine. In like manner, Henry David Thoreau had urged each of his readers in *Walden* to "be a Columbus to whole new continents and worlds within you, opening new channels, not of trade, but of thought." What is travel, he asked, "but an indirect recognition of the fact, that there are continents and seas in the moral world" that remain to be explored? It is easier to sail "through cold and storm and cannibals . . . than it is to explore the private sea, the Atlantic and Pacific Ocean of one's being alone."[30]

Dickinson willingly accepted Thoreau's challenge, but like Melville, as she plied the "ocean of her being," she had to brave those storms that lash the self "voyaging through strange seas of thought, alone."[31] For it was, after all, the same person who both madly pursued the whale and dispassionately analyzed the desperate quest, just as from the one poet the lava of self-expression flowed even as the cooling breezes of her "disengaged rational [and critical] control" fanned across it. Taylor concludes that "a modern who recognizes both these powers [of passion and analysis] is constitutionally in tension." Dickinson and Melville embodied that tension in their works even as they endured it in their lives.[32]

Dostoevsky and the Promise of Dialogue

The religious divisions that drove Herman Melville to the Holy Land and Emily Dickinson to the brink of her inner Vesuvius also assailed some of their greatest contemporaries and most influential successors. In this

30. Henry David Thoreau, *Walden*, in *A Week, Walden, The Maine Woods, Cape Cod*, ed. Robert F. Sayre (New York: Library of America, 1985), p. 578.

31. The phrase is from William Wordsworth, *The Prelude: A Parallel Text*, ed. J. C. Maxwell (New York: Penguin, 1971), p. 103. It comes from Book III, line 63 of the 1850 version of the poem.

32. Taylor, *Sources of the Self*, p. 390. Or as Taylor has put the matter recently: "The modern cosmic imaginary . . . has opened a space in which people can wander between and around all these options without having to land clearly and definitively in any one. In the wars between belief and unbelief, this can be seen as a kind of no-man's-land." *A Secular Age* (Cambridge, Mass.: Belknap Press of Harvard University Press, 2007), p. 351.

tradition of "nimble believing," we find, among others, two remarkable writers from modern Russia: the nineteenth-century novelist Fyodor Dostoevsky, and Mikhail Bakhtin, Dostoevsky's most insightful twentieth-century critic. Together, these two weave together many strands of the arguments that have informed our explorations of belief, unbelief, and the conflict of interpretations.

Dostoevsky staked his life on the outcome of the struggle between belief and unbelief, and in many respects the history of his sustained engagement with the subject dates to his arrest in the middle of the night on April 23, 1849. Along with several dozen others, he was taken in for questioning concerning his role in a loosely knit group of artists and intellectuals who met in St. Petersburg to discuss politics, economics, and social reform. The arrest led to several months of interrogation in prison followed by a formal Commission of Inquiry, which ruled that although the members of this group (called the Petrashevsky Circle after its most famous participant) were united in opposition to the government, there was no evidence of their having plotted against the Tsar or of their having engaged in intrigue with foreign powers.

Nonetheless, in a decision whose consequences would dramatically alter the course of Dostoevsky's life, the Commission decided that twenty-eight of those in custody had committed crimes. Tsar Nicholas I then appointed a mixed military and civil tribunal to set the sentences, and in mid-November the judgment came down: fifteen of the accused, including Dostoevsky, were to be shot by a firing squad. A subsequent appellate review by the highest military court upped the ante by imposing the death sentence on all twenty-eight. Then, in a move orchestrated to allow the Tsar to exercise with his right hand a leniency that the severity of his left had just refused, the tribunal urged him to impose the sentences and then immediately commute them.

This was a common practice during the reign of Nicholas, but in this particular instance the Tsar wished to drive home his point by altering the standard procedure. In normal cases involving the commutation of a death sentence, the prisoner was informed of the reprieve but then required to endure a mock execution meant to demonstrate the depth of imperial grace. But with this group of artistic and intellectual adversaries, the Tsar gave explicit instructions that they were to be taken en masse to the place of execution and prepared for death *before* they were to be told their lives had been spared.

All of this — the verdict, the death sentences, as well the commutation of the sentences — took place without the prisoners having learned anything of the outcome of their cases. For more than two months, they languished in an imprisoned limbo, until early in the morning of December 22, 1849, when, without warning or explanation, they were pulled from their cells, packed into carriages, and sent off to an undisclosed destination. After about half an hour, the procession came to a halt, and the prisoners were deposited in a city square ringed with troops and marked by an elevated platform with several gray stakes planted in the ground next to it.

Once they had ascended the platform, a uniformed official passed before each prisoner and read out his sentence, which invariably included the phrase, "The Field Criminal Court has condemned all to death sentence before a firing squad, and on December 19 His Majesty the Emperor personally wrote, 'Confirmed.'" At the conclusion of this ritual, the prisoners were dressed in white blouses and peasant caps (their burial shrouds) and offered a final opportunity to repent and confess before a priest.

When that was finished, the first three men in one row were taken and bound to the stakes with the hoods of their caps pulled down over their eyes. Dostoevsky was in the next group of three and had to stand, watch, and listen as the drum roll signaled the impending volley from the firing squad. This period of unbearable uncertainty lasted only for a minute but seemed to go on forever; it was, according to one of the prisoners, a "terrible, repulsive, frightening" experience. Then suddenly, the drum roll began beating retreat, and as an ex-Army officer, Dostoevsky realized his life had been spared. Within minutes, his sentence was read — four years in Siberia — and within three days, he was sent into exile.[33]

Years later, Dostoevsky offered a thinly veiled fictional account of this trauma in *The Idiot.* Early in that novel, Prince Myshkin relates what "a certain man" had told him a year earlier about his harrowing experience. Knowing that he had only five minutes to live, the man quickly discovered that it "seemed to him that in those five minutes he would live so many lives that there was no point yet in thinking about his last

33. For my account of Dostoevsky's arrest, trial, and mock execution, I am indebted to Joseph Frank, *Dostoevsky: The Years of Ordeal, 1850-1859* (Princeton: Princeton University Press, 1983), pp. 32-66.

moment, so that he even made various arrangements." He set aside two minutes to bid farewell to his comrades, two minutes for self-reflection, and a final minute to take in his surroundings. At that moment, sunlight glancing off the golden dome of a nearby cathedral caught his eye:

> It seemed to him that those rays were his new nature and in three minutes he would somehow merge with them. . . . The ignorance of and loathing for this new thing that would be and would come presently were terrible; yet he said that nothing was more oppressive for him at that moment than the constant thought: "What if I were not to die! What if life were given back to me — what infinity! And it would all be mine! . . ." He said that in the end this thought turned into such anger in him that he wished they would hurry up and shoot him.[34]

One of the men condemned to die along with Dostoevsky that day later reported that as the moment of execution approached, "Dostoevsky was quite excited, he recalled *Le dernier jour d'un condamné* [*The Last Day of a Condemned Man*] of Victor Hugo, and, going up to Speshnev, said 'Nous serons avec le Christ' [We shall be with Christ]. 'Un peu de poussière' [A bit of dust] — the latter answered with a twisted smile."[35] Joseph Frank says of this exchange and of the passage from *The Idiot* that they reveal in Dostoevsky "an attitude of uncertainty rather than one of either conviction or resignation." He clearly believed in "some sort of immortality," but was uncertain enough in this belief that his fear "came from the possibility that *no* such 'new life' waited beyond the grave." The contrast is striking between Dostoevsky's "tormented and uncertain faith — tortured by fear" yet clinging to the promises of Christ, on the one hand, and the stoicism of Speshnev, "ruefully accepting that after death he would be nothing but dust," on the other. It was precisely because he could not help believing in some form of eternal life that Dostoevsky was tormented by his inability to rest in an unambiguous assurance of immortality.[36]

Shortly after he was released from prison, Dostoevsky explained the influence of his near-death experience and imprisonment on his evolv-

34. Fyodor Dostoevsky, *The Idiot*, trans. Richard Pevear and Larissa Volokhonsky (New York: Knopf, 2002), pp. 60-61.

35. F. N. Lvov, quoted in Frank, *Dostoevsky: Years*, p. 58.

36. Frank, *Dostoevsky: Years*, pp. 57-58.

ing religious creed. He did so in a letter to Natalya Fonvizina, a Russian woman who had given him a copy of the New Testament just before his four-year exile began. This famous passage places Dostoevsky squarely at the center of the nineteenth-century discovery of unbelief and the subsequent efforts to believe again:

> I will tell you that I am a child of the century, a child of disbelief and doubt, I am that today and (I know it) will remain so until the grave. How much terrible torture this thirst for faith has cost me and costs me even now, which is all the stronger in my soul the more arguments I can find against it. And yet, God sends me sometimes instants when I am completely calm; at those instants I love and I feel loved by others, and it is at these instants that I have shaped for myself a *Credo* where everything is clear and sacred for me. This *Credo* is very simple, here it is: to believe that nothing is more beautiful, profound, sympathetic, reasonable, manly, and more perfect than Christ; and I tell myself with a jealous love not only that there is nothing but that there cannot be anything. Even more, if someone proved to me that Christ is outside the truth, and that *in reality* the truth were outside of Christ, then I should prefer to remain with Christ rather than with the truth.[37]

When Dostoevsky reentered Russian society after his imprisonment, he once again became embroiled in the intellectual and religious disputes sweeping through the culture. Yet he had moved far away from the radical and quasi-socialist positions of the Petrashevsky Circle, and as is so often the case, he became as a convert a relentless critic of the very beliefs he had so recently espoused. In particular, Dostoevsky found himself taken up with the question of *nihilism* as the writers of the 1860s and 1870s were posing it. For the Russian intellectuals of that period, James Billington explains, nihilism was an exercise in political consciousness

37. Fyodor Dostoevsky, quoted in Frank, *Dostoevsky: Years*, p. 160. For an illuminating comparative study, see Richard Gill, "*The Rime of the Ancient Mariner* and *Crime and Punishment:* Existential Parables," *Philosophy and Literature* 5 (1981): 131-49. Gill says both Coleridge and Dostoevsky "acknowledge the impossibility of intellectual certitude in matters of ultimate belief" and thus "remain susceptible to the anguish of doubt." They "both display a remarkable openness and even fascination with opposition and contradiction; where their coreligionists might strive for the comfort of settled beliefs, both gave the rationalist adversary his due, to the point of admitting him within the gates" (p. 145). In this, they distinctly resemble Dickinson and Melville, among others.

rather than an expression of spiritual despair. In contrast to their counterparts in France and Germany, the Russian radicals had not experienced the failure of a revolution, and a mood of intense hope and heightened expectation saturated the culture at the very time that Dostoevsky was setting out on his novel-writing career. Through their pursuit of nothingness and the practice of destruction, the radicals sought to transform their social order and remake their history. They passionately desired to possess "some scientific, secular set of beliefs about history and social change that purported to universal validity." So it was that "the nihilist became the intelligent. He had moved from iconoclasm to ideology."[38]

Where his radical contemporaries anticipated a day of renewal after a night of destruction, Dostoevsky could spot nothing but darkness in the nihilistic dawn. He dealt with this subject in *Demons* in the early 1870s, but that book did little to calm his fears about the damaging power of persistent unbelief. As a result, he came to the writing of *The Brothers Karamazov* still filled with anxiety concerning the destructive power of nihilism over Russian culture and the Russian family. Dostoevsky took the collapse of the family structure in particular to be the symptom of a deeper catastrophic loss of established values that had resulted from the sudden decline, among the educated, of faith in God and in Jesus Christ. In *The Brothers Karamazov,* the novelist set out to reaffirm explicitly Christian values by demonstrating "their linkage to the supernatural presuppositions of the Christian faith, which for Dostoevsky offered their only secure support."[39]

He singled out philosophical rationalism and scientific materialism as primary sources of unbelief, and to combat them, he promoted Christ as the mysterious, irrational alternative. At this point in his life, the novelist did not consider faith to be the reasonable "substance of things hoped for, the evidence of things not seen" (Hebrews 11:1, King James Version). Instead, he took it to be the nonrational core of belief that reason could not touch. Christ was one power, reason another, and the two could neither meet nor be reconciled. This sharp division illuminated

38. James Billington, *Fire in the Minds of Men: Origins of the Revolutionary Faith* (1980; repr., New Brunswick, N.J.: Transaction, 1999), pp. 390-91, 401.

39. Joseph Frank, *Dostoevsky: The Mantle of the Prophet, 1871-1881* (Princeton: Princeton University Press, 2002), p. 570.

Dostoevsky's thought to the end of his life, as well as the action and ideas on every page of *The Brothers Karamazov.* That novel's central theme is "the conflict between reason and faith," with faith seen as the nonrational or suprarational heart of Christian belief and practice.[40]

It is the genius of *The Brothers Karamazov,* however, not to represent the conflict between faith and reason — or between belief and unbelief — primarily as an epic struggle between great forces arrayed outside the self. Instead Dostoevsky situated the conflict of interpretations and the contest of belief where Melville, Dickinson, and others had come in recent decades to house it: within the human mind and heart. In the novel, the eldest of the Karamazov sons, Dmitri, frames the clash of forces and values in terms reminiscent of our discussion of "nimble believing." "I can't bear it," Dmitri tells his brother Alyosha, "that some man, even with a lofty heart and the highest mind, should start from the ideal of the Madonna and end with the ideal of Sodom." He finds it even "more fearful" that "someone who already has the ideal of Sodom in his soul does not deny the ideal of the Madonna either, and his heart burns with it, verily, verily burns, as in his young, blameless years." The problem is that men and women have an internal range that is too vast for their own good. "No, man is broad," Dmitri complains, "even too broad, I would narrow him down." He realizes that "what's shame for the mind is beauty all over for the heart. . . . Here the devil is struggling with God, and the battlefield is the human heart."[41]

For each main character in *The Brothers Karamazov* — including the three brothers, their father, and the Russian Orthodox Elder, Father Zosima — this raging heart is the burden he must bear, the battle he must endure. The conflict between belief and unbelief lacerates each of them in its own way and in its own time. Its torments prove especially intense for Ivan, the brother who rejects God and the idea of good and evil, even as he strives to bring an end to the suffering of innocent children.

40. Frank, *Dostoevsky: Mantle,* p. 570.

41. Fyodor Dostoevsky, *The Brothers Karamazov,* trans. Richard Pevear and Larissa Volokhonsky (1990; repr., New York: Farrar, 2002), p. 108. The inner divisions of the human person serve as a constant theme in much of modern literature, philosophy, and theology. Reinhold Niebuhr constructed an entire theological system on the shaky foundation of self-conscious awareness: "This essential homelessness of the human spirit is the ground of all religion." *The Nature and Destiny of Man: A Christian Interpretation,* vol. 1, *Human Nature* (1941; repr., New York: Scribner, 1943), p. 14. See esp. pp. 12-25.

When introduced to Ivan, Father Zosima asks him, "Can it be that you really hold this conviction about the consequences of the exhaustion of men's faith in the immortality of their souls?" Ivan admits that he believes there can be no virtue without immortality, and to this Zosima replies that Ivan must be "most unhappy," because "in all likelihood you yourself do not believe either in the immortality of your soul or even in what you have written about the Church. . . . For the time being you, too, are toying, out of despair, with your magazine articles and drawing-room discussions, without believing in your own dialectics and smirking at them with your heart aching inside you." Zosima correctly senses that this inner turmoil has exhausted Ivan. "The question is not resolved in you," the Elder tells him, "and there lies your great grief, for it urgently demands resolution."[42]

Ivan seeks to resolve his dilemma by rejecting God's created order. He calls this "returning the ticket" of salvation, which would have gained him entry into heaven and its eternal harmony. If accepting that "ticket" requires one also to embrace the moral standards that govern a world in which the innocent are permitted to suffer hideous pain and cruelty, then Ivan will have nothing of it. He believes that by rejecting creation, he will drive himself and others to build a more just world, one in which innocent children will no longer endure brutal suffering. "It's not God that I do not accept, you understand, it is this world of God's, created by God, that I do not accept and cannot agree to accept," he informs Alyosha.[43] In the words of Diane Thompson, Ivan has arrived "from an intellectual milieu (the university and journalism) where . . . Christianity is under attack from atheism in alliance with the rapid rise of science

42. Dostoevsky, *Brothers Karamazov,* p. 70.

43. Dostoevsky, *Brothers Karamazov,* pp. 245, 235. Several years before he began *The Brothers Karamazov,* Dostoevsky wrote a sketch of Vissarion Belinsky, an influential radical whom he had known years before. Elements of Ivan's character and arguments can be found in this portrait, which describes Belinsky's belief that the burden of Christianity — of Christ — had to be lifted, before men and women could be free to create a moral world. Belinsky, reports Dostoevsky, "'screeched one evening' that man was too weak to bear the burden of moral responsibility imposed on him by Christ. 'Do you know that man's sins cannot be counted against him and that he cannot be laden down with obligations and with turning the other cheek when society is set up in such a foul fashion that a man cannot help but do wrong; economic factors alone lead him to do wrong, and it is absurd and cruel to demand from a man something which the very laws of nature make it impossible for him to carry out, even if he wanted to.'" Frank, *Dostoevsky: Mantle,* pp. 90-91.

and the new ideas of socialism and positivism." Attracted to elements of the Christian hope but repulsed by the tenets of orthodox theology, he seeks nothing less than to have "the Christian memory . . . deliberately destroyed, 'wiped out of mind' by a regime of compulsory collective amnesia."[44] Consign the memory of God to cultural oblivion, he wagers, and you will have rid yourself and the culture of interpretive confusion and of the riddling ambiguities of belief.

What Ivan treats with deadly seriousness, his father, Fyodor Karamazov, approaches with sarcasm, as evidenced by the curious religious cross-examination he administers to his sons one evening.

> "But still, tell me: is there a God or not? But seriously. I want to be serious now."
>
> "No, there is no God."
>
> "Alyosha, is there a God?"
>
> "There is."
>
> "And is there immortality, Ivan? At least some kind, at least a little, a teeny-tiny one?"
>
> "There is no immortality either."
>
> "Not of any kind?"
>
> "Not of any kind."
>
> "Complete zero? Or is there something? Maybe there's some kind of something? At least not nothing?"
>
> "Complete zero."
>
> "Alyosha, is there immortality?"
>
> "There is."
>
> "Both God and immortality?"
>
> "Both God and immortality. Immortality is in God."
>
> "Hm. More likely Ivan is right. Lord, just think how much faith, how much energy of all kinds man has spent on this dream, and for so many thousands of years! Who could be laughing at man like that? Ivan? For the last time, definitely: is there a God or not? It's the last time I'll ask."
>
> "For the last time — no."
>
> "Then who is laughing at mankind, Ivan?"
>
> "Must be the devil," Ivan smirked.

44. Diane Oenning Thompson, *The Brothers Karamazov and the Poetics of Memory* (Cambridge: Cambridge University Press, 1991), p. 186.

"And is there a devil?"
"No, there is no devil, either."[45]

In what she calls this "carnivalised catechism," Thompson sees Ivan working towards a goal of the "final annihilation" of the memory of God by means of an "absolute denial which can serve as its philosophical foundation."[46] This denial surfaces overtly in Ivan's declaration that since God does not exist, "everything is permitted," which is his way of claiming that a Hobbesian "war of all against all" rages in the conflict of interpretations as it does elsewhere in life. Albert Camus argues that "with this 'everything is permitted' the history of contemporary nihilism really begins."[47]

Viewed another way, however, Ivan's claim looks less like a radical beginning in modern thought than a plausible destination reached near the journey's end. Ivan Karamazov's interpretive radicalism reads like a late scene in a drama of many acts, with the cycle of revolution and reaction that began in France in 1789 at the center of that drama. According to Isaiah Berlin, the French Revolution hastened the pace of changes that had already begun to transform a two-thousand-year-old view of reality. According to this view, "there existed an unalterable structure of reality," and great men and women were those "who understood it correctly either in their theory or their practice." To be great — to pursue the good, the true, and the beautiful — meant "getting the answer right" to the question posed to every one of us by that reality.[48]

By the beginning of the nineteenth century, however, "the criterion of greatness" no longer involved providing the right answers to life's questions. Instead, it now had to do with putting nature itself to the question. In the romantic period, Berlin explains, the hero was "no longer the discoverer . . . but the creator," for "in the life of the spirit there were no objective principles or values — they were made so by a resolve of the will which shaped a man's or a people's world and its norms; action determined thought, not vice versa." What Berlin calls "the attack upon the

45. Dostoevsky, *Brothers Karamazov,* p. 134.

46. Thompson, *Brothers Karamazov and Poetics,* p. 187.

47. Albert Camus, *The Rebel: An Essay on Man in Revolt,* trans. Anthony Bower (1956; repr., New York: Vintage, 1991), p. 57.

48. Isaiah Berlin, *The Crooked Timber of Humanity: Chapters in the History of Ideas,* ed. Henry Hardy (1990; repr., Princeton: Princeton University Press, 1997), p. 231.

world of appearances" assumed many different forms in the nineteenth century. In their most extreme versions, these attacks "are not innocent flights of fancy but spring from a deranged imagination in which the will is uncontrolled and the real world proves to be a phantasmagoria."[49]

In the works of Schopenhauer, Nietzsche, and Dostoevsky, this will spawned nightmarish visions in which the world was driven by a "blind, aimless" power fiendishly at work beneath "the irrelevant surface of things." The "real world" for some nineteenth-century writers, suggests Berlin, was one "without frontiers or barriers," in which the will is supreme and absolute values clash "in irreconcilable conflict." Appearing under the guise of Fascism and Marxist-Leninism in the twentieth century, this worship of the will led to "the monstrous fallacy that life is, or can be made, a work of art, that the aesthetic model applies to politics, that the political leader is, at his highest, a sublime artist who shapes men according to this creative design." This line of thought, promoted in the late nineteenth century by Ivan Karamazov and others, produced "dangerous nonsense in theory and savage brutality in practice." With their vision of a society that would be modeled after a work of art, Ivan and others established "an ideal for which more human beings have, in our time, sacrificed themselves and others than, perhaps, for any other cause in human history."[50]

More perceptively than any other writer of the late nineteenth century, Dostoevsky saw how the "dangerous nonsense" of his day was destined to become the "savage brutality" of the age to come. As Camus admitted, Ivan Karamazov's rejection of creation required nothing less than the denial of "the basic interdependence, introduced by Christianity, between suffering and truth." Ivan must reject God's creation, even if God exists, because he refuses to accept "that truth should be paid for by evil, suffering, and the death of innocents." Of course, that means Ivan also "refuses salvation," because Christianity claims the suffering of the innocent can only be overcome through the suffering of the innocent One.[51]

In a series of articles and conversations, Ivan declares that for anyone "who believes neither in God nor his own immortality," the moral

49. Berlin, *Crooked Timber,* pp. 231, 233.

50. Berlin, *Crooked Timber,* pp. 233-34, 237.

51. Camus, *Rebel,* p. 56.

law must be spurned and its opposite embraced; "egoism, even to the point of evildoing, should not only be permitted to man but should be acknowledged as the necessary, the most reasonable, and all but the noblest result of his situation."[52] Once he decided to promote this idea, "Ivan compelled himself to do evil so as to be coherent. He would not allow himself to be good." Yet this quest for coherence tears at Ivan's soul, because the same man who trembles at the thought of a child's suffering has found himself driven to declare "the legitimacy of murder. Ivan rebels against a murderous God; but from the moment that he begins to rationalize his rebellion, he deduces the law of murder."[53] This is the conflict of interpretations as a self-lacerating force.

Diane Thompson cautions against reading Ivan solely in the light of his dreadful deduction of murder. As she says, "Ivan is not motivated by pure malice," even as he subconsciously plots his father's death. His despair is genuine, and so is his terror at the prospect of living in a world abandoned by God. The conflict that rages within him between faith and atheism "leads to a constant nagging internal dialogue which gradually splits his personality." When he conducts his "Grand Inquisitor" conversation with Alyosha, Ivan does almost all the talking, but "the tone of his 'tirade' is unmistakably dialogic," for as he speaks, his torments surface and his mind is like a barren landscape on which ideas maraud and clash without ceasing.[54]

As events in the Karamazov drama unfold, both Alyosha and Ivan must undergo spiritual crises that follow closely upon the deaths of the novel's two father figures — the spiritual father, Zosima, and the biological one, Fyodor. In the wake of Zosima's death, Alyosha moves through his initial despair to a deepened faith in Christ, while Ivan plays his role as Oedipus Rex to the end, until his internal torment compels him at last to accept his responsibility for his father's murder. *The Brothers Karamazov* concludes with Alyosha boldly affirming the resurrection and freely embracing a ministry of reconciliation, while Ivan's fate remains uncertain. As he ponders his brother's destiny, Alyosha assures himself that "God will win!" At the same time, he realizes that Ivan "will either rise into the light of truth, or . . . perish in hatred, taking revenge

52. Dostoevsky, *Brothers Karamazov,* p. 69.

53. Camus, *Rebel,* pp. 57-58.

54. Thompson, *Brothers Karamazov and Poetics,* p. 190.

on himself and everyone for having served something he does not believe in."[55]

Interpretation and the Forms of Fiction

Mikhail Bakhtin was fascinated by Dostoevsky's ability to pit radical doubt against confessional belief in his fiction. In *The Brothers Karamazov,* this meant that even as Alyosha chose "to join the chorus and proclaim with them 'Hosanna!'" the novelist permitted Ivan to resist that call and to reject that chorus. To Bakhtin, it was this willingness to grant broad ideological independence to his characters that made Dostoevsky the creator of the *polyphonic* novel, and what unfolds in "his novels is not a polyphony of reconciled voices but a polyphony of battling and internally divided voices."[56] According to Bakhtin, such a model of character development and presentation offers a creative way of engaging the conflict of interpretations, and it presents tantalizing possibilities for a Christian approach to that conflict.

Bakhtin's own relationship to Christianity remains a matter of dispute. Some claim him openly for the faith, while others see his interest in theology as one phase in a long career. Nevertheless, in the words of Gary Saul Morson and Caryl Emerson, what is unmistakable is that at times "Bakhtin's prophetic tone verges on the theological," as he "envisages Christ as the One" whose incarnation — his "live entering into the world without ever losing his divine outsidedness" — provided Bakhtin with a model for understanding Dostoevsky's creation of the polyphonic novel and its dialogic model of the truth.[57]

55. Dostoevsky, *Brothers Karamazov,* p. 655.

56. Mikhail Bakhtin, *Problems of Dostoevsky's Poetics,* trans. and ed. Caryl Emerson (Minneapolis: University of Minnesota Press, 1984), pp. 249-50.

57. Gary Saul Morson and Caryl Emerson, *Mikhail Bakhtin: Creation of a Prosaics* (Stanford: Stanford University Press, 1990), p. 61. Alexandar Mihailovic claims that "Bakhtin's transformative model of dialogue is also grounded in later christological paradigms . . . concerning the twin natures of Christ. . . ." *Corporeal Words: Mikhail Bakhtin's Theology of Discourse* (Evanston: Northwestern University Press, 1997), p. 125. Ben Quash, however, cautions against situating Bakhtin fully within the Christian tradition: "Bakhtin saw the provisional possibility of the Church representing a kind of polyphonic unity, . . . [but] he afterwards rejected the comparisons. He concluded the Church is 'too static, too

Bakhtin was convinced that through the dialogical model Dostoevsky had broken the stranglehold of *monologic* thought upon the modern mind. For several hundred years, Western thought had been ruled by what Bakhtin took to be a perverse idea, which was that truth could be contained within a single system (Newton, Hegel, Marx) or lodged securely within a single consciousness (Descartes). The monological thinker does not need to know other persons or points of view in order to complete his or her own understanding of the truth, and a monological system requires neither correction nor development, for it has already grasped the truth in its totality.

According to Bakhtin, monologism was a mode of thought poorly suited to fiction. In works written according to its dictates, ideas become objects placed in the mouths of characters who represent a fixed understanding of truth and reality. Under these conditions, the idea actually "loses its direct power to mean" and becomes "a mere aspect of reality, . . . indistinguishable from any other manifestation of the hero." So considered, the idea has no essential relationship to the person who expresses it, and it could be as easily inserted into one mouth as another, just so long as it does "not jeopardize the verisimilitude of the image of him who utters it. Such an idea, in itself, belongs to *no one*" but merely expresses "the systematically monologic worldview of the author himself."[58]

The "monologic artistic world" cannot recognize the vibrant thoughts of others as fit objects for representation, because in its understanding of reality, all ideas either belong to an ensemble of convictions gathered within an author's consciousness or they are rejected thoughts that have been cast into the fictional outer darkness. In the first case, when the author approves of the ideas, the validated thoughts "strive to shape themselves in the purely semantic unity of a worldview" that is meant to be affirmed in a particular novel. The rejected thoughts, which are "untrue or indifferent from the author's point of view," end up being "either polemically repudiated, or else they lose their power to signify directly and become simple elements of characterization, the mental ges-

closed . . . and too easy to conflate into an ideological and monologic unity.'" "Real Enactment: The Role of Drama in the Theology of Hans Urs von Balthasar," in *Faithful Performances: Enacting Christian Tradition*, ed. Trevor A. Hart and Steven R. Guthrie (Aldershot, England: Ashgate, 2007), p. 27. See also Susan M. Felch and Paul J. Contino, eds., *Bakhtin and Religion: A Feeling for Faith* (Evanston: Northwestern University Press, 2001).

58. Bakhtin, *Problems*, p. 79.

tures of the hero or his more stable mental qualities." This means that "in the monologic world, *tertium non datur* [there is no third way]: a thought is either affirmed or repudiated; otherwise it simply ceases to be a fully valid thought."[59] There is no place for nimble believing in a monologic world, and no character or author is compelled to endure the conflict of interpretations.

The monologic principle found a congenial home in the philosophical idealism that dominated thought from the early seventeenth century to the early nineteenth. Here the "affirmation of the unity of *existence*" is "transformed into the unity of the *consciousness*." According to Bakhtin, idealism takes consciousness in general to be the place where truth resides, while individualized consciousness, or the experience of the single person, can only be considered to be a site of error. The personal point of view is taken to be an aberration or an instance of fallible thought, for "from the point of view of truth there are no individual consciousnesses. Idealism recognizes only one principle of cognitive individualization: *error*." For the monologic point of view, truth abides solely in the unity of consciousness; "there is no need for a multitude of consciousnesses, and no basis for it."[60]

By the time Dostoevsky began writing novels in the late nineteenth century, monologism had permeated every area of modern thought, having been promoted for several hundred years by "European rationalism, with its cult of a unified and exclusive reason, and especially by the Enlightenment." Bakhtin notes that during the Enlightenment "the basic generic forms of European artistic prose" — including the novel — "took shape. All of European utopianism was likewise built on this monologic principle," as was "socialism, with its faith in the omnipotence of the conviction. Semantic unity of any sort is everywhere represented by a single consciousness and a single point of view." This faith in the sufficiency of the "single consciousness" is the "profound structural characteristic" of modern intellectual and artistic life.[61]

Although Bakhtin does not make the explicit connection, there are

59. Bakhtin, *Problems,* pp. 79-80.

60. Bakhtin, *Problems,* pp. 80-81. Gary Saul Morson and Caryl Emerson speak of Bakhtin as having "rejected the Hobson's choices of modern thought: either there is a system or there is nothing; either there are comprehensive closed structures or there is chaos." *Mikhail Bakhtin,* p. 233.

61. Bakhtin, *Problems,* p. 82.

clear links between what he calls monologism and the Christian heresy of Docetism, which denied the humanity of Christ and sought to protect his divinity by claiming that in the incarnation God effectively borrowed a human body to house the spirit of his Son. The agony in the Garden of Gethsemane, the suffering on the cross, the cry of dereliction — "My God, my God, why hast thou forsaken me?" — these were the experiences of the human Jesus and not the sufferings of the divine Christ. For the Docetists, the Son of God never truly enters into our embodied world, but stands as a soul apart, gazing upon our hostile environment but never sharing fully in its sorrows or its joys.

In like manner, in what Helmut Thielicke terms the "anthropological Docetism" of modernity, a similar truth holds for human consciousness in its encounter with the disenchanted cosmos. Beginning in the late nineteenth century, he argues, an increasing number of people began to consider the external world as a hostile and restrictive environment. The world about us is "the sphere of the technically useful," but it is also "a meaningless reality," and in contrast to the "unconditional radiance of authentic existence," the natural order becomes a "dark foil which sets in relief the burning light of existence."[62]

In docetic views of Christ and the human condition, the eternal remains perfect because it never truly indwells a mortal form. The docetic Christ is not Jesus, who was born of Mary and suffered under Pontius Pilate but, instead, a God who used the human form without making it his own and who only appeared to share our experience, even our sorrow and suffering. In Bakhtin's terms, the docetic world is a monologic one, for its God is a single entity, a lonely Unitarian master distant and detached from the world. In denying the humanity of Christ, Docetism is also denying, in the words of Karl Barth, "that the Word of God did actually become a real man and that therefore the life of this real man was the object and theatre of the acts of God, the light of revelation entering the world."[63]

Bakhtin flatly rejects the monologic view that the truth must be a

62. Helmut Thielicke, *The Evangelical Faith,* vol. 1, *Prolegomena: The Relation of Theology to Modern Thought Forms,* trans. and ed. Geoffrey W. Bromiley (Grand Rapids: Eerdmans, 1974), p. 384.

63. Karl Barth, *Church Dogmatics,* ed. G. W. Bromiley and T. F. Torrance (Edinburgh: T. & T. Clark, 1956-62), I.2.147.

unified (or Unitarian) entity that can be retained within a single consciousness:

> It should be pointed out that the single and unified consciousness is by no means an inevitable consequence of the concept of a unified truth. It is quite possible to imagine and postulate a unified truth that requires a plurality of consciousnesses, one that cannot in principle be fitted into the bounds of a single consciousness, one that is, so to speak, by its very nature *full of event potential* and is born at a point of contact among various consciousnesses. The monologic way of perceiving cognition and truth is only one of the possible ways. It arises only where consciousness is placed above existence, and where the unity of existence is transformed into the unity of consciousness.[64]

In the monologic scheme of things, such "interaction of consciousnesses" and "genuine dialogue" are impossible. They can become viable realities only when the plurality of human voices, as well as the internal divisions of the individual consciousness, are no longer seen as roadblocks to the truth but as avenues to it. In the closing sentence of the Dostoevsky book, Bakhtin issues a call to aesthetic renewal that might also serve as a cry for theoretical and theological reform: "We must renounce our monologic habits so that we might come to feel at home in the new artistic sphere which Dostoevsky discovered, so that we might orient ourselves in that incomparably more complex *artistic model of the world* which he created."[65]

64. Bakhtin, *Problems,* p. 81. For a practical sense of what Bakhtin means by "the unity of existence," we might consider what Erich Auerbach says about figural interpretation. Such interpretation incorporates within a single narrative events that are temporally distant and seemingly unrelated. It "establishes a connection between two events or persons in such a way that the first signifies not only itself but also the second, while the second involves or fulfills the first. The two poles of a figure are separated in time, but both, being real events or persons, are within temporality. They are both contained in the flowing stream which is historical life, and only the comprehension, the *intellectus spiritualis,* of their interdependence is a spiritual act." *Mimesis: The Representation of Reality in Western Literature,* trans. Willard R. Trask (Princeton: Princeton University Press, 1953), p. 73. As Hans Frei argued persuasively in *The Eclipse of Biblical Narrative,* until the eighteenth century, the biblical narrative was considered to be perfectly capable of encompassing *the unity of existence.* With that narrative unifying life, there was no need for consciousness to seek or claim to do so.

65. Bakhtin, *Problems,* p. 272.

What exactly is to be discovered at the heart of the "complex artistic model of the world" that Bakhtin credits Dostoevsky with having created? It is the *polyphonic* model of discourse. This term has had a complex history over the past several decades of theoretical reflection, and Bakhtin never put forward a comprehensive definition of it. Perhaps his fullest explanation appears in the opening pages of *Problems of Dostoevsky's Poetics: "A plurality of independent and unmerged voices and consciousnesses, a genuine polyphony of fully valid voices is in fact the chief characteristic of Dostoevsky's novels."* Instead of a "single authorial consciousness," Dostoevsky presents us with a world peopled by a *"plurality of consciousnesses, with equal rights and each with its own world."* The heroes of his fiction are not only objects of the author's discourse; they are also *"subjects of their own directly signifying discourse."*[66] In a traditional model of novelistic discourse, the power to mean belongs to the author alone, but in a polyphonic novel, multiple voices share and exercise this power. "By surrendering his monologic powers," Gary Saul Morson and Caryl Emerson claim in their study of Bakhtin, "Dostoevsky created a way to embody a dialogic conception of truth."[67]

Morson and Emerson point out that Bakhtin saw a vast difference between a truth that is irreconcilably contradictory and one that merely "requires two or more voices" for its articulation. Bakhtin's point is decidedly not the Nietzschean claim that "truths are illusions about which one has forgotten that this is what they are."[68] Instead of arguing that all truth claims are interpretations and all interpretations lies, Bakhtin is claiming that to know the truth we must hear it proclaimed and tested among a potential multitude of voices. In the case of *The Brothers Karamazov,* this means that while Dostoevsky calls Alyosha his hero, he refuses to close off the powerful opposing discourse of Ivan. By allowing Ivan's arguments to develop with considerable force, Dostoevsky deliberately places himself and his readers at risk. "Dostoevsky's novels are designed to turn readers not into analyzers of character, action, and circumstance, but into dialogic partners of the characters and author," and

66. Bakhtin, *Problems,* pp. 6-7.

67. Morson and Emerson, *Mikhail Bakhtin,* p. 239.

68. Friedrich Nietzsche, "On Truth and Lie in an Extra-Moral Sense," in *The Portable Nietzsche,* trans. and ed. Walter Kaufmann (1954; repr., New York: Penguin, 1976), p. 47.

in a genuine conversation, no single participant can control its direction or its outcome.[69]

This is an intriguing model for a Christian view of literature at a time when the idea of the artist as a creator *ex nihilo* appears to be as culturally exhausted as it is theologically suspect. What would the act of writing look like, if we traded images of godlike power for models of freely-chosen suffering? A particular strength of nineteenth-century thought was its emphasis on the validating power of freedom. If God has taken the risk of creating free creatures, might not Christian artists follow Dostoevsky's lead and champion the freedom of their own creations? Colin Gunton suggests as much when he asks us to consider God's relationship to the world to be "that of an author or playwright" who writes the story but does so in such a manner as "to allow the characters to develop according to its and their intrinsic logic."[70] Hans Urs von Balthasar developed his entire theological project out of this metaphor of the theater, as he explored the mystery of human freedom in the divine drama:

> Theologically speaking, the only thing that makes it possible to have history, in the deepest sense, within the space thus opened up is the fact that this space is an opening within the utter freedom of God (what could be more free, more completely unconditioned and grace-given, than the plan of the Incarnation and its accomplishment?); and hence that it is itself an area of freedom: freedom of God giving space and scope to the freedom of man. Within this space man is free to make history happen. But since this space belongs to Christ, it is in no sense an empty space but one that is shaped and structured and completely conditioned by certain categories. . . . Man cannot fall out of this space which is Christ's, nor out of the structural form created by his life. This is indeed the 'prison' in which God has shut up all in 'their rebellion, only to include them all in his pardon' (Rom 11:32). . . . Each situation in the divine-human life is so infinitely rich, capable of such unlimited application, so full of meaning, that it generates an inexhaustible abundance of Christian situations.[71]

69. Morson and Emerson, *Mikhail Bakhtin,* p. 249.

70. Colin E. Gunton, *The Christian Faith: An Introduction to Christian Doctrine* (Malden, Mass.: Blackwell, 2002), p. 64.

71. Hans Urs von Balthasar, *A Theology of History* (1963; repr., San Francisco: Ignatius, 1994), pp. 70-71. Kevin Vanhoozer makes the helpful connection between Bakhtin's

In the notes he compiled for a possible revision of the Dostoevsky book, Bakhtin drew parallels between the freedom characters enjoy in a polyphonic novel and our freedom as creatures who live in God's world and play parts in the divine drama. In establishing himself as one actor in a larger drama, Dostoevsky was not seeking to serve as a passive agent who merely reports the views of others. An author of this kind would be nothing but a pale copy of the deistic God who had been benignly gazing down upon the educated elites of the eighteenth and nineteenth centuries. Dostoevsky had no interest in such a god, nor as a writer did he wish to be patterned after him.

Instead, according to Bakhtin, Dostoevsky considered the novelist to be "profoundly active" in a "special *dialogic*" manner. The monologic author is "active in relation to a dead thing," which is the voiceless material he or she assigns to a character. The polyphonic author, on the other hand, is, like God, "active *in relation to someone else's living, autonomous consciousness*." In engaging his own characters, the author undertakes "a questioning, provoking, answering, agreeing, objecting activity." To press his case, "Dostoevsky frequently interrupts, but he never drowns out the other's voice, never finishes it off 'from himself.'" In following this course, the polyphonic author imitates the God of the Hebrew Bible and the New Testament:

> This is, so to speak, the activity of God in His relation to man, a relation allowing man to reveal himself utterly (in his immanent development), to judge himself, to refute himself. This is activity of a higher quality. It surmounts not the resistance of dead material, but the resistance of another's consciousness, another's truth.

Because it is rooted in the integral otherness of God and humanity, this dialogic struggle is open-ended and unfinalizable. "In its structure Job's dialogue is internally endless," explains Bakhtin, "for the opposition of the soul to God — whether the opposition be hostile or humble — is conceived in it as something irrevocable and eternal."[72]

---

dialogic view and Balthasar's metaphor of drama: "Bakhtin himself works with a dialogic view in which truth emerges from the conversation between different voices. But this is precisely what happens in a play. . . . The essence of drama is *dialogical action*." *Drama of Doctrine*, p. 270.

72. Bakhtin, *Problems*, pp. 285-86, 280.

As fruitful as Bakhtin's concept of the polyphonic novel may prove to be for Christian thinking about interpretation, these passages also expose its limitations. Like most conversational models of the truth that have emerged in recent decades, Bakhtin's model extols conversation without end as a cultural ideal. To be sure, Balthasar argues, the Christian faith provides ample support for the model of dialogue, because at the center of the biblical revelation "lies the Covenant between God and man." That covenant is a story of freedom, human as well as divine. It encompasses both our capacity to answer the call of God and our freedom to spurn it. There is an absurdity in saying "No" to the truth, Balthasar acknowledges, "but God prefers to accept this absurdity rather than overwhelm his creature from the outside." He chose instead to woo those creatures from the inside, through the sacrifice and sorrow of the Word made flesh. In Balthasar's words, the incarnation "opens up the perspective on both sides: on the one hand, it reveals the primal dialogue in God himself" and "puts the internal human dialogue of mankind in an entirely new light." This conversation is *about* something, and it has a definite *end* in sight.[73]

There are, then, limits to the language and practice of dialogue. If, in Bakhtin's words, that dialogue is "internally endless" and the struggle between God and humankind is "irrevocable and eternal," is there any place for hope in such a model of conversation? Balthasar reminds us that Christian hope is something more than a historical horizon "simply open to the future, according to which world history is hastening toward the 'happy end' of a gradually emerging Kingdom of God." Instead, he argues, a Christian view of dialogue and interpretation recognizes that the world must fully pass "through the mystery of death and resurrection" in order to reach the "absolute" goal "beyond this death." In the end, "dialogue can achieve something when both partners are looking in the same direction. It can fail when the horizons prove to have no common ground at any point."[74]

When such shared horizons disappeared in the late nineteenth century, the "soul's opposition to God" became a poignant activity. How do we struggle with a foe who has vanished and left us nothing but a

73. Hans Urs von Balthasar, *Theo-Drama: Theological Dramatic Theory,* vol. 1, *Prolegomena,* trans. Graham Harrison (San Francisco: Ignatius, 1988), p. 34.

74. Balthasar, *Theo-Drama,* pp. 36-37.

shadow to spar with? Some, like Emily Dickinson, could not resist the opportunity to grapple with the "long shadow — on the Lawn" cast by the setting "Sun" (#487). Weeks before she died, the poet told a friend that she continued to wrestle with God, even in his absence: "Audacity of Bliss, said Jacob to the Angel 'I will not let thee go except I bless thee' — Pugilist and Poet, Jacob was correct — ."[75]

Melville, Dostoevsky, and Dickinson knew that in their own lifetimes the theological ground had shifted beneath their feet. They understood that the emergence of open unbelief called for a new kind of nimble believing. Of the three writers we have dealt with in depth in this chapter, Melville found that new model of belief most daunting, and he wearied of the pursuit more readily than Dostoevsky or Dickinson did. For them, the affirmations were stronger than for Melville, but the doubts remained as well.

In their works, Melville, Dickinson, and Dostoevsky haltingly imagined how the "opposition of the soul to God" would call forth new and dynamic approaches to theological belief and interpretive practice; in the twentieth century these approaches were to include everything from an unprecedented interest in divine suffering to a renewed emphasis upon God as the one who is Wholly Other. However partially and in however preliminary a fashion, these nineteenth-century writers recognized that from that point forward, the experience of belief would of necessity include within itself a correlative possibility of unbelief. They understood that the way to truth would be through the dialogical struggle of the conflict of interpretations, through the soul's sometimes hostile, sometimes humble opposition to itself and to God.

75. Dickinson, *Letters,* 3:903.

CHAPTER 5

Reading

SPEAK OF THE art of *interpretation,* and you are likely to have the word *reading* in mind. In everyday conversation, we often refer to "getting a read" on someone's motives, we strain to "read" the body language of a colleague, or we ask a friend how she "reads" a difficult situation. According to the Oxford English Dictionary, such uses date back to as early as the ninth century. Long before "to read" came to mean "to scan something written with understanding," our Anglo-Saxon ancestors were already reading, as they "interpreted and discerned" the details of their lives, "discovered the meaning" of their dreams, and "reckoned" the value of their possessions.

Yet despite the wide range of reference this word has, when we in the modern world step back from our common usage and consider reading as a practice, we almost always have in mind a single activity, that being the silent scanning of the printed page. And when we ponder this activity, more often than not, our thoughts are troubled. Every few months, it seems, we learn of a new study decrying "Reading at Risk," or we hear of a speech predicting an apocalyptic future for the printed page.

For example, in the fall of 2005, former Vice President Al Gore delivered a major address that touched upon this subject and sounded the customary notes of alarm. The speech began ominously — "I believe that American democracy is in grave danger" — and it went on to cite a decline in reading as a simultaneous cause and consequence of the crisis. Gore spoke of "the sudden explosion of literacy and knowledge after Gutenberg's disruptive invention" of the printing press, which he credited with having ushered in the "Rule of Reason" in Western life. But now "newspapers are hemorrhaging readers," and "reading itself is in sharp decline, not only in our country but in most of the world. The Republic of Letters has been invaded and occupied by television."[1]

The Gore speech echoed findings that had been published to considerable fanfare a year earlier, and here again, the news had been reported to be uniformly bad. In the first sentence of its account of "Reading at Risk," the *New York Times* described America as "caught in a tide of indifference when it comes to literature." The "sobering profile" offered by the National Endowment for the Arts study "describes a precipitous downward trend in book consumption by Americans."[2] This news story was followed days later by a column lamenting the "crisis in reading," which Andrew Solomon then linked to a series of other crises in American public life. The "crisis in national health" has to do with rising "rates of depression" and "escalating levels of Alzheimer's disease" that have followed upon reading's decline; the "retreat from civic to virtual life" has created a parallel "crisis in national politics"; and all of these difficulties point to a grave, ongoing "crisis in national education." The art of reading is "the essence of civilization," and by Solomon's account, the barbarians already have stormed past the library's gates and shredded their way through its stacks.[3]

An observation Dietrich Bonhoeffer once made in a vastly different context may be pertinent to these jeremiads about the fate of reading. In a letter sent from prison in 1944, the German Lutheran pastor first mentioned "religionless Christianity," a theme that was to loom large in his later letters as well as in the theology of the postwar world. Bonhoeffer explained to Eberhard Bethge that he wished to discover whether "religion" per se had a future. Would it survive in anything like its present form? For two thousand years, Christian preaching and theology have rested "on the 'religious *a priori*' of mankind," he noted. "'Christianity' has always been a form — perhaps the true form — of 'religion.'" But

1. Al Gore, "Text of Gore Speech at Media Conference," New York City, October 5, 2005, http://www.breitbart.com/news/2005/10/06/D8D2IU703.html. The vice president's speech eventually became part of his bestselling book *The Assault on Reason* (New York: Penguin, 2007).

2. Bruce Weber, "Fewer Noses Stuck in Books in America, Survey Finds," *New York Times,* July 8, 2004.

3. Andrew Solomon, "The Closing of the American Book," *New York Times,* July 10, 2004.

what if it turns out that there is no such thing as the timeless entity we have come to know as "religion"? What if we discover that religion was "a historically conditioned and transient form of human self-expression?" If that proves to be the case, then the crucial question becomes a simple one of asking "what Christianity really is, or indeed who Christ really is, for us today."[4]

In like manner, in the wake of sweeping social changes and technological developments, we might wonder what reading is for us today and what it may become tomorrow. What are we to do if the age in which the silent scanning of printed texts has been central to our practices proves to have been but one phase in the long history of modernity? If there has been a decline in reading — if we no longer practice it carefully as an art or prize it highly as a cultural activity — what will be the consequences? As we think of its future, what are we to do, to paraphrase Bonhoeffer, if serious, widespread reading proves to have been a historically conditioned and transient human activity?

To ask this question is hardly to assume that reading will pass away and readers vanish, any more than in speaking of a religionless Christianity Bonhoeffer anticipated the disappearance of Christian belief and believers. Reading will survive and thrive, even if, like the church, it no longer enjoys what Stanley Hauerwas might call the Constantinian dominance it knew just a century or so ago.[5] At the same time, the questions raised by reading's decline do press us to confront the historically situated nature of all cultural activity.

In the particular case of reading, asking those questions may lead us to realize that, as Joseph Epstein says, "serious reading has always been a minority matter." By "serious reading," he means the study of those works of poetry and prose "that make the most exacting efforts to honor their subjects by treating them with the exacting complexity they deserve." In these terms, St. Paul was a serious reader, as was St. Augustine; Dante

4. Dietrich Bonhoeffer, *Letters and Papers from Prison*, enlarged ed., ed. Eberhard Bethge (New York: Collier, 1972), pp. 280, 279. In questioning "religion" as a category of human experience, Bonhoeffer followed the lead of Karl Barth, who famously wrote, "We begin by stating that religion is unbelief. It is a concern, indeed, we must say that it is the one great concern, of godless man." *Church Dogmatics*, ed. G. W. Bromiley and T. F. Torrance (Edinburgh: T. & T. Clark, 1956-62), I.2.299-300.

5. See Stanley Hauerwas and William H. Willimon, *Resident Aliens: Life in the Christian Colony* (Nashville: Abingdon, 1989).

read in this manner, and so did Dickinson. Yet as profitable as this activity is, reading has always been the passionate pursuit of the few rather than the shared delight of the many. Serious readers we will always have with us, but in small numbers. As for "Reading at Risk" and its "crises," Epstein concludes, "serious reading . . . isn't at stake here. Nothing more is going on, really, than the críse du jour, soon to be replaced by the report on eating disorders, the harmfulness of aspirin, or the drop in high-school math scores."[6]

Like Epstein, I raise these questions as a passionate believer in reading and not as a skeptic. I have an abiding faith in the potential of books and reading to transform lives, and I agree with Edmund Fuller that the printed word "gives us the extraordinary freedom to choose the intellectual company we will keep, to select those with whom, in spirit, we will walk. That is a privilege." In fact, "in the highest sense it is a duty. . . . Paraphrasing Joshua, 'Choose this day whom you will read.'"[7]

In addition, I do not look back nostalgically to the oral cultures of antiquity, nor do I gleefully await the arrival of some post-print cyberculture. As Walter Ong suggested, after having spent his career charting the transition from oral to print culture, "orality is not an ideal, and never was." To consider its positive aspects is not at all to advocate it as an ideal state, for literacy creates human possibilities that would be "unimaginable without writing" and reading. Oral cultures may agonize over the loss of their traditions, Ong notes, "but I have never encountered or heard of an oral culture that does not want to achieve literacy as soon as possible."[8]

That said, we still have good reason to wonder about the alarms being sounded in many quarters today whenever the subject of reading arises. To make sense of things here, what we need perhaps more than anything else is a sense of context. The opening section of this chapter will seek to provide one through an exploration of silent reading's history. That discussion of the past will lead, in turn, to a look at the future. As we ponder the prospects of reading, I will suggest that in thinking about this practice, we would be wise to downplay the visual metaphors

6. Joseph Epstein, "Is Reading Really at Risk?" *The Weekly Standard,* August 16-23, 2004, p. 23.

7. Edmund Fuller, "A Critic's Notes," *The Wall Street Journal,* May 5, 1987, p. 34.

8. Walter J. Ong, *Orality and Literacy: The Technologizing of the Word* (1982; repr., London: Routledge, 1988), p. 175.

that have dominated Western thought and to highlight instead the aural imagery that lies at the heart of a biblical approach to human understanding. As always, our central concerns will be with nineteenth-century contexts and contemporary consequences.

The Silent Voice of Reading

Her name was Nancy, and by the luck of the alphabetical draw, she sat beside me in the back row of Miss Marelli's class in Jackson School. By a six-year-old boy's standards, she was a nice enough girl. She had a sweet smile, a pleasant manner, and the niftiest braids in the first grade. But there was one big problem with Nancy. It was that this otherwise quiet girl whispered whenever we read from our primers, mouthing the words for each "Sally" and "Tom" and "Spot" she came across. And whenever she did that, it drove my little first-grade mind mad.

One day, when Nancy had come down with an unspecified sickness, Miss Marelli organized a field trip to visit her. We walked to her house, sang to her, chatted awhile, and stuffed ourselves with cookies before trundling back to school. As we made our way across the playground, I "told on" Nancy. "Do you know," I asked Miss Marelli in dismay, "what Nancy does when we have our silent reading time every day? She moves her lips, and she whispers the words!" I don't remember Miss Marelli's response, but whatever it was, it disappointed me, because she clearly didn't share my sense of alarm over Nancy's practices.

To me, the offense was clear and unambiguous. In whispering as she read, Nancy was breaking a taboo that ranked up there with the other great "forbiddens" of the 1950s, including the prohibition against swimming within an hour of a meal or the warning against sticking anything smaller than your elbow in your ear.[9]

When I complained about Nancy, of course, I had no idea that these

9. Marshall McLuhan provides a cultural context for my childhood sense of the silent reading taboo: "The hushing up of the reader has been a gradual process, and even the printed word did not succeed in silencing all readers. But we have tended to associate lip movements and mutterings from a reader with semi-literacy, a fact which has contributed to the American stress on a merely visual approach to reading in elementary learning." *The Gutenberg Galaxy: The Making of Typographic Man* (Toronto: University of Toronto Press, 1962), p. 83.

seemingly universal strictures against audible reading had had a beginning, nor could I imagine that they might someday come to an end. At that time and for a long time after, it would never have occurred to me that reading had a history and that its practices had changed, sometimes dramatically, over time. In turn, an ignorance about reading's history has often led me and others to confusion about its future.

George Steiner has worried about that future for more than four decades. As a case in point, in 1972, he published an essay presciently titled "After the Book?" An air of anxiety hangs over that title, which hints at the disappearance of something — the printed book — that has been a staple of cultural life for more than five centuries. What will replace the book when it disappears? It is in our nature to ask such questions, Steiner explains, and he assures us that he does not press them "in a spirit of indifferent inquiry" or "nihilistic play." On the contrary, he poses his questions about the future of the book simply "because we find ourselves in a social, psychological, technical situation" which makes such questions pertinent and inevitable.[10]

Over the years, Steiner's answers to these questions have been mixed. Like Joseph Epstein, he acknowledges that whatever else happens, serious reading will always remain a minority affair. For that reason, the ideal of a full literacy seems inapplicable "to the majority in a populist society." If we don't require everyone in this society to become a "trapeze artist," he asks, why should we demand that all citizens become serious readers? But at the same time, even though relatively few will seek to do so, Steiner says we must see to it that those who wish to learn how to read with care are given "the critical space and freedom from competing noise in which to practise their passion," for in "our fantastically noisy, distracted milieu," it is not easy to find even "minimal room for private response."[11]

As for the pressures of that "noisy milieu," Steiner described them in a book published only months before "After the Book?" appeared. "This is being written," he reports in that longer work, "in a study in a college of one of the great American universities." The walls in his room throb steadily to the sounds of amplifiers throughout the building. This wall of

10. George Steiner, *On Difficulty and Other Essays* (New York: Oxford University Press, 1978), pp. 186-87.

11. Steiner, *On Difficulty,* p. 202.

sound beats around the clock, and enveloped in its "constant throb," we are in danger of forfeiting the blessings conferred on us and our culture by centuries of silent reading and inward attentiveness. "Reading, writing, private communication, learning, previously framed with silence, now take place in a field of strident vibrato," Steiner complains. Under the onslaught of this wall of sound, the intimate qualities of reading and writing become "adulterated," and they become "vestigial modes" of an outmoded "logic" of human communication and understanding. Indeed, on every front, "a sound-culture seems to be driving back the old authority of verbal order." What will become of reading in this new "global sound-sphere"?[12]

In recent decades, many Protestants have tried to make their peace with this "sound-sphere" by welcoming it into their sanctuaries and harnessing its pulse to drive their services. We do not know what the long-term effects will be of this shift away from text-centered worship, but we have good reason to think they will be considerable, because for half a millennium Protestants have been by definition a "people of the book." For Roman Catholicism and Eastern Orthodoxy, the reading of the Bible is one aspect of a multi-faceted visual and liturgical reality, while for Protestants, historically at least, it has long been more or less the whole gem. Particularly in the flourishing evangelicalism of the North Atlantic cultures, the Bible has proven remarkably important and resilient as a shaping force. As David Lyle Jeffrey notes, for many cultures "the first written texts ever produced in their language have been a portion of the Bible. For all such cultures, the Bible becomes the founding text in their own subsequent national literature," and at times in Protestant cultures it has exercised "the force of exclusionary singularity."[13] Even if reading is not radically "at risk" as the alarmists would have it, it is worth asking what the changes already well underway may augur for a religious subculture whose roots are sunk so deeply in a single book.

Before we think about reading's future, however, we begin by considering an incident from its past. It has to do with a man who is undoubtedly, after the biblical writers themselves, the most important reader and

12. George Steiner, *In Bluebeard's Castle: Some Notes Towards the Redefinition of Culture* (New Haven: Yale University Press, 1971), pp. 115-16, 118.

13. David Lyle Jeffrey, *People of the Book: Christian Identity and Literary Culture* (Grand Rapids: Eerdmans, 1996), p. xiv.

writer in the history of the Christian faith: St. Augustine. The incident took place not long after his conversion to Christianity and his baptism by Ambrose, Bishop of Milan, in 387. The sermons of the brilliant bishop provoked the young convert. "There were questions I wanted to put to him," Augustine reported, "but I was unable to do so as fully as I wished," due to the crowds of people who came to speak with Ambrose at his lodgings. Because the bishop did "not forbid anyone access" to his rooms, Augustine and others would often sit and watch as he spent his "very scant" free time "refreshing either his body with necessary food or his mind with reading." Ambrose's method of reading seemed highly curious to Augustine, because "when he read his eyes would travel across the pages and his mind would explore the sense, but his voice and tongue were silent." Augustine and others would sit for a "long time in silence" and stare at the bishop who was himself reading in silence, "for who would have the heart to interrupt a man so engrossed?" Augustine considered a number of possible reasons for Ambrose's habit of silent reading and could only imagine, "whatever his reason, that man undoubtedly had a good one."[14]

Alberto Manguel believes that Augustine's response to Ambrose's behavior confirms how unusual it was in the early Christian era for readers to peruse the written page in silence. In fact, Manguel claims, "Ambrose's silent reading (including the remark that he *never* read aloud) is the first definite instance recorded in Western literature," and "not until the tenth century does this manner of reading become usual in the West."[15]

Whether Ambrose represents the first recorded instance of silent reading is debatable, but without question this practice did take hold

14. St. Augustine, *The Confessions,* trans. Maria Boulding, O.S.B. (1997; repr., New York: Vintage, 1998), pp. 99-100. For Augustine's relationship to Ambrose, see Peter Brown, *Augustine of Hippo: A Biography* (Berkeley: University of California Press, 1967), pp. 81-87.

15. Alberto Manguel, *A History of Reading* (1996; repr., New York: Penguin, 1997), p. 43. Over the past decade, a number of scholars have questioned whether the practice of silent reading was as rare as Manguel and others have made it out to be. The positions taken on this issue vary widely, but the consensus is that silent reading was a more common practice in antiquity than Manguel acknowledges, even if it was not the norm, as we in the modern period have assumed it to have been. See A. K. Gavrilov, "Techniques of Reading in Classical Antiquity," *Classical Quarterly* 47 (1997): 56-73; M. F. Burnyeat, "Postscript on Silent Reading," *Classical Quarterly* 47 (1997): 74-76; Paul Saenger, *Space Between Words: The Origins of Silent Reading* (Stanford: Stanford University Press, 1997); and William A. Johnson, "Toward a Sociology of Reading in Classical Antiquity," *American Journal of Philology* 121 (2000): 593-627.

and become widely established over the course of the Middle Ages. Its growth was slow, however, because there were precious few books to read and even fewer skilled persons to read them. As a result, until the sixteenth century, reading largely remained a privileged activity undertaken in isolated places, and there was no widespread need for silence as a social courtesy or practical necessity. If we look in the ancient world for silent readers where we would find them today — in modest homes, public libraries, or schools — we will find few of them.

Because ancient cultures had neither a practical need nor a theoretical justification for silent reading, until the early modern period, the act of "reading" meant "reading aloud, or even a kind of incantation."[16] In the silence of modernity, we have lost the intimate sense the ancients had of a word's meaning being bound to its sounding. Written words were meant to be pronounced, and the sound of a word contributed to its sense as much as a printed mark on a page did. The Latin phrase *scripta manent, verba volant* meant at that time the opposite of the connotation it has taken in modern usage. To us, it carries the sense, "spoken words fly away, written words remain," but originally the phrase indicated that a spoken word could soar under its own power, while written words required human breath to bring them to life. It was the reader's duty to "lend voice to the silent letters, the *scripta,* and to allow them to become, in the delicate biblical distinction, *verba,* spoken words — spirit."[17] Or in the words of the Apostle Paul, we are "ministers of a new covenant, not of letter but of spirit; for *the letter kills,* but *the Spirit gives life*" (2 Cor 3:6, emphasis added).

Whether they were written on the page or uttered through the lips, words never stopped speaking in the ancient world, for in oral cultures words are spirited agents of action; only in written cultures do they become lifeless labels attached to ideas or neutral signs pointing to things. In Hebrew, for example, the same term — *dabar* — means both word as "thing" and word as "event." Without risk, a hunter may stand before a buffalo, smell it and touch it, even taste it, just so long as the animal is dead. "But if he hears a buffalo," writes Walter Ong, "he had better watch out: something is going on." Those whom Ong calls "deeply typographic folk" — all of us who live in print and reading cultures — lose sight of the

16. McLuhan, *Gutenberg Galaxy,* p. 84.
17. Manguel, *History of Reading,* p. 45.

fact that words are primarily oral in their nature. Instead, for us, "words tend rather to be assimilated to things, 'out there' on a flat surface." We may consider words to be signs or labels, but this is something that "real, spoken words cannot be."[18]

In the centuries stretching between Ambrose and Gutenberg, the silent reading of written texts gradually became more widespread as a practice among the clerical and scholastic elites, while for those in the general culture, information continued to be transmitted largely through oral repetition and visual representation. For most people, the only "texts" to be read were the paintings, sculptures, and stained-glass windows that graced the churches and the liturgical performances that were enacted within their walls. In the words of Alberto Manguel, each week in the medieval church "people lifted their eyes to the images that adorned the church walls and later the windows, columns, pulpits, even the back of the priest's chasuble as he was saying mass . . . and [they] saw in those images myriad stories or a single, never-ending story."[19]

The Rise of Reading, the Loss of a World

It is an irony of modernity that the same technologies that swiftly dispersed and distributed this "single, never-ending story" of the gospel — the printing press and the book — also served to splinter that story into a seemingly endless array of fragments. In the early modern era, the rapid spread of literacy and the proliferation of the printed page coincided closely with the fragmentation of the Christian church and the larger culture.

One nineteenth-century observer who understood this process well was Henry Adams, a grandson and great-grandson of presidents who was himself a quintessential product of the culture of the book. If we think of Augustine as having been present, in Ambrose's rooms, at the dawn of the culture of silent reading, then Adams considered himself an ambivalent witness to its twilight decline at the end of the nineteenth century. He "felt a kinship" with Augustine, for in the words of his biographer, "living in a time of great crisis in the Roman world, feeling the

18. Ong, *Orality*, pp. 32-33.
19. Manguel, *History of Reading*, p. 107.

shock of Alaric's sack of Rome, Augustine [had] dramatized his disenchantment and revulsion in the very spirit of Adams's own *fin de siècle*."[20]

Although Adams's investment in the culture of print and silent reading had paid handsome dividends in the form of intellectual authority and acclaim, he never stopped longing for the voluble, visual world of the Middle Ages. In his study of French cathedrals, the historian concluded that even today at Chartres, "one sees her [the Virgin Mary's] personal presence on every side. Anyone can feel it who will only consent to feel like a child. Sitting here any Sunday afternoon," with "your mind held in the grasp of the strong lines and shadows of the architecture" and "your eyes flooded with the autumn tones of the glass," you could, if "you cared to look and listen, feel a sense beyond the human ready to reveal a sense divine that would make [the] world once more intelligible." Here, under Adams's nostalgic gaze, the love of the Virgin Mary shines forth in a depth of feeling "more eloquent than the prayer-book" and "more beautiful than the autumn sunlight." Even at the dawn of the twentieth century, those windows remained open to "reading . . . without end."[21]

But to Adams, the problem was that such "reading without end" belonged to a lost world whose values no longer held sway over modern life. The Virgin Mary had unified medieval culture and had given it a vision that saw divine power as personal, gracious, and loving. In the modern world, Adams argued, the Virgin has been displaced by the Dynamo, a symbol of impersonal, efficient, and indifferent force. For those whom Adams considered the great artists of the late nineteenth century, such as Augustus St. Gaudens and Matthew Arnold, the Virgin was not experienced as power but "felt . . . only as reflected emotion, human expression, beauty, purity, taste, scarcely even as sympathy." A "railway-train" was a perfect embodiment of power, but the problem was "that the power embodied in a railway-train could never be embodied in art. All the steam in the world could not, like the Virgin, build Chartres."[22]

20. Ernest Samuels, *Henry Adams* (Cambridge, Mass.: Belknap Press of Harvard University Press, 1989), p. 386.

21. Henry Adams, *Mont Saint Michel and Chartres,* in *Novels, Mont Saint Michel, The Education,* ed. Ernest Samuels and Jane N. Samuels (New York: Library of America, 1983), p. 505. For an illuminating discussion of Adams's "lyric nostalgia" for the unity of the Middle Ages, see Samuels, *Henry Adams,* pp. 355-68.

22. Henry Adams, *The Education of Henry Adams,* in *Novels, Mont Saint Michel, The Education,* p. 1074.

The way of "reading" that inspired the building of Chartres was visual, spatial, and comprehensive, while the practices that led to the steam engine were silent, disembodied, and idiosyncratic. How was it that Western culture moved from the one set of practices to the other? What strong ties came to bind the mechanized world of modernity to the world of print culture, the book, and silent reading? These are difficult questions to answer, but a particularly fruitful way of approaching them can be found in the rich account of literary and cultural history provided in Erich Auerbach's *Mimesis,* the literary historian's study of the "representation of reality in Western literature."

Auerbach argues that two styles, grounded in the Homeric epics and the Old Testament narratives, have exercised a determining influence on the representation of reality in the Western tradition. In the epic, there is little historical development, events unfold in the foreground of the story, and the meanings of things are clear and unmistakable; here we find a clear description of external appearances and events, with "all events in the foreground, displaying unmistakable meanings" and with little or no emphasis on historical or psychological development. In the biblical pattern of representation, on the other hand, we discover "certain parts brought into high relief, others left obscure, abruptness, suggestive influence of the unexpressed, 'background' quality, multiplicity of meanings and the need for interpretation, universal-historical claims, development of the concept of the historically becoming, and preoccupation with the problematic."[23]

Auerbach contrasts the skeletal leanness of biblical narration to the fleshly abundance of Homeric storytelling. When we read the stories of the Hebrew Bible, we are struck by how much remains tacit in their accounts of human waywardness and divine faithfulness. "They are fraught with 'background' and mysterious, containing a second, concealed meaning," Auerbach notes, and he trains his sights particularly on what he calls the "dark and incomplete" story of Abraham and Isaac. There is a dazzling emptiness in this account, and in many respects what isn't stated seems more important than what is. In Genesis 22, it would be unthinkable to have a description of the tools Abraham carries with him or the landscape through which he and his son travel. No inner depths are

23. Erich Auerbach, *Mimesis: The Representation of Reality in Western Literature,* trans. Willard R. Trask (Princeton: Princeton University Press, 1953), p. 23.

sounded here, nor are any amplifying details included about the actors in this drama. We hear nothing of the internal struggles of Abraham and have no clue as to what Isaac might be thinking in the midst of a cryptic uncertainty. These voids exist as the result of deliberate narrative choices; all the elements, including even Abraham and Isaac, are simply "there to serve the end which God has commanded; what in other respects they were, are, or will be, remains in darkness."[24]

Over the course of Christian history, that darkness was gradually filled with the light of visual images, and that silence was broken by the drama of the Mass and the liturgical practices that grew out of it. The biblical accounts cried out for elaboration, for expansive reading and creative interpretation. How did Abraham reconcile God's terrifying command with his reassuring promise? What were the distraught father and confused son thinking as they set out? Why would God put his beleaguered servant to such an unthinkable test? With so much left unsaid in the scriptural narratives, they not only invite "subtle investigation and interpretation," Auerbach says, "they demand them."[25]

Because the Bible made "claim[s] to absolute authority," its silences called forth a stream of commentary and conjecture. In the medieval period, these elaborations of the text most often took shape in the form of iconographic displays and dramatic representations. The liturgy and statuary of the churches stretched the spare biblical accounts and packed them with images and incidents that served a crucial role in transmitting biblical authority. They were like relay towers carrying the signal of revealed truth across time and into the lives of men and women of every station. What later scholars were to call the "eclipse of biblical narrative" was virtually unknown in the medieval world, where the scriptural story blazed without obstruction and flooded virtually every corner of experience. "Far from seeking, like Homer, merely to make us forget our own reality for a few hours, it [the biblical narrative] seeks to overcome our reality," writes Auerbach. "We are to fit our own life into its world, feel ourselves to be elements in its structure of universal history."[26]

"As late as the European Middle Ages," it was still "possible to represent Biblical events as ordinary phenomena of contemporary life," and at

24. Auerbach, *Mimesis,* pp. 15, 9.

25. Auerbach, *Mimesis,* p. 15.

26. Auerbach, *Mimesis,* p. 15.

that point in history, the symbols of Christian art and worship still had the capacity to place distant events and present realities side by side in the same visual fields. Yet at the same time, the growing historical distance and newly emerging historical consciousness were taking their toll on this sense of immediacy and authority. According to Auerbach, the further removed our situation becomes from that of the Bible, the more difficult it is to make the events of our lives fall within the scriptural compass. In the fifteenth and sixteenth centuries in particular, large-scale intellectual and cultural changes combined with the "awakening of a critical consciousness" to widen the gap considerably between the ancient text and the modern age. Auerbach concludes that as a result, in early modernity, the biblical "claim to absolute authority" was jeopardized, and the medieval mode of interpretation was now treated with scorn. In this context, "the Biblical stories become ancient legends, and the doctrine they had contained, now dissevered from them, becomes a disembodied image."[27]

That disembodied image, however, had some distinct advantages. It could be set in type; copies of it could be made endlessly and inexpensively; and those copies could be distributed efficiently to interested parties down the road or across the world. Johannes Gutenberg produced his first Bibles in the early 1450s, and within two decades, presses appeared across the European landscape, first in Italy, then in France, Spain, England, and Holland. For the first time since writing had appeared, it had become possible to reproduce reading material rapidly and on a hitherto unimaginable scale.[28] The practice of reading was changed forever, and the transition from the Virgin's personal world to the Dynamo's impersonal domain was well underway.

27. Auerbach, *Mimesis,* pp. 15-16. For a concise account of the effects of this "awakened critical consciousness," see Robert M. Grant, *A Short History of the Interpretation of the Bible,* rev. ed. (New York: Macmillan, 1963), pp. 139-52. See also Jaroslav Pelikan, *The Christian Tradition: A History of the Development of Doctrine,* vol. 4, *Reformation of Church and Dogma (1300-1700)* (Chicago: University of Chicago Press, 1984), pp. 304-31. Erwin Panofsky sums up the situation of historical distance: "The Renaissance came to realize that Pan was dead — that the world of ancient Greece and Rome . . . was lost like Milton's Paradise and capable of being regained only in the spirit. The classical past was looked upon, for the first time, as a totality cut off from the present; and, therefore, as an ideal to be longed for instead of a reality to be both utilized and feared." *Renaissance and Renascences in Western Art* (New York: Harper, 1969), p. 113.

28. Manguel, *History of Reading,* p. 134.

The Reformation quickly harnessed this new technology and laid on its shoulders the burden of carrying the meaning of the ancient stories into the heart of modern experience.[29] Luther attempted to make the grand drama of salvation fresh and relevant by drawing it deep into the struggles of the human conscience. With his account of the wrenching conflict between law and gospel, he began to shift the center of divine activity from the cosmos beyond the self to the soul within it. To be sure, Luther earnestly affirmed the historic doctrines of the faith; he trusted in the sovereignty of God and believed in the resurrection of the body, just as he embraced the forgiveness of sins and longed for life everlasting. But at the same time, with his stress upon the inner struggles of saints and sinners alike, Luther became a pioneering explorer of the uncharted territory of the modern self.

The printing press was but one of many intellectual, cultural, and technological developments that widened the gulf between the private and public spheres and heightened the isolation of the modern individual. These forces included the nascent capitalist economy, with its power to atomize the social order into discrete units of production and consumption; liberal individualism and the democratic impulse, both of which focused particularly upon the concerns of private experience; Cartesian consciousness, with its fixation upon first-person certainty and its fascination with the validating power of self-awareness; and the Reformation's emphasis upon liberty of conscience, the lay reading of the Bible, and the energizing power of the inner life. As widely as their interests diverged at points, such developments appeared to work in concert to create the private domain, and in doing so, they drew silent reading from the margins of the Western experience and set it at the center of cultural life.[30]

29. See Steven Ozment, "The Revolution of the Pamphleteers," in *Protestants: The Birth of a Revolution* (1992; repr., New York: Image, 1993), pp. 45-66.

30. Among the consequences of late medieval silent reading, Paul Saenger notes, were the "revival of the antique genre of erotic art" and an intensification of the "depth of lay religious experience. Private, silent reading in the vernacular gave lay readers the means of pursuing the individual relationship to God that had been the aspiration of erudite Christians since Saint Augustine." *Space Between Words,* pp. 274, 275.

Nineteenth-Century Contexts, Contemporary Consequences

Having begun its rise in the mid-fifteenth century, the culture of print and silent reading grew in strength and prominence over the next several hundred years. The pamphlet — first religious, then political — became a staple of European and North American life in the sixteenth and seventeenth centuries, and its proliferation eventually led to the creation of the modern newspaper and the periodical magazine. As we saw in an earlier chapter, the development of the concept of "the news" also had powerful repercussions, both social and spiritual, for the citizens of early modernity. As the rate of literacy grew dramatically in eighteenth-century England, one observer notes, the "explosion of newspapers and magazines, and the emergence of Grub Street" brought about a "proliferation of new-minted truths, discoveries and visions."[31]

Of the many innovative developments made possible by print culture and the world of the news, one of the most important proved to be that of the novel, which first took recognizable form in the seventeenth century, became a considerable cultural force in the eighteenth, and assumed a dominant status in the nineteenth.[32] The novel served as an ideal genre for exploring the moral landscape of modernity, for unlike the epic and the romance, it made no pretense of drawing a map of the cosmos or of being responsible to represent the interventions of supernatural forces in human affairs. Instead, it took itself to be free to anatomize the conflicts of belief and values that had become central to the nineteenth-century experience. Over the span of a few decades, England produced Austen and Dickens, Eliot and Hardy, and the Brontë sisters; America had Stowe, Hawthorne, Melville, Twain, and Henry James; in France, Hugo, Flaubert, Balzac, and Zola flourished; and from Russia came two of the greatest of all novelists, Dostoevsky and Tolstoy. From the 1840s to the end of the century, the novel enjoyed an unrivaled status as the central genre of the cultures of the North Atlantic.

During that period, readers of novels turned up everywhere. They were scattered across the prairies of North America, nestled in the vil-

31. Roy Porter, *Flesh in the Age of Reason: The Modern Foundations of Body and Soul* (New York: Norton, 2004), p. 22.

32. Michael McKeon, *The Origins of the English Novel, 1600-1740*, 15th anniversary ed. (Baltimore: Johns Hopkins University Press, 2002), pp. 25-89.

lages of New England, and packed in the population centers of the New World and the Old. In addition, even as it was flourishing in mainstream culture, the novel began, however tentatively, to become an object of study in the growing academic industry of literary criticism. Not coincidentally, in the era of George Eliot and Fyodor Dostoevsky, American colleges and universities also began for the first time to grant credit for the study of literature in the vernacular, and as the discipline of English studies developed in the decades after the Civil War, the practices of readers provided paradigms for this new class of critics to employ.[33] In Victorian England and postbellum America, earnest professors began to urge eager students to read the lyrics of Wordsworth and the plays of Shakespeare as though they were gospels and epistles for a disenchanted age. Where Ambrose had poured over the Septuagint in silence, undergraduates were now being sent off to the library to scan the pages of Dickens for solace and significance.

The study of literature in the vernacular was part of a much larger movement to promote the arts in late-nineteenth-century Western culture. Museums began to crop up across America after 1870, donations to colleges and universities increased dramatically, and a host of voluntary societies sprang up for the promotion of culture and the fine arts. James Turner attributes this sudden growth to "a craving for an ersatz public spirituality as religion began to disentangle itself from central institutions of national life." In an era of vast expansion and acquisition, the study of music, painting, and literature hinted that something deeper than financial gain, and more universal than a person's parochial context, "inhered in life." For many, religion continued to provide such meaning, but for others — particularly for those members of the late-nineteenth-century elite who produced or analyzed the fine arts — Protestant Christianity began "to fade into a nebulous other world and a set of social rituals" or, in some cases, "even to evaporate altogether."[34]

33. For a survey of these developments see James Turner's chapters on "The Humanities" in the book he co-authored with Jon H. Roberts, *The Sacred and the Secular University* (Princeton: Princeton University Press, 2000), pp. 75-106. See also Gerald Graff, *Professing Literature: An Institutional History* (Chicago: University of Chicago Press, 1987), as well as James Turner's rejoinder to Graff in *Language, Religion, Knowledge: Past and Present* (Notre Dame: University of Notre Dame Press, 2003), pp. 97-102.

34. James Turner, *The Liberal Education of Charles Eliot Norton* (Baltimore: Johns Hopkins University Press, 1999), p. 318.

The American variant that Turner describes is an offshoot of what George Steiner has called "the 'myth of the nineteenth century' or the 'imagined garden of liberal culture.'" This was an era when literacy was high and novel writing and silent reading ruled the day, and Steiner says that in hindsight it looks like a "squandered utopia." Our imagination "locates that garden in England and western Europe between ca. the 1820s and 1915." In contrast to our present spiritual poverty and intellectual barrenness, this lost Eden was marked by a high and rising rate of literacy, a firm view of the "rule of law," and a general, widespread sense of social well-being. Steiner notes that we can all call up images of "well-ordered households," stately processions through "the Sunday parks," and "real bookstores and literate parliamentary debate," all of which slipped from our grasp when the nineteenth century passed.[35]

At the center of that lost culture lived a group of "uncommon readers" who for Steiner are perfectly embodied in an eighteenth-century representative of their class: the reader depicted in Jean-Baptiste Siméon Chardin's painting "Le Philosophe Lisant" ("the philosopher reading"). As embodied by this attentive, formally-attired gentleman, the ideal reader does not engage the book casually or in a state of disarray. There is nothing haphazard about his encounter, and his demeanor and behavior are marked by "*cortesia,* a term rendered only imperfectly by 'courtesy.'" He prepares to read his book — and to greet the author who waits in its pages — as though he is entering into the presence of royalty. "It is a courteous, almost a courtly encounter, between a private person and one of those 'high guests' whose entrance into mortal houses is evoked by Hölderlin in his hymn 'As on a festive day'. . . . The reader meets the book with a courtliness of heart" that signals a generous and receptive spirit.[36]

To Steiner, such "courtly" reading is a miracle. Through a series of biological and chemical processes and by means of imaginative empathy, we enter into a world set down by hand or cast in print centuries earlier. In Steiner's terms, when we approach the text in such a courteous manner, we become humble "readers" rather than skeptical "critics." The reader accepts the words on the printed page as "data," in the archaic

35. Steiner, *In Bluebeard's Castle,* pp. 4-6.

36. George Steiner, *No Passion Spent: Essays 1978-1995* (New Haven: Yale University Press, 1996), pp. 1-2.

sense of that word as "that which is given to us." To the reader, poems and novels are not aesthetic objects whose value is grounded in romantic theories of the imagination; instead, written works are "presences" whose power Steiner calls "transubstantiational." For the "reader," books convey a sense of "real presence," and the sensitive reader peruses a book "*as if* the text was the housing of forces and meanings, of meanings of meaning, whose lodging within the executive verbal form was one of 'incarnation.'"[37] For Steiner, reading is a sacramental act for a secular age, and it mediates the only experience of holy presence we are likely to have in a disenchanted world.

Yet however luminous Steiner considers reading's nineteenth-century past to have been, he fears its future may prove to be dark indeed. If the "garden of liberal culture" was only recently filled with avid readers, in our current "post- or subliterate" climate, there has been a "general 'retreat from the word,'" and the sensate masses wander across a blighted landscape. From some possible vantage point in the not so distant future, "Western civilization, from its Hebraic-Greek origins roughly to the present, may look like a phase of concentrated 'verbalism.'" We will look back wistfully to a time when "spoken, remembered, and written discourse was the backbone of consciousness" rather than being the "caption to the picture" that it has become in our day. Through most of Western history, the lofty status of "the word" had been "expressive of . . . a hierarchic value-system" and had served as a symbol of transcendence. "The sinews of Western speech" drove "the power relations of the Western social order" and ordered everything from the relationship between the sexes to the tension between actual history and the utopian dream. Diminish the "sovereign, almost magically validated role" of language, Steiner warns, "and you will have begun to demolish the hierarchies and transcendence-values of a classic civilization. Even death can be made mute."[38]

As striking as these observations may be, there is another way of thinking about the loss of the "golden age of reading," and Steiner himself has put it forward in a series of essays. In "To Civilize Our Gentlemen," for example, he questions the inwardness of reading culture instead of championing it.

37. George Steiner, *George Steiner: A Reader* (Oxford: Oxford University Press, 1984), p. 85.

38. Steiner, *In Bluebeard's Castle*, pp. 111, 113, 114.

Steiner describes his family's narrow escape from the Holocaust and reports that the terrible events of those years have made him question the "confident link" the nineteenth century had detected between literature and humane values. The "simple yet appalling fact" is "that we have very little solid evidence that literary studies do very much to enrich or stabilize moral perception, that they *humanize*." Indeed, the evidence seems to point the other way, for throughout the Nazi era, "the literary imagination gave servile or ecstatic welcome to political bestiality," and a sophisticated delight in poetry proved "no bar to personal and institutionalized sadism."[39]

Instead of refining our moral sensibilities, "close reading" may deaden them. It may be "that the focusing of consciousness on a written text," which is at the heart of the teaching and reading of literature, lessens or even blunts altogether our moral response to actual events. The cry in the poem may sound more urgent than the cry in the street, and "the death in the novel may move us more potently than the death in the next room. Thus there may be a covert, betraying link between the cultivation of aesthetic response and the potential of personal inhumanity. What then are we doing when we study and teach literature?"[40]

Steiner's essay appeared in 1965, at the very time when the Vietnam War and the powerful surge of the civil rights movement were provoking similar questions about the value of liberal education in a war-torn world. A decade after Steiner's essay appeared, Paul Fussell raised similar questions in a trenchant study of the impact of World War I on the English language and the literate culture it served. Fussell's book contains, among other things, a number of sharp, sometimes abrasive set pieces. In one of them, set in two columns, he lists on the left side a series of plain phrases describing combat, while on the right side he provides the Victorian euphemism for the same reality. His point is that within the nineteenth-century "garden of liberal culture," the elegant phrases dulled the senses and obscured the horrors of war. For the young men who blithely went off to die in 1914, and to the culture that hurried them on their way, mechanized warfare was heroic "strife" in which young "comrades" sought to "vanquish" their "foe" with "gallant" actions and "ardent valor." When the battle ended and the bodies of dead soldiers lay

39. Steiner, *Language and Silence: Essays on Language, Literature and the Inhuman* (New York: Atheneum, 1970), pp. 60-61.

40. Steiner, *Language and Silence*, p. 61.

scattered across a sodden field beneath a leaden sky, to the euphemistically inclined, this was a scene where "the fallen" had given the "sweet wine of youth" and surrendered their "limbs" under the watchful gaze of "the heavens." Fussell notes that in 1914, British soldiers were "not merely literate, but vigorously literary," because the First World War began at a particular moment in history "when two 'liberal' forces were powerfully coinciding in England." They were a "belief in the educative powers of classical and English literature" and a faith in "popular education and 'self-improvement' [that] was at its peak" just before the war broke out.[41] The war, it might be said, brought the attenuated sentiments of the age of the Virgin face to face with the harsh realities of the Dynamo's ruthlessly efficient reign.

The poetry of the American expatriate Ezra Pound offers a sharp contrast between the rhetoric that yearned for conflict and the poetry that lamented war's destructive fury after the fact. First, the pre-war (1909) exercise in violence and braggadocio:

> Damn it all! all this our South stinks peace.
> You whoreson dog, Papiols, come! Let's to music!
> I have no life save when the swords clash.
> But ah! when I see the standards gold, vair, purple, opposing
> And the broad fields beneath them turn crimson,
> Then howl I my heart nigh mad with rejoicing.[42]

Only a few years later, after the war (1920), Pound sounds chastened, and a certain relish for conflict has given way to bitterness over its human cost. Here there is no rejoicing over fields "turned crimson" with blood, and there is no longer any disdain for the "stink" of peace.

41. Paul Fussell, *The Great War and Modern Memory* (New York: Oxford University Press, 1975), pp. 21-22, 157. Fussell's book documents the disillusionment of the artists and intellectuals with the First World War *after the fact.* In does not indicate as clearly how eager many of those artists and intellectuals had been for conflict. For an illuminating study of the attitudes held by intellectuals at the start of the war, see Ronald N. Stromberg, *Redemption by War: The Intellectuals and 1914* (Lawrence: Regents Press of Kansas, 1982).

42. Ezra Pound, *Selected Poems* (New York: New Directions, 1957), p. 7. This is only a poem, of course, and not a war propaganda screed, yet as Ronald Stromberg notes in referring to Pound, "the conventional wisdom [pre-1914] . . . held that war was impossible, making imaginative speculation about it the more apparently harmless." *Redemption by War,* p. 180.

There died a myriad,
And of the best, among them,
For an old bitch gone in the teeth,
For a botched civilization,

Charm, smiling at the good mouth,
Quick eyes gone under earth's lid,

For two gross of broken statues,
For a few thousand battered books.[43]

Just decades earlier, Matthew Arnold had extolled the healing powers of poetry and the saving grace of literary culture, but for Pound "the cultural heritage has been reduced to the status of a junkman's inventory," and to him there seems to be little to live for, let alone to die for, in the culture of solitude — with its myriad books and cherished practices of silent reading — that so many had given their lives to preserve.[44]

Hearing Voices: Reading Beyond the View

Over much of the period we have covered in this chapter, from early modernity to the twentieth century, one set of images dominated discussions of reading as well as explorations of larger questions of knowledge, interpretation, and human understanding: metaphors of *sight.* Until recently, their supremacy largely remained unquestioned and unchecked.[45] Only in the past century has "ocularcentrism" come under a sustained attack in certain intellectual quarters, but even at that, such theoretical criticism has done little to dull a peculiarly strong Protestant appetite for visual imagery. To this day, metaphors of sight set the parameters for Christian theories of human understanding, and the loosely defined term "worldview" rests at the heart of Protestant apologetics.

If, for example, you are anxious about your worldview, or that of

43. Pound, *Selected Poems,* p. 64.

44. Hugh Kenner, *The Poetry of Ezra Pound* (1951; repr., Lincoln: University of Nebraska Press, 1985), p. 172.

45. For a comprehensive survey of the reign of sight and the recent stringent critique of it in Western thought, see Martin Jay, *Downcast Eyes: The Denigration of Vision in Twentieth-Century French Thought* (Berkeley: University of California Press, 1993).

another person, help is but a few keystrokes away. At "worldview.org" you can book a week for your teenager at a "worldview" camp; "christianworldview.net" will link you up with an endless supply of "worldview" leaders and resources; and if you are so inclined, you may register at "worldviewweekend.com" for the annual "Worldview Weekend Family Reunion" in Branson, Missouri. And the use of this term is not only to be found on the fundamentalist side of things. Visit the web sites of such mainline denominations as the PCUSA (Presbyterian) and the United Methodists, and you will find a good deal of worldview talk as well; even the Unitarian-Universalists tout "the Unitarian worldview" as "a gift to our increasingly secular society."

So it is that as heirs of the nineteenth century, contemporary Protestants remain in key ways bound to sight and limited by the vision its metaphors afford. For the sake of intellectual clarity and theological authenticity, these branches of the larger church would do well to subdue their passion for *getting the picture* and cultivate instead the art of *hearing voices.*

It is not as easy as it may seem, however, to shift from visual to auditory imagery in thinking about belief, for the bias against hearing remains deeply ingrained in the vocabulary of modernity. I can explain what I mean by describing an experiment I conducted not long ago with the assistance of Google and Microsoft Word. I typed the above two phrases into Google, and the following entries appeared among the first ten results in each case:

Getting the Picture. The Art of the Illustrated Letter.
Getting the Picture: Observations from the Library of Congress on Providing Online Access to Pictorial Images.
Getting the Picture: Communicating Data Visually. According to US census estimates.
Getting the Picture! Video Integration with iMovie and Digital Cameras.

Or

Hearing Voices Network. Welcome. If you hear voices, HVN can help.
Hearing voices when there are none to be heard is a classic symptom of mental illness.

Hearing Voices Service is a project helping people who hear voices to cope with this phenomenon.

The Hearing Voices Network Dundee is a self-help group for those who hear "auditory hallucinations."

The implication is clear, is it not? If you *get the picture,* you are as normal as can be, but if you *hear voices,* you are a bit daft, or worse.

Near the end of this chapter, I use the phrase "in the service of the divine *Logos,*" which is the Greek term for *word* that the Gospel of John applies to Jesus. When I first typed the word *"Logos"* into my manuscript, Microsoft Word immediately signaled a spelling alert. I checked on this and was informed that the correct term for that sentence would be, "in the service of *that logo.*" That pretty much says it all. From the dawn's first light to when we close our weary eyes at night, we are always seeing *logos* and *getting the big picture.* Yet woe unto him, or her, who might claim to have *heard* the voice of God.

In an earlier chapter, we met Pip, a character in Melville's *Moby Dick* who had just finished listening to a number of the ship's crewmen give their "readings" of the symbols on a gold coin nailed to the mainmast. "I look, you look, he looks; we look, ye look, they look," he declaimed. Having heard Pip conjugate the verb in this matter, Ishmael, the ostensible narrator of the novel, mutters to himself, "Upon my soul, he's been studying Murray's Grammar!" Then Pip calls out twice again, "I look, you look, he looks; we look, ye look, they look."[46]

With his simple conjugation of this perspectival verb, Pip shows that he and his crewmates live in what Martin Heidegger has called "the age of the world picture." As for what a "world picture" is, Heidegger explains that "world" is a "name for what is, in its entirety." It encompasses not just the cosmos and nature but also history and "the ground of the world." By "picture," he does not mean a painting or copy but has in mind the sense that "sounds forth in the colloquial expression, 'We get the picture' [literally, we are in the picture] concerning something." Even at that, however, Heidegger says, "the essence of the picture is still missing" from our understanding of what it means to have a "world picture" or "worldview." For "'to get the picture' throbs with being acquainted with

46. Herman Melville, *Moby Dick,* 2nd ed., ed. Hershel Parker and Harrison Hayford (New York: Norton, 2002), p. 335.

something, with being equipped and prepared for it." When we have a "picture of the world," it "stands before us — in all that belongs to it and all that stands together in it — as a system." When we employ the image of a "worldview" to describe our knowledge, Heidegger says we are making a decision "regarding what is, in its entirety. The Being of whatever is, is sought and found in the representedness" of what is.[47]

"The fact that whatever is comes into being in and through representedness transforms the age" and makes our cultural period distinct from any era before it. According to Heidegger, the uniqueness of our understanding means that we cannot consider the "modern world picture" as a contemporary phenomenon that is somehow to be contrasted with an earlier "world picture," because *"the fact that the world becomes picture at all is what distinguishes the essence of the modern age"* (emphasis added). The people of the ancient world and medieval period could no more hold "worldviews" than they could possess "selves" as we understand such things to be. For the age of Aquinas and Dante, what *is* did not consist of what could be *represented* but of *everything* that had been brought into being by "the personal Creator-God." In the Middle Ages, to *exist* meant to stand not *before* a world that could be taken in as a picture but *within* "the order of what has been created." Never in the medieval period does the essential "Being of that which is consist . . . in the fact that it is brought before man as the objective, in the fact that it is placed in the realm of man's knowing and of his having disposal."[48] In other words, no one "got the picture" in the Middle Ages, except for God, because everyone and everything else was a subject for the camera, an object lodged in the divine gaze and caught in the heavenly snapshot of the world.

In the end, the language of *worldview* proves unsatisfying, because it isolates human understanding within the concept of the "point of view," and in doing so, it invariably leads to the reduction of convictions to the status of preferences.[49] In the mid-nineteenth century, Ralph Waldo Emerson evocatively described the dilemma of perspectival subjectivity.

47. Martin Heidegger, *The Question Concerning Technology and Other Essays,* trans. William Lovitt (New York: Harper, 1977), pp. 129-30.

48. Heidegger, *Question Concerning Technology,* p. 130.

49. For a sanguine view of this development, see Richard Rorty's "Nineteenth-Century Idealism and Twentieth-Century Textualism," in his *Consequences of Pragmatism* (Minneapolis: University of Minnesota Press, 1982), pp. 139-59.

"Dream delivers us to dream, and there is no end to illusion," he lamented. "Life is a train of moods like a string of beads, and, as we pass through them, they prove to be many-colored lenses which paint the world their own hue, and each shows only what lies in its focus." We would like to believe that objects are solid and that we can know them as they are, but the painful truth of the matter is that "we animate what we can, and we see only what we animate. Nature and books belong to the eyes that see them."[50] In the realm of the *world picture,* we can do little more than cultivate a mutual toleration of our incommensurable perspectives. It is with good reason that Karl Barth warns us that "we must beware as Christians, and the Church must beware of establishing itself on the basis of any sort of *Weltanschauung.*" The Christian faith, he reminds us, is bound to Jesus Christ, and not to any "definite world-picture."[51]

Matters *sound* very different when we move from sight to hearing. Heidegger is again important here. "Almost perversely," writes Theodore Kisiel, the German philosopher focused upon *hearing* as the central act in which speaking achieves the end for which it is intended. "For speaking finds its completion in the communication, in being received or accepted by the auditor who undergoes or 'suffers' the speech."[52] For the ancient Greeks and the modern Heidegger as well, it is not what our eyes see but what our ears hear that brings us to the truth. "The connection of discourse with understanding and intelligibility becomes clear through . . . hearing," writes Heidegger. It is no accident "that we say, when we have not heard 'rightly,' that we have not 'understood.' Hearing is constitutive for discourse." Without it, we have no openness to God (*Da-sein* or Being, for Heidegger) or other selves, and we remain trapped within our solitude and incapable of *hearkening* to what is addressed to us.[53]

50. Ralph Waldo Emerson, *Essays and Lectures,* ed. Joel Porte (New York: Library of America, 1983), p. 473.

51. Karl Barth, *Dogmatics in Outline,* trans. G. T. Thompson (1949; repr., New York: Harper, 1959), p. 59.

52. Theodore Kisiel, *The Genesis of Heidegger's "Being and Time"* (Berkeley: University of California Press, 1993), p. 296.

53. Martin Heidegger, *Being and Time,* trans. Joan Stambaugh (Albany: State University of New York Press, 1996), pp. 153-54. Jean Grondin notes that for Heidegger *hearing* remained central to understanding. For him, hermeneutics "is most readily understood from the Greek verb *hermeneuein,* which means 'the exposition which brings tidings be-

Heidegger had little interest in the triune God of Christianity, but in prizing sound over sight as he did, he was echoing the priorities of the biblical writers. From the opening verses of Genesis to the benedictions that close many of St. Paul's letters, the Bible makes the aural and the auditory central to the apprehension of the truth, while visual metaphors play an important but secondary role. It is the *sound* of the Lord God walking in the Garden that drives the shamed Adam and Eve into hiding, the *voice* of God that calls the prophets and commands Moses, and the *preaching* of the gospel that spreads the good news across the first-century Mediterranean world. Icons, images, and visions are certainly there to be seen in the Bible, but they are signs along the secondary roads. Speaking and hearing — these make straight in the desert a highway for God.

The psychological significance of the auditory is clear. Sight is the most imperial of the senses, sound the most vulnerable. The romantic painters and poets understood that fact, and that is why they so often set their heroes on mountaintops, so that they could survey the tangled landscape that stretched before them into infinity. With its depiction of a solitary man above the clouds, Caspar David Friedrich's "Wanderer Above the Mists" is an iconic symbol of modern visual power. An ascendant visual glory is also celebrated near the close of William Wordsworth's *The Prelude,* another classic work from the early nineteenth century. After climbing Mount Snowdon in Wales, the poet watches a sublime scene unfold:

> Meanwhile, the Moon looked down upon this show
> In single glory, and we stood, the mist
> Touching our very feet; and from the shore
> At distance not the third part of a mile
> Was a blue chasm.

---

cause it can listen to a message.' Prior to every interpretation, the hermeneutical manifests itself as 'the bearing of message and tidings'. . . . Most simply expressed, hermeneutics means the exposition of tidings that call for a hearing." *Sight* does not even make an appearance in Heidegger's formulation of the interpretive dynamic, save as the imperializing function that is celebrated in modern reflective philosophy and enshrined in the modern technological project. *Introduction to Philosophical Hermeneutics,* trans. Joel Weinsheimer (New Haven: Yale University Press, 1994), p. 104.

Wordsworth then speaks of a "meditation" that rose in him that night upon the mountain,

> when the scene
> Had passed away, and it appeared to me
> The perfect image of a mighty mind,
> Of one that feeds upon infinity,
> That is exalted by an underpresence,
> The sense of God, or whatsoe'er is dim
> Or vast in its own being, above all
> One function of such mind had Nature there
> Exhibited by putting forth, and that
> With circumstance most awful and sublime,
> That domination which she oftentimes
> Exerts upon the outward face of things.

To the poet, the power that nature "thrusts forth upon the senses" in the scenes before him

> is the express
> Resemblance, in the fullness of its strength
> Made visible, a genuine counterpart
> And brother of the glorious faculty
> Which higher minds bear with them as their own.
> That is the very spirit in which they deal
> With all the objects of the universe:
> They from their native selves can send abroad
> Like transformation; for themselves create
> A like existence.[54]

Sight is imperial, because we own what lies within our gaze and we avert our eyes from whatever we would rather not see. For instance, at the beginning of *Nature,* Emerson celebrates the colonizing power of the eye by noting that "Miller owns this field, Locke that, and Manning the woodland beyond. But none of them owns the landscape." The deed to that belongs to him "whose eye can integrate all the parts, that is, the

54. William Wordsworth, *The Prelude: A Parallel Text,* ed. J. C. Maxwell (New York: Penguin, 1971), pp. 512, 514.

poet." This capacity of the inner poetic "eye" yields to us "the best part of these men's farms, yet to this their warranty-deeds give no title." Through the powers of the eye, we become a part of God. "Standing on the bare ground, — my head bathed by the blithe air, and uplifted into infinite space, — all mean egotism vanishes," Emerson declares. "I become a transparent eye-ball; I am nothing; I see all; the currents of the Universal Being circulate through me; I am part or particle of God."[55] Emerson's transparent eyeball, to be sure, has a worldview.

Matters stand differently with the ear. To understand this difference, we only need to consider our own experiences in dorms, apartments, and neighborhoods. We rarely care, do we, about what we are not seeing in the apartment above us or in the room across the hall. If there are scenes we would rather not witness, shades and walls neatly do the trick of letting us avert our gaze. But if the bass is cranked up next door, or drunken voices are crying out across the lawn, how can we get away from the sound? We rule the field of sight, but sound exposes our vulnerability to the word that calls us and demands a response.

The shift from the auditory to the visual is a hallmark of our modernity, and few have mapped the changing sensory terrain more brilliantly than Walter Ong. An early work finds Ong probing the dominance of the visual through a focus upon the career of Peter Ramus, an influential sixteenth-century rhetorician. He is intrigued by the catalogues Ramus devised to organize knowledge along spatial lines, and according to him, these organizational systems were indicative of trends that began "to run riot" in the early modern period and eventually led to "modern encyclopedism." They are evidence of a strong push to comprehend not only the visible universe but the act of "thought itself in terms of spatial models apprehended by sight." In the modern model, the notion of knowledge as *word*, as well as the *personal* conception of cognition and the created order "which this notion implies, is due to atrophy. . . . Persons, who alone speak, . . . will be eclipsed insofar as the world is thought of as an assemblage of the sort of things which vision apprehends — objects or surfaces."[56]

Atrophy did set in, as the Ramist system and other historical phe-

55. Emerson, *Essays*, pp. 9-10.

56. Walter J. Ong, *Ramus, Method, and the Decay of Dialogue: From the Art of Discourse to the Art of Reason* (1958; repr., Cambridge, Mass.: Harvard University Press, 1983), pp. 314, 9.

nomena that accompanied the invention of the printing press silenced the cosmos and paved the way for the rule of sight. The phenomena that clustered around printing included the emergence of the Copernican cosmos, which is decidedly "more truly spatial" than the "directional space" of Aristotelian cosmology; the growth of "the painters' feeling for a similar, abstract space" that reaches its climax in the work of the fifteenth-century Flemish painter Jan van Eyck; and the philosophical systems of early modernity, with their concept of a "mental space analogous" to the spheres of the Copernican system. Ong notes that the preoccupation with spatial metaphors gave birth to a passion for the concept of "bodies" of knowledge. In turn, this led to the "fad of performing intellectual 'anatomies,' which are analyses or 'dissections' of such 'bodies' of knowledge." To this tradition we owe Lyly's *Anatomy of Wit* and Burton's *Anatomy of Melancholy,* as well a spate of now-unread Latin "dissections" from that period.[57]

Ramus conceived of knowledge as a means of opening ideas as though they were boxes, and Ong says it is important to note that the centuries after Ramus produced any number of systems that claimed to provide "'keys' to one thing or another." At the same time, the notion of content was extended from books to words and statements themselves, so that the sense of ideas as "'containing' truth" emerges, and the habit of thinking "of truth as 'content' begins to appear." These shifting notions of knowledge led to a vast industry of "method" from the seventeenth century to the nineteenth. All conceivable ways of knowing were reduced to "box-like units laid hold of by the mind in such a way that they are fully and adequately treated [only] by being 'opened' in an analysis."[58] Such "content" can be scanned and surveyed, but no one would think to claim that it could be *heard.*

This nineteenth-century concept of a "key" to knowledge calls to mind the pathetic career of Edward Casaubon, Dorothea Brooke's husband in George Eliot's greatest novel, *Middlemarch.* When Dorothea marries this lonely pedant, he has been laboring for years on his "Key to All Mythologies." He is determined to catalogue the whole of the mythological past, but not for the purposes of enriching the present or creating the future. "I live too much with the dead," he explains at the beginning of

57. Ong, *Ramus,* pp. 314-15.
58. Ong, *Ramus,* p. 315.

the novel. "My mind is something like the ghost of an ancient, wandering about the world and trying mentally to construct it as it used to be, in spite of ruin and confusing changes." Dorothea dreams of assisting her husband with his lofty enterprise, but all the while he accomplishes nothing and staggers towards death beneath the burden of "a mind weighted with unpublished matter."[59] As Casaubon dissects the past, history remains as silent, dead, and impotent to him as he is to his wife. Under his listless scalpel, the bodies of knowledge that comprise history and religious belief are divvied up and scrutinized in a deathly silence.

Ong might say of Casaubon that, like the modern period in general, he has been marked by a "hypertrophy of the visual imagination" that "crowds spatial models . . . into the universe of the mind." This explosive proliferation of visual models is one of many witnesses "to the evolution in human thought processes which is simultaneously producing the Newtonian revolution, with its stress on visually controlled observation and mathematics, and its curiously silent, nonrhetorical universe." Whatever good it may have accomplished, the Ramist system also joined with other intellectual and cultural forces to eliminate "sound and voice from man's understanding of the intellectual world and helped create within the human spirit itself the silences of a spatialized universe."[60]

The discovery of a "curiously silent, nonrhetorical universe" implies the corresponding loss of a cosmos that once spoke and ached to be heard. Stars that sing and books that talk had been, after all, powerful tropes in Western experience, as medieval literature and early modern

59. George Eliot, *Middlemarch,* ed. Rosemary Ashton (New York: Penguin, 1994), pp. 18, 198. Spatial metaphors even crowd into Dorothea's own anguished efforts to come to terms with her own misery. On her honeymoon she muses, "How was it that in the weeks since her marriage, Dorothea had not distinctly observed but felt with a stifling depression, that the large vistas and wide fresh air which she had dreamed of finding in her husband's mind were replaced by ante-rooms and winding passages which seemed to lead nowhither?" (p. 195).

60. Ong, *Ramus,* p. 318. In spite of the sharpness of his critique of Ramist practice and the spatialized and visual world that emerged out of it as a dominant cultural force in modernity, Ong had no desire to turn back the clock and reestablish the prerogatives of the vanquished oral culture. Orality can never represent the ideal, he claimed. "To approach it positively is not to advocate it as a permanent state for any culture. Literacy opens possibilities to the word and to human existence unimaginable without writing." In the end, he concludes, "both orality and the growth of literacy out of orality are necessary for the evolution of consciousness." *Orality,* p. 175.

slave narratives both demonstrate.[61] Ong's image is of special relevance to the late nineteenth century, when nature and God — along with the text that both of them had written — go silent suddenly and seemingly without warning. In many respects, the subject of the death of God, which first surfaces with force at the nineteenth century's close, merely followed upon the prior question of the silencing of nature and nature's God.

As a case in point, both Emily Dickinson and Herman Melville linked God's silence to his death. "I dreaded that first Robin, so," begins a Dickinson poem from 1862. The source of the speaker's fear in this poem is the simple fact that nature's creatures — be they robins, daffodils, or grasses — have nothing to say to her. She cannot bear the thought that "the Bees should come," and instead wishes "they'd stay away," because "In those dim countries where they go,/What word had they, for me" (#347)? Another poem finds its speaker preparing to pray but missing "a rudiment —/Creator — Was it you?" She tramps off in search of "this Curious Friend" but hears no sound and finds no sign of God; instead, all that stretches before her are "Vast Prairies of Air/Unbroken by a Settler —." Eventually "The Silence condescended —/Creation stopped — for me —/But awed beyond my errand —/I worshipped — did not 'pray' —" (#525). The human heart's deepest secrets may be known to God, but they remain secure, because "The Jehovahs — are no Babblers —" (#692). There was a point in history when the heavens sang and the mountains spoke of the majesty of God, but that was *then,* and *now* we live with silence, since the hand of God has been "amputated," and he is nowhere to be found (#1581).

Images of this kind saturate Melville's fiction, with a particularly pointed example to be found midway through *Moby Dick.* Captain Ahab is gazing one evening upon the head of a whale hanging from the side of his ship. He probes the bloody form with a spade and calls upon it to talk to him. "Speak, mighty head, and tell us the secret thing that is in thee," he demands. That head has dived among "this world's foundations" and has slept by "many a sailor's side." It has witnessed "locked lovers" sink "beneath the exulting wave" and has watched pirates toss a murdered

61. For the trope of the "talking book," see Henry Louis Gates Jr., *The Signifying Monkey: A Theory of African-American Literary Criticism* (New York: Oxford University Press, 1988), pp. 127-69.

mate into the ocean's "insatiate maw." Yet not a word breaks the awful silence of this inscrutable countenance. "O head! thou hast seen enough to split the planets and make an infidel of Abraham, and not one syllable is thine!"[62] As Ahab suggests with his images of orphaned humanity — "Where is the foundling's father hidden?" — for many, creation's silence was a sign that God had abandoned it.

The Sound of Silence: Modernity and the Voice of God

For more than a century, theologians and theorists alike have been seeking to comprehend this silence and to imagine it ringing once again with speech. Karl Barth's vast theological enterprise was an effort to attend to the *speech* of God, as it resounds in revelation, "that event in which the *being of God* comes to word."[63] Similarly, Dietrich Bonhoeffer's reflections on religionless Christianity and the suffering of God were efforts to meet the challenge posed by spatial models of the cosmos and visual conceptions of knowledge. Among Catholic theologians, Hans Urs von Balthasar produced a grand multi-volume theological aesthetics that, in the words of one of his most perceptive critics, gave "the primacy to hearing when we survey the whole range of the human sensorium. Hearing is *the* central theological act of perception."[64]

At the same time, over the course of the twentieth century, key philosophers and literary theorists worked diligently to reestablish a balance between the visual and the auditory. Among others, this group included Kenneth Burke, America's most brilliant modern theorist of rhetoric and culture; Mikhail Bakhtin, whose extraordinary work on Dostoevsky yielded the theory of the polyphonic novel and the dialogical model of truth; and Hans-Georg Gadamer, who placed the art of the question and the act of conversation at the center of reading and interpretation.

The exemplary figure of Paul Ricoeur also belongs here, because for half a century he sought to restore *hearing* to its rightful place in the theory of human understanding. Ricoeur did give visual metaphors their

62. Melville, *Moby Dick,* p. 249.

63. Eberhard Jüngel, *God's Being Is in Becoming: The Trinitarian Being of God in the Theology of Karl Barth,* trans. John Webster (Grand Rapids: Eerdmans, 2001), p. 27.

64. Edward T. Oakes, *Pattern of Redemption: The Theology of Hans Urs von Balthasar* (New York: Continuum, 1994), p. 137.

due. He acknowledged, for instance, that structuralism, the twentieth-century theoretical product of nineteenth-century linguistics, had provided powerful tools for picturing the workings of language. Structuralism's dominant visual and spatial images gave us a way of mapping the intricate grid that channels the flow of language, and it proved to be interested in systems rather than in history. "For historicism, understanding is finding the genesis, the previous form, the sources, and the sense of the evolution," Ricoeur observes. "With structuralism, what is first given as intelligible are the arrangements, the systematic organizations in a given state."[65]

Yet metaphors of sight and systems of structure are not sufficient for an understanding of language, Ricoeur argues, because "to understand is to hear. In other words, my first relation to speech is not that I produce it but that I receive it."[66] The structuralist approach lends itself well to "the great task of nourishing men, of satisfying their needs by mastering nature through planetary technique," but it does not speak to our deepest spiritual longings or moral needs. That is why in the age of structuralist discourse, when language has become "more precise, more univocal, [and] more technical," we long more than ever "to recharge our language." Having emptied that language of its sacred significance by "radically formalizing it," we now wish to see it filled anew with meaning. "Beyond the desert of criticism, we wish to be called again."[67]

With his twofold theory of the hermeneutics of suspicion and the hermeneutics of faith, Ricoeur articulated his understanding of such a *calling.* His "hermeneutics of suspicion" quickly assumed iconic status in theoretical discourse, serving as shorthand for the art of visual distancing that animates Freud, Marx, and Nietzsche in the nineteenth century as well as Foucault, Bataille, and Baudrillard in the twentieth. The "her-

65. Paul Ricoeur, *The Conflict of Interpretations,* ed. Don Ihde (Evanston: Northwestern University Press, 1974), p. 31. Ricoeur believed that although structuralism has limited value, it is not an alien method forced upon the human sciences. Instead, it "stems from the very sphere of language" and "belongs, from birth so to speak, to the domain of the human sciences, and indeed to a leading science in this domain: linguistics." *Hermeneutics and the Human Sciences,* trans. and ed. John B. Thompson (Cambridge: Cambridge University Press, 1981), p. 157.

66. Ricoeur, *Hermeneutics and the Human Sciences,* p. 59.

67. Paul Ricoeur, *The Symbolism of Evil,* trans. Emerson Buchanan (1967; repr., Boston: Beacon, 1969), p. 349.

meneutics of faith," on the other hand, has received scant attention of late in the lecture halls of Paris or the English departments of North America. Ricoeur says the "first imprint of this faith in a revelation through the word is to be seen in the care or concern for the *object*." What he calls the "bracketing of absolute reality" is a given in the visual projects of the modern age, from the physics of Newton to the epistemology of Descartes to the archaeology of knowledge promoted by Foucault. The scientist may bracket the object, but "the philosopher . . . must not avoid the question of the absolute validity of his object. For would I be interested in the object, could I stress concern for the object, through the consideration of cause, genesis, or function, if I did not expect, from within understanding, this something to 'address' itself to me?" Language speaks to us, before it is spoken by us, for we are "born into language, into the light of the logos 'who enlightens every man who comes into the world.'"[68]

Ricoeur is quoting here, of course, from the opening of John's Gospel, which assumes speaking and hearing to be central to the faith, as do the book of Acts and the letters of St. Paul. "For, 'everyone who calls upon the name of the Lord will be saved.' But how are men to call upon him in whom they have not believed? And how are they to believe in him of whom they have never heard? And how are they to hear without a preacher" (Rom. 10:13-14)? As Karl Barth reminds us, the scriptures are "the record of a unique hearing of a unique call and a unique obedience to a unique command" that is delivered to us through the life, death, and resurrection of Jesus Christ, the divine *Logos.*[69]

In the service of that *Logos,* Dietrich Bonhoeffer gave his life in the final days of the Second World War. In the year before his death, Bonhoeffer wrote from prison a series of letters that contained a sustained radical critique of the idea of a Christian *worldview.* In a letter I quoted at the opening of this chapter, he began, on April 30, 1944, to reflect on the question of who Christ is as Lord of a now religionless world. "If religion is only a garment of Christianity," he asked in a letter to Eberhard Bethge, his former student and confidant, "then what is a religionless Christianity?" His complaint in this letter is that "religious

68. Paul Ricoeur, *Freud and Philosophy: An Essay on Interpretation,* trans. Denis Savage (New Haven: Yale University Press, 1970), pp. 28-30.

69. Karl Barth, *Church Dogmatics,* I.1.115.

people speak of God when human knowledge . . . has come to an end, or when human resources fail," and at that point, they drag "the *deus ex machina*" into the scene to make all things right. "I should like to speak of God not on the boundaries," he told Bethge, "but at the centre."[70]

Over the next few months, Bonhoeffer's thoughts on this subject came out in a host of observations, brief discourses, and asides, all of which were tucked into letters smuggled out of his Berlin prison cell. In late May, he wrote that he had been absorbed in the reading of Carl Friedrich von Weizsäcker's *The World-View of Physics.* This book brought home to him "quite clearly how wrong it is to use God as a stop-gap for the incompleteness of our knowledge," because when the boundaries of knowledge are pushed back, God is "pushed back with them, and is therefore continually in retreat." Rather than looking for God at the margins of our knowledge or just beyond the edge of the known universe, Bonhoeffer says God would have us find him "in what we know, not in what we don't know."[71]

As he thought his way through these matters, Bonhoeffer began to speak of a book project he hoped to tackle, if and when he won his release from prison. That work would have covered much of the historical territory we have traversed in this book, and on its own terms, it would have focused on the modern tension between *believing still* and *believing again.* We get an initial hint of what the book might have been like in a letter from early June 1944, in which Bonhoeffer says he wishes to focus on "the movement that began about the thirteenth century . . . towards the autonomy of man." That movement has reached its "undoubted completion" in the twentieth century, he explains, and its central consequence has been that men and women have learned to deal with themselves "in all questions of importance without recourse to the 'working hypothesis' called 'God.'"[72]

According to Bonhoeffer, Protestant and Catholic apologetics have seen this development as "the great defection from God," and they have sought to "play off God and Christ against it." They have attempted "to prove to a world thus come of age" that it cannot and will not thrive without "the tutelage of 'God.'" In questions of science, art, and ethics, even

70. Bonhoeffer, *Letters and Papers,* pp. 280-82.

71. Bonhoeffer, *Letters and Papers,* p. 311.

72. Bonhoeffer, *Letters and Papers,* p. 325.

the apologists realize the battle has long since been decided, so the Church has retreated to the "so-called 'ultimate questions' — death, guilt — to which only 'God' can give an answer." But what will happen, Bonhoeffer asks, if even those questions receive even a partially satisfying secular solution?[73]

That question is well taken because, as we have seen in our discussions of subjects ranging from sacramental poetics to the culture of silent reading, there is a strong degree of nostalgia for re-enchantment among many Western Christians. In North American Protestantism, this nostalgia has assumed a number of particularly powerful guises. It has surfaced as an effort to resurrect the nineteenth-century argument from design; it can be heard in the aesthetic call to transfer incarnational and sacramental powers from the history of redemption to the workings of the imagination; and we encounter it in popular apologetics in the frequent use of the idea of a "God-shaped void" that every human possesses and God alone can fill.

All these efforts might be seen as instances of what Bonhoeffer calls "the attack by Christian apologetic on the adulthood of the world," and in his June 8 letter to Bethge, he dismisses them as being "pointless, ignoble, and unchristian." They are "pointless" because they seek to force the human race back into a state of adolescent dependence; they are "ignoble" in that their goal is "to exploit man's weakness for purposes that are alien to him"; and Bonhoeffer considers them "unchristian" because they confuse "Christ with one particular stage in man's religiousness, i.e. with a human law."[74]

Several letters from the summer of 1944 sketch the historical background that Bonhoeffer planned to fill in when the time came to write his book. In different intellectual disciplines and in a series of social and cultural practices, he spots evidence of the irreversible growth of human autonomy. Instead of reprimanding the world for having attained this degree of independence, Bonhoeffer asks that we see it as a historical development that Jesus Christ, as Lord of the world, has suffered to come to pass. By mid-summer, he was stating his point boldly, even brazenly. "The God who is with us is the God who forsakes us (Mark 15.34)," he wrote. "The God who lets us live in the world without the working hy-

73. Bonhoeffer, *Letters and Papers,* p. 326.

74. Bonhoeffer, *Letters and Papers,* p. 327.

pothesis of God is the God before whom we stand continually. Before God and with God we live without God. God lets himself be pushed out of the world on to the cross."[75]

As this passage indicates, Bonhoeffer hardly considered a religionless world to be a *world without Christ.* Or to put the point more positively, he expected the Church to continue to proclaim the good news of Christ crucified and Christ risen from the dead. On June 27, 1944, he complained to Bethge that modern Protestantism had sold the gospel short by reducing redemption to a release "from cares, distress, fears, and longings . . . in a better world beyond the grave." To Bonhoeffer, this misses the point of the Christian hope of resurrection, which unlike "the mythological hope . . . , sends a man back to his life on earth in a wholly new way." There is no line of escape for the Christian, who must, "like Christ himself ('My God, why hast thou forsaken me?'), . . . drink the earthly cup to the dregs." Only in the Christian's "doing so is the crucified and risen Lord with him, and he crucified and risen with Christ." The "redemption myths" arise from fear at life's boundaries, "but Christ takes hold of a man at the centre of his life."[76]

In his understanding and practice of the Christian faith, Bonhoeffer in the war years turned completely from metaphors of sight to those of hearing. "The great masquerade of evil has played havoc with all our ethical concepts," he wrote of the Nazi regime in a document meant to encourage his small band of co-conspirators in early 1943. The crucial question, he said, is "who stands fast?" in a world in which unbridled evil is readily "disguised as light, charity, historical necessity, or social justice." To answer this question, Bonhoeffer runs through a list of failures — all of which have to do with the *surveying* of the world from the vantage point of an abstract principle. Reason, zeal, conscience, duty, private virtue — none of these principles can provide a solid ground for viewing the world of the Nazis or for acting responsibly in it.[77]

Bonhoeffer then repeats the question, "Who stands fast?" And his answer is that only the person who *hears* the call of God in the scriptures, the sacraments, and the circumstances of this evil day can stand fast. "Only the man whose final standard is not his reason, his principles, his

75. Bonhoeffer, *Letters and Papers,* p. 360.

76. Bonhoeffer, *Letters and Papers,* pp. 336-37.

77. Bonhoeffer, *Letters and Papers,* pp. 4-5.

conscience, his freedom, or his virtue, but who is ready to sacrifice all this when he is called to obedient and responsible action in faith and in exclusive allegiance to God — the responsible man, who tries to make his whole life an answer to the question and call of God. Where are these responsible people?"[78] That is a good question. Will those who dwell in the solitude of a sensate age have ears to hear it?

78. Bonhoeffer, *Letters and Papers,* p. 5.

CHAPTER 6

Beauty

LIKE MANY THINGS we take for granted and assume to be timeless — such as the notion that each of us possesses a godlike faculty called the imagination or the view that the exclusive purpose of writing poetry is self-expression — beauty as we know it was born in the eighteenth century and came into its maturity in the nineteenth. That said, in case you wonder, I am not claiming that until then no lover's heart raced at the sight of his beloved or that no voice gasped in the presence of the sublime. On these matters, I am a realist of the kind Isak Dinesen had in mind in one of her remarkable stories, "The Supper at Elsinore." If we doubt the persistence of beauty, we only need to take a minute to look around us in a crowd and consider what one character from that story observes: "What a strange proof, [Fanny De Coninck] thought, are these . . . bodies here tonight of the fact that young men and women, half a century ago, sighed and shivered and lost themselves in ecstasies."[1]

Yes, beauty and its ecstasies have been around for a while, and even if we were to fail to recognize the proof of them that we carry in our bodies, we would know this fact from the remarkable history of reflection on beauty's meaning. Plato worked this theme ceaselessly and set beauty near the good at the peak of his scale of values, and in the history of the Christian church, from Augustine to Aquinas and beyond, beauty has been a source of wonder and a path to the divine.[2]

1. Isak Dinesen, *Seven Gothic Tales* (1934; repr., New York: Vintage, 1991), p. 238.

2. Under the pressure of political events and social change, beauty was significantly eclipsed as a subject of academic interest in the last decades of the twentieth century, but

In that sense, beauty was not born in the eighteenth century, but what did come into being at that time was the concept of beauty as the subject of a unique discipline within the larger philosophical enterprise. The development of this new disciplinary understanding was sudden — unfolding as it did over the brief span of several decades at mid-century — yet its influence proved lasting and extensive. From the concept of a separate discipline of aesthetics, there soon followed the idea of beauty as a surrogate for a seemingly discredited system of Christian belief. For many of the nineteenth century's most ardent apologists for beauty, the process that Emily Dickinson named "the abdication of belief" made urgent the need to press the case that beauty belonged on the abandoned throne.

My subject in this chapter is "the beauty of belief," and in the closing section, I will address that theme directly, but before we reach that point, we have historical ground to cover and a correlative theme — beauty *as* belief — to explore.

The Birth of Aesthetics

We begin in 1735, when a young German scholar, Alexander Baumgarten, published a treatise called "Philosophical meditations on some requirements of the poem" and in it introduced the idea of aesthetics as an independent philosophical discipline. At first, Baumgarten had in mind the modest goal of defending the relevance of sensory perception and demonstrating that it could produce valid knowledge. Only later would he and others expand the scope of aesthetics to make it a rigorous "investigation of art and a [general] theory of beauty and ugliness."[3]

Why at this particular point in history did the likes of Baumgarten and Moses Mendelssohn feel driven to defend sensibility and secure a special domain for art? A number of extraordinary books written in the

---

in the past decade that interest has begun to rise once again. Works such as Elaine Scarry's *On Beauty and Being Just* (Princeton: Princeton University Press, 1999) and Denis Donoghue's *Speaking of Beauty* (New Haven: Yale University Press, 2003) are representative of a vibrant, renewed emphasis upon the centrality of beauty in literary and cultural studies.

3. Kai Hammermeister, *The German Aesthetic Tradition* (Cambridge: Cambridge University Press, 2002), p. 4.

past century — from Martin Heidegger's *Being and Time* to Hans-Georg Gadamer's *Truth and Method* to Charles Taylor's *Sources of the Self* — have sought to answer that question. But for our purposes, I want to turn to a poet rather than a philosopher to clarify the issues at stake.[4] The poet is W. H. Auden, and his critique of modern aesthetics can be found in an essay titled "The Poet & The City," in which he examines "four aspects of our present *Weltanschauung* which have made an artistic vocation more difficult than it used to be."[5]

The second of those four aspects provides the backdrop for understanding the eighteenth-century emergence of aesthetics. Auden describes this particular development as *"the loss of belief in the significance and reality of sensory phenomena."* To explain what he means by the use of this term, he cites two towering figures from the early modern era, Martin Luther and René Descartes. The father of the Reformation drove a wedge between the inner dynamics of the spirit's experience and the outward realm of public deeds; he did so, Auden claims, by questioning the significance of sensory phenomena through his denial of "any intelligible relation between subjective Faith and objective Works." To use a distinction borrowed from Dietrich Bonhoeffer, it was hardly Luther's primary motive to sever the connections between inward spirit and outward nature, but the eventual cutting of this tie did prove to be a troubling secondary consequence of his thought.[6]

A century after Luther, "with his doctrine of primary and secondary qualities," Descartes struck a devastating blow against the senses and the evidence they provide to the mind and spirit.[7] For Descartes, the primary qualities of objects were such things as extension in length, width, and depth, along with the properties of substance and duration; the sec-

4. See Martin Heidegger, *Being and Time,* trans. Joan Stambaugh (Albany: State University of New York Press, 1996); Hans-Georg Gadamer, *Truth and Method,* 2nd ed., trans. Joel Weinsheimer and Donald G. Marshall (New York: Crossroad, 1989); and Charles Taylor, *Sources of the Self: The Making of the Modern Identity* (Cambridge, Mass.: Harvard University Press, 1989).

5. W. H. Auden, *The Dyer's Hand and Other Essays* (1962; repr., New York: Vintage, 1989), p. 78.

6. "One wonders why Luther's action had to be followed by consequences that were the exact opposite of what he intended, and that darkened the last years of his life, so that he sometimes even doubted the value of his life's work." Dietrich Bonhoeffer, *Letters and Papers from Prison,* enlarged ed., ed. Eberhard Bethge (New York: Collier, 1972), p. 123.

7. Auden, *Dyer's Hand,* p. 78.

ondary qualities — what our senses, and the arts, consider the "good stuff," such as sound, light, color, taste, and touch — may either exist in the object or be projected from the subject. We simply cannot know for certain which is the case.[8]

Auden says a conception of "sacramental analogies" had governed thinking about the phenomenal world for centuries before Luther and Descartes, and it had served efficiently the needs of the saint as well as the demands of the artist. In that system of analogies, the senses offered outward evidence of inward and invisible realities, and both the inner sign and the outer manifestation were considered to be real, valuable, and substantial. That is not to say that the testimony of those senses was unambiguous. As Erich Auerbach argues, Christian history has been permeated by an "antagonism between sensory appearance and meaning," because of the distinction between "event" and "meaning" that a doctrine of revelation requires.[9]

Nevertheless, for the medieval man or woman, a basic spiritual assurance remained, which was that a measure of truth about the God the heart worshipped could be discovered in the wonders the eyes beheld. According to Auden, it is this confidence that has been steadily eroding over the past 150 years, as science, abetted by philosophy and theology, "has destroyed our faith in the naïve observation of our senses" by informing us we cannot know what the world really *is like.* We can only know our subjective notions about reality, and those have more to do with the "particular human purpose[s] we have in view" than with the actual nature of things.[10]

In turn, this view of the self and reality "destroys the traditional conception of art as *mimesis,* because there is no longer a nature 'out there' to be truly or falsely imitated." As a result, the poet or artist can only be *true* to his or her "subjective sensations and feelings." To highlight this point, Auden cites William Blake's famous remark that "some people see

8. Charles Taylor says of the Cartesian "objectification of nature": "[According to Descartes] we also have to clear up our understanding of matter and stop thinking of it as the locus of events and qualities whose true nature is mental. And this we do by objectifying it, that is, by understanding it as 'disenchanted', as mere mechanism, as devoid of any spiritual essence or expressive dimension." *Sources of the Self,* pp. 145-46.

9. Erich Auerbach, *Mimesis: The Representation of Reality in Western Literature,* trans. Willard R. Trask (Princeton: Princeton University Press, 1953), p. 49.

10. Auden, *Dyer's Hand,* p. 78.

the sun as a round golden disc the size of a guinea but that he sees it as a host crying Holy, Holy, Holy." Blake may have abhorred Newton's science, but he accepted its division "between the physical and the spiritual." The poet simply turned the tables on the physicist, as he lauded the spiritual imagination, consigned the material universe to the status of "the abode of Satan," and refused to attach any "value to what his physical eye" looked upon.[11]

In the early eighteenth century, then, Alexander Baumgarten found himself thrust into the middle of this debate about the senses. He not only had to work against the influence of philosophical naturalism, but he also faced the considerable challenge of Protestant pietism and its denigration of the splendors of the created order. If Descartes had dismissed their evidence as episodic, unmethodical, and subjective, and if people such as Blake were to take them to disclose little more than the measurements of Satan's dwelling place, how were the senses to be defended?

To rehabilitate sensory perception, Baumgarten set about analyzing the obscure images and unfocused reflections that fall somewhere between the disjointed world of private perception and the ordered domains of science and rational thought. Following the lead of Leibniz, he called this the realm of *confused cognition,* and to account for the activities within its borders, he proposed a "science of sensual cognition" called aesthetics. This new discipline would work the night shift, sifting through and making sense of the mass of rough, raw perceptions that pour into the mind each day. To Baumgarten, this confusion "is a necessary condition for the discovery of truth, because nature does not make leaps from obscure to distinct thought. Out of the night dawn leads to daylight."[12]

The sensations of dawn needed a theory to explain the rules that governed them, and the aesthetic doctrine of beauty was created to provide this. To be sure, for Baumgarten the beauty revealed in art paralleled the harmony to be found in the mind of God and the order of the world. Yet he was not greatly concerned with questions of theology or apologetics, because his primary focus was on the power of art to shelter, organize, and preserve the immediacy of experience and the intricacy of perception. According to Kai Hammermeister, in the end, the "truth of

11. Auden, *Dyer's Hand,* pp. 78-79.

12. Alexander Baumgarten, quoted in Hammermeister, *German Aesthetic Tradition,* pp. 7, 8.

art for Baumgarten is not a mere preparation for logical truth, nor . . . is it accessible by means of logic." Instead, it remains "sensual" and "unconceptualized." At first, Baumgarten may have intended aesthetics to "be a prop for the perfection of rationality," but in his wake the discipline "no longer defended its usefulness by reference to its helpfulness for logical modes of thought. Instead, it presented itself both as independent of and even productively opposed to rationality."[13]

The separation of aesthetics and rationality — of art and reason — soon became a commonplace of Western thought. To use the terms of Immanuel Kant, the preeminent figure of late eighteenth-century aesthetics, both reason and art worked with the sensory manifold, that array of unorganized particulars furnished to the mind by the experience of the senses. Rationality worked upon these phenomena for its own particular purposes, unifying them through the synthesizing powers of the understanding and organizing them for the purposes of scientific description and technological control.

In the meantime, as reason charted the workings of the kingdom of necessity, art was busy building a separate fortress of freedom. In his *Critique of Judgment,* Kant defined art as being "distinguished from nature as doing *(facere)* is from acting or producing in general"; the product of artistic activity proves to be a "work," whereas nature only produces an "effect." "By right," Kant argues, "only production through freedom, i.e., through a capacity for choice that grounds its actions in reason, should be called art."[14] This power of choice is a sign of consciousness freely at labor, and it marks the distinctiveness of art. Here, at least, freedom is alive and vital, and the human mind and affections have their chance to make a mark, to leave a durable and indelible impression upon an indifferent universe.

In this same passage, Kant draws a sharp distinction between *art* and *handicraft,* or between what we might call the *fine* and the *useful* arts. In his words, the first (fine art) "is called liberal" and the second, the useful, is termed "remunerative art." Fine art can be successful "only as play, i.e., an occupation that is agreeable in itself; the second [useful art] is regarded as labor, i.e., an occupation that is disagreeable (burden-

13. Hammermeister, *German Aesthetic Tradition,* p. 13.

14. Immanuel Kant, *Critique of the Power of Judgment,* ed. Paul Guyer, trans. Paul Guyer and Eric Matthews (Cambridge: Cambridge University Press, 2000), p. 182.

some) in itself" and is attractive only because it brings payment.[15] Once again, we have a world of freedom — the playful domain of art that does not look beyond itself for its ground or purpose — and a province of bondage — that being the realm of the crafts in which we labor with the tools of our trade.

For Kant, as for Baumgarten and many others who were to come after them in the nineteenth century, beauty was the central category for understanding the "fine arts." "Only that which has the end of its existence in itself," wrote Kant, "[i.e.,] the human being, who determines his ends himself through reason, . . . this human being alone is capable of an ideal of beauty." Animals may find things agreeable, but only human beings can appreciate them for their beauty, which is an end in itself and serves as a marker of the unique supremacy of art. "Beauty is the form of the purposiveness of an object, insofar as it is perceived in it without representation of an end."[16] For Kant the "experience of the beautiful is . . . an experience of 'purposiveness without purpose,' a sense that things fit together according to a purpose that we cannot state."[17]

By the end of the eighteenth century, then, a new and powerful understanding of beauty and the arts had planted its flag on the Western intellectual landscape and staked its claim to a sizable plot of cultural ground. The aesthetic realm was governed by a set of interlocking assumptions that had at their base the belief that science disclosed a cosmos governed by law and necessity, while the spirit's inner drama played itself out in oppositional freedom. Yet as highly as modernity prized this inner realm, it worried about its epistemological status and struggled to reaffirm the *"significance and reality of sensory phenomena."* The creation of an aesthetic domain and the elaboration of a doctrine of the fine arts were meant to establish the epistemological authority of sensory perception and to secure the spiritual rights of beauty. To that end, the eighteenth century placed the arts side by side with the sciences in a setting in which each was to become increasingly impervious, even incomprehensible, to the other.

It was no coincidence that the dream of a domain of beauty arose at

15. Kant, *Critique,* p. 183.

16. Kant, *Critique,* pp. 117, 120.

17. Terry Pinkard, *German Philosophy 1760-1860: The Legacy of Idealism* (Cambridge: Cambridge University Press, 2002), p. 72.

the same time that new intellectual and social realities were causing a great deal of unrest for Christians across the theological spectrum. Over the course of the eighteenth century, a number of new forces brought sharp challenges to the Christian tradition, as rationalism subjected the concept of miracles to a withering critique, the historical-critical method called the trustworthiness of the scriptures into question, and Enlightenment ideals of universality and fairness questioned the particular and exclusive claims of Christian revelation.

In these theological crises of the eighteenth century, Hans Frei sees clear evidence of "the centrifugal pressure of modernity," as the religious thought of northwestern Europe moved toward a polarized opposition between those who saw revelation as a unique and saving event and those who rejected altogether the idea of revelation in favor of an unspecified theism or natural religion.[18] In the late eighteenth century, the advocates of this "natural religion" included almost all who championed the realm of the aesthetic and found in beauty a rich alternative to the poverty of a material world. The harder it became to trust in the God of Abraham, Isaac, and Jacob — and of Jesus Christ — the more beguiling it became to believe in beauty, entire and alone.

Beauty as Belief

At first, the advocates of beauty worked to tether it to a concept of reality, divine or natural, in order to keep it from being carried away by any gusts of human subjectivity. For some, such as Samuel Taylor Coleridge, Christian belief provided the anchor; to the end of his life he remained convinced that religious belief could be reconciled with "nineteenth-century scientific thought," just as he believed it possible to reconcile historic Christianity with the modern discovery of the self and the modern passion for scientific rationalism and technological control.[19] For William Wordsworth and others, it was not Christian orthodoxy so much as ordinary nature that would secure the rights of the spirit in an

18. Hans W. Frei, *The Eclipse of Biblical Narrative: A Study in Eighteenth and Nineteenth Century Hermeneutics* (New Haven: Yale University Press, 1974), pp. 62-63.

19. Richard Holmes, *Coleridge: Darker Reflections, 1804-1834* (New York: Pantheon, 1999), p. 539.

increasingly material world; to them, Christian belief and the Bible were "the grand store-house of enthusiastic and meditative Imagination" that pointed to the primary revelation to be found in the interaction of the human mind and nature.[20]

As the nineteenth century wore on, however, art's ties to both Christian belief and the natural world continued to fray, and by century's end they had snapped. The poetry and letters of John Keats show the difficult challenges a brilliant mind faced, as it labored to maintain the bond between beauty and nature at the beginning of that century. Having trained for a career in medicine and having been drawn to the secular skepticism that was in the cultural air of his day, Keats had little interest in Christian thought and practice per se. Yet he retained a passionate concern for the questions of truth that had occupied Christian thought for centuries, and he intuitively understood the ongoing debate about beauty in his own day. Specifically, like Baumgarten and Kant, he had a strong spatial sense of beauty and believed it might offer a retreat from the world of mortal toil and sorrow. The opening lines of his long poem, *Endymion,* capture this sense evocatively:

> A thing of beauty is a joy for ever:
> Its loveliness increases; it will never
> Pass into nothingness; but still will keep
> A bower quiet for us, and a sleep
> Full of sweet dreams, and health, and quiet breathing.[21]

If the foxes have holes, and the birds of the air have nests, may not beauty offer those who bear the burdens of consciousness a place to lay their heads?

In "Ode on a Grecian Urn," Keats offered one of his most extensive — and certainly most well known — poetic treatments of beauty and belief. The poem opens with a tribute to the "still unravish'd bride of quietness," the "foster-child of silence and slow time" that is the urn.[22] After posing a

20. William Wordsworth, quoted in M. H. Abrams, *Natural Supernaturalism: Tradition and Revolution in Romantic Literature* (New York: Norton, 1971), p. 32.

21. John Keats, *Selected Poems and Letters,* ed. Douglas Bush (Boston: Houghton, 1959), p. 39.

22. All references to the text of "Ode on a Grecian Urn" are taken from *Selected Poems,* pp. 207-8.

series of questions — "What men or gods are these? . . . What mad pursuit? What struggle to escape? What pipes and timbrels? What wild ecstasy?" — it unfolds as a meditation on human mutability and historical process. Everything depicted in the second stanza fades or fails over the course of ordinary experience, but in the extraordinary timeless world of the urn, these realities endure. Here, in the scene depicted on the urn, the "fair youth's" song never ends, and the trees will never lose their leaves. The bold lover cannot win his beloved, but "do not grieve," the speaker instructs him, for "she cannot fade" and "for ever wilt thou love, and she be fair!"

Walter Jackson Bate notes that at this point the poem's sympathies begin "to desert the urn for the painful world of process, of which the urn is oblivious."[23] The urn may preserve mutable experience, but it always will remain a "Cold Pastoral." There is a limit to the powers of preservation, for in the words of one of Keats's greatest poetic descendants, William Butler Yeats, "the mountain grass/Cannot but keep the form/Where the mountain hare has lain."[24]

Still, the power of this beautiful "silent form" remains:

When old age shall this generation waste,
Thou shalt remain, in midst of other woe
Than ours, a friend to man, to whom thou say'st,
"Beauty is truth, truth beauty, — that is all
Ye know on earth, and all ye need to know."

According to Bate, these final words are meant to convey what Keats called the "greeting of the Spirit," that dynamic encounter of the imagination with nature which "is itself as much a part of nature, or reality, as is its object." With the "harmony ('beauty,' 'intensity') of the greeting mind and its object," writes Bate quoting Keats, "we have a fresh achievement altogether within nature: a 'truth — whether it existed before or not' in which reality has been awakened further into awareness."[25]

A year before he composed this ode, Keats had outlined in a letter

23. W. Jackson Bate, *John Keats* (Cambridge, Mass.: Belknap Press of Harvard University Press, 1963), p. 513.

24. William Butler Yeats, *Selected Poems and Four Plays*, 4th ed., ed. M. L. Rosenthal (New York: Scribner, 1996), p. 63.

25. Bate, *John Keats*, pp. 517-18.

his view of religion and the theory of poetry that followed from it. "You know my ideas about Religion," he told Benjamin Bailey, who was concerned about his friend's spiritual uncertainty. Keats had "a mind so left to itself — an orphan mind," Bailey was to write decades after the poet's death, that it was hardly surprising he was given to skepticism. "Yet he was no scoffer, & in no sense was he an infidel," Bailey wrote of his friend.[26] In his own letter to Bailey, Keats explained, "I do not think myself more in the right than other people and that nothing in this world is proveable," but he also admitted that he could not, even for a "short 10 Minutes," enter into this subject as eagerly as his friend was able to do. He was too skeptical of the outmoded doctrines of Christianity and too committed to his own "system of Salvation" to take the Bible's claims seriously.[27]

At times, Keats confessed to Bailey, he even looked skeptically upon poetry itself and considered it to be "a mere Jack a lanthern to amuse whoever may chance to be struck with its brilliance." Since, "as Tradesmen say everything is worth what it will fetch," it may be that "every mental pursuit takes its reality and worth from the ardour of the pursuer — being in itself a nothing." Still, despite the conjuring powers of ardent pursuit, there are many "Things real" and "things semireal" in the world. Substantial realities, such as the "Sun Moon & Stars and passages of Shakspeare," can stand on their own without the support of human willing or imagining, but many things of value, "Things semireal such as Love, the Clouds" do "require a greeting of the Spirit to make them wholly exist."

These "semireal" things are not called out of nothing by the mind but are made vital through their contact with it. They require the vivifying power of the imagination to bring to life their latent form and vitality, and without a "greeting of the Spirit," they remain mute and incomplete, because they are objects in desperate need of the subjects who alone can make them whole. In turn, they are to be distinguished from what Keats identifies as a third class of "things." These are the fantasies of human imagining, the "Nothings which are made Great and dignified by an ardent pursuit — Which by the by stamps the burgundy mark on the bot-

26. Benjamin Bailey, quoted in Bate, *John Keats,* p. 217.

27. Keats, *Selected Poems,* p. 268. The reference to "system of Salvation" is quoted in Abrams, *Natural Supernaturalism,* p. 67.

tles of our Minds, insomuch as they are able to '*consecrate whate'er they look upon.*'"[28]

This celebration of the "greeting Spirit" follows a series of similar observations Keats had made in previous letters to Bailey and to his own brothers. Even as he was writing his great odes and entering his death struggle with tuberculosis, Keats was forging in his vision of beauty as belief a romantic variation upon the aesthetics of Baumgarten and Kant. "What the imagination seizes as Beauty must be truth," he wrote to Bailey. "The Imagination may be compared to Adam's dream — he awoke and found it truth. . . . O for a Life of Sensations rather than of Thoughts!"[29] A few weeks later, he told his brothers of his conviction that "the excellence of every Art is its intensity, capable of making all disagreeables evaporate, from their being in close relationship with Beauty & Truth." Keats cherished most of all a quality he believed "Shakespeare possessed so enormously." He called it "Negative Capability" and defined it as the capacity for remaining "in uncertainties, Mysteries, doubts, without any irritable reaching after fact & reason."[30] This was Kant's disinterestedness given a Keatsian twist, just as the theory of the imagination was an intuitive variation upon the Kantian theme of synthetic judgment.[31]

What Keats held together at the start of the nineteenth century — the countervailing demands of spirit and nature — began to come asunder as the century unfolded. Romanticism depended upon a spiritualized view of nature to drive its system. It relied on the spirit's complex courtship of nature, which in theory the romantics considered to be a spouse capable of responding to the intricate demands and growing

28. Keats, *Selected Poems,* pp. 268-69. Keats was troubled by such a mind-centered understanding of poetry, but many of his poetic descendants thrilled to the prospect of these special capacities. For example, in 1936, William Butler Yeats memorably wrote that once the mind had discovered its own creative powers, it had to press even further: "that soul must become its own betrayer, its own deliverer, the one activity, the mirror turn lamp." Quoted in Richard Ellmann, *Yeats: The Man and the Masks* (1948; repr., New York: Norton, 1978), p. 284.

29. Keats, *Selected Poems,* pp. 257, 258.

30. Keats, *Selected Poems,* pp. 260, 261.

31. Walter Jackson Bate notes that it was during his brief but intense friendship with Benjamin Bailey that Keats first began to use the term "disinterestedness," and within a year "the word and all it represented were to become something of a polar star." *John Keats,* p. 202.

powers of the imagination. If beauty was to be something more than one of those "Nothings" made great by an ardent pursuit, there had to be a "something" in nature with which spirit could unite.

For the romantics, that "something" varied from one writer to another. For Wordsworth it was something like the spirit of God that brooded over the world and coursed through nature and the human soul alike. Why should paradise be a "history only of departed things,/Or a mere fiction of what never was?" the poet asked,

> For the discerning intellect of Man,
> When wedded to this goodly universe
> In love and holy passion, shall find these
> A simple produce of the common day.[32]

In the early works of Ralph Waldo Emerson, a similar intimacy was considered to be a given. For him, spirit and nature were all but identical, because "nature is the opposite of the soul, answering to it part for part. One is seal, and one is print. Its beauty is the beauty of his own mind. Its laws are the laws of his own mind."[33] And if in the poetry and letters of Keats the sense of nature often seemed more material than spiritual, he nevertheless labored to keep imagination and nature wedded to one another and to make certain that the spirit stayed faithful to its partner. As long as that relationship held, beauty could claim a lineage both in nature and in spirit, even as it earnestly set about completing the tasks that lay before it as a surrogate of belief.

With this account, I have been describing a historical drama of sorts, and in it Kant, Keats, and others have played crucial parts. We have reached the point, however, where Charles Darwin walks on stage, and with his entry, the scene changes, the plot takes a new direction entirely, and the actors find their roles transformed in the very middle of the act. There were others, such as Charles Lyell in geology, who had appeared in scenes before Darwin, and many others who came after him. Yet in the drama of nature and spirit, he was the one who broke up the marriage by revealing the irreconcilable differences between the workings of the for-

32. William Wordsworth, "Preface" to *The Excursion,* quoted in Abrams, *Natural Supernaturalism,* p. 467.

33. Ralph Waldo Emerson, *Essays and Lectures,* ed. Joel Porte (New York: Library of America, 1983), p. 56.

mer and the aspirations of the latter. As John Dewey explains, with Darwin, intellectual "interest shifts from the wholesale essence back of special changes to the question of how special changes serve and defeat concrete purposes." It shifts from a preoccupation with a divine "intelligence that shaped things once for all" and turns its attention to "the particular intelligences which things are even now shaping."[34]

Although some sentimentalists and popularizers would try to do so, it was hard to romanticize the survival of the fittest, and if the romantics had originally relied upon the marriage of spirit and nature to produce a sanctuaried beauty, their union was now being dissolved. If beauty was to have permanent strength and status, by the latter decades of the nineteenth century, it would be that of a "Nothing" whose dignity was a gift bequeathed to it by the "ardent pursuit" that had conjured it into being *ex nihilo.*

The poetry of Emily Dickinson provides an illuminating guide to the remarkable transition that takes us from the clear confidence of Kant and Keats to the troubled and turbulent world of contemporary aesthetics. Dickinson was an avid student of science, a keen reader of intellectual culture, and a brilliant artist who treasured her poetic prerogatives and longed to believe in the spirit's possibilities. In her childhood and adolescence, she took comfort from the argument from design and eagerly studied the evidence nature offered for everything from the existence of God to the resurrection of the body.[35] Even more than Keats, she lamented the modern loss of belief:

> The abdication of Belief
> Makes the Behavior small —
> Better an ignis fatuus
> Than no illume at all — (#1581)

34. John Dewey, *The Influence of Darwin on Philosophy and Other Essays* (1910; repr., Amherst, N.Y.: Prometheus, 1997), p. 15.

35. In her educational training, Dickinson was strongly influenced by the work of Edward Hitchcock, a prominent antebellum geologist who taught at the Amherst Academy and served as President of Amherst College. Later in life, the poet wrote to a friend: "When Flowers annually died and I was a child, I used to read Dr Hitchcock's Book on the Flowers of North America. This comforted their Absence — assuring me they lived." *The Letters of Emily Dickinson,* ed. Thomas H. Johnson and Theodora Ward (Cambridge, Mass.: Belknap Press of Harvard University Press, 1958), 2:573.

Many readers of this poem, which begins with the image of God's "Right Hand" being "amputated," assume that "abdication" serves as a synonym for "abandonment" and take the poem to be faulting the modern world for having discarded belief. But Dickinson's sense of things is less clear, because it is belief itself that has abdicated the throne and left the ungoverned human race to its own devices.

To Dickinson, it often appeared that only the poets could compensate for this loss. In 1863, she composed a poetic hymn in praise of the poets of beauty. "I reckon — When I count at all — ," she wrote, "First — Poets," then the sun, summer, and the heaven of God. But why value all these different things equally, when one — the poet — "comprehends the whole?" Poets create a summer that never falls away, and their sun is "extravagant" by any standard. And even if the "Further Heaven" proves to

Be Beautiful as they prepare
For Those who worship Them —
It is too difficult a Grace —
To justify the Dream — (#533)

The poets, as another poem would have it, have the "Essentials Oils" wrung from their lives by means of that suffering which is "the gift of Screws." Their lives will perish, but their works will endure:

The General Rose — decay —
But this — in Lady's Drawer
Make Summer — When the Lady lie
In Ceaseless Rosemary — (#772)

If "The Definition of Beauty is/That Definition is none," Dickinson concludes in another poem, then all we can know is that it is "Of Heaven, easing Analysis,/Since Heaven and He are One" (#797).

But as is so often the case with Dickinson, that is only half the story. For every poem of hers that lauds poetry and declares it to be an everlasting boon, another draws art back within the circuit of mortality. The most famous of these poems is a commentary on the "Beauty is truth, truth beauty" lines of Keats's ode. Dickinson's ironic takeoff begins with the poetic speaker announcing,

I died for Beauty — but was scarce
Adjusted in the Tomb

When One who died for Truth, was lain
In an adjoining Room —

These two chatter into the night, declaring, "Themself are One." This sibling talk would go on forever, were it not for the stubborn fact of death, which claims their lives, their lips, and at last, their names:

And so, as Kinsmen, met a Night —
We talked between the Rooms —
Until the Moss had reached our lips —
And covered up — Our names — (#448)

Dickinson's confidence in poetry as beauty's sanctuary was shaken by post-Darwinian science, which undermined the idea of intelligent design upon which romantic poetics and Protestant apologetics had been grounded. In a poem from early adulthood, she took a stock image of nineteenth-century evangelical apologetics — the emergence of the butterfly from its cocoon — and gave it a skeptical slant. In her treatment of this figure, the butterfly is a mindless winged creature that emerges on "a Summer Afternoon —/Repairing Everywhere —/Without Design — that I could trace." The butterfly flutters in a field "Where Men made Hay — " and struggles "hard/With an opposing Cloud —." There is nothing to meet in nature but "Parties — Phantom as Herself —" which

To Nowhere — seemed to go
In purposeless Circumference —
As 'twere a Tropic Show —

Upon this carnival of random beauty in senseless motion, God looks down without interest, for "This Audience of Idleness/Disdained them, from the Sky — " (#610). Deprived of its divine audience, the "phantom" self can only play its part in a "Tropic Show," an endless play of signs without design. No longer a *type* of a higher spiritual reality, nature in this poem can only prompt *tropes* of human longing.[36]

36. In this study of the "purposeless Circumference" that is "a Tropic Show," Dickinson uncannily anticipates poststructuralist views of language as a system of endless tropes and infinite differences. In the latter decades of the twentieth century, such a vision of language was often employed to attack or dismantle modernist notions of beauty and aesthetic form.

The silence of this God who is the "Audience of Idleness" is mirrored by the silence of nature. Nature had shouted to Wordsworth and Henry David Thoreau and spoken softly to Keats, but it now stood silent, having been rendered mute by a process that had taken several centuries to unfold. "About two hundred years ago, the idea that truth was made rather than found began to take hold of the imagination of Europe," Richard Rorty notes. It was in the nineteenth century that men and women began to realize that the world outside themselves had nothing to say to them. The idea of a truth that is "out there" in the world is the legacy of an era when "the world was seen as the creation of a being who had a language of his own." According to Rorty, by the end of the nineteenth century, some of the more enlightened among us came to realize that such a being — i.e., God — does not exist. And in light of this fact, we can only conclude "the world does not speak. Only we do."[37] Nature may endure, but for Dickinson at times, as for Rorty always, she has nothing to say:

> We pass, and she abides.
> We conjugate Her Skill
> While She creates and federates
> Without a syllable — (#798)

According to Albert Gelpi, throughout her life, Dickinson kept raising the same fundamental questions: "Do I know myself only in connection with, even in submission to, something beyond self? Or must I make my own meaning in a murky universe?" And "when I behold Nature," is there some inherent connection between "the phenomenon and its significance, between the concrete thing and its universal relevance, between physics and metaphysics?" In the terms of poetry and aesthetics, "the question is whether Nature is type or trope."[38]

In Rorty's categories, *types* are truths as they are supposedly found; *tropes* are truths as they are actually made. If nature is a *type,* it is grounded in a higher reality, and each of its elements points to that reality. This was the Puritan view of nature in the New World, just as it had

37. Richard Rorty, *Contingency, Irony, and Solidarity* (Cambridge: Cambridge University Press, 1989), pp. 3, 5, 6.

38. Albert J. Gelpi, *Emily Dickinson: The Mind of the Poet* (1965; repr., New York: Norton, 1971), p. 153.

been, in modified form, the dominant understanding of reality in medieval Catholic Europe. By the early nineteenth century, however, Puritanism had all but disappeared as a vital intellectual force, and at the same time, idealist philosophy and literary romanticism had begun to trumpet the newly discovered powers of the imaginative self. As we have seen, nineteenth-century romanticism initially attempted to balance its emerging view of nature as a *trope* anchored in the creative human mind with the more ancient understanding of it as a *type* of transcendent reality. Over the course of the century, the balance shifted, and by the time Dickinson began to write poetry, *types* had all but given way to *tropes.*[39]

We recall Auden's observation concerning the way in which the modern understanding of the cosmos destroys the idea of "art as *mimesis,* for there is no longer a nature 'out there' to be truly or falsely imitated." Although Dickinson did not give up on the idea of design entirely, she did question the viability of beauty as a surrogate for belief. If what some of her poems were beginning to imagine was true — that truth and beauty are "Nothings" spun off by the energy of "ardent pursuit" — it would be difficult for the heavy laden to find rest in them. Along with others in the late nineteenth century, she anticipated what we have already seen to be one of the central dilemmas of contemporary cultural life: How are we to believe in anything, if we consider truth to be something that has been *created* entirely by our desire to believe rather than something that has been *discovered* through our capacity to learn and to receive?

Friedrich Nietzsche set this challenge more clearly than anyone else in the late nineteenth century. In *Twilight of the Idols,* he wrote bluntly about the origins of beauty in the will to power and scuttled all efforts to ground it in nature or the transcendent self or in the offspring of their union. There is nothing essential about beauty, he claimed, because "nothing is so conditional, let us say *circumscribed,* as our feeling for the beautiful." We may believe "the world itself is filled with beauty," but our belief is based upon our forgetfulness, for we are the ones who have created this beauty. We alone have "bestowed beauty upon the world — alas! only a very human, all too human beauty."[40]

39. For a fuller discussion of these issues and their implications for poetics and aesthetics, see Roger Lundin, *Emily Dickinson and the Art of Belief,* 2nd ed. (Grand Rapids: Eerdmans, 2004), pp. 44-48, 218-20.

40. Friedrich Nietzsche, *Twilight of the Idols* and *The Anti-Christ,* trans. R. J. Hollingdale (London: Penguin, 1990), p. 89.

To Nietzsche beauty was not a product of the marriage of spirit and nature but a matter of "man . . . [transforming] things until they mirror his power — until they are reflections of his perfection. This *compulsion* to transform into the perfect is — art." In analyzing what he terms the "psychology of the artist," Nietzsche describes the process by means of which the artist fabricates the beautiful. "From out of this feeling [of plenitude] one gives to things, one *compels* them to take, one rapes them — one calls this procedure *idealizing*."[41]

There is much we can learn about beauty from this nineteenth-century journey from the imagery of intimacy to that of violation. "Is the world actually made beautiful because *man* finds it so?" Nietzsche asks rhetorically. His answer is simple: "Nothing is beautiful, only man: on this piece of naïvety rests all aesthetics, it is the *first* truth of aesthetics." The second truth, which follows upon it, is that "nothing is ugly but *degenerate* man — the domain of aesthetic judgment is therewith defined." In language that haunts after Auschwitz, Nietzsche boasts of being able to measure ugliness "with a dynamometer." When a man feels depressed, he can assume "the proximity of something 'ugly,'" and this ugliness represents a clear threat to "his will to power, his courage, his pride." In the presence of degrading ugliness, "a feeling of *hatred* then springs up; what is man then hating?" The answer is the *"decline of his type."* And this he hates "out of the profoundest instinct of his species." Indeed, "it is the profoundest hatred there is. It is for its sake that art is *profound*."[42]

41. Nietzsche, *Twilight,* pp. 82-83. With Nietzsche, the persistent question is to know how seriously to take his pronouncements. Are they exercises in ironic suggestiveness? Or are they earnest, angry efforts at self-assertion? Charles Taylor offers a balanced assessment: "One after the other, the authoritative horizons of life, Christian and humanist, are cast off as shackles on the will. Only the will to power remains. The power and impact of Nietzsche's work come from his fierce espousal of this destructive movement which he pushes to the limit." Nevertheless, Nietzsche "also seems to have held that the will to power of self-defining man would be disastrous. Man as a purely self-dependent will to power must be 'overcome', to use Zarathustra's expression." Charles Taylor, *Hegel* (Cambridge: Cambridge University Press, 1975), p. 563. That Nietzsche's rhetoric celebrated violence and violation is unquestionable; it is less clear that he found a way of "overcoming" disastrous self-will. For Hans Urs von Balthasar's ambivalent reading of Nietzsche on this score, see Edward T. Oakes, *Pattern of Redemption: The Theology of Hans Urs von Balthasar* (New York: Continuum, 1994), pp. 90-93.

42. Nietzsche, *Twilight,* pp. 89-90.

Nietzsche had contempt for Kant's ideal of aesthetic perception as a disinterested apprehension of the beautiful, just as he did for the views of art-for-art's sake that had flowed from the Kantian source. He rejected the idea that aesthetics had to do with a unified experience set apart from science and granted the right to rule over its own limited domain. Nietzsche had no desire to rest in any Keatsian bowers or gaze disinterestedly upon any Grecian urns, for he was too busy trying to establish the rule of aesthetics over every domain of knowledge and action. From epistemology to ethics and beyond, everything became for Nietzsche a matter of art, and beauty was no longer a surrogate for belief but a product of the will to power, that source and substance of all beliefs.

The Beauty of Belief

In his recent study of the German aesthetic tradition, Kai Hammermeister calls Nietzsche's endeavor a "remarkable" attempt to effect "nothing less than an aestheticization of philosophy at large" and of all moral, cultural, and spiritual endeavors.[43] On behalf of art, Nietzsche sought not provincial rule — with the aesthetic serving as a kind of Switzerland of the spirit — but centralized control.

In claiming this ground for aesthetics, Nietzsche hardly acted alone. In analyzing the Nietzschean declaration of war against Christianity ("Hear me, for I am he; do not at any price mistake me. Am I understood? — Dionysus versus the Crucified"), Karl Barth says the philosopher was merely saying "with less restraint" and "greater honesty" what "Goethe, Hegel, Kant and Leibniz" had long been arguing, and indeed, what "the spirit of all European humanity as fashioned and developed since the 16th century" had been intimating with increasing boldness. If Nietzsche is to be blamed for everything from reactionary Fascism to leftist perspectivalism, according to Barth the fault ultimately lies with "the European spirit during the last centuries." In its most distinguished representatives, that spirit has lustily promoted the belief that the human mind in its "last and deepest isolation" is alone "the eye and measure and master and even the essence of all things. What Goethe [and others] quietly lived out Nietzsche had to speak out continually with the nervous vi-

43. Hammermeister, *German Aesthetic Tradition,* p. 146.

olence of ill-health."[44] Nietzsche, that is, was harvesting and marketing in the late nineteenth century cultural crops that others had planted generations before him.

Yet what was it that Nietzsche, gleaning from the European tradition, found "absolutely intolerable and unequivocally perverted" in the Christian faith? The answer, Barth says, can be discovered in his declaration of war: "Dionysus versus the Crucified." Dionysus, Zarathustra — indeed, Nietzsche himself, as he wished to envision himself — this was the ethical and spiritual ideal, "the lonely, noble, strong, proud, natural, healthy, wise, outstanding, splendid man, the superman." In contrast to this lofty figure — a real beauty, so to speak — Christianity has offered a far different ideal, of which Nietzsche says, "this ideal we contest."[45]

The Christian faith sets against the Dionysian ideal what Barth calls the gospel's "blatant claim that the only true man is the man who is little, poor and sick, . . . who is weak and not strong, who does not evoke admiration but sympathy, who is not solitary but gregarious — the mass-man." Christian belief goes a step further and speaks of a crucified God; it identifies "God Himself with this human type" and demands of all men and women "not merely sympathy with others but that they themselves should be those who excite sympathy and not admiration." In Nietzsche's words, it is disgusting that in Christianity "the neighbour is transfigured into a God." He concluded that if God had indeed chosen "what is weak and foolish and ignoble and despised in the eyes of the world" as his standard of beauty and virtue, there is nothing for us to do but to resist Christianity, which "is the greatest misfortune of the human race thus far."[46]

Once again, Barth says, the context is important, because in his aestheticizing opposition to the Crucified One, Nietzsche was only trumpeting at the close of the nineteenth century what a host of others had been murmuring in muted tones for decades. "Goethe, too, had no great time for Christianity," but he made his repudiation of it "cool and good-tempered and mild." The same was true "of the great philosophical Idealists of the time, of Kant, Fichte, Schelling and Hegel," according to Barth. They had little use for the Christianity of the New Testament but were

44. Karl Barth, *Church Dogmatics,* ed. G. W. Bromiley and T. F. Torrance (Edinburgh: T. & T. Clark, 1956-62), III.2.236, 232.

45. Barth, *Church Dogmatics,* III.2.239.

46. Barth, *Church Dogmatics,* III.2.239.

"restrained and cautious and sparing" in their critiques, and even their materialist descendants, such as Strauss and Feuerbach, stopped short of proposing that Dionysus take on the Crucified.[47]

What Barth calls the "new thing in Nietzsche" was "the development of humanity without the fellow-man," which was, after all, the secret humanity of the post-Cartesian ideal. Christianity confronts this Nietzschean "superman" with "the figure of suffering man." It places before the Olympian man the "Crucified, Jesus, as the Neighbour," and in his person "a whole host of others who are wholly and utterly ignoble and despised in the eyes of the world (of the world of Zarathustra, the true world of men), the hungry and thirsty and naked and sick and captive, a whole ocean of human meanness and painfulness." Christianity audaciously informs Dionysus-Zarathustra that he is not a god and says that if he wishes to be redeemed, he must belong to the Crucified One and be in "fellowship with this mean and painful host of His people."[48]

Barth credits Nietzsche with having recovered Christian truths that modernity had been content to misconstrue or ignore. Nietzsche uncovered the gospel, he explains, "in a form which was missed even by the majority of its champions, let alone its opponents, in the 19th century." This advocate of Dionysus did the servants of the Crucified One a service by "bringing before us the fact that we have to keep to this form [of the gospel] as unconditionally as he rejected it, in self-evident antithesis not only to him, but to the whole tradition on behalf of which he made this final hopeless sally."[49]

To Barth, "keeping to the form" meant holding to Christ at the center of the theological enterprise, and the Christological turn in twentieth-century theology does indeed have crucial implications for the story I have told and for a contemporary Christian understanding of beauty. The first has to do with overcoming the dichotomies that Auden uncovered in modern views of the arts. If we believe in the incarnation and accept that the same mind is to be in us that was in Christ Jesus,

> who, though he was in the form of God,
>   did not regard equality with God
>   as something to be exploited,

47. Barth, *Church Dogmatics,* III.2.240.
48. Barth, *Church Dogmatics,* III.2.240-41.
49. Barth, *Church Dogmatics,* III.2.242.

but emptied himself,
  taking the form of a slave,
  being born in human likeness.
And being found in human form,
  he humbled himself
  and became obedient to the point of death —
  even death on a cross

— and if, as Yeats's Crazy Jane tells the Bishop, it is true that "Love has pitched his mansion in/The place of excrement" — then who are we to deny *"the significance and reality of sensory phenomena"?*[50]

In addition, the Barthian revival of Christological thought and trinitarian theology addressed the problem of impersonal power that had led to the birth of aesthetics in the first place. As we have seen, the turn to beauty took place in reaction to a rising view of nature as an intricate mechanism ruled by impersonal laws. In the words of H. Richard Niebuhr's stinging critique of the "Christ against culture" position — a position embraced by, among others, the fundamentalist ancestors of contemporary evangelicalism — this view led to "an ontological bifurcation of reality." The position was built upon a deep "suspicion of nature and nature's God," and it readily gave way to a temptation "to divide the world into the material realm governed by a principle opposed to Christ and a spiritual realm guided by the spiritual God." For, as Niebuhr says, "at the edges of the radical movement the Manichean heresy is always developing," as the "relation of Jesus Christ to nature and to the Author of nature" is obscured or denied.[51]

One could argue that the history of aesthetics from Baumgarten to Nietzsche is the story of the slow but steady emergence of a thoroughly modern Manicheanism.[52] Although Wordsworth, Keats, and others had tried to sustain the tie between spirit and nature, in the end, beauty as a surrogate for belief depended upon a Manichean view that posited "an

50. Yeats, *Selected Poems,* p. 149. The scriptural text is from Paul's letter to the Philippians 2:6-8.

51. H. Richard Niebuhr, *Christ and Culture* (New York: Harper, 1951), p. 81.

52. For a comprehensive discussion of the connections between Christian belief and materialistic paganism, both ancient and modern, see Charles Norris Cochrane, *Christianity and Classical Culture: A Study of Thought and Action from Augustus to Augustine* (1940; repr., London: Oxford University Press, 1944), pp. 399-516.

absolute rift between man and that in which he finds himself lodged — the world."[53] With its renewed emphasis upon the "relation of Jesus Christ to nature and to the Author of nature," the robust Christology of Barth, Dietrich Bonhoeffer, and others sought to repair that rift and to reject the idea of a radical opposition between outward banality and inward beauty.

The Christological vision enabled the likes of Barth and Hans Urs von Balthasar to reestablish for the contemporary world a *dramatic* understanding of the architectonic beauty of Christian belief. To understand what Barth and Balthasar were attempting to accomplish on this front, we might do well to remind ourselves of the framework established by C. S. Lewis in *The Discarded Image*. In that work, Lewis compares the felt differences between a medieval and a modern vision of the universe. In describing what it meant to "see the sky in terms of the old cosmology," he depicts that cosmos as an immense spatial structure that is undeniably intricate in its complexity but unmistakably finite in its totality. It has an architectural harmony that the eye can see and the heart can rest in. To gaze at "the towering medieval universe" is like looking up "at a great building." We behold "an object in which the mind can rest, overwhelming in its greatness but satisfying in its harmony."[54]

The modern view of the universe is something else entirely. One cannot rest in the spatial dimensions of this cosmos, nor is it feasible to construct a satisfying structural model of the whole of it, for in the words of Lewis, "to look out on the night sky with modern eyes is like looking out over a sea that fades away into mist, or looking about one in a trackless forest — trees forever and no horizon." This "space" of modern astronomy can "arouse terror, or bewilderment or vague reverie," but it cannot offer a satisfying structural or visual harmony.[55]

For that harmony, we must turn to other models, in which the structural intricacy of God's creative and redeeming love can be told, sung, and heard. In twentieth-century theology, as we have seen, the most powerful models proved to be those that employed metaphors of drama or patterns of narrativity to capture the majesty of God's activity. The greatest systematic expressions of the faith in the past century — Hans

53. Hans Jonas, *The Gnostic Religion: The Message of the Alien God and the Beginnings of Christianity*, 2nd ed. (Boston: Beacon, 1963), p. 327.

54. C. S. Lewis, *The Discarded Image: An Introduction to Medieval and Renaissance Literature* (Cambridge: Cambridge University Press, 1964), pp. 98, 99.

55. Lewis, *Discarded Image*, p. 99.

Urs von Balthasar's multivolume *Theo-Drama* and *The Glory of the Lord: A Theological Aesthetics,* as well as Karl Barth's *Church Dogmatics* — display an architectural brilliance of the kind Lewis attributes to the medieval picture of the universe. In their own way, these are all "objects in which the mind can rest, overwhelming in their greatness but satisfying in their harmony."

The *Church Dogmatics* may be the St. Peter's Basilica or St. Paul's Cathedral of Barthian thought, but we will conclude our look at beauty by examining a passage to be found in one of the outlying structures he put up in preparation for that larger project of a lifetime. It comes near the close of his *Ethics.* It concerns the arts, and it evidences Barth's passionate concern to situate all human activity in a Christological and eschatological context.

"Art must be considered in an eschatological context," Barth argues, "because it is the specific external form of human action in which this cannot be made intelligible to us except as play." Along with humor, art is an activity of which "only the children of God are capable," and like humor, it is "sustained by an ultimate and very profound pain" and is "born of sorrow." Art is the creation of children (1 John 3:2ff.) who play away in a world "whose corruptibility they cannot overlook or ignore. . . . Only those who have knowledge of the future resurrection of the dead really know what it means that we have to die," Barth reminds us.[56]

He sees art as accepting the essential homelessness of human experience east of Eden. "The artist's work is homeless in the deepest sense," Barth says, and he presses the case so far as to claim that it is "precisely in their strange and rootless isolation from all the works of present reality [that works of art] live so totally *only* by the truth of the promise" of God. By means of art, we learn "not to take present reality with final seriousness in its created being or in its nature as the world of the fall and reconciliation." In Barth's words, "true aesthetics is the experiencing of real and future reality." And to this extent, "art *plays* with reality" by refusing to let present reality "be a last word" in its fallen and partial state:

> [Art] transcends human words with the eschatological possibility of poetry, in which speech becomes, in unheard-of fashion, an end in it-

56. Karl Barth, *Ethics,* ed. Dietrich Braun, trans. Geoffrey W. Bromiley (New York: Seabury, 1981), pp. 506, 507.

> self, then to a higher degree — although we are still dealing only with the sound and tone of the human voice — with the eschatological possibility of song, and then — still with the intention of penetrating to what is true and ultimate, of proclaiming the new heaven and the new earth, but now using the voices of the rest of creation — with the eschatological possibility of instrumental music.[57]

In case the eschatological gravity of all this singing and versifying threatens to make us too serious, Barth reminds us that to the end of our lives we remain the *children* of God. Whether we envision a transformed world in our poetry or seek to bring it into being through political struggle, we "must not try to view our work as a solemnly serious cooperation with God." Instead, we forever "play in the peace of the father's house that is waiting for us." At all costs, we strive to avoid allotting "final seriousness to what we do here and now." We play and we wait, "because the perfect has still to come beyond all that we do now. . . . We cannot be more grimly in earnest about life than when we resign ourselves to the fact that we can only play."[58]

But play we do, and play we will, throughout time and in eternity. At least that's what the Reverend John Ames believes we will do. He is the main character in Marilynne Robinson's much-lauded novel *Gilead.* Near the close of his life, Ames reports that he feels like "a child who opens its eyes on the world once and sees amazing things it will never know any names for and then has to close its eyes again." He knows this world is only a "mere apparition" compared to the one to come, "but it is only lovelier for that. There is a human beauty in it." In fact, Ames refuses to believe that when we have all "put on incorruptibility" we will somehow forget the fantastic drama of mortality and impermanence, "the great bright dream of procreating and perishing that meant the whole world to us. In eternity this world will be Troy," he believes, "and all that has passed here will be the epic of the universe, the ballad they sing in the streets." However great the future will be, he says, "I don't imagine any reality putting this one in the shade entirely, and I think piety forbids me to try."[59]

That is the beauty of belief. So it always has been and so it always will be, world without end.

57. Barth, *Ethics,* pp. 507-8.

58. Barth, *Ethics,* pp. 504, 505.

59. Marilynne Robinson, *Gilead* (New York: Farrar, 2004), p. 57.

CHAPTER 7

Story

SEVERAL DECADES AGO, the distinguished literary critic Wayne Booth commented on the proliferation of studies of metaphor, which he claimed had "multiplied astronomically in the past fifty years." The increase, he said, was not simply parallel to a general growth in scholarly studies in the twentieth century, because while critics of Homer, Shakespeare, and Dickens have undoubtedly multiplied, "students of metaphor have positively pullulated." To his audience in 1977, Booth announced, "I have in fact extrapolated with my pocket calculator to the year 2039; at that point there will be more students of metaphor than people."[1]

A person assessing the status of narrative today might reach a similar Boothian conclusion about the prodigality and promiscuity of the students of story. Studies of narrative are legion, and the language of narrative theory has worked its way into every area of everyday life. Just decades ago, only a handful of critics knew that *closure* existed, but now every one of us eagerly seeks it for each crisis we face and each transition we endure. In the distant past of cultural time — say, a century or so ago — a relatively small number of people kept diaries, but now many of us *journal,* or are encouraged to do so, as we struggle to articulate the stories of our lives.

There has been a similar explosion of interest in narrative on the scholarly level. It has surfaced where one would expect to find it, in studies of fiction and historiography, but it has also made its presence felt in

1. Wayne Booth, "Metaphor as Rhetoric: The Problem of Evaluation," *Critical Inquiry* 5 (1978): 49.

major ways in everything from systematic theology to moral philosophy to cosmology. As a category of human understanding and as a conduit for divine revelation, narrative has acquired unprecedented stature in recent decades, and it has become an indispensable element of contemporary thought about God, the self, and the created order.

Sound and Fury

To understand how we developed our current passion for narrative, we begin with a story that itself begins in an unprepossessing manner. It is dated Saturday, April 7, 1928, and its first two sentences read as follows: "Through the fence, between the curling flower spaces, I could see them hitting. They were coming toward where the flag was and I went along the fence."[2] This is in many ways an unremarkable opening, and if the whole of the story were to develop along these lines for several hundred pages, the prospects for boredom might be considerable.

But that is not to be the case with this story, because after a paragraph of plodding autobiographical description, the details start to blur, the account begins to break into disjointed fragments, and we are thrown into a succession of incidents without context or connection. At the point that the confusion sets in, the narrator is describing a group of golfers at their game. One calls out, "Here, caddie," hits the ball, and walks down the fairway with his playing partners. This sets our narrator to crying inconsolably. "I held to the fence and watched them going away. 'Listen at you now,' Luster said. 'Aint you something, thirty three years old, going on that way. . . . Hush up that moaning.'"[3]

As readers of William Faulkner's *The Sound and the Fury* know, Benjy Compson never stops moaning throughout this novel, but merely pauses temporarily between agonized cries. The reasons for his anguish only become clear in the final section of the novel — or, for many readers, after a second or third reading of the entire work. We learn that for Benjy, "caddie" is not a golfer's assistant but the sound of the name of his sister, the only person who ever loved him faithfully and fully and who now has

2. William Faulkner, *The Sound and the Fury* (1929; repr., New York: Vintage, 1990), p. 3.

3. Faulkner, *Sound,* p. 3.

been lost to him forever. In her absence, Benjy cries each time he hears her name, and his suffering is compounded by the fact that the course on which the golfers play had once been Compson pasture land, which the family had had to sell to fund Quentin Compson's Harvard education and Caddy's hastily arranged wedding almost two decades earlier.

Ever since Caddy vanished, Benjy has bellowed out his loss. Daily he experiences that loss afresh, because he cannot place it in the past, fix it in his memory, or learn once and for all that he never again will know Caddy's sheltering love. As each morning dawns, he believes she is about to appear, and as each afternoon unwinds, he awaits her return from school. *"Aint nothing going to quiet him, T. P. said. He think if he down to the gate, Miss Caddy come back."*[4] But Caddy never returns, and Benjy never learns, so he cries without ceasing. His wounds and outrage are new every moment, because he can neither understand the story of his family's life nor situate his own experience in any coherent narrative form. "We enter human society, that is, with one or more imputed characters — roles into which we have been drafted," and we must learn what those roles are in order to "understand how others respond to us and how our responses to them are apt to be construed," writes Alasdair MacIntyre. "Deprive children of stories and you leave them unscripted, anxious stutterers in their actions as in their words."[5]

Our confusion over these "stutterings" is precisely what Faulkner intends, for he has taken his title from Shakespeare's *Macbeth* and has tried to imagine the narrative an "idiot's tale" would give us:

> Life's but a walking shadow, a poor player
> That struts and frets his hour upon the stage
> And then is heard no more. It is a tale
> Told by an idiot, full of sound and fury,
> Signifying nothing. (5.5.24-28)[6]

4. Faulkner, *Sound,* p. 51.

5. Alasdair MacIntyre, *After Virtue: A Study in Moral Theory,* 2nd ed. (Notre Dame: University of Notre Dame Press, 1984), p. 216. "Benjy, of course, is unconscious of time. Past and present jumble together in his mind, and . . . for Benjy events are related only through some casual and accidental association." Cleanth Brooks, *William Faulkner: The Yoknapatawpha Country* (New Haven: Yale University Press, 1963), p. 328.

6. All references to the works of Shakespeare are taken from *William Shakespeare: The Complete Works,* gen. ed. Alfred Harbage (1969; repr., New York: Viking, 1977).

"The idea struck me," Faulkner said years later, "to see how much more I could have got out of the idea of the blind, self-centeredness of innocence, typified by children, if one of those children had been truly innocent, that is, an idiot."[7]

What Faulkner got was the prompting for one of the most brilliant of literary modernism's myriad experiments in narrative form. In the first two sections of *The Sound and the Fury,* he dismantles our assumptions about consciousness and the stories it tells and then returns to us the flow of that consciousness in its original draft, before the editing has begun or the shaping into sense has gotten underway. Along with James Joyce's *Ulysses* and Virginia Woolf's *Mrs. Dalloway* and *The Waves, The Sound and the Fury* changed the way we think about the way stories are told.

There are deeper questions, however, than those of technique at issue in Faulkner's novel, and they are of great interest to critics of culture who seek to trace the shape of our storytelling world. We might think of them this way: for Faulkner, the technical innovations fed into a more fundamental concern about the prospects for truth and the possibilities of meaning. The more pressing questions are: What do the sound and fury in this story signify? What do they point to? Are they merely a sign of an author's verbal virtuosity, or do they signify the more menacing possibility that the chaos and cacophony of human life mean nothing at all?

Along with the tortured legacy of slavery and race, this question — as to whether the order of stories imitates a deeper order of life — drove Faulkner through two decades of novel writing that remain unparalleled in the history of American literature. To the end, he had a divided mind on questions of truth and meaning, and his ambivalence mirrored the uncertainties of his era. If we trace our way back in time from Faulkner, we see that the conflicts which beset his narrative experiments first emerged with clarity and force in the nineteenth century, and it is to that century that we will return repeatedly in this chapter.

The argument that will inform our study of stories is straightforward. In the nineteenth century, the Protestant cultures of Western Europe and North America underwent a crisis of authority that led to a dra-

7. James B. Meriwether and Michael Millgate, eds., *Lion in the Garden: Interviews with William Faulkner, 1926-1962* (1968; repr., Lincoln: University of Nebraska Press, 1980), p. 146.

matic redefinition of the role to be played in cultural life by the Christian narrative of creation and redemption. Over the course of that century, this transformation involved the internalization in romantic poetry and idealist philosophy of the biblical narrative, a recognition of the rapidly growing power of accounts of material explanation, and finally, at the close of the century, the birth of the "hermeneutics of suspicion" that was to have immediate and long-lasting implications for Christian belief and practice.

To frame my discussion of the nineteenth-century view of narrative, I will call upon the help of a dramatic character who worried his way through his own set of questions about narrative and meaning. He is Hamlet, and he was to the nineteenth-century mind the most fascinating of Shakespeare's characters.[8] Hamlet entered that century's consciousness most forcefully through the powerful reinterpretation offered by Samuel Taylor Coleridge, and he dominated its literary consciousness as an exemplar of anxious and expansive inwardness.[9]

Yet before we turn to Hamlet, narrative, and the nineteenth century, I should perhaps offer a word of clarifying caution. Here as elsewhere in this book I do not intend the following account to be read as a narrative of loss and decline. To be certain, vital elements of Christian belief were abandoned or lost in the nineteenth century, while others were stretched almost beyond recognition. But at the same time, new and salient truths about Christianity and modernity came to the fore over the course of that century. So the picture is mixed, and even where we detect decline,

8. "During the nineteenth century, and through much of the early twentieth, *Hamlet* was regarded as Shakespeare's central and most significant play, because it dramatized a central preoccupation of the age of Romanticism: the conflict of consciousness and action, the sense of consciousness as a withdrawal from action which could make for futility, and yet was all that could prevent action from becoming totally mindless." Northrop Frye, *Northrop Frye on Shakespeare* (New Haven: Yale University Press, 1986), p. 99.

9. In the words of Richard Holmes, Coleridge argued that Shakespeare brilliantly turned the revenge play "into a supremely poetic meditation on the inner workings of the imaginative mind and the tragedy of inaction." *Coleridge: Darker Reflections, 1804-1834* (New York: Pantheon, 1999), p. 282. In the figure of Hamlet, Coleridge says Shakespeare "intended to portray a person in whose view the external world, and all its incidents and objects, were comparatively dim, and of no interest in themselves, and which began to interest only when they were reflected in the mirror of his mind." *The Major Works*, ed. H. J. Jackson (Oxford: Oxford University Press, 2000), p. 655. With this provocative interpretation of his character in place, Hamlet was brought, center stage, into the nineteenth century.

we should proceed wisely and honestly as we recuperate elements of a Christian narrative at the start of the twenty-first century. For as we have seen throughout this book, there is a great difference between believing something *still* and believing it *again.*[10]

The World Within Which Passes Show

Hamlet's first speech comes in response to his mother's question about why his grief for his dead father seems so particular and intense. "Seems, madam?" he responds. "Nay it is. I know not 'seems.'" Neither the wearing of black nor the flowing of tears

> can denote me truly. These indeed seem,
> For they are actions that a man might play,
> But I have that within which passeth show —
> These but the trappings and the suits of woe. (1.2.76, 83-86)

Here at the outset of the seventeenth century, through the figure of Hamlet, Shakespeare glimpsed the growth of inwardness that the next two centuries would nourish and the nineteenth century would bring to fruition. There were few precursors to Hamlet's inwardness, but countless successors.

The history of modern inwardness is complex, and among the many elements that are at play within it, it is often difficult to determine which is a cause and which an effect. Hamlet is a student at Wittenberg, the birthplace of the Lutheran Reformation, and his thoughts and actions reveal a man whose transformed self-understanding presages dramatic changes to come. With the advent of Protestantism, the rise of mechanistic science, the spread of capitalism, and the stirrings of democratic individualism, the early modern centuries began to shift their attention from the "actions that a man might play" to the workings of "that within which passeth show." Keith Thomas's *Religion and the Decline of Magic* documents this move inward through a focused study of the disenchanting of the world in sixteenth- and seventeenth-century England. Through its denigration of miracles and magic and its elevation of the

10. W. H. Auden, *Forewords and Afterwords,* ed. Edward Mendelson (1973; repr., New York: Vintage, 1989), p. 87.

concept of individual faith, "the Protestant Reformation helped to form a new concept of religion itself." In turn, "it was the abandonment of magic which made possible the upsurge of technology, not the other way around." In Thomas's words, "as Max Weber stressed, magic was potentially 'one of the most serious obstructions to the rationalisation of economic life.'"[11] Thomas believes the technological advances of Western science may have been due in good measure to the fact that magic was more readily and rapidly eradicated in early modern Europe than anywhere else.

There was a price to be paid for that technological mastery, however, just as there were to be dramatic consequences for the Western understanding of biblical narrative as a result of it. In tandem with philosophical rationalism and empiricism, Newtonian science promptly rendered the world as a domain of value-neutral objects to which spiritually vital subjects responded. In that newly mechanized realm, the biblical accounts of miracles, along with many details of the scriptural record, began to look problematic. It was one thing to read of a time when the blind received sight and the lame took up their beds and walked, and another to live in an age when the laws of nature seemed to brook no such happy interventions. Over the course of the eighteenth century, Hans Frei argues, the historical events came to "constitute an autonomous temporal framework of their own under God's providential design." And where the biblical narrative had once provided an indispensable point of access to those events of history, it now could only verify them and acknowledge their independent accessibility to any kind of description "either predictively or after the event." Frei concludes that there came to be "a logical distinction and a reflective distance between the stories and the 'reality' they depict."[12]

That gap grew wider throughout the eighteenth century, until by century's end what had opened as a crack now yawned as a chasm. German idealist philosophy and English romantic poetry sprang up as efforts to

11. Keith Thomas, *Religion and the Decline of Magic* (New York: Scribner, 1971), pp. 76, 657.

12. Hans W. Frei, *The Eclipse of Biblical Narrative: A Study in Eighteenth and Nineteenth Century Hermeneutics* (New Haven: Yale University Press, 1974), pp. 4-5. For an insightful analysis of the "crisis of time consciousness" that arose in the middle of the nineteenth century, see Charles Taylor, *A Secular Age* (Cambridge, Mass.: Belknap Press of Harvard University Press, 2007), pp. 718-20.

span the gap, to build a bridge between the province of spirit and the land of fact. Coleridge responded enthusiastically, for example, to the German philosophers' unprecedented celebration of consciousness as a life-giving power in a death-dealing universe. Among others, he aligned Fichte and Schelling with "an older tradition of Christian mystics who denied a purely passive, mechanistic view of the human spirit."[13] In the *Biographia Literaria,* Coleridge credits the pietists and idealists with having enabled him to keep "alive the *heart* in the *head*." They showed him that "the products of the mere *reflective* faculty partook of DEATH"; and in championing the imagination, they had been "always a pillar of fire throughout the night, during my wanderings through the wilderness of doubt, and enabled me to skirt, without crossing, the sandy deserts of utter unbelief."[14] Instead of finding the ideas of the German idealists to be inimical to the Christian faith, Coleridge took them to be essential to its survival.

With some modifications, the Coleridgian view of the imagination informs M. H. Abrams's classic but contested account of romanticism as a vast cultural effort to ground human values in the interaction of the human mind or consciousness with the natural world.[15] In the nineteenth century, a number in the Protestant cultures of the North Atlantic dreamt of supplanting the exhausted deity of Judaism and Christianity with a newly invigorated "cosmic spirit which unfolds in nature [and] is striving to complete itself in conscious self-knowledge, and the locus of this self-consciousness is the mind of man."[16] Ralph Waldo Emerson summed up this dramatic shift in a characteristically epigrammatic journal entry from 1838: "They call it Christianity, I call it Consciousness."[17]

This is Hamlet's territory. The Coleridgian and Emersonian temperaments can readily appreciate the claim that outward gestures are but seeming "actions that a man might play, . . . the trappings and suits of woe." What matters more than the play of the surfaces, however, is the fact that Hamlet possesses within himself "that within which passeth

13. Holmes, *Coleridge: Darker Reflections,* pp. 398-99.

14. Samuel Taylor Coleridge, *Biographia Literaria,* ed. James Engell and W. Jackson Bate (Princeton: Princeton University Press, 1983), 1:152.

15. M. H. Abrams, *Natural Supernaturalism: Tradition and Revolution in Romantic Literature* (New York: W. W. Norton, 1971), pp. 11-16.

16. Charles Taylor, *Hegel* (Cambridge: Cambridge University Press, 1975), p. 44.

17. Ralph Waldo Emerson, *Emerson in His Journals,* ed. Joel Porte (Cambridge, Mass.: Belknap Press of Harvard University Press, 1982), p. 190.

show." The show that is surpassed in Hamlet's mind is the same one that had established the narrative framework for human life in other Shakespearean speeches that made use of theatrical tropes. In those speeches, the stage is the world, the seven ages of man, or life itself, and not the internalized world of human consciousness. "All the world's a stage,/And all the men and women merely players" (*As You Like It* 2.7.139-40), or "Life's but a walking shadow, a poor player/That struts and frets his hour upon the stage/And then is heard no more" (*Macbeth* 5.5.24-26).

Hamlet, however, places the stage within the mind, and in the nineteenth and twentieth centuries, many poets and artists would follow his lead and move to that inner stage where the spirit was busy writing parts more grand than any furnished by the narratives of ordinary life or the myths of the Christian past. Robert Gross describes, for example, how Emily Dickinson concluded that "real life is private life, the events happening in the grand theater of the mind."[18] "When the Audience is scattered/And the Boxes shut" on the larger stage of life, she wrote in 1863 — a year in which tens of thousands of young Americans were dying on the battlefields of the Civil War — the primary drama of the human heart continues to play itself out:

"Hamlet" to Himself were Hamlet —
Had not Shakespeare wrote —
Though the "Romeo" left no Record
Of his Juliet,

It were infinite enacted
In the Human Heart —
Only Theatre recorded
Owner cannot shut — (#776)

To Dickinson's contemporary, Henry David Thoreau, the whole of life had become, by the middle of the nineteenth century, a drama in which the individual both plays the parts and serves as the audience for the show. "[I] am sensible of a certain doubleness by which I can stand as remote from myself as from another," Thoreau explained. "However in-

18. Robert A. Gross, "Lonesome in Eden: Dickinson, Thoreau, and the Problem of Community in Nineteenth-Century New England," *Canadian Review of American Studies* 14 (1983): 11.

tense my experience, I am conscious of the presence and criticism of a part of me," which is not an actor, but the "spectator, sharing no experience, but taking note of it." And "when the play, it may be the tragedy, of life is over, the spectator goes his way. It was a kind of fiction, a work of the imagination only, so far as he was concerned. This doubleness may easily make us poor neighbors and friends sometimes."[19]

This consciousness also isolates us from any idea of narrative as an already established framework into which an individual life might be fit. Alasdair MacIntyre argues that inwardness of the Thoreauvian sort has made it difficult for us moderns to recognize the story-like quality that is built into our very experience. We dream that we are both the authors and spectators of the dramas that are our lives, but in truth, we are "deeply affected by the fact that we are never more (and sometimes less) than the co-authors of our own narratives. Only in fantasy do we live what story we please." We enter life upon "a stage which we did not design and we find ourselves part of an action that was not of our making." We are the main characters of our own dramas but play secondary parts at best in "the dramas of others, and each drama constrains the others." To myself, I am Hamlet or Iago, but in your drama I appear as nothing more than the "Second Murderer" or "A Gentleman." And to me, you may be no more than my "Gravedigger."[20]

19. Henry David Thoreau, *Walden,* in *A Week, Walden, The Maine Woods, Cape Cod,* ed. Robert F. Sayre (New York: Library of America, 1985), pp. 429-30. Robert D. Richardson reminds us that for Thoreau, the purpose of this distancing was to trumpet consciousness, whose triumph shows us why we should not make "too much of the seasonal structure of *Walden*" or "accept the seasonal cycle of nature as final wisdom." In Richardson's reading, Thoreau shares little of Hamlet's melancholy but all of his obsession with consciousness: "Nature teaches us to want to reach beyond nature. The conclusion of *Walden* is a call to everyone, whatever their present position, whether living alone or in crowds, in the woods or in the city, to have the courage to live a life according to the dictates of the imagination, to live the life one has dreamed." *Henry David Thoreau: A Life of the Mind* (Berkeley: University of California Press, 1986), p. 310.

20. MacIntyre, *After Virtue,* p. 213. The isolated nineteenth-century doubts about the truthfulness of stories have become a commonplace of intellectual life. Narrative frameworks are seen as arbitrary contrivances we fashion to suit our purposes and fulfill our needs. We find a typical expression of this view in Daniel Peck's impressive study of Thoreau. "From a late-twentieth-century perspective," he says, Thoreau's efforts to come up with a "'truer' calendar" of nature seem problematic, "because our notion of truth has changed so radically since his day." To Peck, the fictive nature of all narratives is so obvious that no argument needs to be mounted in its favor. We only need to be reminded of this

Both Judaism and Christianity have long-established means of making sense of the events unfolding on that stage. In Jewish history, the concept of the covenant bound the incidents of history within a story of God's providential care and deliverance, and in the Christian tradition, figural interpretation was to perform a similar role. In the words of Erich Auerbach, typological interpretation established "a connection between two events or persons in such a way that the first signifies not only itself but also the second, while the second involves or fulfills the first." Although separated in time, the two poles of a figure are real events or persons abiding within the same temporal framework, and they are carried along by "the flowing stream which is historical life, and only the comprehension . . . of their interdependence is a spiritual act."[21]

Try telling that to Emerson or to Hamlet. To both of them, it would have seemed strange indeed to believe that the meaning of events across time was secured by a force that operated from outside those events to establish and reveal their meaning in the fullness of time. "Time and space are but physiological colors which the eye makes, but the soul is light," Emerson serenely proclaimed. "History is an impertinence and an injury," he explained, "if it be any thing more than a cheerful apologue or parable of my being and becoming."[22] In history, we play and con our parts, shifting as we must to survive and to make possible the vital life of that consciousness "within which passeth show."

---

self-evident truth: "As Edward Said and Frank Kermode have reminded us in different contexts, beginnings and endings are always fictional. . . . And, it may be added, the 'middle' or 'prime' is just as fictional a moment within the flux of duration." *Thoreau's Morning Work: Memory and Perception in "A Week on the Concord and Merrimack Rivers," the Journal, and "Walden"* (New Haven: Yale University Press, 1990), p. 102. For a full exposition of this view, see Frank Kermode, *The Sense of an Ending: Studies in the Theory of Fiction with a New Epilogue* (London: Oxford University Press, 2000), pp. 67-89.

As rejoinder to this view, MacIntyre quotes Louis Mink — "Stories are not lived but told. Life has no beginnings, middles, or ends" — and then asks, "What are we to say to this?" Certainly, in retrospect, we can characterize hopes "as unfulfilled or battles as decisive and so on. But we so characterize them in life as much as in art. And to someone who says that in life there are no endings, or that final partings take place only in stories, one is tempted to reply, 'But have you never heard of death?'" *After Virtue,* p. 212.

21. Erich Auerbach, *Mimesis: The Representation of Reality in Western Literature,* trans. Willard R. Trask (Princeton: Princeton University Press, 1953), p. 73.

22. Ralph Waldo Emerson, *Essays and Lectures,* ed. Joel Porte (New York: Library of America, 1983), p. 270.

This Quintessence of Dust

When we look back at the early nineteenth century, there is something wistful about the lauding of inwardness by Hamlet's romantic descendants. To the poets and philosophers at the close of the eighteenth century, the chief antagonist of spirit was the mechanical view of the cosmos that had been described by the science of Galileo and Newton and defined by the philosophy of Bacon and Descartes. To counter the deadly influence of mechanism, the romantic writers trumpeted the vivifying powers of spirit. William Blake railed against the "dark Satanic Mills" and prayed, "May God us keep/From Single vision & Newtons sleep," while Coleridge was at the same time busy promoting the Imagination as a faculty that "is essentially *vital,* even as all objects (*as* objects) are essentially fixed and dead."[23]

Except perhaps for Blake, most romantic poets and philosophers were willing to give the scientific explanation its due. Even as they lamented the demystifying powers of science, they prided themselves on what the cosmological discoveries revealed about the power of the human mind. It was this pride that Karl Barth noted when he observed that the Enlightenment involved, in effect, a massive displacement of a geocentric view of the universe by an anthropocentric one.[24] For the first half of the nineteenth century, that anthropocentric picture remained securely established. If any force threatened consciousness as Coleridge and Emerson defined it, it was neither the mechanism of nature — for it had been put into perspective — nor historic Christianity's narrative of creation and redemption — for that had been stripped of its historical particularity and given a new dwelling place within human consciousness. For a number of people in the early nineteenth century, the only threat to the anthropocentric narrative came from the consumptive power of the idealist vision itself. Terry Pinkard says the legacy of idealism is "our new self-consciousness of the way in which all our norms are subject to challenge because of that very modern self-consciousness

23. William Blake, "Letter to Thomas Butts, 22 November 1802," in *The Poetry and Prose of William Blake,* ed. David V. Erdman (1965; repr., Garden City, N.Y.: Doubleday, 1970), p. 693; Coleridge, *Biographia,* 1:304.

24. Karl Barth, *Protestant Theology in the Nineteenth Century,* new ed., trans. Brian Cozens and John Bowden (Grand Rapids: Eerdmans, 2002), pp. 23-24.

about them."[25] In a poignant essay, "Experience," Emerson wrote of the engulfing "creative power" of our newly discovered "subject-lenses":

> Once we lived in what we saw; now, the rapaciousness of this new power, which threatens to absorb all things, engages us. Nature, art, persons, letters, religions, — objects, successively tumble in, and God is but one of its ideas. Nature and literature are subjective phenomena; every evil and every good thing is a shadow which we cast.[26]

Such skepticism borders on solipsism, the belief that the self is the only reality we can know and verify, and it has pointed implications for human understanding, as the opening sentences of "Experience" explain. "Where do we find ourselves?" Emerson asks. "In a series of which we do not know the extremes, and believe that it has none." For countless centuries, men and women had known "where they were." They dwelt between heaven and earth, where God had placed them "a little lower than the angels." The "extremes" of which Emerson writes are outlined in Genesis and foretold in the book of Revelation.

For Emerson in "Experience," however, all that had once been clear is now opaque. Acquiring a consciousness of one's situation is like awakening to find oneself "on a stair; there are stairs below us, which we seem to have ascended; there are stairs above us, many a one, which go upward and out of sight." Trapped in the middle, we know our experiences and ourselves only as a series of incidents and episodes that "swim and glitter" without connection. "All our days are so unprofitable while they pass," Emerson laments, "that 'tis wonderful where or when we ever got anything of this which we call wisdom, poetry, virtue."[27]

Yet as powerful as the perspectival challenge would prove to be in the twentieth century, in Emerson's lifetime a more immediate threat to narrative coherence and continuity loomed. Another of Hamlet's speeches — which is poised between a sublime exaltation of the human condition and a ridiculous reduction of it — captures the sense of this challenge:

25. Terry Pinkard, *German Philosophy 1760-1860: The Legacy of Idealism* (Cambridge: Cambridge University Press, 2002), p. 359.

26. Emerson, *Essays,* p. 487.

27. Emerson, *Essays,* p. 471.

> What a piece of work is a man, how noble in reason, how infinite in faculties; in form and moving how express and admirable, in action how like an angel, in apprehension how like a god: the beauty of the world, the paragon of animals! And yet to me what is this quintessence of dust? Man delights not me — nor woman neither. (2.2.300-306)

Or as Hamlet asks in a later scene, "What is a man,/If his chief good and market of his time/Be but to sleep and feed? A beast, no more" (4.4.33-35).

Recall Hans Frei's claim that the eighteenth century witnessed an eclipse of biblical narrative as the means of grounding the human understanding of reality. The Bible claimed to be a "special revelation," and when the concept of revelation itself came into question in the Enlightenment, it was inevitable that Christians would turn to other sources to buttress their claims and ground their beliefs. Catholics had the magisterium, the teaching authority of the Church, to lean upon, but Protestants lacked such a means of support, and in the main they turned instead to nature to fortify the faith. From the early eighteenth century to the mid-nineteenth, Protestant apologists called upon the argument from design to anchor Protestant apologetics in the face of the critique of miracles and the historical criticism of the scriptures.

In the design argument, the proof of God's existence was contingent upon the power of a unifying explanation to account for the intricate order on display in nature and at work within us. As Barth explains, this argument did allow for complementary elements of that explanation to run on what were in effect parallel tracks. When described in a certain way, nature might be seen as a mechanism governed by impersonal laws and developing according to fixed patterns. But it also could be viewed another way, through the animating and integrating prism of consciousness, whether that consciousness was thought of in terms of the categorical imperative of Kant, the creative imagination of Coleridge, or the common sense of the Scottish Realists. Consciousness tethered spirit to nature and ensured that both gave corresponding evidence of their divine origin and design. When the creative scholar sees nature and spirit as they are in their essence, Emerson wrote in 1837, he "shall see, that nature is the opposite of the soul, answering to it part for part. . . . Its beauty is the beauty of his own mind. Its laws are the laws of his own mind. . . . And, in fine, the ancient precept, 'Know thyself,' and the modern precept, 'Study nature,' become at last one maxim."[28]

Only decades after Emerson had written those lines, to "know thyself" and to "study nature" were indeed to become a single maxim, but hardly in the manner he had imagined. In the 1860s, the argument from design collapsed suddenly and completely as a support for Christian belief. To some extent, the harsh realities of the Civil War hastened the demise of this argument, and the corrosive power of industrialization also contributed to its decline. But the primary force was the work of Charles Darwin, which supplied the modern world with an explanatory device that could account for the whole of reality, even for the quickening spark of life and the dynamic power of consciousness, without recourse to a theory of divine origins or an understanding of providential ends. With Darwin, there was no need for a designer to call life into being or to spin it through its endless permutations. The principles guiding nature's development were now seen as nascent forces working their intricate way through living organisms rather than as transcendent powers creating and sustaining life from beyond the system. When *On the Origin of Species* was published in 1859, the time for it was ripe; as Louis Menand explains, "Darwinism dropped into a cultural configuration already aligned to accommodate it. Its fitness was generally appreciated before its rightness was generally established."[29]

The cultural elites of the late nineteenth century eagerly appropriated Darwinian theory. Henry Adams confessed to being "a Darwinian for fun. . . . To him, the current of his time was to be his current, lead where it might." And for those "whose lives were cast in the generation between 1867 and 1900, Law should be Evolution from lower to higher, aggregation of the atom in the mass, concentration of multiplicity in unity, compulsion of anarchy in order." There was no time "to chase doubts as though they were rabbits . . . , no time to paint and putty the surface of Law."[30] To Adams, Darwinism was there for the asking as an explanatory device. It provided an account of human life more compel-

28. Emerson, *Essays,* p. 56. For a helpful background to the question of design, see Taylor, *A Secular Age,* pp. 176-85.

29. Louis Menand, *The Metaphysical Club* (New York: Farrar, 2001), p. 140.

30. Henry Adams, *The Education of Henry Adams,* in *Novels, Mont Saint Michel, The Education,* ed. Ernest Samuels and Jane N. Samuels (New York: Library of America, 1983), p. 932.

ling than any other, including the argument from design. And as Conrad Wright observes, it was precisely the idea of a "purposive adaptation by God between organisms and their environments" that Darwin called into question. In turn, this challenge to the concept of design paved the way for a "purely naturalistic world-view."[31]

In dealing with a grand account of gradual evolution, Darwinism brought narrative back into the intellectual equation, but no longer as a record of God's sovereignty or covenantal care. Instead, the new narrative told how inanimate matter somehow caught or conjured the spark of life and then began developing from the simple to the complex, as it divided into different forms, sexes, and species, one of which at last acquired the curious capacities of consciousness and language. Here in Darwin was an all-encompassing explanation of how the "quintessence of dust" took life and through a grueling process became the noble, reasonable, infinite, admirable, angelic, godlike, and beautiful paragon of animals.

As far as Darwin or anyone else could tell, the purpose of this prolific activity was solely to keep the well-stocked propagation humming along. This is a narrative without ends, which is described by some of its most avid proponents as a spiritual story of nostalgia for the divine. "Romantic assumptions," in the words of Robert Richards, led Darwin "to portray nature as organic, . . . and to identify God with nature, or at least to reanimate nature with the soul of the recently departed deity."[32]

But as any biologist may remind us, recently departed beings leave behind two things — decay and signs that testify to their loss and absence. So it is not surprising that many of the most compelling theological narratives of the late nineteenth century spoke of the death of God

31. Conrad Wright, "Introduction" to *The Religion of Geology and Its Connected Sciences,* by Edward Hitchcock (Hicksville, N.Y.: Regina, 1975), p. 4m.

32. Robert J. Richards, *The Romantic Conception of Life: Science and Philosophy in the Age of Goethe* (Chicago: University of Chicago Press, 2002), p. 516. Richards tries to bridge the gap between Darwinian austerity and Christian assurance, but to do so he must rely upon the talismanic power of Christian symbols whose substance Darwinian theory has undermined. He says that the patterns in "Darwin's nature" first arose and then were altered "through the power of a creative nature *(natura naturans)* — ever fruitful and rich in possibilities, realizing those possibilities in the best interests of her creatures" (p. 553). Richards even claims that "the intrinsic moral aspect of nature also imbued her most developed creatures, human beings" (pp. 553-54). The sentiment is ennobling, but the argument remains unconvincing, given its premises.

and the signs of his absence. Henry Adams gave a moving account of how for him, God stopped being a "Person" and became an impersonal "Substance"; Friedrich Nietzsche offered in *The Gay Science* and elsewhere extended narratives about the death of God and the decay of God's providential influence over human affairs; and Emily Dickinson, in a series of arresting poems, detailed the "abdication of belief" and the loss of God's "amputated hand." These and other writers of the late nineteenth century wondered whether the loss of God would leave human life as a "quintessence of dust" and human beings as "beasts, no more."

One of the most instructive late-nineteenth-century accounts of the loss of God can be found in a conversation that takes place between the imprisoned Dmitri Karamazov and his brother Alyosha in Fyodor Dostoevsky's *The Brothers Karamazov.* As he awaits trial for the murder of their father, Dmitri informs Alyosha that Rakitin, a materialist and atheistic seminarian, has absolved him of guilt. Dmitri had been compelled by his environment to kill his father, Rakitin explained, and blind physical forces had driven his actions. "Imagine: it's all there in the nerves," Dmitri tells his brother. "There are little sorts of tails . . . and when they tremble, an image appears . . . — and that's why I contemplate, and then think . . . because of these little tails, and not at all because I have a soul or am some sort of image and likeness, that's all foolishness."[33]

"And yet, I'm sorry for God!" Dmitri admits. If chemistry explains away the spirit and biology dispenses with God, how are men and women "going to be virtuous without God"? For the prisoner, the only answer is to praise God from the depths of bondage and despair. "Rakitin's lying: if God is driven from the earth, we'll meet him underground! It's impossible for a convict to be without God. . . . And then from the depths of the earth, we, the men underground, will start singing a tragic hymn to God, in whom there is joy. Hail to God and his joy! I love him!"[34] From beneath the earth, this quintessence of dust will offer a model of what the Westminster catechism says is the chief end of all humanity: he will glorify God and enjoy him forever.

It is hardly a coincidence that Dmitri learns these things in prison. Narratives of imprisonment have been central to Christian witness over

33. Fyodor Dostoevsky, *The Brothers Karamazov,* trans. Richard Pevear and Larissa Volokhonsky (1990; repr., New York: Farrar, 2002), 589.

34. Dostoevsky, *Brothers Karamazov,* pp. 589, 592.

the centuries — from the letters of St. Paul to John Bunyan's *Pilgrim's Progress,* from Dietrich Bonhoeffer's *Letters and Papers from Prison* to Martin Luther King's "Letter from Birmingham Jail." Yet it has especially been the case that in the past 150 years the God who has been expelled from the narratives of the surface has often met men and women in the stories of the depths. "Life in a prison cell may well be compared to Advent," Bonhoeffer wrote from his own cell late in the autumn of 1943; "one waits, hopes, and does this, that, or the other — things that are really of no consequence — the door is shut, and can be opened only *from the outside.*"[35]

Must I Remember?

In telling Alyosha of his determination to "meet God underground," Dmitri spoke of the future with greater prophetic insight than he may have realized. For at the same time that powerful narratives of material explanation were appearing in the latter stages of the nineteenth century, another persuasive form of narrativity began to well up, to erupt from within the domain of the human subject and from beneath the citadel of human consciousness.

For our point of entry into this particular form of narrative, we have Hamlet's initial soliloquy. This speech finds him already thinking of suicide and complaining, as is his wont, of "how weary, stale, flat, and unprofitable/Seem to me all the uses of this world!" As Stephen Greenblatt observes in *Hamlet in Purgatory,* the Prince "cannot get his dead father out of his mind":[36]

> That it should come to this,
> But two months dead, nay, not so much, not two,
> So excellent a king, that was to this
> Hyperion to a satyr, so loving to my mother
> That he might not beteem the winds of heaven
> Visit her face too roughly. Heaven and earth,
> Must I remember? (1.2.137-42)

35. Dietrich Bonhoeffer, *Letters and Papers from Prison,* enlarged ed., ed. Eberhard Bethge (New York: Collier, 1972), p. 135.

36. Stephen Greenblatt, *Hamlet in Purgatory* (Princeton: Princeton University Press, 2001), p. 213.

In his study of the sixteenth-century abandonment of the idea of purgatory, Greenblatt describes *Hamlet* as a play in which "a young man from Wittenberg, with a distinctly Protestant temperament, is haunted by a distinctly Catholic ghost." Purgatory and the complex practices that had grown up to serve it had provided "a powerful method of negotiating with the dead." With the demise of this hazy intermediate state — the abode of those who "were at once dead and yet, since they could still speak, appeal, and appall, not completely dead" — the burden of negotiating with the dead and preserving them fell to memory.[37] In *Hamlet,* memory is a haunting force that rises up like a usurping power within the self, and its assaults are as impossible to anticipate as they are to resist.

With memory, it is as though the conscious, ordering self is besieged by an opposing force that is nevertheless also a part of that self. Of the issues surrounding the Ghost at the beginning of the play, Greenblatt writes, "they raise the possibility of a difference between oneself and oneself. The possibility will not be fully explored until much later in the play, where Ophelia is '[d]ivided from herself' and Hamlet 'from himself be ta'en away.'"[38]

"A difference between oneself and oneself" — what Hamlet envisioned in an incident, the nineteenth century once again was to discover as a principle. And here again, we have seen how Emily Dickinson proved to be one of the surest guides to these discoveries. She writes in 1862:

> One need not be a Chamber — to be Haunted —
> One need not be a House —
> The Brain has Corridors — surpassing
> Material Place —

Where some Dickinson poems laud the perfection of the soul and celebrate the triumphs of the aesthetic consciousness, the following poem, as we have already seen, puts consciousness to a severe test by pitting it against an ancient foe that lurks in the background of the self, however modern it might be:

37. Greenblatt, *Hamlet in Purgatory,* pp. 240, 256. Diarmaid MacCulloch refers to belief in purgatory as "a marvelous way of uniting the dead and the living in mutual aid," which had the added benefit of giving "people a sense that they had some control over death." *The Reformation: A History* (New York: Viking, 2004), p. 13.

38. Greenblatt, *Hamlet in Purgatory,* p. 211.

Ourself behind ourself, concealed —
Should startle most —
Assassin hid in our Apartment
Be Horror's least —

The Body — borrows a Revolver —
He bolts the Door —
O'erlooking a superior spectre —
Or More — (#407)

"Ourself behind ourself, concealed —/Should startle most" — here Dickinson anticipates the late-nineteenth-century revolution Paul Ricoeur has outlined in *Freud and Philosophy* and which we explored briefly in an earlier chapter. In speaking of the "hermeneutics of suspicion," Ricoeur designates what he took the three great "masters" — Marx, Nietzsche, and Freud — to hold in common. Each decided "to look upon the whole of consciousness primarily as 'false' consciousness." In doing so, "they thereby take up again . . . the problem of the Cartesian doubt, to carry it to the very heart of the Cartesian stronghold." Cartesianism holds that *things* are doubtful, but it trusts consciousness, because "in consciousness, meaning and consciousness of meaning coincide." With Marx, Nietzsche, and Freud, however, "this too has become doubtful. After the doubt about things, we have started to doubt consciousness."[39] We doubt it, that is, because like our melancholy Danish prince, it is assailed by forces that irrupt from beneath it and well up within it.

These forces have their own narrative histories that cry out for elaboration and interpretation. Like Hamlet's Ghost, they demand, "Remember us." And in Ricoeur's account, this is what the "masters of suspicion" did in the late nineteenth century, as they dismantled consciousness to "clear the horizon for a more authentic word, for a new reign of Truth" to be made possible through "the invention of an art of *interpreting*." They *remembered* history by rearticulating it with new joints and ligatures that stitched together compelling narrative accounts of human action and its cultural record. Beginning with the masters of suspicion, "understanding is hermeneutics: henceforward, to seek meaning is no longer to spell out

39. Paul Ricoeur, *Freud and Philosophy: An Essay on Interpretation,* trans. Denis Savage (New Haven: Yale University Press, 1970), p. 33.

the consciousness of meaning, but to *decipher its expressions*." The discovery of "Ourself behind ourself" — that unconscious signifying force that prompts the conscious self — makes matters such that "a new relation must be instituted between the patent and the latent; this new relation would correspond to the one that consciousness had instituted between appearances and the reality of things. For Marx, Nietzsche, and Freud, the fundamental category of consciousness is the relation hidden-shown or . . . simulated-manifested."[40]

The patent and the latent, the hidden and the shown — can we imagine modernism in the arts without these categories? Freud, Marx, and Nietzsche — can we conceive of the modern critical study of the arts without their powerful narratives of suspicion playing a central role? No doubt at times, when we think of them, we ask with Hamlet, "Must we remember?" And the answer, for a Christian artist or critic, is "Yes." We must remember the powerful discovery of inwardness, the forceful assertions of material explanation, and the narratives of suspicion that have shaped our understanding and given us a renewed capacity to explore, envision, and bear witness to the world in which God has placed us.

The First and the Last

We began with the opening passage of *The Sound and the Fury,* and we close with that novel's final section, the only one to employ a third-person narrator. This section — "Dilsey's section" — is set on April 8, 1928, which is Easter Sunday. We recall that Benjy's section, which was filled with a nameless and implacable grief over the memory of an unbearable loss, was set on Saturday, the day between the crucifixion and the resurrection of Christ. George Steiner says this is one day about which history and scripture make no report, "and it has become the longest of days." Both Christians and non-Christians understand the meaning of Good Friday, because it is filled with the injustice and suffering that make up both "the everyday fabric of our personal lives" and "the historical dimension of the human condition." Only Christians claim to know the meaning of Sunday, which is for them a day filled with the promise of deliverance. Yet for much of modern humanity, Sunday re-

40. Ricoeur, *Freud and Philosophy,* pp. 33-34.

mains out of reach and foreign to their experience. "Ours," Steiner concludes, "is the long day's journey of the Saturday."[41]

Dilsey reads history differently. With Benjy at her side, she attends the Easter morning service at which the fabled Reverend Shegog is scheduled to preach. His topic is the "recollection and the blood of the Lamb," and his sermon sweeps passionately through the Jewish and Christian narratives of redemption. Shegog's sermon has it all: the "blastin, blindin sight" of Calvary, the "widowed God," the "whelmin flood," and the "darkness en de death everlastin." But it also envisions "de doom crack en de golden horns shoutin down de glory, en de arisen dead whut got de blood en de ricklickshun of de Lamb!"[42]

To Dilsey, who is saddled with the care of the decaying Compson family — with the neurotic and hypochondriacal Mrs. Compson, the compulsive and domineering Jason, and the ever-needy Ben — this Easter sermon provides the framework she needs to endure and triumph. Dilsey weeps on her way home from church, and when her daughter Frony tells her to quit, because "we be passin white folks soon," she replies, "I've seed de first en de last. Never you mind me. . . . I seed de beginnin, en now I sees de endin."[43]

Dilsey has indeed seen it all. Over the years, she has seen the Compson family consume itself with its obsessive attention to "that within which passeth show." Lacerated by his own devastating sense of inwardness, Quentin had committed suicide eighteen years earlier, while

41. George Steiner, *Real Presences* (Chicago: University of Chicago Press, 1989), pp. 231-32. See also Hans Urs von Balthasar, *Mysterium Paschale: The Mystery of Easter,* trans. Aidan Nichols (San Francisco: Ignatius, 2000), pp. 148-88.

42. Faulkner, *Sound,* pp. 294-97. Throughout this book, I have referred to ironies of the Protestant tradition, and one of the foremost of them is that the heirs of that tradition (Emerson et al.) have promoted a subjectivity that would have been inimical to the original Reformers. The Compson brothers may be the modern self-conscious descendants of the Protestants, but Revered Shegog and Dilsey sound much more like Martin Luther than the Compsons do. Luther, from his "Sermon on the Afternoon of Christmas Day (1530)": "Who, then, are those to whom this joyful news is to be proclaimed? Those who are fainthearted and feel the burden of their sins, like the shepherds, to whom the angels proclaim the message, letting the great lords in Jerusalem, who do not accept it, go on sleeping." *Martin Luther's Basic Theological Writings,* ed. Timothy F. Lull (Minneapolis: Fortress, 1989), p. 229. For Luther, as for Dilsey, the *object* of faith is more important than our selves as the *subjects* of doubt and anxiety.

43. Faulkner, *Sound,* p. 297.

Benjy has never been able to discover any pattern in his experience, and Jason can never stop running long enough to realize he has no clue to the meaning of his life or any other.

Dilsey has also witnessed the corrosive power of material explanation and the cynicism it has engendered in Quentin Compson and his father. On the day of his death, Quentin thinks of his father having said "that Christ was not crucified: he was worn away by a minute clicking of little wheels." To Mr. Compson, Christ and humanity are the quintessence of dust. "Father was teaching us that all men are just accumulations dolls stuffed with sawdust swept up from the trash heaps where all previous dolls had been thrown away the sawdust flowing from what wound in what side that not for me died not."[44]

And as for the hermeneutics of suspicion, what child of slaves and victim of Jim Crow would not understand the terrible tension between the simulated and the manifested? Dilsey no doubt would have understood Frederick Douglass when he wrote of the need for suspicion. "I have found that, to make a contented slave, it is necessary to make a thoughtless one," he observed. "He must be able to detect no inconsistencies in slavery; he must be made to feel that slavery is right; and he can be brought to that only when he ceases to be a man."[45]

But in seeing it all — the inwardness, the material explanation, and the suspicion — Dilsey has also seen these things as realities situated within a grand narrative of God's freedom to create, to love, to suffer, to die, and to redeem. She understands intuitively a point that Karl Barth made more abstractly about the nineteenth-century embrace of experience as the locus of spiritual authority. This effort to supplant a narrative of revelation with one of experience sparked, Barth argues, a divisive conflict between consciousness and nature. From that conflict emerged a view of God as an impersonal force ruling a material world. The members of the Compson family live in that world, and most of them break under its pressure.

Yet as Barth passionately and repeatedly reminded us, the Christian gospel is not a narrative of necessity and force, but is instead the story of a divine love that freely created the world and graciously entered into its

44. Faulkner, *Sound,* pp. 77, 175-76.

45. Frederick Douglass, *Narrative of the Life of Frederick Douglass, an American Slave,* in *Autobiographies,* ed. Henry Louis Gates Jr. (New York: Library of America, 1994), pp. 83-84.

life, sharing its suffering and bearing its death. Near the end of his career, Barth wrote a short summation of his life's work in the form of an address to theologians. Quoting Romans 6:8 — "If we have died with Christ we believe [we trust] that we shall also live with him" — he writes of theologians, "along with all other men," that "they build on a firm foundation if they work in profound happiness as well as in profound terror." They may act with more than a "'bit of bravery' concerning the solitude, doubt, and temptation" they must endure, and they (and we) will "also know how to endure and bear all this . . . in alacrity, hilarity, and spiritual joy, in the joyousness of the Holy Spirit." We can endure the reversals of history "as the No which is nevertheless only the husk of the Yes, a Yes which is valid even for [us] at this very time and place and which, at the last, will break through with irresistible power."[46]

As Barth suggests here, Steiner and Faulkner are pressing a valid point when they testify to a modern sense of desolation. In many ways, ours is indeed an era of the "long day's journey of the Saturday" that stretches between the certainty of sorrow and the hope of deliverance, between the full exposure of human cruelty and the full disclosure of God's glory. Yet Steiner and Faulkner have it right only to a point, for in the end we live not in the darkened shadow of Good Friday but on ground that has been illuminated by the dawn of Easter Sunday.

For the Christian understanding of history and narrative, another pivotal day may provide a more fitting analogue for our sense of these things. In *Christ and Time,* Oscar Cullmann offers the metaphor of D-Day as an appropriate trope for a Christian understanding of modernity. We have a relationship to the future that is like that of the Allies after that day. *"The decisive battle in a war may already have occurred in a relatively early stage of the war, and yet the war still continues,"* says Cullmann. There is still great suffering to be endured and there are terrible losses to be absorbed, but our deliverance is not in doubt.[47]

Despite such assurances, more often than we like, our modern experience is a source and site of confusion. Our predicament is like the one that the narrator in a W. H. Auden poem wrestles with. The poem is

46. Karl Barth, *Evangelical Theology: An Introduction,* trans. Grover Foley (1963; repr., Grand Rapids: Eerdmans, 1979), pp. 155-56.

47. Oscar Cullmann, *Christ and Time: The Primitive Christian Conception of Time and History,* rev. ed., trans. Floyd V. Filson (Philadelphia: Westminster, 1964), p. 84.

"Compline," and it is one of several interlocking shorter poems contained within a longer work, *Horae Canonicae* ("Canonical Hours"). Within the Catholic tradition, these are the "Offices," the times of day specifically prescribed for worship. *Compline* is the service set at the end of the day, and it is traditionally said or chanted before retiring for the night.

In *Horae Canonicae,* what makes both the whole and each of its parts particularly intriguing is the fact that Auden follows the lead of the "Offices" by setting the events of the poems anachronistically within the context of Good Friday. As a result, when we read each poem, we are brought simultaneously into the general world of the twentieth century and into the events of a particular first-century day. In "Compline," this means that the speaker of the poem is coming to the end of a day that is like every other and yet also unlike any day the world has seen before or since. Now, on the brink of sleep, the speaker reflects,

> now a day is its past,
> Its last deed and feeling in, should come
> The instant of recollection
> When the whole thing makes sense . . .

That moment comes, but the sense — the meaning of the terrible events of this unspeakable day — does not surface with it. Instead, the speaker laments, all

> I recall are doors banging,
> Two housewives scolding, an old man gobbling,
> A child's wild look of envy,
> Actions, words, that could fit any tale,
> And I fail to see either plot
> Or meaning; I cannot remember
> A thing between noon and three.

This is the missing link for meaning — forgetfulness — yet it is anything but an innocent act. Instead, it involves the brutal repression of the truth, the speaker's self-induced failure to remember and to acknowledge his part — *our* part — in the events of this Friday we call "Good":

> Nothing is with me now but a sound,
> A heart's rhythm, a sense of stars

Leisurely walking around, and both
 Talk a language of motion
I can measure but not read: maybe
 My heart is confessing her part
In what happened to us from noon till three.

The final lines of the poem take the form of a prayer that concludes with a picnic, as the poet pleads,

spare
Us in the youngest day when all are
 Shaken awake, facts are facts,
(And I shall know exactly what happened
 Today between noon and three)
That we, too, may come to the picnic
 With nothing to hide, join the dance
As it moves in perichoresis,
 Turns about the abiding tree.[48]

Confession returns us to the drama of our lives not as detached *spectators* or godlike *authors* but as responsible *agents.* In confession, we acknowledge the harm we have inflicted upon ourselves and others and the sins we have committed against God. More importantly, through the mysterious mercy of God, that confession carries us into the drama — the dance — of Father, Son, and Spirit, which is pictured in "Compline" as "perichoresis," the technical term for the eternal communion of the three persons of the Trinity as they turn "about the abiding tree." That tree is the cross of Christ. As Eberhard Busch says in his superb introduction to the theology of Karl Barth, sin's "reality and mystery become recognizable for us only where *God himself engages it.* . . . The event in which God is 'affected and involved' with sin, and in which he wrestles with it, is identical — Barth's decisive discovery — with the event of the *reconciliation* of the world with God in Jesus Christ on the cross (2 Cor 5:19)."[49]

48. W. H. Auden, *Collected Poems,* ed. Edward Mendelson (New York: Modern Library, 2007), pp. 638-39. For the image of the "prayer and picnic," I am indebted to Arthur Kirsch, *Auden and Christianity* (New Haven: Yale University Press, 2005), p. 136.

49. Eberhard Busch, *The Great Passion: An Introduction to Karl Barth's Theology,* trans. Geoffrey W. Bromiley, ed. Darrell L. Guder and Judith J. Guder (Grand Rapids: Eerdmans, 2004), p. 204. Busch's Barthian emphasis upon the priority of the cross for the understand-

In other words, "what happened to us from noon till three" was not a product of blind force or a result of the promptings of conspiratorial power. Quentin Compson may believe "that Christ was not crucified: he was worn away by a minute clicking of little wheels," but Auden implores us to abandon the imagery of victimization and to acknowledge "our part" — our complicity — in the events that unfolded "between noon and three." If we do so, he believed, we will be graciously enabled to hear within the sound and beyond the fury of our lives a tale told by one who freely suffers in love and whose suffering love signifies everything.

---

ing of sin is more explicitly Christological than the general analysis of sin Auden frequently undertook in terms adapted from Reinhold Niebuhr; for this contrast, see Auden's review of Niebuhr's *The Nature and Destiny of Man* in W. H. Auden, *Prose,* vol. 2, *1939-1948,* ed. Edward Mendelson (Princeton: Princeton University Press, 2002), pp. 131-34.

CONCLUSION

Memory

BEFORE WE CAN *believe again,* one can imagine W. H. Auden and Czeslaw Milosz saying, along with Karl Barth and Hans Urs von Balthasar, we must first *remember* what we have forgotten or forsaken. In one sense, throughout this book our efforts to understand the nineteenth century have been an extended exercise in cultural memory, and as we have seen, that century's own relationship to the subject of memory was often tempestuous and always ambiguous. For many in that era, the rupture with the past was a cause for celebration. Recall Thomas Jefferson's excited admission to John Adams: "I like the dreams of the future better than the history of the past. So good night." For others, the loss of the past was a calamity that fueled a desperate hope for renewal. In the essay that gave this book its title, Auden writes of this countervailing impulse in the nineteenth century and traces it to a very specific event: "In terms of religious history, [John Henry] Newman's conversion to the Roman Church in 1845 marks the beginning of our era."[1] As we have seen repeatedly, the concerns that animated Newman within the church have also preoccupied the artists who have often remained poised just outside its doors. For the poets and theologians alike, the power of memory has proved essential to the effort to *believe again.*

As we begin our final exploration of these themes, a word of caution, a reminder, may be in order. It has to do with the purpose of the reflection we have engaged in throughout this book. My introduction opened with an

1. W. H. Auden, *Forewords and Afterwords,* ed. Edward Mendelson (1973; repr., New York: Vintage, 1989), p. 87.

account of an adolescent spiritual discovery, and I wish to keep the idea of personal discovery in mind as we conclude. For in the end, we engage in historical study, theoretical reflection, and theological analysis for the purpose of renewing the life we live in the world in which God has placed us. Our thinking allows us to step back from that world, but we do so in order to be able to return to it with a restored vigor and deepened love.

This is the sort of experience the speaker has in mind in Robert Frost's "Birches," a sly poem that tells of a boy's love of climbing branches "Toward heaven." And so, the speaker says,

> I dream of going back to be.
> It's when I'm weary of considerations,
> And life is too much like a pathless wood
> Where your face burns and tickles with the cobwebs
> Broken across it, and one eye is weeping
> From a twig's having lashed across it open.
> I'd like to get away from earth awhile
> And then come back to it and begin over.

This boy has his trees to climb to gain his fresh vantage point, while we as readers have the poem to read and our discussions to enjoy. But as the speaker reminds us, we always need to climb down from the heights of abstract reflection and set our feet once again on solid ground, the scene of our greatest labors and the place where we pursue our most profound loves.[2] For as the speaker in the poem pleads,

2. In recent decades, a number of philosophers and literary theorists have argued we should never climb down from those branches. They have done so by promoting an ideal of the intellectual life as an endless conversation, and not surprisingly, the university has supplied key metaphors for this conception of the cultural task. The continuation of conversation — subsidized by ample professorial salaries and foundation grants — becomes the point of thinking and talking alike: "The only point on which I would insist is that philosophers' moral concern should be with continuing the conversation of the West, rather than with insisting upon a place for the traditional problems of modern philosophy within that conversation." Richard Rorty, *Philosophy and the Mirror of Nature* (Princeton: Princeton University Press, 1979), p. 394.

"Continuing the conversation" may sound appealing, but what many miss in their passion for the metaphor of conversation is what Frost says in "Birches," and what thinkers such as Paul Ricoeur and Michael Oakeshott have reiterated repeatedly: the point of a conversation is to *say something about reality* and to arrive at a point of understanding, agreement, even truth.

May no fate willfully misunderstand me,
And half grant what I wish and snatch me away
Not to return. Earth's the right place for love:
I don't know where it's likely to go better.[3]

Memory and Love

Memory and love are the twin themes of this epilogue, and memory, specifically in its nineteenth-century context, provides a useful starting point for reflection. We begin with Wordsworth at the opening of the nineteenth century and with a passage to be found near the close of his epic, *The Prelude.* That work painstakingly charts the course of the poet's childhood development, and from the perspective of adulthood his eye focuses in particular on the "god-like hours" he had once spent "in the strength of Nature." The poet also explores the turmoil and aspirations of his adolescence, including his time in that "gaudy congress" that was a Cambridge education.

Then Wordsworth moves from the subject of private development to that of public engagement. Specifically, he charts his complex response to the French Revolution, moving all the way from the bright expectations of its dawn to the blighted hopes of its denouement. When he first arrived in France in July of 1789, Wordsworth was filled with revolutionary ardor, and as he walked "through triumphal arches bedecked with flowers, he sensed joy diffusing everywhere like the perfume of spring," writes Simon Schama.[4] It was of this period in his life that the poet wrote, "Bliss was it in that dawn to be alive,/But to be young was very Heaven!" With "France standing on the top of golden hours,/And human nature seeming born again," the prospects for transformation seemed breathtakingly unlimited.[5]

Yet within two years, everything had changed. Wordsworth "continued to describe the Revolution as a great cyclonic disturbance. But in-

3. Robert Frost, *Collected Poems, Prose, and Plays,* ed. Richard Poirier and Mark Richardson (New York: Library of America, 1995), p. 118.

4. Simon Schama, *Citizens: A Chronicle of the French Revolution* (New York: Knopf, 1989), p. 513.

5. William Wordsworth, *The Prelude: A Parallel Text,* ed. J. C. Maxwell (New York: Penguin, 1971), pp. 440, 224.

creasingly it was no longer the storm that invigorates and cleanses; rather, a dark and potent elemental rage, moving forward in indiscriminate destruction."[6] Repulsed by the gruesome manner in which this drama continued to unfold, Wordsworth shifted his hopes from revolution to education. His "faith in an apocalypse by revolution . . . gave way to faith in an apocalypse by imagination or cognition," and he turned to the recuperative powers of memory and the healing powers of love.[7] As a result, in the "Conclusion" to *The Prelude,* we find him no longer celebrating the overthrow of aristocratic power but championing "a day/Of firmer trust" when the inward "redemption, surely yet to come" will at last have been realized:

> Prophets of Nature, we to them will speak
> A lasting inspiration, sanctified
> By reason and by truth: what we have loved,
> Others will love, and we may teach them how.[8]

"What we have loved, others will love, and we may teach them how" — this seems a particularly engaging way of describing a central impulse behind the vast enterprise of memory and transmission that is the work of culture. There would be no such thing as the church, and indeed we would not have the scriptures, if the members of each generation had somehow failed to teach those of the next what they should love and why they should love it.[9] If we individually and collectively did not "hand on what we in turn have received" (1 Cor. 15:3), we would have no identity beyond that conferred by immediate needs and passing preferences.

In *The Prelude,* Wordsworth says we will teach those who come after us about the objects of our affection, with the goal of bringing them to share the love we hold for those things. We do not train them to develop a technique for acquiring affections, that is, but instead teach them to

6. Schama, *Citizens,* p. 572.

7. M. H. Abrams, *Natural Supernaturalism: Tradition and Revolution in Romantic Literature* (New York: Norton, 1971), p. 334.

8. Wordsworth, *Prelude,* p. 536.

9. "But tradition there certainly was, even before and within the Bible and not simply after the Bible: tradition was, in [Pierre] Grelot's phrase, the 'source and environment of Scripture.'" Jaroslav Pelikan, *The Vindication of Tradition* (New Haven: Yale University Press, 1984), p. 9. To respect tradition, of course, is not to bow before it uncritically; nothing I say about tradition here should be taken otherwise.

love the proper persons, values, and beings. "He lives in justice and sanctity who is an unprejudiced assessor of the intrinsic value of things," writes St. Augustine. "He is a man who has an ordinate love: he neither loves what should not be loved nor fails to love what should be loved." Sinners are not to be loved for their own sake, and all women and men are to be "loved for the sake of God, and God should be loved for His own sake."[10] And while he grounds teaching in the act of transmission, Wordsworth also speaks confidently of the future: "what we have loved,/ Others will love." He delivers this assertion as a promise, managing in two short lines to connect past, present, and future in a narrative of memory and anticipation.

In the section that leads up to the "what we have loved" passage in *The Prelude,* Wordsworth has been rehearsing the tragic course of the French Revolution and its aftermath. He pictures his age in general and his nation in particular as falling "back to old idolatry" and returning "to servitude as fast/As the tide ebbs, to ignominy and shame." Still he hopes "we" may yet be "labourers in a work . . . of their redemption." (Samuel Taylor Coleridge is the other person forming the "we" in these passages.) They will stand as "Prophets of Nature," and will "speak/A lasting inspiration." In teaching others how to love and what to love, Wordsworth promises in this poem's closing lines, he and Coleridge will

> Instruct them how the mind of man becomes
> A thousand times more beautiful than the earth
> On which he dwells, above this frame of things
> (Which, 'mid all revolutions in the hopes
> And fears of men, doth still remain unchanged)
> In beauty exalted, as it is itself
> Of substance and of fabric more divine.[11]

10. St. Augustine, *On Christian Doctrine,* trans. D. W. Robertson Jr. (New York: Bobbs-Merrill, 1958), p. 23.

11. Wordsworth, *Prelude,* pp. 534, 536. Richard Holmes describes how Coleridge proposed to Wordsworth an "overwhelming and epoch-making task which the age itself imperiously demanded. 'My dear friend . . . I wish you would write a poem, in blank verse, addressed to those, who, in consequence of the complete failure of the French Revolution, have thrown up all hopes of the amelioration of mankind, and are sinking into an almost epicurean selfishness, disguising the same under the soft titles of domestic attachment and contempt for visionary *philosophes*.'" *Coleridge: Early Visions, 1772-1804* (New York: Viking, 1989), p. 242. *The Prelude* was the response to this request.

Written in the first years of the nineteenth century, *The Prelude* marks a point at which the arcs of two radically different cultural trajectories cross. The descending line traces the path of a conception of the created universe that had become deeply ingrained in Western consciousness over the course of more than two millennia. This view has many sources, including the Logos philosophy of the Greeks, the Christian doctrine of the incarnation, and the Aristotelian understanding of nature that shaped most facets of medieval Catholicism. According to this view of created reality, the universe is saturated with a *worded significance.* We may now think of ideas as things we make and place in our minds, just as we may be inclined to consider moral values to be personal preferences that people choose for private reasons. But in the older conception of the cosmos, values and ideas are situated not in the human mind and heart but in the world created by God (or the gods); these values inhere in the nature of things and are not merely ascribed to objects by subjects. In terms borrowed from Charles Taylor, for this view of reality, "the order of things embodies an ontic logos," and "correct human knowledge and valuation comes from our connecting ourselves rightly to the significance things already have."[12]

To support his argument, Taylor refers to Walter Ong's book on Peter Ramus, the influential sixteenth-century French logician and educational reformer. In that work, Ong focuses at length on the shifting modern understanding of language's relationship to God, human consciousness, and the world. To get at what he sees as vast differences between our age and the early modern period, he traces the history of the words *honor* and *praise.* We think of these things as qualities that are applied to objects by the human consciousness; *we* honor God, or *we* praise our elders. To the predecessors of Ramus, things would have appeared exactly otherwise; for them, "object[s] somehow emanate honor and praise, in this way performing a kind of personal role." When we praise God, according to the older view of things, we are responding in a secondary manner to the praise that has already flowed from its primary source in God. Our praise is not primarily a work of creative attribution, but one of dependent participation. Ong marshals evidence from *The Merchant of Venice* — "How many things by season season'd are/To their right praise

12. Charles Taylor, *Sources of the Self: The Making of the Modern Identity* (Cambridge, Mass.: Harvard University Press, 1989), p. 186.

and true perfection" — and other works to illustrate his point that "for the sixteenth- and seventeenth-century mind, the value in the object and the praise elicited by the object tend to be viewed as one whole."[13]

This trajectory of thought had already begun its descent by the time Wordsworth wrote *The Prelude,* and during the poet's lifetime, from 1770-1850, the era of the English romantic poets and German philosophical idealists, it intersected with a rising belief in the primacy of the human mind and imagination. The history of early nineteenth-century intellectual life provides a graph of those intersecting trajectories, and from the time of Wordsworth on, we can track for several decades the rising fortunes of consciousness and the decline of nature.

Wordsworth intended *The Prelude* to serve as a brief introduction to a longer epic he never finished. He did complete a "Prospectus" to that proposed work, however, and it is a haunting blank verse poem that develops *The Prelude's* bold claim that the mind is "a thousand times more beautiful than the earth." The "Prospectus" piles image upon image to affirm that nothing — not "Jehovah — with his thunder," nor his "choir/Of shouting angels," nor the pits of hell itself — "can breed such fear and awe/As fall upon us often when we look/Into our Minds."[14]

At this point, the "Prospectus" turns into a wedding verse meant to celebrate the union of "the intellect of Man" and "this goodly universe." M. H. Abrams notes that romanticism relied heavily on marriage imagery in its efforts to reconcile mind and nature, which philosophy and science had been driving apart for two centuries. A number of German and English writers made marriage "the central figure" in a "complex of ideas concerning the history and destiny of man and the role of the visionary poet as both herald and inaugurator of a new and supremely better world."[15] According to the "Prospectus," in "love and holy passion" this "great consummation" will make paradise itself "a simple produce of the common day." The poet's

voice proclaims
How exquisitely the individual Mind

13. Walter J. Ong, *Ramus, Method, and the Decay of Dialogue: From the Art of Discourse to the Art of Reason* (1958; repr., Cambridge, Mass.: Harvard University Press, 1983), pp. 278-79.

14. William Wordsworth, quoted in Abrams, *Natural Supernaturalism,* p. 467.

15. Abrams, *Natural Supernaturalism,* p. 31.

(And the progressive powers perhaps no less
Of the whole species) to the external World
Is fitted — and how exquisitely, too —
Theme this but little heard of among Men,
The external world is fitted to the Mind;
And the creation (by no lower name
Can it be called) which they with blended might
Accomplish: — this is our high argument.[16]

This was to be the "high argument" of the greatest English-language writers of the early nineteenth century — including Wordsworth, Coleridge, William Blake, Ralph Waldo Emerson, and Henry David Thoreau — and at that unique point in intellectual history, the marriage between mind and nature seemed to be secure as a permanent, indissoluble union.

It is crucial to distinguish the view of the mind promoted by Wordsworth and the romantic poets from the understanding of reality that Taylor and Ong describe. In the ancient world and the Middle Ages, both the "value in the object and the praise elicited by" it were God's offspring; subject and object may not have been identical twins, but they carried the same familial DNA. But by the beginning of the nineteenth century, the human person as a subject had become one thing, the natural world as an object another. Theirs was no longer a sibling relationship, but rather one of potential suitors ready for courtship, marriage, and consummation. Exquisitely fitted to each other, they were about to bring into being the restored paradise that God himself, for whatever reason, had failed to this point to create. "Old things seemed passing away," wrote Wordsworth's contemporary, Robert Southey, "and nothing was dreamt of but the regeneration of the human race."[17]

At the beginning of the nineteenth century, many anticipated the end of history as it had been known and experienced ever since Adam and Eve had first headed east on their way out of Eden. The vision of a new heaven and new earth sprang from the human mind whose task, Emerson said, was to effect "the transformation of genius into practical power." It was this transformation for which Wordsworth had waited expectantly at the dawn of the French Revolution.

16. William Wordsworth, quoted in Abrams, *Natural Supernaturalism,* pp. 467-68.

17. Robert Southey, quoted in Abrams, *Natural Supernaturalism,* p. 330.

Why should I not confess that Earth was then
To me what an inheritance, new-fallen,
Seems, when the first time visited, to one
Who thither comes to find in it his home?

The one who inherits this world walks about "the place" in a spirit of gratitude, and then sets out to improve it. He "moulds it and remoulds,/ And is half pleased with things that are amiss,/'Twill be such joy to see them disappear."[18] The sense of being liberated is palpable here, as Jehovah, his choir of angels, and the sorry history over which they have ruled seem to be on the brink of vanishing.

But if the "Mind of Man" was to triumph, if consciousness was going to play ascendant husband to nature's submissive wife, then memory had to be chastened and subdued, for more than any other force it threatened to cripple the consciousness and bring to a halt the work of re-creation. Emerson and Friedrich Nietzsche are key figures in this drama. In the 1830s, having traded his Unitarian pulpit for a lyceum lectern and the genre of the sermon for that of the essay, Emerson set about laying the foundations for a cultural order that was to rise without the support of the Christian creeds and the Triune God. In a series of dazzling essays, he sought to obliterate the distinction between God and human consciousness, because "God incarnates himself in man, and evermore goes forth anew to take possession of the world." He trumpeted the incarnation as an exercise in self-development and self-expansion: God assumes his new and only residence within the self. "That which shows God in me, fortifies me," Emerson declared. "That which shows God out of me, makes me a wart and a wen."[19]

For Emerson, no force has a greater power to "show God out of me" than memory. It makes us foolishly concerned about the consistency of our actions and the continuity of our identities; it trains our minds on the dead letter of the past instead of on the quickening spirit of the present; and it imposes on life's fluidity a pattern that our experience in itself neither detects nor demands. Emerson's disdain for memory is visceral and unyielding. The problem with preaching is that it is rooted in tradition and "comes out of the memory, and not out of the soul"; "when we have new

18. Ralph Waldo Emerson, *Essays and Lectures,* ed. Joel Porte (New York: Library of America, 1983), p. 492; Wordsworth, *Prelude,* p. 442.

19. Emerson, *Essays,* pp. 80, 81.

perception," he writes, we are able at last to discard the "old rubbish" of "memory"; we are burdened not by our sins but by the "corpse of memory" under whose weight we stagger; and God protects us from our past by drawing "down before us an impenetrable screen of purest sky, and another behind us of purest sky. 'You will not remember,' he seems to say, 'and you will not expect.' All good conversation, manners, and action, come from a spontaneity which forgets usages, and makes the moment great." Simply put, "the miracle of life, which will not be expounded, but will remain a miracle, introduces a new element. . . . Life has no memory."[20]

Not surprisingly, the assault on memory was accompanied in Emerson's work by a sharp critique of the art of teaching and the work of the American college. As records of past experiences, books "are for nothing but to inspire." They are for the "scholar's idle times," because when he or she can "read God directly, the hour is too precious to be wasted in other men's transcripts of their readings." The truth, he told the Harvard Divinity School students in 1838, "cannot be received at second hand," for "truly speaking, it is not instruction, but provocation, that I can receive from another soul." The person thus provoked is "the word made flesh, born to shed healing to the nations," and he or she is ready to begin "tossing the laws, the books, idolatries, and customs out of the window." Having been a lackluster student at Harvard, Emerson saw little of value in the cloistered life of higher education. "Life is our dictionary," he declared. "Colleges and books only copy the language which the field and the work-yard made."[21]

The Rediscovery of Memory

In the seventh decade of the nineteenth century, that language of the American field and work-yard was to take on a bloody coloring and ac-

20. Emerson, *Essays,* pp. 86, 271, 265, 483, 484. Emerson was one of the few writers who escaped Nietzsche's wrath and earned his unqualified admiration. The latter's 1874 essay, "On the Uses and Disadvantages of History for Life," condemns memory, because it makes us unable to live as the animals do, *"unhistorically."* "Thus: it is possible to live almost without memory, and to live happily moreover, as the animal demonstrates; but it is altogether impossible to *live* at all without forgetting." *Untimely Meditations,* trans. R. J. Hollingdale (Cambridge: Cambridge University Press, 1983), p. 62.

21. Emerson, *Essays,* pp. 57-58, 79, 275, 61-62.

quire a violent resonance. At this point, the nineteenth-century American story takes a decisive turn, for the Civil War marked a turning point on the cultural matter of belief. "Before the war, Americans spoke of providence. After it, they spoke of luck," Andrew Delbanco pungently observes.[22] For many who lived in the war's aftermath, both the longstanding orthodoxies of Christianity and the more recently minted pieties of the romantic faith quickly became brittle and hollow. As a case in point, Oliver Wendell Holmes survived his wounds from the battle of the Wilderness in 1864 but never recovered from the spiritual shocks of those dreadful years. Although he went on to a distinguished career as a Supreme Court justice, "he never forgot what he lost. 'He told me,' Einstein reported, 'that after the Civil War the world never seemed quite right again.'"[23]

Presided over by a God of Battles so ruthless, efficient, and indifferent that it had no name but Force, the Civil War confirmed what some had already begun to fear more generally. For some poets, novelists, and philosophers, that is, over the course of the nineteenth century, the delight in having been liberated was slowly changing into the fear of being abandoned. This seems to be one of the points being made in the dreadfully gleeful passage on the death of God in Nietzsche's *The Gay Science* — "*We have killed him* — you and I. All of us are his murderers"[24] — just as it is one reason for the nineteenth-century American and English novel's fascination with the figure of the orphan. Take the orphans out of the novels of Dickens, the Brontë sisters, and George Eliot, and what do you have left? What would *Great Expectations* be, if Pip had parents? What is *The Scarlet Letter,* if not the story of a daughter's search to find the father who has abandoned her? Who is Huckleberry Finn, but another orphan drifting down the lazy river of aimless American time?

As the nineteenth century moved into its final decades, mind and nature were in the final stages of divorce proceedings brought on by irreconcilable differences, and their abandoned children were orphans

22. Andrew Delbanco, *The Death of Satan: How Americans Have Lost the Sense of Evil* (New York: Farrar, 1995), p. 138.

23. Louis Menand, *The Metaphysical Club* (New York: Farrar, 2001), p. 69.

24. Friedrich Nietzsche, *The Gay Science: With a Prelude in Rhymes and an Appendix of Songs,* trans. Walter Kaufmann (New York: Vintage, 1974), p. 181. For Nietzsche and "the precarious project of forgetting," see Harald Weinrich, *Lethe: The Art and Critique of Forgetting,* trans. Steven Rendall (Ithaca, N.Y.: Cornell University Press, 2004), pp. 125-31.

cast upon the shores of a strangely different age. Melville asked, "Where is the foundling's father hidden?" and Dickinson wrote of the loss of faith as the most severe of impoverishments:

> To lose One's faith — surpass
> The Loss of an Estate —
> Because Estates can be
> Replenished — faith cannot —
> Inherited with Life —
>
> Belief — but once — can be —
> Annihilate a single clause —
> And Being's — Beggary — (#632)

For Melville and Dickinson, the fear of abandonment and loss aroused a strong desire to bring memory back to life. Memory was to them not a dead hand of the past threatening their identity; it was instead the vital pulse of that identity. For example, *Benito Cereno,* Melville's wrenching account of slavery, race, and the ironies of identity, concludes with the forward-looking American, Amasa Delano, admonishing the broken-hearted Spaniard, Benito Cereno: "But the past is passed; why moralize upon it? Forget it." The sun has forgotten it, "and the blue sea, and the blue sky; these have turned over new leaves." Cereno "dejectedly replied" that they were able to do so, "because they have no memory; because they are not human."[25]

William Spengemann places Melville and Dickinson's view of memory within the context of the larger nineteenth-century drama we have been examining throughout this book. Eighteenth-century American culture had witnessed a slow but steady growth of subjectivism, as the "liberalization of dogma" and the rising power of "scientific empiricism" made necessary a "gradual relocation of the absolute, from the mind of God to the human mind." In the nineteenth century that shift increasingly deprived the culture of a dependable standard to guide their interpretations of nature and experience, and eventually "one man's interpretation came to possess as much authority as any other's." (This is the problem Pip isolates so devastatingly in the "I look, you look" passage from *Moby Dick.*)

25. Herman Melville, *Melville's Short Novels,* ed. Dan McCall (New York: Norton, 2002), p. 101.

Eventually, nature lost its vital connection to human experience, and that "experience became the sole ground of knowledge."[26]

As the Wordsworthian and Emersonian faith in the power of consciousness waned, the passion for memory waxed ever more strongly. "I cannot tell how Eternity seems. It sweeps around me like a sea," Emily Dickinson wrote to her cousins only days after her mother had died in late 1882. "Thank you for remembering me. Remembrance — mighty word. 'Thou gavest it to me from the foundation of the world.'" Several weeks later, she wrote, again in reference to her mother's death, "Memory is a strange Bell — Jubilee, and Knell."[27] It was "Jubilee" because it brought the dead to life and lodged them securely in the mansion of the mind. "My Hazel Eye/Has periods of shutting —/But, No lid has Memory," Dickinson claimed, for "Memory like Melody,/Is pink eternally — " (#869, #1614).

Yet at the same time, memory also sounds the death "Knell," tolling the loss of ones she had loved. "Remorse — is Memory — awake," and the mind that calls the dead to life must at the same time acknowledge that although "The Grave — was finished — ," "the Spade/Remained in Memory — " (#781, #886). For Dickinson, memory's power was without equal as a human capacity, and life without its consolations was unthinkable. "Dear friend," she wrote to a neighbor in 1879, "I think Heaven will not be as good as earth, unless it bring with it that sweet power to remember, which is the Staple of Heaven — here. How can we thank each other, when omnipotent?"[28]

Memory and the Cultural Enterprise

It was hardly a coincidence that in the same decades during which Melville and Dickinson were meditating on memory and the loss of God — from the 1850s through the 1880s — the modern ideal of liberal learning took form and then took hold of American higher education. What memory had done to preserve identity on the personal level, for the likes

26. William C. Spengemann, *The Adventurous Muse: The Poetics of American Fiction, 1789-1900* (New Haven: Yale University Press, 1977), pp. 199-200.

27. Emily Dickinson, *The Letters of Emily Dickinson,* ed. Thomas H. Johnson and Theodora Ward (Cambridge, Mass.: Belknap Press of Harvard University Press, 1958), 3:750, 755.

28. Dickinson, *Letters,* 2:651.

of Melville and Dickinson, it now was to be called upon to accomplish for the culture as a whole. "Development may be forecast; revolution cannot," James Turner writes in the opening sentence of his section of a recent book on the nineteenth-century origins of the modern university. "No one in 1850 could have predicted the dramatic shapes into which academic knowledge would shift by 1900."[29] In that half-century, a new constellation of subjects, known as the humanities, came into being and rapidly supplanted the Greek and Latin-based curriculum that had governed the liberal arts for centuries.

This "rise of the humanities was intimately linked to embarrassments consequent upon secularization," Turner claims. Those embarrassments had to do with the weakening of what the late nineteenth-century Princeton physicist Joseph Henry described as the belief that ought to animate every facet of the modern university's endeavors. "All the phenomena of the external universe, and perhaps all those of the spiritual, [may be] reduced to the operation of a single and simple law of the Divine will," he claimed. According to Turner, this assumption was undermined by the passing of the moral philosophy that had unified college curricula from the Revolution to the Civil War; by the increasingly specialized work of researchers who had neither the need nor the desire "to invoke the Creator or any larger matrix of knowledge"; by the influence of graduate training in Germany, where ties between Christianity and higher learning "had frayed if not snapped"; by the small, growing cadre of agnostics who appeared in universities after the Civil War; and, finally, by the methodological consequences of Darwin and the "shaking of epistemological certainty" that his evolutionary system administered to every aspect of late nineteenth-century intellectual life.[30]

29. Jon H. Roberts and James Turner, *The Sacred and the Secular University* (Princeton: Princeton University Press, 2000), p. 75.

30. Roberts and Turner, *Sacred and Secular,* pp. 76, 91. "Before 1900," Paul Conkin explains, "few influential American intellectuals openly defended a nontheistic position, whatever their private doubts. Every aspect of the existing culture worked against such views." The cultural atmosphere, however, quickly changed, largely through the influence of philosophical naturalism, as "trends in psychology and philosophy, as well as geology, biology, and anthropology, undermined theism. An emerging intellectual elite . . . found the old verities no longer appealing or, more correctly, no longer believable." *When All the Gods Trembled: Darwinism, Scopes, and American Intellectuals* (Lanham, Md.: Rowman & Littlefield, 1998), p. 143.

With a few exceptions, late nineteenth-century American universities and colleges moved with what Turner calls a "buoyant zeal to bring Christian learning up to date" and to subdue "the threat of disciplinary specialization and of intellectual secularization more broadly."[31] Educators of that era deployed literature and the humanities as weapons in the battle to restore coherence to a fragmented array of disciplines. At the same time, they sought to sustain the religious character of learning, even as their schools were shedding their allegiances to particular Christian confessions or creeds. Their indifference to historic Christianity should not surprise us, for the most vocal proponents of the humanities — such as Charles Eliot Norton and Matthew Arnold — were Protestants who had no commitments to Christianity as a way of life involving specific beliefs and practices. These figures were the proponents and products instead of a nineteenth-century religious vision that made universities bastions of what George Marsden has called "liberal Protestantism without Protestantism."[32]

Earlier in the nineteenth century, however, others had set out not just to retrieve the ethos of a remembered past, but to recuperate the living faith that had animated that past. For some, like John Henry Newman and Orestes Brownson, this meant a return to the Roman Catholic Church their ancestors had forsaken centuries earlier. For Newman, tradition was the unselfconscious memory of the faithful; it was a "profoundly democratic concept" that "filtered up from the faithful (who are the church) to become the subject matter for the speculations, controversies, and systems of the dogmatic theologians."[33] Still others in the nineteenth century, such as John Williamson Nevin and Henry Boynton Smith, remained, in the words of Mark Noll, "far less convinced that the

31. Roberts and Turner, *Sacred and Secular,* p. 92.

32. George M. Marsden, *The Soul of the American University: From Protestant Establishment to Established Nonbelief* (New York: Oxford University Press, 1994), pp. 408-28. James Turner writes of Charles Eliot Norton and the "evaporation of belief" in the late nineteenth century: "True religion, he insisted, had nothing to do with 'definite beliefs'.... Religion comprised 'the most private and personal part of the life of every man'; it was thus 'a new, a different, a peculiar thing for each separate soul.' Hence, no creed could possibly be 'broad enough to serve as the exact statement of the religion of two souls.'" *The Liberal Education of Charles Eliot Norton* (Baltimore: Johns Hopkins University Press, 1999), p. 213.

33. Pelikan, *Vindication of Tradition,* p. 30.

natural deliverances of consciousness did as much for theological formation as their American counterparts claimed," and members of this group sought to counter vapid liberalism through the renewal of a creedal Protestantism that took seriously the collective memory of the church: its tradition.[34]

Despite their undeniable importance within the history of Christianity, Newman and Nevin proved to be the exception rather than the rule in the larger culture of the nineteenth century. In the main, the intellectual leaders who shaped the American revival of liberal learning late in that century had little desire to resist the shift in knowledge that Ong and Taylor have outlined. To most of these diffidently Christian humanists, the world was a domain of objects without qualities faced by an array of human subjects who ascribed to these objects what values they could.

To be sure, in many instances, those educators longed to believe that the ineffable mind of God mysteriously held these objects and subjects together within a single purpose, law, and destiny. But however strong their longings for a unified vision were, the Victorian humanists found it increasingly difficult to hold together their "split-screen vision of nature." On one side of this screen we see the universe of modern science, which is vast, baffling, and utterly indifferent to us, even though we can recognize it as being "full of unexpected beauty" and capable of "inspiring awe." On the other side of the divide we discover what Charles Taylor calls our "inexhaustible inner domain," and from this source flow the values and visions that give meaning to life. How this inner world was to relate to the outer one became, in Taylor's words, "deeply problematical" over the course of the nineteenth century, and it remains so to this day. This makes our cultural dilemma vastly different from anything that transpired before the eighteenth century, for up until that time, the scientific explanation of the natural order had remained "closely aligned with its moral meaning. . . . For us, the two have drifted apart, and it is not clear how we can hope to relate them."[35]

The fiction of the late nineteenth century shows the consequences of the split between nature and the moral sense, as characters struggle to

34. Mark A. Noll, *America's God: From Jonathan Edwards to Abraham Lincoln* (New York: Oxford University Press, 2002), p. 249.

35. Taylor, *Sources of the Self*, pp. 416-17.

envision their fate in a materially vital yet spiritually listless world. In Kate Chopin's *The Awakening,* for example, Edna Pontellier cannot bear the tension between her inner experience of freedom and the pressure of social convention and natural necessity that weigh heavily upon her. One night, after having been present while a close friend gave birth to a child, Edna speaks of these conflicts to the physician who delivered the baby. When Dr. Mandelet asks whether she will be "going abroad" soon, she says she will not be traveling, because she does not wish to do so. "I want to be let alone. Nobody has any right — except children, perhaps — and even then, it seems to me — or so it did seem — ." At that point Edna's voice, filled with "the incoherency of her thoughts," trails off. The doctor grasps "her meaning intuitively," and responds by explaining that her troubles have to do with the fact that "youth is given up to illusions," which are "a provision of Nature; a decoy to secure mothers for the race." Were they to see life as it truly is — as a senseless struggle for survival that ends in a sinister slide to death — women would never willingly endure the pain of bringing children into the world. According to Dr. Mandelet, "Nature takes no account of moral consequences," which he calls the "arbitrary conditions which we create." Edna can only nod in agreement with this cynical wisdom, because she concedes that her life has been a "dream," and it might have been better for her to have gone on sleeping, secure in her illusions to the end of her days.[36]

LIKE TURNER'S ACCOUNT of the rise of the research university, this episode from Chopin's novel sounds a variation upon several themes that have resonated throughout this book. In the chapters on history and science, we saw how oppositional thinking — poetry vs. science, imagination vs. reason — has framed many of the crucial debates about ideas and values since the early nineteenth century. The central chapters of the book explored the nineteenth-century emergence of unbelief and its myriad implications for the life of the mind, the activities of culture, and the workings of the spirit. Our concluding chapters on beauty and story offered two different ways of responding creatively to the split between "the scientific understanding of the natural order" and its "moral meaning."

Throughout *Believing Again,* we have seen how some of the keenest

36. Kate Chopin, *The Awakening,* in *Complete Novels and Stories,* ed. Sandra M. Gilbert (New York: Library of America, 2002), pp. 649-50.

theological and artistic minds of the twentieth century — Protestant, Catholic, and Orthodox alike — have engaged the issues of modern belief and unbelief with theological integrity and creativity. No single Christian tradition, let alone any solitary Christian observer, could possibly comprehend the whole as far as these matters are concerned. Rather than attempting to conclude by offering a synthesis of the best elements of these traditions, I would like to close by returning to a subject we discussed at the very opening of the book: the sacrament of communion. For this sacrament brings together love, memory, and the possibility of believing again in extraordinary ways.

The sacrament has many names — the Lord's Supper, Eucharist, or Communion — but one object and one subject. And here again for assistance I call on W. H. Auden, who gave this book its title and who has supplied powerful images and insights for our discussions along the way. Near the end of his life, Auden wrote of what he called "the significance of the Mass." "As biological organisms," he observed, "we must all, irrespective of sex, age, intelligence, character, creed, assimilate other lives in order to live." And "as conscious beings, the same holds true [for us] on the intellectual level: all learning is assimilation." Because we are children of God who are made in his image, "we are required in turn voluntarily to surrender ourselves to being assimilated by our neighbors according to their needs. The slogan of Hell: Eat *or* be eaten. The slogan of Heaven: Eat *and* be eaten."[37]

This idea of "surrendering ourselves to being assimilated by our neighbors according to their needs" has always struck me as a wise and shrewd description of the myriad cultural activities that serve to transmit beliefs and values. We give ourselves up in the service of the books, beliefs, and rituals that have nourished us, and in turn we surrender ourselves to others and to the future, so that they may assimilate us according to their needs.

As we give of ourselves in this manner, we often receive nourishment in return. As a case in point, this is what happened in an incident from my first year of teaching. We had arrived at Emily Dickinson in the syllabus, and as I worked my way stiffly through the poems, we came upon one that had me stumped. The poem begins,

37. W. H. Auden, *A Certain World: A Commonplace Book* (New York: Viking, 1970), p. 134.

A Clover's simple Fame
Remembered of the Cow
Is sweeter than enameled Realms
Of notoriety — (#1256)

I uttered something unmemorable about the idea of memory, and was ready to move on to firmer ground and an easier poem, when one student near the back of the class spoke up. He returned our discussion to the imagery of the poem and implored us to think of how a cow turns clover into milk. He urged us to think of "remembered" not just in the sense of something "being brought back to mind," but of its being "re-*membered*" in the sense of its having been broken, its having died, and its having been transformed.

Dickinson embraced the brokenness of Jesus the Son in the late nineteenth century, even as she spurned the cold serenity of believing in a naturalistic God. Late in life, as we have seen, she wrote to a neighbor that "when Jesus tells about his Father, we distrust him," just as "when he shows us his Home, we turn away, but when he confides to us that he is 'acquainted with Grief,' we listen, for that also is an Acquaintance of our own."[38] As one of her poems about Christ phrases the matter, his "acquaintance" with death does "Justify Him" and makes him that "Tender Pioneer" who leads and guides us every step of the often difficult human way (#727). In the life and death of this one "acquainted with Grief," Dickinson the subject found an object whose qualities she could praise, honor, and grasp. As she wrote to a friend when they were both grieving the death of a man they honored and loved, "the crucifix requires no glove."[39]

In writing about the modern tension between love and knowledge, and between memory and hope, Charles Taylor says "Augustine holds that in relation to God, love has to precede knowledge. With the right direction of love, things become evident which are hidden otherwise."[40] Through acts of *re-membering,* Christian belief and practice are nourished by a love that reveals the hidden and heals the brokenhearted. In the contemporary world, the Christian faith bears witness by remembering that "the Word became flesh and lived among us" and by proclaiming

38. Dickinson, *Letters,* 3:837.
39. Dickinson, *Letters,* 2:603.
40. Taylor, *Sources of the Self,* p. 449.

that the breach between subject and object has been healed through the suffering love of the Son of God. By the light of the incarnation, we may see ourselves as subjects in new ways, and we may learn to see once again the loveliness of objects, even those we once found most unlovely.

Only a month after her mother had died, Emily Dickinson confessed to a friend, "we were never intimate Mother and Children while she was our Mother — but Mines in the same Ground meet by tunneling and when she became our Child, the Affection came."[41] As we engage in the life of culture and strive to teach others to love what we have loved, we do well to remember that the connections between Christ and the life of the mind may be more readily discovered in Emily Dickinson's tunnels than they are to be glimpsed from Robert Frost's treetops. As he dreamt of heaven and thought of his own art at his life's close, William Butler Yeats concluded, "I must lie down where all the ladders start/In the foul rag and bone shop of the heart." Or as we have already heard him assert,

"Love has pitched his mansion in
The place of excrement;
For nothing can be sole or whole
That has not been rent."[42]

So we begin at that point at which our own affection and love came — with our memory of that child who became a man and whose body was rent, broken out of love, so that we might remember it and thus live with the hope of that day when God will re-member us wholly — body, mind, and soul — for eternity. That is a love worth remembering, a promise worth trusting, and a truth worth believing again.

41. Dickinson, *Letters,* 3:754-55.

42. William Butler Yeats, *Selected Poems and Four Plays,* 4th ed., ed. M. L. Rosenthal (New York: Scribner, 1996), pp. 213, 149.

Index